Window

Row 1

Ruggiero
**Vitale &
Trupiano**

Leitman
Palazzolo

Fogelnest
Salamone

Koppelman
V. Badalamenti

Schoenbach
Randazzo

Kennedy
G. Badalamenti

Row 2

Di Chiara
Cangialosi

Moriarty
DeVardo

Bergman
Amato

Schechter
S. Lamberti

Benfante
Mazzurco

Lombardino
G. Lamberti

Row 3

Kimelman/Novack
Ligammari

Ryan
Casamento

Querques/Pisano
Polizzi

Segal/Rosen —
Mazzara

Kaplan
Castronovo

Bronson
Greco

Spectators

Spectators

Window
(operable)

Window

Names in **boldface** = Defendants

THE PIZZA CONNECTION

THE PIZZA

Lawyers,

Shana

WN

CONNECTION

Money, Drugs, Mafia

Alexander

WEIDENFELD & NICOLSON   New York

Published by Weidenfeld & Nicolson, New York
A Division of Wheatland Corporation
841 Broadway
New York, New York 10003-4793

Published in Canada by General Publishing Company, Ltd.

The illustrations in this book appear courtesy of the following: AP/WIDE WORLD PHOTOS: Badalamenti, Buscetta, French Smith, S. Lamberti, Ronsisvalle; © DANIEL AUBRY: Leval; © JILL KREMENTZ: Fisher; *NEW YORK NEWSDAY:* Lewis; *NEW YORK POST:* Mazzara, Conte, Giuliani; UPI: Galante; U.S. DEPARTMENT OF JUSTICE: Bonventre, Catalano, Ganci and Casamento, Ganci and Giuliani, Ganci and Polizzi, Lamberti and Cangialosi, Mazzurco, Polizzi with Bonventre, Ganci and Amato. Attorneys Bergman, Burke, Freeh, Kennedy, Malerba, Martin, and Rosen provided their own photographs.

LIBRARY OF CONGRESS CATALOGING-IN-PUBLICATION DATA

Alexander, Shana.
  The pizza connection.

  Includes index.
  1. Badalamenti, Gaetano—Trials, litigation, etc.
2. Trials (Narcotic laws)—New York (N.Y.) 3. Organized
crime—New York (N.Y.) I. Title. II. Title: Pizza
connection trial.
KF224.B23A44 1988   345.73′0277 88-5771
ISBN 1-55584-027-2   347.305277

Manufactured in the United States of America

Designed by Irving Perkins Associates

First Edition

10 9 8 7 6 5 4 3 2 1

for Hannah Bentley

C'era beddu lu pitrusinu, cii lu' attu e ci piscio.

It wasn't very good parsley to begin with, and then the cat went and peed on it.

—SICILIAN PROVERB

Contents

Preface

THIS is not the book I had intended to write.

I started out to do a panoramic, backstage view of all sides of a contemporary American criminal trial as it was taking place.

My work in the past ten years had confined me for long months in courtrooms from San Francisco to Brooklyn, months of wondering what was really going on—not what the lawyers were saying, but what they were doing, or trying to do. The decade produced three books and a long magazine article. It also produced an unshakable conviction that *nobody* in those courtrooms knew what was really going on, except some of the lawyers and judges some of the time, and they were not disposed to disclose any more than they had to, not even after the verdict was in. We know quite a lot about what doctors do; we know very little about what lawyers do—probably because that's the way doctors and lawyers want it.

It also appeared to me that the people who knew least about what was really going on were the members of the jury. Whenever something important was due to happen, they were sent out of the room. If it was really important, all participants retired to the judge's chambers so that reporters and spectators also were kept in the dark.

What worried me most were the jurors. Although they were the referees of the life-or-death game we were all watching, they were not told the main rules of the game until after it ended, after the evidence and the argument were all in. Then the judge told them the rules—in lawyers' language, he "charged the jury"—and after *that* they were locked in a room and told not to come out until they had reached a unanimous decision as to which side had won.

During the trials, they were diddled and courted and lied to and flimflammed by the lawyers, on both sides; they were bewildered, befuddled, and benumbed by the "expert witnesses" on both sides; they were flattered half to death by the judges; they were coddled and soothed and sometimes held prisoner by federal marshals and sheriff's deputies; they were bored almost beyond human endurance at one time or another by all of these people, and yet . . . and yet . . . I was firmly assured by every judge and every lawyer I talked to—hundreds!—that 99% of the time, juries reach the correct conclusion about the guilt or innocence of the person on trial.

I didn't believe them. I said that I would never serve on a jury myself if I could help it. By nature, I do not like judging people. I would particularly not want to judge them from a jury box, where the information on which to base one's judgment is so thin, so carefully incomplete, so expertly slanted.

Without realizing it, my four trials had set me looking for a fifth, one I could somehow cover from the "inside"—as it was happening—rather than having to reconstruct its dynamics by rereading transcript and interviewing participants after the verdict. It would have to be a case in which lawyers for both sides were reasonably forthcoming, and one which I felt reasonably capable of understanding, and one in which I was not likely to become emotionally involved. A crooked financier, or a child molester, would not do.

When I heard about the forthcoming "Pizza Connection" trial, it sounded like a good possibility. It would be held in the Southern District of New York, the showplace of the federal judicial system, an arena where one is likely to see topflight lawyers and judges in action. The twenty-two defendants, all Sicilian-born, were charged with international drug smuggling on an epic scale, and since each man was entitled to his own lawyer, one could anticipate seeing a great variety of courtroom styles. The charges offered as secure a protection against personal emotional involvement as I could expect to find. I am not *for* drugs, or drug dealing. But I think that drugs, and drink, and illicit sex, and gambling, and other so-called victimless crimes will always be with us because people enjoy them. That being the case, we should educate, and regulate, but not make the foolish mistake of trying to eradicate. Prohibition doesn't work. But that is the subject matter for some other book.

Best of all, from my point of view, I knew and admired several lawyers in the case, and the lead counsel, Michael Kennedy, was a close friend, as was Kennedy's only law partner, his wife, Eleanore. I told the Kennedys I was thinking about writing one last trial book, and maybe this was it. My decision would depend on "how far I could expect to penetrate the counsels of the defense." (I had learned to talk like this from working on the other books.)

"All the way," said Kennedy, to my astonishment. "Of course I speak only for myself. If you decide to try it, I will tell the other lawyers what you are doing, and that I trust you. Then each can decide for himself."

On the government side too, the Pizza Connection strategy was being managed by just the sort of person I needed to make the book work. U.S. Attorney Rudolph Giuliani might not agree with me about victimless crimes, and indeed he does not. But he does believe that members of the public would benefit by a better understanding of how the criminal justice system really works. I told him that was what I hoped to provide, and sent him copies of my previous trial books.

In due course, we made an appointment and I explained my panoramic plans, told him of my agreement with the chief defense attorney, and asked him how far the government would go. As far as the law allows, Giuliani said. He would make available as much background material as possible while the trial was under way. He would keep himself personally available for interviews on and off the record. He would try to arrange interviews for me with the many overburdened lawyers and FBI agents handling the day-to-day prosecution of the case.

Assistant U.S. Attorney Benito Romano would function as a sort of surrogate for all the government employees involved in the prosecution, hard-driven men who would be far too busy to spend much time with me while the trial was in progress. Romano would set up the interviews, and before that he would gather up and make available a massive amount of government paperwork. This would assist me to understand the background of this huge and complex prosecution while it was moving forward, and enable me to follow the case as it developed in the courtroom.

There were delays. Some of the materials were proving hard to gather, Romano said. The delays lengthened, and I waited from November to April before he finally confessed the reason. The lead prosecutor, Richard Martin, had balked. His reason, said Romano, was that one of the defense attorneys had called Martin a "liar" in front of the judge. This of course was Kennedy. Martin said that good lawyers had "higher standards," and better manners. They did not attack a man personally, nor publicly impugn his integrity. Martin had concluded I was unlikely to write a fair book about him, and was not disposed to help me try. Government cooperation thereafter dried up.

So that was the first thing that went wrong. The second thing was worse. Despite the colorfulness of this trial, its excitement, challenge, and bravado, it was turning out to be even harder to follow than the others had been. Despite the increasingly friendly assistance of all the defense lawyers during what became a grueling legal ordeal, despite the generous gift of their time and expertise, and the mountains of background materials they furnished me, I found myself gradually sinking deeper and deeper into legal ooze, swamps of confusion, vast bogs of befuddlement.

Unknowingly, I had elected to describe an anomaly, a new legal mutant of recent years, something lawyers and judges call a "megatrial."

It took me months simply to sort out the players. Not just the defendants were Sicilian. So were most of the witnesses. We had six or eight different Catalanos to keep straight. There were a half-dozen Palazzolos, and a dozen Badalamentis. Not to mention ranks of look-alike defendants named Cangialosi, Casamento, and Castronovo; Amato and Alfano; Mazzurco and Mazzara; Ligammari and Lamberti—many of whom were *not* mentioned, not for months on end.

I struggled. I made myself a scorecard. I pasted a seating chart into my notebook. I carried to court with me each day a diagram that outlined the many charges against each defendant. It helped, but not quite enough. Eventually I found out that most of the people *on* my scorecard, including all of the lawyers, were also keeping scorecards, even the judge. Nobody could follow this thing in his head.

The hapless Pizza jurors were forbidden by the judge to take notes; that could only increase their confusion. But throughout the trial they were provided with visual aids of every kind: charts, maps, diagrams, rebus figures, summaries, code books, translations. They were admonished many times that their duty was to judge each defendant separately.

When they finally retired to the jury room to deliberate, each juror carried a massive stack of documents: a verdict sheet that was 59 pages long; a 100-page copy of the judge's charge; a copy of the 129-page Indictment, a 410-page government-made notebook summarizing—with the aid of still more maps and charts—the government's interpretation of the evidence; and a half-dozen smaller notebooks, provided by various defense lawyers, offering contradictory, relatively benign interpretations of the same evidence.

In the end, the so-called Pizza Connection proved impossible for most observers to connect. It was too big, and too complex and contradictory, and it went on too long. It lasted seventeen stupefying months and cost more than $50 million in taxpayer dollars. It did not make even a slight dent in this nation's desperate drug problem. More heroin, and more cocaine, is on the streets today than before Pizza began. The trial severely overtaxed every branch of our legal system—law enforcement, bench, and bar—and taxed the unfortunate jurors worst of all.

Yet Pizza is a landmark trial well worth pondering. So *use* the courtroom seating chart as you read along. Use the Cast of Characters, the Chronology, the Family Tree, the pictures, the index. Use the margins if you need to. And if you get lost, take comfort in the knowledge that you are not alone, and find reassurance in knowing that such a megatrial is unlikely to occur again.

Wiser judges, people concerned with broader issues of justice than how to lock up drug dealers, are trying not to let it happen. You will meet just such a sagacious judge, the Honorable Jack Weinstein, on page 410. The presence within the federal judiciary of such men lends hope that the megatrial will soon become as invisible as the thing it most resembles, the megalosaur—defined in my dictionary as an extinct, gigantic, carnivorous dinosaur.

A Final Word

I have explained why this is not exactly the book I intended to write. More important, now that the writing is over, is to acknowledge that I did not write it alone, and could not have done so.

The Pizza Connection would never have come about without the many, varying contributions of a remarkable young Irish-born journalist and playwright named Terry George. When I hired him as assistant, researcher, and legman to help me gather and deal with the enormous amount of material in a twenty-two-defendant case, I had no notion of how indispensable to this project he would become. He has been a tireless co-worker and co-writer, a dogged and resourceful reporter, an ever-cheerful and encouraging companion, a loyal and critical friend. His participation in this work is crucial to its existence.

On top of all that, Terry and his wife, Rita, and their children, Oorlagh and Seamus, have in the past two years made me a part of their family, greatly increasing the breadth and pleasure of my off-duty life.

My gratitude, admiration, and affection are beyond measure.

JUNE 1988

THE PIZZA CONNECTION

1. *The Game*

THE COURTROOM. A courtroom is laid out like a cathedral. Members of the public are the congregation, and they are always divided from the clergy by a railing. The jury box takes the place of the choir stalls. In this trial, the jury box is on the left, and opposite it, on the right, is another box, the soundproofed translators' booth. The raised altar at the back is the province of the judge. Or is he high priest, or grand rabbi? No matter. The question is: Who, and what, is being worshiped here?

The government calls it the biggest drug and Mafia case ever to come to trial in the United States. The press calls it the Pizza Connection. The trial about to begin here in the United States Courthouse in Manhattan will attempt to prove the existence within the nation's midst of a conspiracy to import and distribute more than one and one half tons of pure heroin. The street value of this much heroin, the government has said, is one and two thirds billion dollars. A small amount of the loot was discovered at the Palermo international airport in a suitcase

3

shipped from New York City. The cash was wrapped in pizzeria aprons, which made the tabloid title almost inevitable.

The defendants are twenty-two Sicilian-born men, all of them Mafia members, or associates, and nearly all of them in the food and pizza business. They will be represented here by twenty-two trial lawyers, members of the criminal defense bar.

This morning the courtroom is empty—a drafty, two-story vault of brown gloom paneled in dark wood and lit by four dim chandeliers. As in a church, laity and lesser clergy enter first. Members of the Altar Guild, vestrymen, altar boys, sacristans, deacons, and ushers are replaced here by court clerks, court reporters, marshals, translators, bailiffs, FBI men, and sound technicians, each carrying the tools of his trade.

When all has been made ready, the principals take their places. In this trial they are the four prosecutors, the twenty-two defendants, their twenty-two lawyers, the black-robed judge.

"Call the jury, please."

A door opens in the rear wall, and a holy white light shines through. Silence. Then a file of twenty-four ordinary people enters, snaking its way around the big world maps set up on the left end of the bench, and climbing into the jury box. Twelve of them are jurors, twelve more are alternates; a long trial is anticipated.

"Good morning, members of the jury," says the judge. "This is to be a fair trial. There is nothing more important in American justice. . . . Each defendant . . . is entitled to a fair trial. . . . The government is entitled to a fair trial. The people of the United States are entitled to a fair trial. . . .

"It is the jury which has the power to [decide] who wins and loses . . . [you] have become high officials in our system of government.

"The judge, of course, makes important decisions—like what time we break for lunch." His small smile draws tentative return smiles from the jury box. They are nervous, and he is practiced in putting them at their ease.

"The defendants are charged with participation in organized crime, in the trafficking of drugs. . . . The charges include commission of a murder."

The judge explains a few rules of the dangerous game about to begin. "What the lawyers say is not evidence . . . it is argument. What I say is not evidence. I have *no* knowledge of the facts in the case.

"Each defendant is entitled to have his case considered separately by the jury. For each defendant, you will have to reach a separate decision."

The man whose luck it is to be presiding here is the Honorable Pierre N. Leval. At forty-nine, just off the lengthy and difficult General Westmoreland libel case, the blond, bespectacled, deep-voiced, Roman-faced judge is a richly admired and respected jurist, a man at the height of his powers.

He introduces the lawyers for the government, four well-brushed and fit-looking men seated at the long table facing his raised bench: Richard Martin, Louis Freeh, Robert Stewart, Robert Bucknam. Each stands in turn.

He indicates the chief defendant, a small, grizzled man seated in the front pew just to the right of the aisle, his back to the room. "Gaetano Badalamenti is represented by Mr. Michael Kennedy."

A tall, slender man with red-gold hair and gold-wire glasses stands up and tenders the jury a slight bow. "Good morning." A row of counsel tables has been placed in front of the first pew, just inside the altar rail, and Kennedy occupies the aisle seat, directly in front of his client.

Three such double rows of lawyers and clients fill almost the entire spectator section of the courtroom to the right of the center aisle. The front double row bends in a dogleg toward the bench, so that four more lawyers and clients sit directly facing the jury, alongside the translators' booth. This crowded seating plan enables the defense, like the prosecution, to sit *en bloc.* The pews to the left of the aisle are reserved for the press and public, family and friends.

"On the side of the government, and on the side of the defendants, we are fortunate to have very fine lawyers, among the most respected lawyers of their profession," says Judge Leval. "But a trial is not a popularity contest. . . ." He reviews more rules of the game, then gavels his first recess.

Once the jury has departed, the members of the congregation stand and stretch. They wander out the center and side aisles to the granite corridor, which soon turns blue with smoke. The prosecutors have left the courtroom in the opposite direction, disappearing through the two doorways in the rear wall at either end of the bench, the same exits that are used by judge and jury. Ten of the twenty-two Pizza defense lawyers, as well as Judge Leval, are former government prosecutors of considerable experience. A reporter asks one of these ex-prosecutors to describe the jury-selection process which has been going on in this

5

courthouse for more than three weeks. What qualities were the prosecutors looking for?

"The government wanted an old, dumb, black jury," he says, "people who'll believe the Mafia is responsible for bringing drugs into this country and ruining their children."

And the ideal defense juror?

"We want him so goddamn dumb he walks into walls."

The evidence in this massive case has taken the government five years to assemble. It includes 55,000 wiretaps, few of them in English. The Sicilian-born defendants arrived only rather recently in the United States, in the 1960s and 1970s. Earlier Sicilian immigrants refer to these newcomers as "Zips," not an admiring term.

All but three of the twenty-two defendants are charged with being part of a RICO (Racketeer-Influenced and Corrupt Organizations Act) conspiracy, a relatively new law that allows the government to charge that apparently unrelated criminals are in fact acting together to further the aims of an overall criminal enterprise. Organized crime itself, or the Mafia, can be deemed such an enterprise. RICO convictions carry very severe penalties.

Because this is an organized-crime case, a Mafia case, the government has requested an anonymous jury. The identities of jurors and alternates are to be kept secret for their own security, and they will be under the protection of federal marshals at all times.

The defense lawyers object to the entire case. Its sheer size makes it untryable, they say. They have filed numerous pretrial motions to sever it into more manageable parts. The government has opposed the motions on grounds that holding several smaller trials would be time-wasting, repetitive, and needlessly expensive. Defense lawyers also object that the RICO charge may be unconstitutional, and that the existence of an anonymous jury is automatically prejudicial to their clients. Judge Leval has consistently upheld the government's positions.

The person chosen to deliver the government's opening statement is Department of Justice Attorney Robert Stewart, forty-nine, a man who has spent his life in law enforcement in New Jersey, and has accumulated an encyclopedic knowledge of this case. Stewart is an austere figure with pale, angular features, black-rimmed glasses, a black suit, and the voice and manner of an undertaker. He stands at a little oak podium that has been wheeled to face the jury box.

The first four front-row defendants are considered flight risks, too dangerous for bail, and the government has insisted that, for security reasons, they sit together, guarded by marshals. Gaetano Badalamenti, sixty-two, is said to be the most wanted narcotics fugitive in the world, and one-time Boss of Bosses of the entire Sicilian Mafia. In short, he is the *real* Godfather. His elder son, Vito, twenty-eight, sits one seat away to his right. Father and son have been extradited from Madrid. Between them sits Badalamenti's Number One nephew, Vincenzo Randazzo, extradited from Zurich. The fourth jailed defendant is no relation. Salvatore Salamone, scrawny and pale, in T-shirt and rose-colored glasses, is a small-time hood who has been brought here from federal prison where he is serving a twenty-year sentence for illegal gun possession.

These four men reside in MCC (Metropolitan Correctional Center), the federal pen attached to the backside of the courthouse, and they are escorted back and forth to the courtroom each day in handcuffs, which are removed before the jury enters.

The remaining eighteen defendants, seated behind and in front of the incarcerated four, all managed to make bail, though some had to raise as much as $3 million.

Normally, all the pews to the left of the aisle are reserved for reporters, sketch artists, and the public. This morning the first three rows have been cleared. Alone in the front row sits a slender, muscular man, in grey suit, black tie, knees crossed. Beneath a thick mat of black hair is a face white as a Mexican sugar skull, with alert black eyes. Rudolph Giuliani, thirty-nine, is United States attorney for the Southern District of New York. Giuliani is the composer of this entire opera. He has arranged and rehearsed this morning's rousing overture. He will be the mostly invisible maestro of the whole show to come.

Prosecutor Stewart grips the microphone tightly, runs his finger around a too-tight shirt collar, and in a flat voice, with minimal gestures, begins to tell a story. It is really a simple tale, he says: one single commodity bought, shipped, sold, replenished. But the numbers are huge. Stewart mentions "over a ton of pure heroin worth over $333 million, a third of a billion dollars, in the space of little over a year." This is a great deal of money, to be sure, though significantly less than the $1.65 billion the government had first announced.

A group of individuals in the New York–New Jersey area formed a joint business venture, Stewart continues. They then got together with a friend overseas and asked: Can you provide us with this commodity? The overseas friend called *his* friend and said he wanted to buy a certain raw material, then manufacture it into a commodity and transport it

7

to America, where it would be sold to customers. No checks, no bank accounts; the business was to be all cash.

"That's all that happened, ladies and gentlemen, month in and month out. But the commodity"—he pauses for as long as he can bear—"the commodity was massive amounts of contraband. And all the individuals engaged in the enterprise were members of the Mafia, or associates of Mafia members, both in Sicily and in the United States."

The business venture, says Stewart, came about in this fashion. After the breaking of the French Connection, in the late 1960s, the Zips gradually took over heroin distribution in the United States. American Mafiosi did not touch drugs, not directly; it was too dangerous. They left that to the lean, hungry newcomers.

The Zips were concentrated in the Knickerbocker Avenue area of Brooklyn. They were led by an avocado-shaped, bull-necked bakery owner named Salvatore "Toto" Catalano. The FBI believed that Toto's friend and codefendant Giuseppe "Il Bufalo" Ganci, a squat, grey-haired man who is not in court because of illness, coordinated the heroin importation and distribution through a firm known as Pronto Demolition. The business partners in Pronto funded the initial purchases of drugs from their Mafia suppliers in Sicily. The drugs were believed to have been distributed through a series of pizzerias in the East and Midwest.

Mountains of cash earned from the drug trade were collected and boxed by a subsidiary group of restaurant and pizzeria owners in New Jersey. These men, also recent Sicilian immigrants, used their contacts in Italy and Switzerland to set up a money-laundering operation that moved millions of dollars into the secret Swiss bank accounts of the Sicilian Mafia warlords.

The FBI actually saw and followed boxes and suitcases of cash leaving the restaurants in New Jersey. They watched the money couriers scuttle between New Jersey, the businessmen of Pronto Demolition in Brooklyn, and Joe Ganci's house in Queens. Through a network of wiretaps, they were able to eavesdrop on hundreds and eventually thousands of coded conversations, most of them in fragmented, slangy, near-incomprehensible Sicilian. The FBI agents were sure they were on to something big, but they were not quite sure what, and they did not yet have enough solid evidence to make arrests and go to trial. But the case grew more promising with each suitcase of cash smuggled out of the country.

Then two years ago, in 1983, the government got an unexpected break. One of Ganci's key players, a partner in Pronto Demolition, met at La Guardia Airport with the leader of a group of Midwestern Sicilians. These men, most of them pizza-parlor owners, lived in tiny Bible Belt towns in Illinois, Wisconsin, and Michigan. At first it appeared to the FBI that the Zips were enlarging their heroin distribution network to encompass the American heartland.

The Bureau put the Midwest pizza parlors under surveillance and struck gold. The Midwest men were not a heroin outlet for the Brooklyn Zips. They were acting on the instructions of a powerful, mysterious telephone caller from someplace overseas. The caller, code-named "The Uncle," was using the Midwest Sicilians to work out some sort of deal with the Zips of Brooklyn.

Then the FBI discovered the caller's identity. He was no one less than Gaetano Badalamenti, former *capo di tutti capi* of the Sicilian Mafia, the Boss of Bosses, and since 1978 the most wanted man in Italy. In November 1978 Badalamenti had fled Sicily in fear of his life after a brutal takeover by his Mafia enemies during the so-called Mafia wars. All the Midwesterners were his relatives.

The FBI had thrown the net out to catch a group of middle-level Mafiosi in Brooklyn, and into that net had swum the former Sicilian Godfather and his complete American crew.

Again they stepped up the surveillance, and the wiretaps. Soon six-agent teams working eight-hour shifts were listening to forty-seven telephones around the clock, including a number of outdoor public pay phones, which the callers favored for security reasons. By March of 1984 the FBI believed that the Uncle overseas was attempting to deliver something to the Zips in the United States. A great deal of mistrust was evident on both sides, but the conversations indicated something was about to happen within the next month, in Florida.

Then, astonishingly, the agents heard Badalamenti instruct Pietro "Pete" Alfano, his nephew and chief Midwest henchman, to meet him in Madrid, Spain. After nearly seven years in hiding, the Boss of Bosses was about to break cover.

With Badalamenti himself suddenly within their grasp, the American authorities faced a crucial decision. They could wait for the arrival of the Florida delivery, capture what they felt was certain to be a substantial amount of drugs, and have solid evidence to put these Zips away for a very long time. Or they could move now, grab the fox, and take their chances on the drugs.

They went for the second choice, the sexy one. As the leading investigator put it, "Anybody can get heroin. We may not get another shot at Badalamenti for ten years."

The FBI placed several agents on Alfano's KLM flight from Chicago to Madrid. At Madrid airport, Alfano was met by young Vito Badalamenti, the Uncle's elder son, and the FBI men were met by a team of Spanish police. The police and FBI men followed Badalamenti and Alfano to an apartment house in a prosperous section of the city. That night the building was surrounded by Spanish plain-clothes men. The next morning a small man neatly dressed in a grey suit and white socks emerged from the block of furnished flats and headed for the bakery. With him was Alfano. The Spanish police allowed them to move down the street, out of earshot of the apartment, then grabbed the two men and bundled them into a waiting police car.

Six other police officers stormed the apartment and found a petite blonde woman making pasta. Mrs. Badalamenti appeared to know no Spanish. But her son Vito, who emerged dripping from the shower, knew exactly what was happening. He quickly dressed and accompanied the police out the door.

Within minutes of the arrest of Badalamenti, word was flashed to Thomas L. Sheer in New York. He was the flat-bellied, slab-handed deputy director of the FBI in charge of the New York office. The prize was in the bag. Now it was time to pull in the net on five years' work.

Sheer's New York headquarters had assembled enough manpower to serve twenty search warrants and twelve arrest warrants. It also coordinated the simultaneous raids carried out by teams from the FBI's Newark, Philadelphia, Chicago, Detroit, and Milwaukee headquarters. Each squad "generally knew where it was going," Sheer said later, and each squad leader had had time to review the files on his man, count the number of people in the family, the number and location of exits from the house, and calculate the necessary number of men. Each search team was equipped with sledgehammers, pry bars, cameras, flashlights, inventory sheets, and whatever else might be needed.

Each team member had a specific responsibility within the squad: one was designated photographer, another recording agent, a third was in charge of the physical security of his team, so that, as Sheer said, "no one pops out of a closet unexpectedly."

When the minute hand clicked straight up on the clock on the wall, Sheer said, "Execute your warrants," and FBI agents simultaneously banged on suspects' doors from the Bronx to Wisconsin. The agents had all been instructed, "As soon as the subject is in custody, start your search and call in again."

The searches and seizures went on all day. Sheer and his men occupied three tiers of consoles in the FBI's New York command post.

Observers and officials from the Drug Enforcement Administration and the New York Police Department were also on hand. The smoke of pipes and cigars was soon overwhelming; at noon, sandwiches arrived.

From Queens, New York, to Oregon, Illinois, the search teams turned up plenty of guns. Ganci had four semiautomatic rifles and three pistols. Alfano's little Midwest pizzeria had a rifle, a silenced machine pistol, three handguns, two flak jackets, and a dart gun for anaesthetizing horses. But the only drugs found that day were one ounce of cocaine hidden in a filing cabinet in Temperance, Michigan.

Such, according to Stewart, is the case the government will prove. The evidence, he says, has two themes. One deals with the mechanics of smuggling: how you get the drugs in, the money out. He promises that the government will show in detail how these defendants moved more than $40 million in cash to Sicily alone. This does not include money sent to Brazil, he adds with a thin smile.

"The second theme involves the dynamics of the Mafia . . . the secret criminal organization which provided the cement which held this conspiracy together." The Mafia is extremely disciplined, Stewart explains. These men had no ability to enforce their contracts under law. But they had a secret criminal society, and Mafia discipline is so strict it enables a man to walk down a dark alley with $1 million in cash and fear no ambush.

Stewart moves on to the sizzle of his presentation, aided by the big electrified map boards at the left end of the bench. As he speaks, these light up and twinkle in Brooklyn, then Rio, Paris, Palermo, linking his story together like a flashy TV documentary. To add drama and flow, Stewart tosses in subplots about bad drugs, deadly betrayals, and secret codes, all to be explained later.

Stewart has begun struggling to identify for the jury each member of the cast of characters in his baroque tale, no easy task, since they are almost all small, dark Sicilian men of middle years, and—to American ears—their names tend to run together in a rushing torrent of liquid vowels.

The leader of the New York group, says Stewart, is Salvatore "Toto" Catalano, "seated over there in front of the window, behind his attorney, Ivan Fisher." Catalano's eyes are narrowed to slits, and he has tilted back in his chair so that his bullet-shaped head is pillowed against a metal filing cabinet. "Mr. Catalano is also known as 'The Baker,' because he owns a bakery in Queens. Now, Mr. Catalano is a very quiet and modest man. He drives no Mercedes. He does not, like some other of these defendants, stand out for hours on street corners in freezing weather waiting for pay phones to ring."

Catalano's chief lieutenant was Giuseppe Ganci. He is not here, because of illness. His lawyer, Mr. Mario Malerba, is here, sitting next to Mr. Fisher.

Stewart flicks a page and turns around to point at the second row of defendants, seated behind the incarcerated four. "Three of these men stood out in the snow on cold winter nights taking the phone calls." They are Giuseppe "Joe" Lamberti, on the aisle, his cousin Salvatore Lamberti, and, seated between them, Salvatore Mazzurco, who is a brother-in-law of Joe Lamberti. Three chunky, greying, balding men stare into their laps. Distinctions have begun to blur.

Stewart now points to two defendants seated side by side in the back row. One is lean and hawk-faced; the other is stocky and has a full head of curly silver hair. "In New Jersey, Gaetano Mazzara and a man named Frank Castronovo were business partners in the Roma Restaurant and Pizzeria in Menlo Park. These then are the seven individuals— Toto Catalano, Giuseppe Ganci, Joe Lamberti, Sal Lamberti, Sal Mazzurco, Gaetano Mazzara and Frank Castronovo—who bought, sold and distributed the heroin."

Next Stewart turns to Toto Catalano's overseas suppliers. Their leader was Gaetano Badalamenti, of Cinisi, a small town west of Palermo, Sicily. He supplied the men in New York and New Jersey with heroin between 1978 and 1980, "when he was compelled to relocate to Brazil." Hearing this, Badalamenti worms his big head around to the left to gaze mildly upon the prosecutor and jury. He has pebbly ivory skin, a grim mouth, eyes like lumps of coal; the unreadable visage of a Pharaoh.

"Mr. Badalamenti was operating through his nephew Pietro Alfano, who lived in northern Illinois, just below the Michigan border." Alfano in turn gave orders to other family members who also lived in tiny towns in the Midwest. All of these people were related to Gaetano Badalamenti by blood or marriage: Salvatore Evola, Giuseppe Trupiano, Giuseppe Vitale, and Emmanuele Palazzolo. Stewart mumbles the lyrical Sicilian names as if his mouth were filled with peanut butter. Small, pathetic, spaniel-eyed Palazzolo shrinks back slightly, as though to hide from the accusation.

The prosecutor again approaches his map. As Stewart mentions each city, a flashing green light twinkles in the appropriate spot. "New York City"—sparkle! sparkle!—"was the center of operations." Another light indicates Rio de Janeiro, Brazil, the primary location of defendants Gaetano Badalamenti, his nephew Randazzo, and his son Vito.

"Pietro Alfano, another nephew, was located in Oregon, Illinois." Flash! "His people held and delivered packages, and collected money for transfer to Brazil."

A second group of suppliers operated from the small town of Partinico, Sicily. Twinkle! They sent a messenger to America. The messenger was defendant Cangialosi, seated in the second row, who dealt with defendants Lorenzo DeVardo and Giovanni Ligammari. The drug suppliers needed investors. They brought in the wealthy restaurant owner Frank Polizzi and the buyer Filippo Casamento.

These more or less obscure defendants, somewhat outside the main drama, are mostly arrayed along the right-hand side of the defense block, under the high windows, lost in the quagmire of Sicilian names and defiant lawyers. The exception is Ligammari, a sour-faced man with thick grey curls, who stands propped against the paneled wall. This so-called investor is by profession a ditchdigger. He crushed his back one day in a job accident, and now lives in chronic pain.

And how did they deal with the huge profits, the third of a billion dollars? Stewart says that Sal Salamone, the scraggly young front-row hood in the T-shirt, changed small bills into large bills. Defendant Sal Greco, the pencil-thin, silver-haired, elegant-looking man in the back-row aisle seat, sent it out of the country.

"So much for the lengthy indictment," says prosecutor Stewart, as though all has now been explained, each defendant fixed in the jury's eye, every nuance of law illuminated. The jurors seem to be trying to look both attentive and impassive, all except for #4, an elderly black man in the front row. He works as a night janitor, and has fallen fast asleep.

Stewart outlines the government's case, listing like a menu the sequence of bloody and chemical dishes the government will set before the jury. First will come the notorious Mafia defector Tomasso Buscetta, to tell of Mafia rules, structure, and involvement in narcotics.

The prosecutor mentions certain inferior narcotics, and how some of these defendants traveled to Sicily in 1980 to inspect future shipments, and how the following month some of the commodity in question was captured by the police in Milan. Stewart is building toward higher drama. The government will go back even further, he promises, back to the 1970s, to show the arrival in the United States of the Zips, the rise to Mafia power of their leader, Salvatore Catalano, and how the ruthless American Mafia don Carmine Galante was removed from office to make way for the Zips and their drug deals.

A BROOKLYN DOG DAY.   The temperature was 88°, humidity an energy-sapping 80%. Joe Turano, owner of Joe & Mary's Restaurant, at 205 Knickerbocker Avenue, had already stripped down to his undershirt. The heat of the pasta cooking in the restaurant kitchen pushed the indoor temperature to 100°. It was midday. The afternoon would be unbearable.

Constanza Turano, Joe's daughter, was behind the small bar at the front of the restaurant, dusting around the bottles of red wine and grappa. Her brother John was setting tables on the small rear patio. He took particular care with the central table, the long rectangle partially shaded by grapevines and placed facing the doorway into the darkened restaurant.

His father, Joe Turano, was expecting his cousin Carmine Galante. Galante, released six months earlier from federal prison, was not making a social call. The Bonanno Family boss had arranged the lunch so that he could reconcile two former friends.

The sixty-nine-year-old Mafia chieftain entered the restaurant soon after noon. He was alone. This was unusual, because he rarely traveled anywhere without his two young Sicilian bodyguards—the handsome, suntanned blond one and the black-haired Donatello ideal.

Galante stopped to sit and talk for a few moments with the old grandmother Turano. They both had been born in Castellammare del Golfo, a small village on Sicily's northwest coast, and they spoke of the cool breeze off the Tyrrhenian Sea that allowed no humidity ever to hang over Castellammare.

Joe Turano greeted his cousin with great respect. He pointed to the vine-hung patio and invited him to escape the heat of the kitchen. Turano suggested antipasto and some wine and fresh bread. Galante nodded in agreement.

Joe Paravati, another lunchtime diner on that inferno of a day, had been reluctant to remain when he saw that the small restaurant did not have air conditioning. But his friend Joe Polizzi insisted. The food would be a gift in return for the ride from the Bronx that Paravati had given him. Polizzi's partner joined them at the rear table to the left of the patio doorway. Polizzi had eaten here before. He said the fish was good. They were the only customers inside the restaurant. Joe Paravati ordered the fish, rubbed the sweat from his hands, and spread the napkin on his lap.

The street door opened, and two tall young men entered. They wore aviator sunglasses. One was blond and one was dark. Joe Paravati wasn't sure what it was, but something about them looked wrong. Then he realized they were wearing leather jackets, blazer-cut leather jackets, buttoned, in 90° heat. Paravati decided to pay attention to his meal.

Cesare Bonventre, the blond man, wore his curly hair fashionably long, emphasizing the classic features of his tanned Roman face. The aviator sunglasses and black leather blazer gave him the look of a young and arrogant Hollywood star. Baldassare "Baldo" Amato, the other man, was equally handsome, with alabaster skin and thick, jet-black hair. The two young gangsters were accompanied by Leonard "Nardo" Coppolla, a close associate of Carmine Galante and former friend of Joe Turano. Coppolla had been summoned by Galante so that a reconciliation could take place.

In February of 1979 Coppolla and Turano had quarreled. Coppolla had an arrangement with Mary Turano, Joe's wife, that she would make payments for him to an insurance broker. The broker claimed that he had not been paid on several occasions, and Coppolla accused Mary Turano of keeping the money. Joe Turano ordered Coppolla never to enter his restaurant again. The dispute had come to Galante's attention and he had designated July 12 as the day for the meet when these grievances would be heard.

Coppolla and the two bodyguards sat at a table just inside the front door of the restaurant. John Turano offered them espresso. He would serve the coffee, then he would tell Mr. Galante that they were here. He placed the silver pot and three small cups on the table.

The patio door was in the back wall. The right wall was interrupted by a small pantry storeroom, and the swinging door to the kitchen. A line of tables ran along the left wall. From Joe Paravati's table at the far end of the line he could see into a corner of the garden. He thought it might be nice to have lunch out there. Then he noticed the young waiter in the patio doorway hailing the two leather coats at the front. Paravati put his head down and studied the bluefish *oreganato* on his plate as the three men made their way out onto the patio.

Carmine Galante sat facing the doorway in the middle of the long side of the center table. Joe Turano sat at one end. Galante greeted Coppolla and invited the three men to join him. The Bonanno boss knew his bodyguards' leather jackets were worn to conceal the pistols in their belts. Galante had many enemies. Upon his release from prison he had plunged the Bonanno Family into the heroin trade. He had set up a network of Sicilians to replace the supply lines broken up by the smashing of the French Connection drug ring. He had ignored the warning of the more traditional Mafia dons about dealing drugs. Worse, he refused to share any of the profits of his network with any of the other families. "To hell with them" was his attitude. If they weren't prepared to take the risks, why should they get the benefits? Soon his wealth would make him the strongest boss in America, and he could tell the other old men to get lost. They were getting soft. Their American soldiers were weak, corrupt. Their own sons wanted nothing to do with old-country ways; they wanted to go to college. Galante had the Zips, the young Sicilians of Knickerbocker Avenue, men who had been in the United States only since the late 1960s. Earlier immigrants called them Zips because they spoke the native language so fast. The Zips knew about *omerta* and wars and vendettas. They grew up with these things. It was their heritage. He had brought them to America to strengthen the stock. They were his right arm, his mules, and his soldiers, as well as his bodyguards.

As Joe Paravati cut into the soft flesh of the bluefish, the phone rang. Young John Turano moved from the kitchen to answer. It was James Galante, the nephew and sometime driver of Carmine. "Is my uncle still there?"

Turano knew the caller. He had come to the restaurant to pick his uncle up many times. Turano answered, "Yeah, he's here."

"I'll be right over," replied Galante.

Less than a minute later a four-door blue Mercury Montego pulled up outside the restaurant. It was 2:40 P.M. The packed pavements and blaring traffic of a Knickerbocker lunch hour had subsided, and the avenue was quietly baking in the heat. The doors of the blue Mercury opened and from each door emerged a masked man. The driver stepped out onto Knickerbocker. He wore a red-striped ski mask over his head, and held a .3030 M1 carbine at his side. His three passengers moved at a quick jog to the door of Joe & Mary's and pushed it open.

Constanza Turano was still behind the bar. She was transfixed at the sight of the three gunmen, unable to move or call out. Joe Paravati looked up from his bluefish. A tall man in dark clothes and an olive grey ski mask was bearing down on him. The masked man had a pump-action shotgun cradled in his arm. Behind him came a medium-built masked man with a double-barreled shotgun swinging at his side, and following behind was a small potbellied gunman waving a pistol and spinning round to check on Constanza, who had begun to make pathetic whining sounds.

Her brother heard his sister and stepped out of the kitchen to see what was wrong. The first man raised the shotgun, pointed it at John Turano, and said, "Keep your fucking mouth shut." He turned to the gunman behind and said, "In the back, Sally."

The three men rushed toward the door to the patio. As they passed Paravati's table the tall man with the pump-action stopped, turned his head. The shotgun he cradled in his arm was leveled at the table. "Don't move," he barked.

John Turano screamed "Papa!" He ran to the little storeroom alongside the kitchen. He knew that in a box on the top shelf was a .38 special revolver, loaded and ready to fire.

The small, potbellied gunman saw John run. He turned, swearing. John managed to reach the storeroom and to close the door. He reached toward the shelf for the gun while trying to hold onto the door. It flew open. He could hear his father shout, *"What are you doing?"* The potbellied gunman shot John Turano once in the back as he tried to dive for cover.

Constanza crawled behind the refrigerator beside the door and closed her eyes as the explosions went off in front of her. The man with the pump-action stepped out onto the patio.

The gunman with the double-barreled shotgun fired first, straight at Carmine Galante. Thirty pellets of buckshot hit him in the stomach as he tried to stand. The pump-action opened up, hitting him in the face and throat and spinning him on his side.

Joe Turano screamed, *"What are you doing?"*

The shooter with the pump-action, who was standing beside Turano, turned, placed the barrel against Turano's chest and fired. The oo buckshot ripped his chest apart. The paper wadding from the shotgun shell imbedded itself in his shoulder.

The pump-action turned again to Galante. The second blast of buckshot tore lumps of muscle from the old man's right arm. As he slumped forward, the assassin holding the double-barrel fired into his back.

Nardo Coppolla tried to push back from the table. He never saw Bonventre pull and fire the .38 automatic pistol. Galante's "bodyguard" hit Coppolla once in the forehead, then fired five shots into his chest. As the dead Coppolla fell off his chair, the pump-action stepped forward and blew the back of his head off, then fired one more blast into the body. Bonventre stood up unscathed.

Constanza stared in horror through the patio doorway. She could see the black-haired "bodyguard," Baldo Amato, crouching behind an overturned table, a .38 special revolver in his hand.

Migdalia Figuero lived in the third-floor walk-up apartment at 202 Knickerbocker Avenue, across the street from Joe & Mary's Restaurant. Twenty-four years old and just married, she was preparing the midday meal. The heat from the stove made the apartment almost unbearably hot. She had opened wide the windows overlooking Knickerbocker Avenue. As she stood at the stove she heard shouts, screams, then silence. Knickerbocker was a tough street, always full of fights, always drunks and voices screaming in Italian or in Spanish. Migdalia continued cooking. The silence was strange. The constant hum of traffic was gone. Then she heard the bangs, fireworks perhaps. It was just eight days after the Fourth of July, and there were still nights broken by the pop of cherry bombs. No, these explosions had a beat, a staccato that sounded more ominous. Migdalia thought she heard cries. She went to the window.

A masked gunman stood in the street, at the side of a double-parked car. She heard him shout, "Get on the ground, get on the ground!" His rifle was pointed at several passers-by crouched or lying on the pavement. Others were running away. The shots seemed to be coming from Joe & Mary's. The Sicilians. Mafia. The three masked gunmen ran out.

Inside, the two bodyguards, Amato and Bonventre, looked at their boss. The cigar he had been chewing was shattered by buckshot and drooped from his mouth like a snapped twig. The bodyguards turned and fled. Joe Turano moaned.

Joe Paravati sat frozen in his seat in fear as he watched the masked men flee. He was about to get up when Amato and Bonventre marched quickly through the room. Paravati let them leave, then ran around the room trying the doors to the kitchen, the storeroom, searching for another exit. His friend Polizzi grabbed him, and they ran, shouting, out the front door. Paravati was breathless, panic-stricken, wanting only to get away from the smoke and the noise.

As Migdalia Figuero stared down at the gunman in the street, the door of the restaurant burst open and three masked men rushed out. One ran around the blue car. They all opened doors and jumped in. The car sped off. 270 NYU. She saw it. 270 NYU. The door of the restaurant burst open again. 270 NYU. Two men emerged, half running, looking around, almost hopping across the street, walking as though to run was to condemn themselves as killers, yet to walk was to be caught. Both wore leather coats. The tall, blond guy's arm hung by his side. He was carrying a pistol. 270 NYU.

Just as they disappeared out of sight, the door burst open again, and a young man staggered out. His chest was covered in blood. He was crying, screaming, "Help, Jesus help!" Three more frightened men, Paravati and his two friends, pushed past the wounded man, running, not stopping. The blood-covered man staggered back inside. The other men ran. Migdalia's baby started to cry. A crowd was gathering now, moving cautiously. The baby cried. 270 NYU. She wrote it down.

New York policeman Robert Dixson, of the 83rd Precinct, an eleven-year veteran of the force, sat in his police car. He and his partner, John Bobot, had been assigned to patrol the Charlie-David sector of the precinct. As they drove along Gratton Street, the radio crackled. "Report of shots. Knickerbocker Avenue. Any units in the area to respond." Dixson and Bobot were three blocks away. Dixson switched the siren on. Knickerbocker Avenue was astir. Kids were running toward a crowd gathering around Joe & Mary's Restaurant. It was a Zip joint. More trouble. Dixson pulled to a halt outside the restaurant.

Bobot drew his gun, ran to the door, and cautiously walked inside. A few seconds later he emerged. Dixson had just finished locking the car. Bobot was shocked, disgusted. "Tell them we've got two down and two going."

Dixson picked up the handset and called for ambulance, backup, homicide, and crime scene.

Detective Bill Clark of the Queens Homicide Task Force pulled up just as the ambulance was taking Joe Turano and his son to the hospital. It was 3:00 P.M., ten minutes after the shooting. Clark walked past the thronging crowd of kids, through the horde of cops and paramedics, into the dark restaurant. The patio out behind was splattered with blood. The right-hand wall had brain matter splashed along its concrete face. Clark instantly recognized the figure lying wedged between the wall and a tumbled-over chair, the cigar, shot to pieces, still jammed in his mouth. Every detective in Queens knew Carmine Galante.

. . . THURSDAY MORNING, OCTOBER 24, 1985.

THE COURTROOM. "Now Sal Catalano had it all!" exclaims Stewart, winding up his description of the slaughter around the table at Joe & Mary's, and how the murder propelled into prominence the gang of recent Sicilian immigrants, the Zips, who figured so importantly in this case.

In the second row, defendant Baldo Amato has listened attentively, alert but cool, as Stewart fingered him as a participant in the killing. Baldo's pal Bonventre is one of thirteen men indicted in this case who are not present in the courtroom. Twelve have vanished, fled, or managed to get their indictments quashed. A few weeks after the arrests, the thirteenth man, Bonventre, turned up in three barrels of glue in New Jersey, his legs in one barrel, his head and shoulders in another, his torso in the third. This is one of many lurid facts in the Pizza case that the defense will succeed in keeping from the jury as "inflammatory," "prejudicial," or "irrelevant."

"Why all this shooting?" the gaunt, black-clad prosecutor asks, and answers himself, "Vast amounts of money." Stewart reels off deals and swaps, illicit flights and furtive meetings. He describes millions being moved in chartered jets, overloaded banks in the Caribbean, vanishing suitcases stuffed with cash. The money-laundering narrative segues into accounts of drug deals, of multi-kilos sold between Philadelphia and New York. The story races toward a conclusion. "In 1983 the conspirators got over-extended. They over-bought and ran out of cash," says Stewart in tones implying complete inner knowledge of the workings of the cartel. "Meanwhile, Gaetano Badalamenti says: 'I want cash on the barrelhead.' *They* want credit. So it's a standoff. Until, in March, 1984, they find a way to get the money to Badalamenti. . . .

"Alfano is ordered to meet Badalamenti in Madrid, Spain. When he does, everyone—Badalamenti, his son Vito, his nephew Alfano—is arrested." Coordinated raids in the United States pick up thirty-two more alleged conspirators. The ensuing searches produced narcotics records, narcotics paraphernalia, weapons, including "39 hand guns, and three silencers . . . which have no particular use in the restaurant business." So saying, Stewart gathers his papers from the podium and walks back to the prosecution table.

Judge Leval announces a brief recess. The jury leaves looking pole-axed, dizzy with drugs and money, and a veritable phone book of Italian names. Have they noticed yet, defense lawyers wonder as they straggle out, that amid all this mayhem of blood and guns, nobody has turned up any narcotics?

... OCTOBER 14, 1982.

THE WHITE HOUSE. On a bright Thursday morning the smiling President of the United States watched the Brazilian soccer star Pelé juggle a leather soccer ball in front of a prepicked crowd of vigorous, healthy American children. Ronald Reagan's first term was almost half over. Congressional elections would occur in less than a month's time, and it was important that the President dominate the public eye.

The President and the soccer star had been brought together to encourage the youth of America to participate in healthful sports. Reagan beamed his best Hollywood smile, the air hummed with the whirr of the superfast autowinders on cameras, and the White House press corps unleashed the usual barrage of questions.

It was the first photo opportunity of the day. The Reagan White House basked in the glory of a continual flow of public-opinion polls showing that the former movie star was shaping up as the most popular president in U.S. history. Many of his top aides credited his success to their masterful manipulation of the media. The Reagan team met each morning to decide the message of the day, a message to be pounded home to the waiting press corps, and channeled to a select group of loyal journalists and columnists—George Will, William F. Buckley, Jr., Evans & Novak—known to look with favor on the growing neoconservative power bloc best epitomized by Reagan himself.

Today's message was not about child-health or soccer-development programs. Not at all. The little press show in the Rose Garden was just a wonderful opportunity to show Reagan as the shepherd of the nation's young and pure, a gentle man dedicated to preserving the innocence of youth.

October 14 had also been selected by his media advisers as the day Ronald Reagan would take out a contract on the mob. The President would talk law and order. The catchword of the day would be *strength*. Strength was one of the key themes that had propelled the former governor of California into the White House with one of the largest majorities in history: strength against Communism, might against terrorists, toughness on crime, war on drugs.

President Reagan was scarcely the first president aiming for reelection to declare all-out war on drugs. Eisenhower had tried it, and

Nixon. So had Herbert Hoover, for that matter, if you considered alcohol a drug; and you could probably find some ringing words about the evils of marijuana in the speeches of Franklin Roosevelt. Drug wars are politically sexy, especially in puritan America. They are high-voltage. Nobody is *for* drugs.

The Reagan entourage—bulletproof limousines, Secret Service "war wagons," Cherokee Chargers with blackened windows, a fully equipped emergency ambulance, police vans filled with cops and sniff dogs—rolled out the rear of the White House and set off on the short drive to the headquarters of the Department of Justice.

Attorney General William French Smith had ordered the entire Department of Justice staff to assemble in the building's imposing Great Hall. As thousands of prosecuting attorneys, agents of the FBI, DEA, Immigration and Naturalization Service, and other law-enforcement agencies, their secretaries and clerks, streamed in and took seats in the vast, formal blue-velvet auditorium, swagged with gilded rope and watched over by the immense golden eagle on the Great Seal of the United States, Attorney General Smith was joined on the stage by the director of the FBI, Judge William Webster. Just behind Judge Webster and the attorney general stood the white-faced, black-thatched master-mind of the plan the President was about to outline.

At age thirty-seven, Rudolph Giuliani had lost none of the fervor that as a youth had made him seek out the seminary of the Montfort Fathers, a French order with missions in Malawi, Peru, and India. Giuliani was the ambitious son of an Italian-American pizza-restaurant and bar owner. His aspirations reached beyond the parochial schools of Brooklyn. After he finished at the seminary, he and his school pal Alan Palca hoped to be accepted to study for the priesthood.

Giuliani explained later that his enthusiasm for the work of God had been tempered by his attraction to the opposite sex. "I could not understand how to live the rest of my life either not being married or without women." The would-be seminarian opted for a career in law, while his pal Palca went on to become a priest.

After graduating with high marks from the University of Maryland Law School in 1968, Giuliani began clerking for U.S. District Court Judge Lloyd McMahon, a man who later described his twenty-five-year-old clerk as a "natural lawyer" and "a regular Pied Piper." In 1970 Giuliani joined the U.S. Attorney's Office for the Southern District of New York. Within weeks the new man was juggling several cases, and by the end of his first year he had prosecuted eighteen cases and won most of them. The following year the workaholic prosecutor hit the headlines with two cases that rocked the police and political structure in New York.

Giuliani supervised the New York City Police Department corruption cases, which later formed the basis for the book and movie *Prince of the City.* In the fall of 1974 he prosecuted Congressman Bertram Podell in another corruption case, and mauled the defense team so badly that on the tenth day of trial the defendant decided to throw in the towel and plead guilty.

In 1975 one of Giuliani's mentors, Southern District federal judge Harold Tyler, was appointed deputy attorney general. Tyler took Giuliani with him to Washington as his associate deputy. Two years later they left the government and went into private law practice together.

The landslide victory of Ronald Reagan brought Giuliani back to the Department of Justice, this time as associate attorney general, the nation's number-three man in law enforcement. He was thirty-four years old.

Almost immediately Giuliani caused waves. The day before he was sworn into office, he and his aide Ken Caruso met with the general counsel for the McDonnell Douglas Corporation, which was facing charges in a highly visible foreign-payments scandal. Giuliani dropped the charges and almost precipitated open courtroom rebellion by attorneys from the Justice Department's Criminal Division.

Caruso denounced the Criminal Division as a bunch of crybabies. Giuliani admits that his relations with the Criminal Division were adversely affected, but he was not about to let interdepartmental feuding stymie his plans. He was anxious to implement that part of the Reagan Doctrine which called for more action against crime. His experience as head of the U.S. Attorney's Office narcotics unit in New York had convinced him that the FBI was the organization best staffed, structured, and equipped to tackle the massive illegal drug problem, and he was instrumental in the crucial decision to expand the powers of the FBI to assume direct responsibility for all narcotics investigations.

Thus, in the tradition of the Pied Piper, Giuliani set about leading his tight group of cohorts in a strategy aimed at expanding the dominion of the FBI and mounting an all-out federal assault on drug traffickers. Caruso called it Giuliani's "Great Coup."

During his first year in office Giuliani submitted budgets for several ambitious programs. All were rejected out of hand by White House budget chief David Stockman. It was inevitable. Besides promising to do something about crime, Reagan had also campaigned to cut federal spending, and to keep one promise required sabotaging the other. But the smart, aggressive young men around Giuliani were not going to be held back by mere inconsistency. They decided to bypass Stockman and appeal directly to the law-and-order instincts of Ronald Reagan. Giuliani's office came up with a strategy. They would go to the attorney general with a well-defined program, and convince him to present it to the President and his cabinet in person. They would do this in secrecy, so that the miserly Stockman would know nothing of the expensive plan until he heard it from the President's own mouth.

This bright October morning as President Reagan drove to the Justice Department, Rudolph Giuliani was already at the podium, happy in the knowledge that his Great Coup was about to come off. The plan had been kept so tight that even members of the department's Criminal Division were unaware of its existence. Giuliani stood on the blue-carpeted stage watching the head of the Criminal Division enter through the metal detectors at the distant doorway and take a seat in the audience.

Ronald Reagan advanced to the podium and set about doing what he did best: communicate a written message via television to the great American public. He turned his head in mid-sentence from the clear-glass Teleprompter on his left to the Teleprompter on his right, where the same text appeared. To the viewing audience it was as though he were master of all he surveyed, addressing first those far off to the left in his live audience, and then those far off to the right. At moments when he could remember a phrase or sentence, he gazed levelly ahead, eyeball to eyeball with the nation.

The man was talking action. He was asking Congress today for a $100-million war chest. He intended to reorganize and streamline the nation's drug-fighting forces. The beleaguered Drug Enforcement Administration would be put under the control of the crack new Federal Bureau of Investigation. Twelve new drug and organized-crime task forces would be set up in key cities throughout the nation: New York, Los Angeles, Atlanta, Chicago, Boston, Houston, St. Louis, Baltimore, San Diego, San Francisco, Denver, and Detroit. The regional forces would be modeled on one already operating in Florida and would target, prosecute, and ultimately cripple organized crime in America. Reagan spoke of a vast nationwide criminal syndicate whose power had reached awesome new heights, an invisible, lawless empire. The beefed-up task forces would be equal to the mighty job. The government was planning to hire and train 900 new FBI special agents, 200 new assistant U.S. attorneys, and a new support staff of 400. The cost would be fearful, but the urgency was great. Organized crime and drugs were sapping the nation's strength, rotting her moral fiber. Nothing less than all-out war was required.

Not surprisingly, the Republican majority in the House and Senate, also facing reelection, voted the money. By January 1983 the Organized Crime Drug Enforcement Task Force was ready to go into action. It had $100 million to spend, and good people to spend it. What was needed was a big case, something to highlight the administration's all-out commitment, a very public win.

In Washington, Giuliani was growing restless. He had become further embroiled in the ongoing internal politics of the Justice Department. The initial clash over the dropping of the McDonnell Douglas charges had left deep scars, and Giuliani's brash public style continued to annoy some of the more staid figures in the administration.

In New York, in February, the U.S. attorney for the Southern District, John Martin, Jr., let it be known he planned to resign. Soon several key figures in Justice were suggesting to Giuliani that the Southern District spot might be a job where he could stretch his wings. In New York he would be the boss again, unfettered by codes of conduct or office politics. In technical terms it was a demotion, a career plunge, but this baseball fanatic from Brooklyn recognized a base-stealing opportunity when he saw one.

By April he had moved his baseball souvenirs and law books into the executive office at One Saint Andrew's Plaza, the modern red-brick-and-black-glass structure attached umbilically to the old limestone courthouse that houses both the offices of the Southern District and the inmates of MCC. Giuliani had arrived in Manhattan at the precise moment when the Organized Crime Drug Enforcement Task Force was expanding a Brooklyn-based drug-trafficking investigation into a massive international surveillance of the world's most powerful drug cartel: the Sicilian Mafia.

Giuliani could now quite legitimately claim that he had conceived the plans for the war against the mob and drugs, that he had personally designed and lobbied in Washington for the legislative and law-enforcement tools needed to do the job, and that he was now back in New York to put them to work on the streets. Here was a man who got what he wanted.

2. *The Players*

. . . JULY 1985.

UPPER EAST SIDE, NEW YORK CITY.   The phone rang in the elegant, one-man law office of Michael Kennedy, a tall, slender trial lawyer of forty-eight years, red-gold hair, and deadly reputation. The caller was a professor at the University of Chicago Law School, expert in extradition law. He talked about an unusual federal prisoner who for some months had been kept discreetly cooling his heels in New York City.

The man had been arrested in Madrid, along with a son and a nephew. All three had false papers and stubbornly denied their true identities. But the FBI never doubted whom they had. He was Gaetano Badalamenti, once the leader of the entire Sicilian Mafia. Until 1978 Badalamenti had been *capo di tutti capi.* He had tumbled into the FBI's net completely by accident. It was as if they had been trolling for bass and pulled up the Loch Ness Monster.

Now, more than a year after his arrest, and only a few weeks before his trial was to begin, Badalamenti wanted to change lawyers.

"I don't represent heroin dealers," Kennedy said.

"Not even if the guy's innocent?"

"How do you know that?"

"The government has a snitch in with the Old Man. He says so."

Kennedy agreed to talk to Badalamenti. They spoke through an interpreter. The lawyer liked this little, grizzled man with eyes like burning coals. His grave, superior manner was as courtly as Kennedy's own. "You know, Meester Kennedy," he said, after a bit, "certain things a man must do in life." Kennedy understood this as a reference to Badalamenti's lifelong criminal career. In Italy he had been accused of many crimes: tax evasion, smuggling, fraud, extortion. He was wanted there now for numerous crimes, including ultimate responsibility for the deaths of numerous magistrates and other officials assassinated in Sicily's ongoing, bloody Mafia wars. But Badalamenti denied dealing drugs. He loathed drugs, repudiated them *assolutamente.* He did not profess a moral point of view; he spoke as a businessman, a lifetime outlaw and professional smuggler, mostly of tobacco. Drugs were bad business. The money was never worth the risk. Only greedy pigs touched drugs. Badalamenti's views were well known throughout Italy. Kennedy could check. The Old Man had been exiled from Sicily, thrown out of the Mafia and forced to flee for his life precisely because he would not bend with the times, would not go along with the new Mafia ways, would not abandon his conservative stance, would not deal drugs. The lawyer believed the Old Man.

Kennedy pitched a figure—$250,000. Badalamenti said it was far too much. He didn't have it.

"I understand you. You must understand me," Kennedy said. "You are asking me for six months of my life."

Several more money talks followed. Neither man bent. The lawyer and his wife left for their vacation cottage in Ireland. By the time they came back, he had made clear, it would be too late to take on the Badalamenti defense.

Kennedy and his brainy, beautiful wife, the former Eleanore Baratelli, are an unusual couple. In private they are in many ways complementary personages: He is fair, she is dark; he is Irish, she is Italian; he is from the Far West, she is from New Jersey; he is book-minded, she is a connoisseur of pop culture; he is basically reserved, she is joyous and outgoing; he cares little for display, she is an interior designer and cares much. Since they got together, some years ago, under great difficulties, because each was married to someone else, they have not spent a night apart. They have adopted each other's tastes and enthusiasms without surrendering their own.

In public, which is to say in the courtroom, these two complementary figures become, in a sense, one person, or a double person, someone who is entirely focused on winning an acquittal for the client. Almost always, they do. The Kennedys specialize in political cases, and their victories are a part of sixties and seventies American history. Wounded Knee Native Americans, Puerto Rican draft resisters, drug guru Timothy Leary, the porn star Marilyn Chambers, and various members of the Black Panther Party, the Weather Underground, and the Chicago Seven owe their freedom entirely or in part to the Kennedys' courtroom skills. The Kennedys smelled politics all over Badalamenti's forthcoming trial.

Eleanore is a paralegal, not an attorney, but her courtroom smarts often outstrip her husband's. Her specialty is jury selection, an area of trial law that many practitioners say is 90% of the case. In every trial, Kennedy makes his wife an official member of the defense team. Together, they have tried more than 100 cases. Law school for Eleanore at this point, they agree, would be a waste of time.

The day the couple returned from Ireland, an urgent message was waiting. Kennedy went down to the jail, and Badalamenti said he had the money.

Kennedy had only weeks to master a wealth of complex evidence and charges, not only against Badalamenti, but against the seven family members who were his codefendants. This was essential because Badalamenti was more than Kennedy's client; he was the absolute, feudal leader of his clan, and they took orders only from him. They were more likely to listen to him, and trust him, than listen to or confide in their own attorneys.

Kennedy also had to position himself and shore up alliances, where possible, with more than twenty-eight other defense lawyers. Because the indictment named Badalamenti as the chief defendant, his attorney automatically was lead counsel. But this was a very different batch of lawyers from Kennedy's colleagues in his last multidefendant case. That time, the clients were seven diehard Irish-American patriots accused of running guns to Northern Ireland. Kennedy had been lead counsel then too, captain of a happy group of revolutionary-minded courtroom cowboys who called themselves "The Seven Samurai," and who won seven acquittals by convincing the Brooklyn jury that the gunrunners were not terrorists but patriots.

Most of the Pizza lawyers Kennedy did not know at all. They were not seven samurai but twenty-one wildly various, mutually suspicious, unequally competent, divergently experienced, diversely principled,

28

highly theatrical human beings. Every one of them was endowed with—or stuck with—the truly massive ego that criminal-defense work demands. Looking them over, it was hard to know whether this ill-assorted company was embarking on a contemporary pilgrimage to Canterbury, or whether a modern-day Ship of Fools was setting out to sea.

Most prominent among the lawyers were probably Ivan Fisher, Mario Malerba, Marvin E. Segal, and Paul Bergman. Fisher, forty-two, representing Salvatore Catalano, was a brilliant trial lawyer immensely respected yet widely mistrusted, both for the imperceptibility of his loyalty to anyone save his client and for his grand passion, which was money. Malerba, on retainer to the absent Joe Ganci, by now terminally ill with lung cancer, had at one time or another represented a great many Sicilians embroiled in both civil and criminal cases. Some called Malerba the *consigliere* of Knickerbocker Avenue.

Marvin E. Segal, attorney for Gaetano "Tommy" Mazzara, the handsome, hawk-faced New Jersey restaurateur, had been a federal prosecutor in the Southern District in the same period as Pierre Leval. Segal was the most seasoned and perhaps most cynical of the Pizza lawyers.

Paul Bergman, lawyer for Baldassare Amato, was a partner in the firm headed by James LaRossa, the man presently personally defending the Gambino Family boss, "Big Paul" Castellano. This was another major Giuliani anti-Mafia prosecution, taking place in the same court-house as Pizza, two floors above. Bergman had also been a Southern District prosecutor with Leval, and he knew the law better than any other man on the team except perhaps for David Lewis, twenty-seven, a sort of dented legal prodigy with a photographic memory. Lewis had been the youngest of the seven attorneys on the IRA case, and he and Kennedy had developed a superficially prickly but secretly fond father-son relationship. Lewis had been in the Pizza case from Day One, representing Salvatore "Sam" Evola, husband of Badalamenti's favorite niece, and he knew the case backward and forward.

As for the rest of the Pizza lawyers, it would be an understatement to describe them as a motley crew. Of the twenty-two, ten were former prosecutors, federal or state. Five were former Legal Aid lawyers. Five were Italian-American, four were Irish-American, nine were Jewish-American. Three were women. Twelve were paid, more or less hand-somely, by their clients. Ten were being paid by the American taxpayer, at rates of approximately $2,500 a week, under the Criminal Justice Act statute, which provides free legal services to any accused person who can prove himself indigent. Sixteen were more or less experienced drug lawyers. Six had never handled a drug case. Nine had never before been involved in an organized-crime case. Three had practiced law less than five years. One or two had earlier in their lives faced and beaten back disciplinary proceedings for questionable practices. Six came from big law firms. Eight were solo practitioners. The one characteristic many of the lawyers had in common was that fifteen of the twenty-two were the ambitious, self-made sons or daughters of immigrant parents, the first person in their families to get beyond high school.

... THURSDAY, OCTOBER 24, 1985.
THE COURTROOM. After lunch on Day One, Michael Kennedy formally greets judge, jury, and counsel. He tenders a slight bow to his client, and declaims, " 'Oh, what a tangled web we weave, When first we practice to deceive.' . . . If this case were what was presented to you by the prosecution, I would not be here.

"My name is Michael Kennedy. I represent Gaetano Badalamenti. I speak for him. I speak for no one else."

Badalamenti, small and waxen, dressed in a worn grey suit, sweater, white socks, gives the jury a regal nod. Kennedy next introduces his client's family. Seven younger men, most wearing Windbreakers or leather jackets, stand up in turn and offer a modest bow or nod to the jury box.

"All these people are related to Mr. Badalamenti by blood or marriage." Kennedy speaks in a rich baritone, and has a formal but friendly, slightly pedagogic manner. "A family, particularly a Sicilian family, is an extraordinary unit. . . . Gaetano Badalamenti is a proud man, a simple man. He speaks . . . a little English."

The lawyer notes "a profound irony." His client has been brought into this courtroom "not because he is the Boss of Bosses, not because he is the world's biggest drug dealer—but because he refused to have anything to do with drugs! He was brought here for reasons of politics."

A lawyer in the back row mutters, "Only Kennedy could make a political pitch in a heroin case."

"In November, 1984 . . ." Kennedy begins to tell his story. Perhaps it is merely his ringing voice, but the lawyer has caught the judge's attention; Leval listens intently.

"In Italy, he faces charges of being a member of the Mafia. Here [in the United States], he is not charged with currency violations. He is charged with racketeering [a reference to the RICO charge]. He is charged with *conspiring*. He is charged with maintaining a continuing criminal enterprise.

"We will show you that Gaetano Badalamenti dealt no drugs. Did he participate in money-laundering? No, he did not. He has violated no United States laws, with one exception. Yet he is being held here, against his will, jailed in the Metropolitan Correctional Center—the federal prison next door.

"In 1947, my client entered the United States illegally. . . . And that is the only United States law that Gaetano Badalamenti ever violated.

"Now let me speak to you for a moment about the Sicilian family." There follows a little anthropology lesson on Sicilian customs. For some reason, a reason probably rooted more in Kennedy's unconscious than in his training in the theater of advocacy, the lawyerly voice has taken on a faint Irish brogue. In Sicily, "the family is the most basic unit. The family is the source of energy, the source of power, the source of honor. To defend the honor of the Sicilian family, one does not turn to the authorities. The government in Sicily is distrusted, and frequently discredited. In Sicily when one has problems, one solves them himself."

Sicily has other curious ways. "There are Sicilians who do not consider themselves Italians. The Sicilian language, quite different from Italian, is a strange dialect. It is a secretive language. Like Yiddish, like Gaelic, it comes out of a history of oppression." Kennedy is aware that the jury foreman is Jewish, and two or three others are all or partly Irish. "The people speak to one another in a guarded way."

Next comes a little bit of history. The Mafia came out of a nineteenth- and even eighteenth-century "secret Sicilian society, the *Beati Paoli,* the beautiful people. The *Beati Paoli* defended the weak against the oppression of the Bourbons. This is Gaetano Badalamenti's tradition.

"You will hear a lot of talk about honor in this case. But the most important honor is the honor of the United States government, and the honor of the law.

"During World War II, the United States kicked the *fascisti* out of Italy." Every time Kennedy speaks an Italian word or phrase, he is careful to enunciate slowly, with practiced and perfect inflection. The effect is to convey a deep respect for all things Italian. "After the Italians and Germans had been defeated, it was the United States government which put the Mafia family heads back in power. They were the natural community leaders, disgraced and disavowed during the Mussolini years."

In the 1960s Badalamenti prospered. He grew in power and respect. He became known as a "Man of Honor." He was still a Man of Honor in 1978 when, "in some sudden reversal of fortune, Gaetano Badalamenti was forced out of Sicily. He flees to save the life of himself and his family."

His "difficulties," Kennedy tells the jurors, had to do with his adamant refusal to have anything to do with narcotics trafficking. "Who says Gaetano Badalamenti dealt drugs? I don't know. Who made up this mythology?" Here the magnificent voice drops dramatically. "Who made up this mythology is what this case is ultimately about."

Kennedy allows himself the risk of long silence, to let this sink in, then returns to the business at hand. "Much of the evidence in this case is based on tapes, on phone conversations secretly recorded. The voices of Gaetano Badalamenti and members of his family are heard on a very few of the tapes. We will bring as much light and sunshine as possible onto this matter.

"Remember that words have more than one meaning. Remember that the Sicilian language is designed to avoid being understood. Also, Sicilian is a language designed to convey information with circumspection. . . ."

Kennedy mentions the government's star witness, Tomasso Buscetta, the first high-level Mafioso ever to betray his oath of secrecy and become an informer. "Tomasso Buscetta will say to you that Gaetano Badalamenti did not deal drugs, or launder money. Tomasso Buscetta is a very unusual man—an admitted *Mafioso,* an admitted liar, an admitted criminal who says he is a Man of Honor.

"I ask you to treat Gaetano Badalamenti as the proud, dignified individual he is—and not push him into a group. . . . We will say: The charges are not proved."

It is 2:00 P.M. Without a recess, Judge Leval calls on the second-ranking defense counsel, Ivan Fisher, attorney for Salvatore Catalano, to give his opening remarks. Fisher rises, unfolds, looms out of his chair. Pale, with longish black hair dribbling over his outsize shirt collar, bearlike in bulk yet eel-like in movement, this almost six-and-a-half-foot-tall man commands any room. His most frequent expression is an enigmatic Etruscan smile that looks sometimes beatific, sometimes satanic. Fisher discharges enormous kinetic energy, and he has bad knees. Together these give him the never still, ever-rocking stance of a tethered elephant. In the excitements of his long-awaited opening statement, his normal rocking gait expands into a full, trapezelike swing.

A New York–raised, former San Francisco Legal Aid lawyer, Fisher is considered a top member of the New York criminal bar. His grateful clients have included the late shady international financier Michele Sindona, recently poisoned by cyanide in his Italian prison cell, whose relationship with the Vatican earned him the sobriquet "God's Banker." He has successfully represented both Norman Mailer and Norman Mailer's pet convict, Jack Henry Abbott, who knifed a young waiter to death the same week Mailer/Fisher got him out of prison.

Pacing the breadth of the courtroom, the entire thirty-foot span between the jury rail and the interpreters' booth, and cuddling a hand mike in his enormous paw, Fisher says, "The government suggests this is a two-lane highway, with drugs in one lane and money in the other lane." Smile.

"How do you prove you are *not* a member of the Mafia?" He spreads wide his gargantuan arms, palms upward, in a massive Jewish shrug. The jurors already love Ivan Fisher. They sit upright in their seats; they smile at the swooping inflections of the boyish voice.

The lawyer half turns toward his glowering, thick-necked client. "May heaven forgive you for working in a bakery!" he exclaims. "A bakery within walking distance of Knickerbocker Avenue . . ."

The government will show lots of evidence of this man carrying bags, and visiting Sicily. "Well, we will prove to you that the bags are full of bakery products, and we will show you that Sal Catalano returned to Italy to get married!

"The government has a lot of theories about what my client was doing. Well, the government also has lots of theories about the Kennedy assassination . . . that doesn't prove anything."

To save his client, Fisher must bury star witness Tomasso Buscetta, the government stool pigeon, and he sets about the work of character demolition with the gusto of Iago. He tells a long and unpleasant story about Buscetta's excellent opinion of himself as a ladies' man, and how he went to a woman's house "with flowers, and a derringer . . . and relieves her of everything."

At 2:14 P.M. Fisher has finished. He sits down like a man who has hugely enjoyed his own show.

Leval dismisses the jury, but not without reminding them that the Pizza trial runs Monday through Thursday, that court resumes at 9:15 next Monday morning, and that promptness is essential. "If one juror is late, seventy people are held up. Seventy times fifteen minutes is a lot of wasted hours."

The long week is finally at an end. To celebrate, the Kennedys head for Umberto's Clam House, the notorious Little Italy mob hangout where Joey Gallo was gunned down in the early 1970s. Their car is a Checker taxi converted to a limousine. Many of these lawyers drive expensive cars with working telephones: Bergman has a new Porsche, Fisher a grey stretch limo, Malerba a spotless new Mercedes-Benz town car. Joseph Benfante and Lawrence Bronson, the attorneys for Salvatore Mazzurco and Salvatore Greco, each drives a red Mercedes two-seater convertible. But the Kennedy car is special—a square, high old taxicab repainted a burnished maroon, reupholstered in tan leather, equipped with small bar and TV set (usually broken), telephone, and radar fuzz-buster.

With them today are David Lewis and Joseph Calluori, Kennedy's young "stunt lawyer." The term derives from the Hollywood stunt man, the anonymous cowboy who does the dangerous work, and the boring work, for the star. In truth, Calluori is a younger assistant who drafts motions, looks up the law, and occupies the senior man's seat on unimportant days.

"I don't think Catalano looks so scary," Calluori says.

"Wait 'til you see him smile," says his boss.

... **MONDAY, OCTOBER 28, 1985.**
THE COURTHOUSE CAFETERIA across from Judge Leval's courtroom. Today the cafeteria is hung with cardboard pumpkins and twisted streamers of brown and orange crepe paper. Looking at the cheap decorations, one realizes that the pumpkins will give way to turkeys and Pilgrim hats, and then to Christmas tinsel and Santa beards, and after that to lilacs and Easter bunnies, before daylight, or breath, or serenity, or natural rhythm, or order returns to any of these people's lives. The lawyers gulp their coffee and queue at the metal detector.

9:53 A.M. "All rise!" declaims the clerk.

Richard Martin, leader of the prosecution team, is a man of middle height, in his late thirties, with a well-exercised, powerful torso inside his sharply tailored suit. He has dark curly hair, a toothbrush mustache, an alert, terrierlike manner, and a pugnacious nature. He relishes a fight, and in a few moments the jury will get its first sight of the chief prosecutor in action.

Leval is brisk. "Good morning, gentlemen. Next on the menu is Mr. Lombardino. Call the jury, please."

But before this can happen, Larry Bronson, Sal Greco's lawyer in the back row, shouts out, "The government and Mr. Stewart *lied* about my client."

Dick Martin is on his feet immediately. "We're very careful with that word," he snarls. "We never use it in front of the jury." But this grossly understates Martin's fanatical sensitivity to the term *liar*. Pizza's chief prosecutor is extremely righteous. To him, the very word *lying* or *liar* is searingly shameful; is filled with magic dread; is his very own "word that dare not speak its name." Before the year is out, however, the question of Martin's own candor will become a key issue in the trial. By the time it is over, nearly every one of the defense lawyers will have directly challenged Martin's veracity, and even Judge Leval will have termed him "uninformative," in reference to his propensity for not always telling the whole truth.

The marshals have by now lined up the jurors in the wings so that they will march in to their seats in the proper order. The three-tiered jury box contains three rows of green leather swivel armchairs, eight to a row. The first row holds jurors #1 through #8. #1 will be closest to the witness box, and #8—who enters first—sits closest to the spectators. The second row holds jurors #9 through #12, and alternates #1 through #4. The last eight alternates are seated in the high back row. These people have almost no chance of being called to serve. They are human props, present in the courtroom for symbolic more than actual reasons, the flesh equivalent of the cafeteria pumpkins and Santas.

Thus the jury parade is always led by #8, identified during jury selection as a middle-aged, unmarried accountant. He has rehennaed his hair over the weekend. Behind him always come #7, a transportation supervisor, and #6, the giggling bank teller who takes her shoes off and flirts with #5, the young black data processor—back to #1, the Jewish sanitation-man foreman. The second row is led by alternate #4, an ample, coffee-colored social worker with dancing eyes. Leading the back row is alternate #5, a licensed practical nurse and Marvin Hagler look-alike in T-shirt and Hitler mustache.

"Good morning, members of the jury."

Like a bright chorus of schoolchildren: "Good morning, your Honor."

Now the ritual lateness lecture: "There are several reasons this trial could not start on time. One, a juror was forty minutes late. And the marshals forgot Mr. Badalamenti at MCC." Leval's eyes twinkle behind his glasses. The jurors twitter appreciation of the little joke. They have begun to adore Leval. ". . . But every late individual means sixty person-hours or more wasted." It takes him four minutes to deliver this sermon.

The jurors tilt back in their comfortable leather chairs. They are about to have their first experience of the preposterous side of this huge conspiracy trial—eighteen more opening statements, eighteen more lawyers trotting out varying exhortations, supplications, and denunciations of government impropriety.

Over the next three days, the jury will listen to the "it's not him, it's his brother" defense; the "he has an alibi, he was getting married at the time" defense; the "he only came here looking for a job" defense; the "hard-working man" defense; the "immigrant makes good and can't help having all this money" defense; a host of "the government is out to get him" protestations; several insinuations of anti-Italian bias on the part of the government; and at least one plea of "I don't even know why he's here."

For the younger lawyers, this is the most important case of their entire careers. They would like to summon up all their considerable legal and oratorical talents to impress this jury. Yet by Day Two of the defense opening statements, the witty and good-looking Gerald Di Chiara, lawyer for the "I only came here for a job" defendant, Giovanni Cangialosi, is compelled by honesty to confess to the jury, "I'm the 15th attorney to address you. It's hard to be original."

Each defendant has his own well-defined, plausible, even alluring tale to tell. But to pile these stories on top of one another in this manner is to encourage in the virgin juror the cynicism of the veteran courthouse reporter. That is one reason the government favors large, multi-defendant trials.

Michael Kennedy may be theoretical captain of the defense team, but his client's interests very seldom mirror the interests of other defendants, even within his own family. Indeed, on a great many occasions they will be antithetical. Yet the Kennedy/Badalamenti strategy depends on maintaining a tight formation among the eight defendants who make up the family group. After all, as Kennedy has reminded the jury, in Sicily, family fealty is everything. Hence the Badalamenti-group lawyers, while sworn to protect their clients' best interests, in fact have to operate within the context of the Old Man's strategy. Badalamenti calls the shots. But he does not quite call them openly. As Kennedy has said, Sicilians are naturally secretive. They do not like to disclose their strategy, not even to their lawyers.

The family sits together. Next to Badalamenti is his nephew, the foxy-looking Vincenzo "Enzo" Randazzo, represented by Lawrence Schoenbach, whose ample whiskers tend to emphasize rather than obliterate the baby face beneath. Enzo's only crime, Schoenbach assures the jury, is that he was misidentified by the government on several phone calls.

Faithful son Vito is represented by the quiet Robert Koppelman, one of the shrewdest men in the room. His opening remarks are a model of brevity. "I want a fair trial and a verdict based on the evidence."

The next lawyer in line is an odd character with lank grey hair and droopy mustache, unknown to the lawyers on either side of him. Robert Fogelnest looks a little bit like a hippy relic left over from San Francisco in the 1960s. In fact, he has just moved up from Philadelphia; this is his first New York case. His imprisoned client, Sal Salamone, accused of being the conspiracy's chief money changer, has an unemployed wife, two small children, and is dead broke. As payment for services, he could offer the lawyer only a second mortgage on his house, an arrangement Fogelnest accepted. One wonders how he plans to collect. He has arrived in Manhattan without space to work or live. He sleeps temporarily on another lawyer's office couch, and sometimes looks it. But he is very smart, and goofily engaging.

Patrick Burke, a handsome, modest, former Marine Corps lieutenant colonel and devoted father of four teen-age sons, represents Pietro "Pete" Alfano, of Oregon, Illinois, Badalamenti's nephew and main contact in the United States. Burke is the antithesis of the flashy Manhattan criminal lawyer. He spends every free moment as a volunteer high-school athletic coach, and he loads his Pizza briefcase into the trunk of a BMW sedan already filled with basketballs, football helmets, soccer boots, and hockey jerseys. Always fiercely patriotic, Burke began his law career as assistant U.S. attorney on the Organized Crime Strike Force for the Southern District of New York.

To Burke's right sits young David Lewis, bearded like Nebuchadnezzar and shaped like a fireplug. His client, Salvatore "Sam" Evola, a former construction worker in his late forties, is blond and blue-eyed, more Norwegian-looking than Sicilian, and a testament to the many invaders who have ravaged and ruled the island, from Carthaginians to Saracens to Vikings to Bourbons. Evola is the one fully fluent English speaker in the Badalamenti family. His wife, Christine, a beautiful, very carefully groomed and coiffed American-born Sicilian with dark hair and high color, is in daily attendance in the courtroom, translating for other family members.

The other Badalamenti defendants are three husbands of other Badalamenti nieces, modest-looking little men who are also small-town pizza bakers. (Family relationships are complex. The three sisters of defendant Trupiano are married to defendants Alfano, Vitale, and Palazzolo.) Giuseppe "Joe" Trupiano and Giuseppe "Joe" Vitale, both from the little town of Paris, Illinois, have decided to pool their resources and share the same lawyer. He is Lawrence Ruggiero, a former prosecutor and Martin's one-time senior colleague.

Low man on the Badalamenti totem pole is the dewy-eyed Emmanuele Palazzolo. This gentle-looking fellow is represented most days by an equally gentle-seeming young woman, Genay Leitman, twenty-six, who for a long time could not decide whether she wanted to be a lawyer or an actress. Now, as stunt lawyer for the always-absent David DePetris, she finds herself thrown into one of the most complex legal dramas ever played out in the United States federal courts.

The first two lawyers in the second row represent two of Joe Ganci's partners in Pronto Demolition, members of the loose affiliation the government calls "the Catalano faction." On the aisle sits the attorney for Giuseppe "Joe" Lamberti, Anthony Lombardino, who will be the third defense lawyer to address the jury. He is a hulking man with eyes like black olives set in a face modeled from unbaked dough. Another former prosecutor, a Queens County district attorney, Lombardino is one of several Pizza attorneys who are also businessmen. He operates a legal-messenger service and owns a construction-sand business.

The lawyer-entrepreneur mops his brow with a florid silk handkerchief. He has a cold and coughs as he walks to the podium, but his foghorn voice can probably be heard in the next courtroom. His client is a square, middle-sized man who wears an eerie, perpetual smile. Joe Lamberti is a legitimate businessman, the lawyer tells the jury, a partner with his brother-in-law Mazzurco in a legitimate wrecking company.

Next up after Lombardino is his courtroom neighbor, Joe Benfante, who brought his pal Lombardino into the Pizza case. Benfante represents Sal Mazzurco, Lamberti's brother-in-law. The muscular young lawyer nods and smiles toward the jury box and, in deliberate mimicry of Johnny Carson, says, "Welcome to the Pizza Case." Already he has endeared himself to the jury.

At the mention of his name, Mazzurco, a tiny man, no more than five feet three inches, with a very high, suntanned forehead, stands up.

His granny glasses are pushed high on his domed brow. Mazzurco is not only a partner in Pronto; he also owns a successful roller-skating rink and a nearby dress shop in the Hudson Valley. Why would he be involved in anything illegitimate, Benfante asks.

Next in line is Salvatore Lamberti, Joe Lamberti's cousin, a small, ashen-faced man in his fifties who has known Badalamenti for forty years. His lawyer is Marvin Schechter, a man with horn-rimmed glasses, angry complexion, and a terribly sincere manner, acquired during his ten-year hitch with Legal Aid. He tells the jury that his client came to the United States only two years ago, has since developed kidney cancer, and is just recovering from surgery.

To Schechter's right is Paul Bergman, another oddity. Baldo Amato's attorney is a loner, a compulsive, nonstop talker, and so serious-minded as to make his neighbor Schechter seem frivolous. Bergman is dapper, bespectacled, and slim, and from the front appears to have a luxuriant grey Afro. From the rear, one sees a balding tonsure. One sees it often, because Bergman is on his feet, talking, at every opportunity. His style is continually to interrupt and object, and he sees himself as dutybound to utilize his superior knowledge of legal precedent.

To his right is a smiling, freckled, prematurely grey Irish lawyer, James Moriarty, representing the fringe character Lorenzo DeVardo, a small-time painter and hood who seems to have fallen into this particular case by accident. And at the end of the second row sits tall, robust, red-cheeked, and black-mustached Gerry Di Chiara. His client, Giovanni Cangialosi, is a truckdriver who arrived from Sicily only weeks before the April 9 arrests. Young Di Chiara's overall strategy is to disappear with his client into the general jumble of Pizza faces and Italian names, seeking further to minimize Cangialosi's already minimal role.

In sum, the middle row of lawyers can be thought of as a line of loose cannons, openly trying to protect only the interests of their individual clients, yet much affected by the invisible undertows and hidden currents that swirl around all men with heavy Mafia associations. The same could be said of the back-row men, with the additional fact that most are from New Jersey. On the aisle, representing Sal Greco, is former Hudson County prosecutor Larry Bronson, a stocky, smiling man in glasses and a brown suit, who exudes the unmistakable air of his native New Jersey. He is cheerful and unpretentious, hangs out at trendy cafés, and likes the ladies. Bronson tells the jury his client works twelve-hour days running a small, break-even pizza parlor on the Jersey Shore. His trip to Sicily has been misrepresented by the government. He went there to visit his mother.

Greco's robust cousin, Frank Castronovo, sits beside him, frequently leaning forward to whisper to his lawyer, lanky, stooped, mustached Kenneth Kaplan, another former federal prosecutor.

Castronovo's Roma Restaurant partner is the hawk-faced and narrow-eyed Gaetano "Tommy" Mazzara, who has retained Marvin Segal, the elder statesman of the Pizza defense. Segal is small, wiry, and perfectly tailored. He favors expensive light-grey suits and yellow ties. He works with a pair of horn-rimmed glasses balanced on the end of his nose. For a number of years he has maintained a many-balconied apartment overlooking the Mediterranean, south of Rome, and he is perpetually suntanned.

Alongside Mazzara is the man the government has called the "investor," big, jovial-looking Francesco "Frank" Polizzi, who owns a thriving construction company and a motel-and-restaurant complex in New Jersey. He is a rich man, worth several million dollars and, unlike his fellow defendants, he looks it. He dresses well and has the expansive, natural benignity common to many men of wealth. His lawyer is the quietest person here. Michael Querques is small and intense, with white skin, black glasses, delicate features. He brings his lunch each day in a paper bag, and spends the lunch hour silently doing deskwork.

"A case is like a coin," he lectures the jury today. "It has two sides, head and tail. So I was surprised, unless I fell asleep, not to hear three words: *speculation, conjecture* or *surmise.*"

Alongside Querques sits Joseph Ryan, a fiesty little ex-DA from Long Island who has represented Filippo Casamento for some years, and is irate that his client has been called an investor. Ryan insists that the little rooster-faced, white-thatched man with twinkling eyes is only a Brooklyn mozzarella-maker and distributor, the hard-working owner of a *salumeria* and of the Eagle Cheese Company. What Ryan does not tell the jurors, and what the government is prevented by law from telling them, is that the merry little cheese distributor has also been known to distribute heroin, and has served time for it. Casamento is the only Pizza defendant with a prior drug conviction.

The crippled Giovanni Ligammari has hired Steven Kimelman to represent him. But Kimelman has decided he cannot waste time sitting in this courtroom for months to listen to a mere hour or two of testimony against his client. So, in his opening remarks, Kimelman introduces his associate Carol Novack, a dark-haired, free-spirited young woman who writes poetry, and is another of the stunt lawyers.

The one lawyer who does not make an opening statement is Mario Malerba, fifty, a knowing, suave, bright-eyed former Golden Gloves boxer who today has one of the more prosperous law practices in the Borough of Queens, New York. Like the Irishman Burke, whom he resembles in many ways, Malerba is invariably courteous and well spoken. His Italian wardrobe is beautifully made. Malerba's father and grandfather were Sicilian-born, and Mario speaks the dialect fluently and readily tunes in to the special, secretive Sicilian mind set.

Malerba is the long-time lawyer for defendant Giuseppe Ganci. But when Ganci developed lung cancer, his lawyer won him a medical severance. Malerba remains in the case, however, as co-counsel to Sal Catalano. It was he who brought in Ivan Fisher to argue to the jury. Fisher asked for a $500,000 fee in advance, and got it. This became known when prosecutor Richard Martin moved to seize the fee, under the 1984 Comprehensive Forfeiture Act, on grounds that the money came from illegal drug dealing. Fisher insisted it was a Constitutional right-to-work issue, and Judge Leval ruled in his favor.

Little Joe Ryan is the last of the defense lawyers to address the jury. "The more Mafia evidence they put into this case, the more it proves they have no other evidence! . . . And now it is time to begin. God bless each and every one of you. Thank you very much." He sits down. It is nearly lunchtime on the third court day devoted to defense opening statements.

3. *The Informants*

THE COURTROOM. "The government will call its first witness,"
says Leval. At the far right end of his bench sits a pretty clerk with fluffy
blond hair, here to see the big action. She does not have long to wait
before the government's star witness enters through the jury door on
the left.

Tomasso Buscetta has a droopy bloodhound's face, baggy eyes, liver-
ish complexion. The space between his nose and mouth is exceptionally
long. The shock of glossy black hair falling over his forehead in bangs
is surely a wig. He is not very tall, and wears a well-cut, dark-blue
Italian suit, blue-grey shirt, narrow black tie. To hide himself from his
enemies, he has undergone extensive face lifting at U.S. government
expense. One tries without success to imagine what he looked like
before the plastic surgery. The new face looks like less than the sum of
its former parts.

"Your Honor, the government's first witness is Tomasso Buscetta."
The chief prosecutor's words are accompanied by an all but audible

drum roll. Buscetta has been advertised in the British and European, particularly the Italian, press, and to a lesser degree in the United States, as the biggest Mafia turncoat of all time.

Martin first draws out the man's reason for appearing as a witness for the United States. The Mafia is not what it used to be, he explains in Italian, speaking through a woman interpreter who sits at his side in the witness box. Her words are retranslated into Italian, and into Sicilian, by other interpreters, in the soundproof booth. They also translate Martin's English questions. Cordless radio headsets carry these translations to every defendant who cares to wear his earphones.

The Mafia is an organization of killers now, not Men of Honor, says the witness. Martin elicits information about Mafia structure and customs. The organization is divided into units called "families." Each family bears the name of the town or village where it is headquartered. Members are assigned military ranks, and a member may proceed upward from *soldato* to *capodicine* (chief of ten) to *consigliere* (counselor) to *sotocapo* (underboss) to *capo.*

A member of the Mafia must behave in an appropriate way. He must always speak the truth to a brother. He must always observe *omerta*— the rule of absolute secrecy. He must not look at other men's wives. He must not steal. He must always stop what he is doing to hurry to the aid of a brother.

And the penalty for breaking any of these rules?

"Death."

Martin's examination continues. The jury hears that the Mafia initiation rite requires the new member to prick his finger, rub blood onto the picture of a saint, then set fire to the picture and say, "If I should betray the organization, may my flesh burn like this saint."

How do Men of Honor recognize one another, Martin asks. "*Cosa Nostra* means Our Thing. If you use these words, it means: I belong to the Mafia family." If one family member introduces someone to another family member with the words *This is our friend,* it means the newcomer is also a Man of Honor. If one says, *This is my friend,* it means he is not a Mafia member but the speaker is prepared to vouch for him.

Recess. Defense attorneys huddle in the corridor, debating how the star witness appears to the jury. Buscetta is a stock character, they tell one another, straight from the pen of Mario Puzo. He cannot hurt their clients, he knows nothing, he's all display, intended to impress the press and jury. None of this Mafia voodoo is relevant, just more scare tactics by the government. What does it have to do with the Pizza Connection?

. . . WEDNESDAY, OCTOBER 30, 1985.
THE COURTROOM. The star witness, looking imperturbably waxen, almost embalmed, is back in the box. Martin asks Buscetta if any Cosa Nostra people are present. "Kindly look around this courtroom and see if anybody is here who was introduced [to you then] or [in your presence] in the manner you just described?"

The bloodhound eyes flicker toward Gaetano Badalamenti, not fifteen feet away. "Si." The witness goes on to identify as Mafiosi Sal Catalano, Sal Lamberti, Gaetano Mazzara, Filippo Casamento, and ends up, "Over there is Badalamenti's son Vito, and his nephew Vincenzo Randazzo."

Martin returns to the prosecution table for a photo album, which he hands to Buscetta. "Your Honor, I would like this marked Government Exhibit #102." Buscetta identifies photographs of defendants Catalano, Ganci, and a man named Giuseppe Bono.

As soon as Martin begins asking questions about defendants, Paul Bergman asks that the jury be sent out. "Write your objection and send it up to me," orders Leval. Other attorneys have other objections, which become a small blizzard of paper as the lawyers scribble notes.

The clock inches toward 4:00 P.M. Marshals covertly glance at their watches, checking the minutes before they go into overtime. Leval declares a recess, and as the jurors stream out their special door, the defense is still listing objections to the photos in question. They are the five-year-old wedding pictures of a certain Giuseppe Bono. . . .

. . . 1980.
This had been a big year for Mafia weddings. In February the defendant Sal Catalano had traveled to the village of Cimina, not far from Palermo, Sicily, to marry Caterina Catalano, a young woman who bore the same surname but was no relation. The wedding, a simple ceremony, was followed by a six-month wait before Signora Catalano's U.S.

immigration papers were straightened out. In September, soon after her arrival in New York, a large reception was held for the newlyweds at the Marina del Rey Restaurant, in the Throgs Neck section of the Bronx. The affair was attended by a good number of made members of the Bonanno Family, a leading New York Mafia clan. "Made members" are men who have been formally sworn into a Mafia family, as Buscetta was sworn. The FBI had a field day identifying wedding guests and photographing their cars.

Five days later, four persons who had been noted as guests at the Catalano reception were observed driving to the County Courthouse on Queens Boulevard. They were defendant Joe Ganci and his wife, Margarita, en route to witness the second marriage of Giuseppe Bono.

Bono, don of the Bolognetta Family, was an important figure in the Sicilian Mafia, who, in 1978, had decided to take up residence in the United States. He arrived in New York in April of that year, and within days he had married an American citizen, Carmen Figuero, and bought a large house in the Pelham Manor section of the Bronx.

In less than two years Bono's lawyer, Mario Malerba, had obtained a divorce and, on September 15, 1980, Bono married one Antonina Albino at a quiet wedding in Queens. The wedding reception, however, was one of the most elaborate Mafia get-togethers in recent memory.

On the evening of November 16, the main ballroom of the Pierre Hotel on Fifth Avenue in Manhattan was bedecked with flowers. Tables overflowed with champagne and food. Two dance orchestras played nonstop. Among the 500 guests was almost every major figure in the New York Mafia. The hotel's $62,000 bill was paid in cash.

Outside, on 61st Street, law-enforcement agents tripped over each other photographing the mob figures arriving and departing in limos and taxis. Inside, hired wedding photographers busily posed the wedding guests for their family albums and souvenir collections.

These are the photographs that Martin now seeks to introduce in order to show associations, friendships, and Mafia connections. Joe Ryan roars from the back that the true purpose of offering the wedding album is not to show a *conspiracy* among the defendants, which is what they are charged with. "The purpose is to show the Mafia connections of the defendants. But Mafia is not a crime in this country!" Martin agrees to withdraw the album, for now. Leval gavels a recess.

Kennedy at this point is focusing on his crucial cross-examination of the unknown quantity Buscetta, which likely will begin tomorrow. He has prepared and written out on 5"-by-8" index cards three separate cross-examinations, which he thinks of as "hard, soft, and other." He must be prepared for an ambush. He also reminds himself that, for him to cross-examine to maximum effect, Buscetta needs to understand certain things about Badalamenti's new lawyer.

During Martin's direct examination, Kennedy had four times stood up and stooped to whisper to his client, "so Buscetta would be sure to *capice* which one I was.

"Buscetta will know the Old Man will not have picked a fool for a lawyer. He'll know that he will have told his hand-picked lawyer some damaging things about Mr. Buscetta, things that the United States government knows nothing about. That way, if he doesn't stay in line, we'll unload on him like a cement truck. They go back a long way together."

. . . THURSDAY, OCTOBER 31, 1985.

As the courtroom fills with lawyers, translators and observers, Martin is already arguing that, yes, he did so give the defense the Bono wedding photos. The rules of discovery require the government to provide the defense with all government evidence and background materials—known as "3500 material" and "Brady material"—before they are presented to the jury.

Did not, says Lewis.

Did so, snaps Martin.

"I don't care. Please!" Leval is irritated.

Buscetta is unhappy. The translators continually interrupt him; he needs a notepad to keep track.

Buscetta's Mafia identifications continue. Gaetano Mazzara, of the Noce Family, seated in the back row, smiles at him like a knife.

Martin leads Buscetta back into recent Mafia history once more, and the informer tells of the night the Sicilian and American Mafia compared notes. . . .

... OCTOBER 12, 1957.

PALERMO. Charles "Lucky" Luciano, the notorious American Mafia chieftain exiled to Italy, had taken the ferry across the Strait of Messina for a highly secret rendezvous. Luciano had been tried and found guilty in New York in 1936 of running white-slavery and prostitution rackets, and sentenced to thirty to fifty years in prison. Early in World War II, he was released and deported to Italy on his promise that he would enlist the help of the Sicilian Mafia in protecting Allied ports from the Nazis, and assisting in preparations for the Allied invasion of Sicily. Luciano made good on his promise, and after the war took up residence in Naples.

On this night Luciano joined a number of Mafia bosses at a formal banquet in the Spano Restaurant in Palermo to honor an important American guest. Among the company were Gaetano Badalamenti, Leonardo Greco—Mafia boss of the ruthless Greco Family of Ciaculli, and older brother of defendant Sal Greco—and Tomasso Buscetta.

The guest of honor that night was Joseph Bonanno, boss of the New York Mafia family that bore his name. Bonanno was on his first trip back to his birthplace, and he was being treated like visiting royalty. He had been greeted by delegations of church leaders and local politicians. At the airport, a member of the Italian government had been standing on the tarmac. Bonanno was accompanied by his junior advisers and underbosses. One was a tough street hood named Carmine Galante.

Once the proper Sicilian formalities and the rituals of food and drink had been observed, the rulers of this international brotherhood of crime got down to comparing notes on the growth of their organization in the Space Age. Bonanno drew Buscetta and Greco aside and advised them that the old days of blood feuds and vendettas must be abandoned. The Sicilian Mafia needed to follow in the modern footsteps of its American counterpart and appoint a ruling council to arbitrate all interfamily disputes. Sicily needed to set up a *Commissione,* just as New York organized-crime figures had set one up two decades before.

That night Buscetta and Greco were assigned the task of putting together such a body.

. . . THE COURTROOM.

Within minutes of Buscetta's mention of the Luciano meet, Leval again sends the jury out. He is not sure that this information will be in furtherance of the government's conspiracy case—the sole grounds on which it would be admissible. Therefore the proceedings will continue as a voir dire hearing: testimony elicited to determine if the jury should hear it.

In the absence of the jury, the defense lawyers hurl a host of objections at the judge. One problem, they say, is where contact with a Man of Honor stops. Pete Alfano's lawyer, Pat Burke, elaborates on the point. "Badalamenti is a Man of Honor," says Buscetta. But Burke's client, the Old Man's nephew, is merely an associate of a Mafioso.

Furthermore, adds Genay Leitman, "my client, Palazzolo, as an associate of Alfano's, is an associate of an associate." Where does Mafia contamination cease? The judge agrees to think it over. Leval already has emphasized the need for caution to safeguard against his deepest fear, a mistrial.

As the courts empty for the weekend, maestro Giuliani is working the building. This morning he has been portrayed in an essay written by the head of the American Civil Liberties Union, and published on the *New York Times*'s Op-Ed page, as an overenthusiastic prosecutor and dangerous zealot. Finding himself in an elevator full of reporters, Giuliani says, "I figure I must be doing something right if the ACLU is after me." Then, fixing his fellow passengers with his burning black eyes, he adds, "Those men have ice water in their veins. You were sitting in a roomful of murderers."

. . . MONDAY, NOVEMBER 4, 1985.

THE COURTROOM.   The night has brought chill winds down from Canada, and the lawyers stamp their feet while divesting themselves of mufflers, hats, gloves. *"Buon giorno! Come 'sta?"* they greet one another. How soon this bunch of warring egoists has become a group, a single organism, however divided against itself. Already the Ship of Fools has navigated the harbor and passed out to sea; the voyage is under way.

Icy drafts play around the lawyers' feet. The old courtroom, closed all weekend, is impossible to heat, impossible to cool in summer. A drama of opening and banging shut the one huge operable window, on the left, next to the jury and spectator benches, soon becomes an ongoing war between the marshals and the lawyers.

"Where's Mr. Martin?" the judge asks.

"Delayed, your Honor," says Stewart.

"Probably working Buscetta over with a rubber hose," one lawyer whispers.

When Martin rushes in moments later through the rear door, Leval interrupts the daily haggle of prejury pleading and argument. "Let me pause at 9:30 AM to welcome Mr. Martin, and to tell him how appreciative we are that you have decided to come and join us today."

The jury enters. Buscetta wears a new wig; the part in his glossy mop has changed from left to right. Martin returns to the identification process. He shows Buscetta several photographs. The witness dons gold-rimmed glasses. He knows only this man's nickname, he thinks it is "Lilo" [Carmine Galante], whom he first met in 1957, in Palermo. They were introduced with the words "He is a friend of ours."

Buscetta looks down at another photo. "These are the Adamita brothers." Buscetta first met Emmanuele Adamita in 1965 or 1966, in New York, and was told he was not a member of the Mafia.

A fusillade of "Objection!"'s flies from the defense lawyers. Bergman again wants both jury and witness banished. The procession of jurors, only one or two showing frustration, winds back out to the jury room.

The Adamita brothers were part of a major heroin importation plot in 1980. The government intends to show involvement by several Pizza defendants in the same scheme. But by extracting from Buscetta the fact that one of the importers was not an actual Mafia member, Martin has hit an extremely sensitive nerve.

Leval raises his hand to halt the defense barrage. "Mr. Martin, you say this witness is going to testify that a Mafia member may employ a non-Mafia member to help him in a project?"

"Yes, sir."

"And in doing so he is under obligation to communicate some rules to him?"

Martin explains that an associate of a sworn Mafia member is told the rules of the Mafia, and he takes on the responsibilities dictated by these rules. If he in turn contracts with or brings in other associates, he passes on the same Mafia restrictions and cautions he has received.

Uproar from the defense benches. Alfano's lawyer is the first to catch Leval's eye. "Mr. Burke."

"This is the most pernicious part of Martin's umbrella conspiracy theory—that he's trying to use the umbrella to taint associates outside the umbrella." Burke fears that this formulation could mean there are no limits to the spreading tentacles of the conspiracy, and that Martin could widen the net sufficiently to snare all the defendants—Mafia men such as Catalano and Badalamenti, associates such as Alfano and Mazzurco, and now associates of associates, little fish like Palazzolo and Cangialosi—in the overall drug-conspiracy charge.

Leval decides to give himself more breathing space. "Let's put the witness back on and hear what he has to say." Once more the government must make an offer of proof: Buscetta will testify out of hearing of the jury to determine whether his evidence is fit for their ears.

The debate rages. Buscetta details his dealings with Mafia associates. Martin seeks always to expand the net. The defense lawyers challenge every word, looking for a legal flaw, a moment of definition so loosely constructed by Martin and Buscetta that the defense can declare it outside the witness's scope of knowledge. They are all caught up in the dangerous word game.

Leval steps in and questions the witness directly. "The rules in dealing with associates were what?"

"The inside person, not the outside person, was responsible."

"Were there any rules requiring you to say *anything* to an associate?"

Yes. Buscetta mentions the stricture of *omerta.*

"Any rules on how you conveyed that information to an associate?" Leval appears to think that the Mafia has rules the same way that the law has rules, or the local Elks Club has rules. But the law's rules are codified, and *omerta* is based on unwritten rules, unspoken rules. There is something absurd about a federal judge questioning a washed-up Mafioso one-on-one about the rules of *his* game.

"So far, Mr. Martin, I don't think Mr. Buscetta's testimony has borne out your offer of proof."

Martin asks, "If not a rule, was there a *practice* . . . ?"

Buscetta says, "There are no written rules in the Mafia. There are *attitudes.* " The old wreck has come up with the *mot juste* at last.

Bob Fogelnest, Salamone's lawyer, says he has reason to believe that Buscetta does understand a good deal of English. He has noticed that when the defense gives the reasons behind an objection, Buscetta tailors his next answer to obviate the objection.

The jury is brought back, and Leval instructs Buscetta in its presence that he may not use the terms *omerta* or *associates* in his testimony. Throughout the following inquiry, the defense objects to every question containing the word *Mafia*. The grounds are sometimes relevancy, sometimes competency, or hearsay, or lack of foundation. All objections are overruled.

. . . NOVEMBER 1972.

PUNTA RAISI INTERNATIONAL AIRPORT, outside Palermo. Tomasso Buscetta stepped down the stairway from the Alitalia jet in handcuffs. Fifteen years after the 1957 Luciano meeting, the Sicilian Mafia was once again in a period of relative nonbelligerence. The Luciano meeting had led to the formation of the Sicilian Commissione, the ruling body of the capos of each of the Mafia families. But it had scarcely been fifteen years of uninterrupted harmony.

Back in 1963, another bloody war had broken out among the various Mafia families. Two families, the Grecos of Ciaculli and the powerful family from the fierce and sullen mountain village of Corleone—the Corleonese—had emerged strongest from the slaughter. The war reached a climax on June 30, 1963, in what became known as "the Ciaculli Massacre," when a Mafia car bomb exploded and killed seven police officers. The massacre brought an immediate response from the Italian government. Hundreds of Mafia members were arrested. The Commissione was forced out of existence, and the Sicilian families were decimated by the succession of trials that followed.

Tomasso Buscetta was one of the Mafiosi who fled Sicily in the wake of the police crackdown, after the Palermo police issued a warrant for his arrest on charges of kidnapping and murder. He traveled to the United States by way of Switzerland, Mexico City, and Canada. Buscetta spent six years in and around New York City operating pizzerias and, according to the FBI, dealing in narcotics with defendant Filippo Casamento, among others. He was arrested and deported to Mexico in August 1970, and drove through Central America to Brazil.

In 1972 Brazilian police arrested a network of Corsican heroin smugglers operating out of São Paulo and Rio. One of the men gave police information that led to the arrest of Buscetta. Two months later he was deported from Brazil.

Buscetta arrived back in Palermo's infamous old dungeon-fortress, Ucciardone Prison, where he had served a previous sentence for cigarette smuggling. This time he was there to serve three years for Mafia association, a crime of which he had been convicted in his absence.

The U.S. government moved swiftly to have Buscetta extradited to face charges of heroin trafficking while in Brooklyn. The Italian government did not respond directly to the request. Instead it used the United States indictment as the basis for similar charges in Palermo, and Buscetta was sentenced to fourteen years. The murder indictment that had been hanging over his head since the early sixties was dropped for lack of evidence.

The police roundups in the wake of the Ciaculli Massacre had resulted in the notorious "Trial of the 114," a Mafia trial held in Calabria, on the Italian mainland. One of the accused was Gaetano Badalamenti. The trial wandered on for over a year. In 1967 minor sentences were returned against only a third of the defendants, Badalamenti among them.

By 1969 the Sicilian Mafia had again shown its phoenixlike ability to survive family wars and government crackdowns. La Cosa Nostra was back in business. Honor had been restored. Three senior Sicilian Mafia leaders had laid the groundwork for the new Mafia order. Gaetano Badalamenti was one of the ruling triumvirate.

Badalamenti was the powerful don of Cinisi, a small town lying just west of Palermo across the coastal plain. The municipality benefited greatly from the construction of Sicily's new jet airport a few kilometers outside Cinisi. Punta Raisi International Airport, constructed with hundreds of thousands of tons of Badalamenti cement, is a literal monument to the power of Badalamenti, or "Don Tanino," as he was locally known. It is built at the foot of a mountain, Don Tanino's mountain, and many a pilot will testify that in bad weather it can be one of the most harrowing places to land a jet in all of Europe and Africa. The unusual proximity of runways to mountain is made more curious by the miles of lush, verdant flatland that lie between Cinisi and Palermo. But Don Tanino owned the mountain and he owned the quarry on the other side of the mountain, and that was where the airport was going to be built.

Badalamenti held both the airport and the town under his firm personal control. When the FBI asked the Italian authorities about him, they were told, "His power is such that he can call upon almost all the male population of Cinisi to serve him."

Badalamenti's ally in the Mafia triumvirate was Stefano Bontate, a suave, sophisticated man who was comfortable—as the peasant-born, misanthropic Don Tanino was not—among Palermo's ancient, elegant, and often sclerotic nobility. Bontate was also an avid patron of the opera. He ran a country club and shooting range on the outskirts of Palermo, and he numbered among his patrons high-ranking police officers and members of Italy's ruling Christian Democratic Party.

Badalamenti and Bontate were the traditional conservatives within the Mafia's ruling triumvirate. The third man was Salvatore Riina, acting head of the Corleonese. The Corleonese had displayed a considerable amount of independence from the other families, even during the period of relative tranquillity in the late 1950s when the Commissione was strong. They had always insisted on keeping the numbers and identity of their Mafia soldiers a secret, to the annoyance of Don Tanino, who complained bitterly to the Commissione.

Despite these tensions, it had been agreed that Don Tanino would head the Commissione, and that the leaders of the major families would constitute the membership. Badalamenti's position was supported by Bontate, and by a strong ally of Bontate's, one Salvatore Inzerillo. The Corleonese were represented by Salvatore Riina.

Just after the Commissione was restructured, Badalamenti and Bontate were once again arrested. While they stewed in the Ucciardone, the Corleonese consolidated their position.

A series of ransom kidnappings carried out by the Corleonese, despite Commissione rules forbidding such activity, made clear that the men from Corleone constituted a law unto themselves. The growing rift between the traditionalists and the Corleonese was heightened by the changing nature of the criminal enterprises in which the Sicilian Mafia engaged.

The island of Sicily was enjoying an economic boom. Rome had decided to embark on a program of massive construction in the poverty-stricken south of the country, and had voted billions of lire to help the poor and homeless. A vast amount of money wound up in the regional banks of Palermo. The Mafia families who controlled these banks now had access to vast resources of capital with which to finance their criminal enterprises. They looked around for a wise investment for the government's funds. The answer had already been provided by the New York Police Department.

In October 1961 New York Police Detective Eddie Egan and his partner, Sonny Grosso, had stopped for a drink at the famous Copacabana nightclub in Manhattan. At the bar they spotted a low-level mobster named Pasquale Fuca tipping lavishly and waving a huge wad of money around. They decided to check out the high roller. Their investigation soon became famous as the French Connection case. It had led to the capture of fifty-one kilos of almost pure heroin shipped to New York aboard the transatlantic liner *United States,* hidden in a Buick Invicta. Arrests and further investigations in New York and France continued for nine more years, and eventually led to the smashing of the French Connection heroin ring. Secret laboratories and packaging plants around Marseilles, run by French and Corsican dope dealers, were destroyed. The Sicilian Mafia had been involved in the transportation of morphine base to the French laboratories, but police had no evidence to show that the Mafia had progressed into the sophisticated field of heroin processing. With the destruction of the French Connection, some Sicilian Mafiosi saw the opportunity to establish a monopoly in one of the world's most lucrative enterprises: the production, distribution, and sale of heroin.

A small, extremely violent, immensely wealthy group of Turkish businessmen and Lebanese warlords had always brokered the harvest of the poppy fields of Turkey, Iran, and Southeast Asia. They took the gooey paste known as "morphine base" and sold tons of it to the highest bidders, at something between $3,000 and $10,000 a kilogram. All one needed to get into the game was a few million dollars; a small navy to rendezvous on the Mediterranean high seas with the ships of the morphine dealers; a small army for self-protection in the ruthless world of drug dealing; a skilled chemist to process the precious morphine base into even more precious heroin; a hidden laboratory in which to do the work; and a network of buyers. These buyers would take care of the retail distribution.

The Sicilians had access to tens of millions of dollars of Italian government subsidies. They had a flotilla of high-powered speedboats, which they had used for years to smuggle cigarettes from Turkey and Greece, avoiding Italian and other tobacco taxes. They had more than enough muscle to make even the most insane drug warlord think twice before double-crossing them. And they had a long-established, highly secure organization of brokers in New York City, hub of the richest drug market in the world.

The Sicilian Mafia was perfectly placed to inherit the world's most lucrative criminal enterprise. When the American heroin franchise came up for grabs, the ruthless, pragmatic Corleone family decided to move. By the time Gaetano Badalamenti and Stefano Bontate emerged from prison, in 1975, the Corleonese had taken effective control of the Commissione, and now formed a strong, secret cabal within a secret society. Their next move was to eliminate all opposition. Gaetano Badalamenti was marked as first to go. . . .

. . . WEDNESDAY, NOVEMBER 6, 1985. THE COURTROOM.   Paul Bergman wants talk of cigarette smuggling by Buscetta excluded. Kennedy wants it left in. In the old days, Badalamenti and Buscetta dealt in contraband tobacco together, and Kennedy must persuade the jury that the Old Man has not changed his ways. Bergman drones on, determined to dissect and discuss every legal nuance. He does not seem to understand, or care, that Kennedy needs this evidence because it occurs at a time when the Mafia switches from tobacco to heroin, a switch that coincides with Badalamenti's expulsion from the Mafia. It strengthens his argument: Mafia turns to drugs, Mafia throws out Badalamenti; therefore Badalamenti must have been thrown out because he is against drugs.

But Bergman is impervious to the need. Kennedy fumes. The jury is called in. Their step is a millisecond slower, the faintest hint of familiarity and boredom beginning to show.

Bergman makes a second request: "Your Honor, my mike is not working."

"I'm sorry," says Leval dryly. "I can't fix that."

"Michael has pulled his plug," Eleanore whispers.

Buscetta resumes testimony on his meetings with Badalamenti in Brazil. But within minutes he is stopped, and the jury sent out once more.

Kennedy wants all of the day's testimony stricken from the record. Buscetta is now dealing with the period after Badalamenti's expulsion from the Mafia, so it is irrelevant to charges against his client. Additionally, the prosecutors have already said that the Mafia is the cement that holds this whole Pizza conspiracy together. If that is the case, a man who is out of the Mafia must also be out of the conspiracy.

Martin counters, "The evidence will show that although Badalamenti withdrew his name and presence, and despite his expulsion, he continued to be active in the Mafia."

Leval quickly moves to cut off Kennedy's route. "There are two kinds of glue in this case, Mafia glue and narcotics glue. Motion denied. Let's take a recess."

"I'm so nervous," says Eleanore. "The next fifteen minutes *is our case.*"

But just as Michael Kennedy rises to begin his carefully choreographed cross-examination of Buscetta, Martin interrupts. The prosecutor wishes to clarify a mistranslation of something the witness says he was told by a fellow Mafioso, Saca Catalano, a cousin of defendant Salvatore, before he left Sicily. "See my cousin for a *posto* when you get to America." The word *posto* had been translated as job. Did not Buscetta intend the less common meaning, "place"?

Buscetta appears to reply on cue. He meant *una casa,* a house to hole up in.

The change is fundamental. Instead of saying that Saca told him, "See my cousin for a job," the government now says the message was, "See my cousin for a place to hide out." The new translation throws sinister, criminal light on defendant Catalano.

The courtroom rings: "Objection!" "Objection!"

Catalano's lawyer, Ivan Fisher, is on his feet. His writhings suggest a multi-armed buddha attacked by fleas. He stares heavenward as if beseeching the deity to shed light in this dark corner; he juggles the microphone like a rock in his glove. Did he, Buscetta, speak to Mr. Martin regarding this conversation during the recess? No.

"The word *posto.* What does it mean to you?"

"For us, house . . . or a place where one can stay."

". . . A place to stay in hiding?"

"For me, yes."

"So when *you* used the word *posto,* it means a place where one stays in hiding, is that right?"

Fisher, using his most sarcastic tone, is illustrating that this witness will take and cling to any position the government hints it wants. The interpreter had translated the word *posto* as job. Buscetta had let it pass. He had already demonstrated that, after six years in Brooklyn, he knows the English language reasonably well. No matter. Once Martin had corrected the translation to suit the government's arguments, Buscetta means to stick to the government's designated translation no matter what Fisher says.

Several defense lawyers think they sniff prosecutorial misconduct.

They rise to question. But by the time they sit down, hours later, the incisive, precision cuts of Fisher's scalpel have been gradually blurred and destroyed by the broadsword swings of the pack. This pattern will be much repeated in the months to come. Thoughtless, stupid, or openly hostile moves by one's fellow lawyers are almost certainly the greatest danger in multidefendant trials. To guard against them requires defense solidarity and unanimity of purpose, strict discipline, firm leadership, and nightly strategy-planning meetings attended by all defense counsel.

The translator of the disputed word, a proper Englishwoman, is called to the stand to test her for collusion with the government. Cecile Horner had participated in a pretrial interrogation session with Buscetta in the U.S. Attorney's Office. She was overheard warning another translator to be cautious in the presence of a member of the defense team. This has led the defense to suspect that she may be overly sympathetic to the prosecution, if not hand in glove. The defense wants the woman fired for bias. Leval will think on the matter overnight.

Eleanore Kennedy fears that this entire flap is a stall, a maneuver to permit the government to caucus before Kennedy's cross-examination. She is unhappy. Her husband, she explains, "is like a race horse," all prepared to cross-examine, who has now been forced to spend an entire day cooling his heels pending the resolution of the *posto* affair.

. . . THURSDAY, NOVEMBER 7, 1985. THE COURTROOM. Michael Kennedy walks down the center aisle with measured tread and deposits on his front-row table a gigantic Italian dictionary. It is good psychological warfare, suggesting as it does that Kennedy is prepared and equipped to destroy the embattled court interpreter.

The tough Brooklyn lawyer Joe Benfante is attacking Martin's veracity by chopping at the woman. Though sometimes inarticulate, Benfante characterizes better than any other lawyer the reasons for the mass defense demand that Ms. Horner be replaced. "Tomasso Buscetta was given a feeling he was safe in her hands."

In fact, Benfante insists, the government's background material clearly shows Buscetta to be a "flippant, unscrupulous person who has delusions of grandeur . . . and his testimony must be stricken, or a mistrial declared."

Leval prefaces his ruling with a stern comment: "For starters . . . I'm extremely angry at the prosecutor. He made all of this necessary by making inaccurate statements to the court."

The judge now rereads aloud the relevant portion of the transcript from last month. Leval had asked Martin whether the translators under discussion had been employed by the U.S. Attorney's Office. Martin had said no, but that two of them had asked to hear Tomasso Buscetta's voice, to become familiar with his speech patterns.

"That statement by Mr. Martin did not accurately apprise the court of what happened . . . it was just learned that the interpreter had had some contact with the U.S. Attorney's office, not only with Buscetta, but with another witness X."

Additionally, Horner had served as interpreter in a preview run-through of Buscetta's testimony held in Martin's office. Here even Judge Leval questions Martin's veracity. "I don't know and I don't need to know for present purposes why Mr. Martin's answer was so uninformative. I don't know if it was his intention to conceal the true nature of the occurrences, or was it just extraordinary sloppiness? That answer, which misled court and counsel, led to long delay over what I regard as an issue of no substance."

This said, Leval gets down to business. "Ms. Horner is a superbly qualified interpreter of great experience. . . . So, while a lot of heat has been generated on this matter, it is not my intention to disqualify [her]. Many defense counsel feel I have been had, by Mr. Martin's statement. I sympathize. But nothing I have heard impugns her qualifications."

The clock shows 12:56 P.M. The morning is gone.

A day late, the cross-examination begins. Kennedy walks over to stand beside his client, mike in hand. He turns back to the witness box. "Good morning, Mr. Buscetta. Permit me to introduce myself." The lawyer places his right hand on the shoulder of his seated client. "This is a person you have known at least thirty-five years, yes?"

Kennedy treats the baggy old informer with the utmost courtesy, playing on his self-image as a Man of Honor.

"Was Gaetano Badalamenti personally engaged in narcotics trafficking?" The lawyer again places a hand on his client's shoulder.

For a moment, silence. Then: "Personally, no."

Now it is Kennedy's turn to leave a split second of silence, to let this answer reverberate in the jurors' minds.

His next question changes tack. Was his client, he wonders, ever an ally of Salvatore Greco—not the Sal Greco in the back row, but the old Mafia chieftain.

The lawyers for the Catalano faction are instantly on their feet, shouting objections. They discern Kennedy's strategy, they think, and find it in direct conflict with the interests of their own clients. Kennedy's question was intended to remind the jury of the Mafia wars, and to position his client at the heart of the struggle. Fisher and Malerba, who represent Catalano, and Schechter and Lombardino, who represent the Lambertis, oppose any mention of Mafia membership. This, they feel, can only dye their clients blacker than they have already begun to look. The conflict within the defense is so sharp as to seem an echo of the bloody Sicilian hostilities of the past.

. . . 1977.

PALERMO. Gaetano Badalamenti was having increasing difficulty keeping control within his own fiefdom of Cinisi. Several mysterious crimes had taken place on his turf. In Palermo, a new wave of Mafia-inspired murders startled even that hardened population by their audacity. One of the first victims was a famous *carabiniere* colonel, Giuseppe Russo, gunned down by Pino Greco, a ruthless new ally of the Corleonese.

Badalamenti complained bitterly that the authority of the Commissione was being ignored. The Corleone group charged that Badalamenti was intellectually incapable of ruling so sophisticated a body as the modern Sicilian Mafia Commissione. The Corleonese leader Luciano Leggio openly mocked Badalamenti's lack of eloquence at meetings.

In highly secret and controversial circumstances, Gaetano Badalamenti, don of the Cinisi Family, was ousted both from his position on the Commissione and from leadership of his own family. No one of a number of informers has been able to state the precise facts regarding the Badalamenti expulsion, and he of course, true to his oath of *omerta,* says nothing.

In late 1978 Badalamenti fled Sicily in fear of his life. The Cinisi Family was taken over by his cousin and long-time enemy, Antonino Badalamenti. The Commissione was reorganized, with Michele Greco (no relation to defendant Sal Greco), a leading figure in the Corleonese alliance, named as Boss of Bosses. As for the ousted Badalamenti faction, they soon had a new sobriquet in the Sicilian press. They were "the Losers."

It was 1979, and La Cosa Nostra, the *Beati Paoli,* the beautiful people of Sicilian folklore, the Robin Hood characters who fought the French invaders and defended the weak and brought justice upon tyrannical landlords, had now become an organization of dope dealers and extortionists. Soon the Corleonese, in their lust for power, threatened the very fabric of the Italian state. Within their own Mafia ranks they inaugurated a purge that left the streets of Palermo streaming with blood.

On July 21, 1979, Palermo's top detective, Boris Giuliano, entered the Bar Lux for his morning cappuccino. Giuliano was active in fighting the Mafia's booming trade in heroin, and lately had made several important busts. It was he who had discovered $497,000 wrapped in American-made pizzeria aprons in a cheap blue suitcase at Punta Raisi Airport, and assisted U.S. agents in tracking down the source. Giuliano finished his coffee. As he rose to leave, another customer walked up behind him and shot him many times in the head and back.

Not long after the slaying, Michele Reina, provincial secretary of the Christian Democratic Party, was murdered. Next to die at the hands of the Corleonese was Cesare Terranova, a judge who had mounted a lonely campaign against the Mafia, focusing particularly on the Corleonese chief Luciano Leggio.

Leggio, Riina, and the other Corleonese bosses increased the pressure. They claimed that Badalamenti's ally, and the real strong man behind the traditionalist group—the opera patron Stefano Bontate— was out of touch with what was going on in Sicilian politics. Bontate was outraged. He was out of touch with whoever was killing moderate Mafiosi and key police and political figures within his territory. That, he claimed, was his only fault. He confided to Tomasso Buscetta that he had decided it was time to move against Salvatore Riina. It was chiefly Riina, Bontate said, who was behind the new wave of political killings. These latest victims soon became known in the Sicilian press as "the Brilliant Cadavers."

Riina by his actions had offered Bontate terrible personal humiliation. In retaliation, Bontate decided to shoot Salvatore Riina dead, and shoot him in the only setting where he could be sure to encounter him face to face: across the table at a meeting of the Mafia Commissione.

Buscetta was horrified at Bontate's proposal. His insane plan made it clear how desperate, and how isolated from reality, Bontate and his ally Inzerillo had become. Though Buscetta was able to persuade Bontate to hold off, at least temporarily, defeat was already inevitable. The Corleonese had by then so effectively infiltrated both the Bontate and Inzerillo families that, within two days, Riina was aware of Bontate's threat to assassinate him.

Buscetta's mediation efforts ended abruptly when the head of his own Mafia family tricked Buscetta's son into accepting a gift of ransom money, then had him arrested and charged with kidnapping. For Tomasso Buscetta it was the last straw. He decided to return with his family to Brazil.

Stefano Bontate threw a lavish farewell party for Buscetta at his $500,000 mansion. Soon after, Buscetta drove to Paris and used a false passport to board a flight for Rio de Janeiro. He had left Palermo just in time. Within weeks, many of those who had gathered to bid him farewell were dead.

Bontate was the first to go. He made the mistake of telling an informant within his family of his plan to spend the weekend at his country estate. He would drive himself, and have his bodyguard precede him in another car. When a red light separated the Mafia chieftain from his guard, the Corleonese moved. A car pulled up beside Bontate. A Kalashnikov AK-47 assault rifle was pushed out the passenger window. Bontate saw it and pulled a silver Colt .45 automatic pistol from his shoulder holster. But he was too late. The high-velocity bullets from the Kalashnikov blew the side of his face off.

Salvatore Inzerillo, head of the Rigano Family, and the last remaining boss of the Losers faction, was now extremely worried. But he was certain he had at least a few weeks' grace, thanks to an outstanding financial debt. He had obtained fifty kilos of heroin from Salvatore Riina and had yet to pay him. Still, precautions needed to be taken, so Inzerillo bought himself an armor-plated Alfa Romeo. . . .

In the courtroom, Kennedy is continuing to battle to get across to the jury Buscetta's crucial message about his client. The answer must be very clear. "Gaetano Badalamenti was against drugs, and did not deal in drugs . . . is that your answer, Mr. Buscetta?"

"I was *certain* he was not working in drugs."

When Buscetta first knew Badalamenti, in Cinisi, what sort of work did he do?

"Farming and livestock."

"And you knew Mr. Badalamenti first as a *soldato,* then as a *sotocapo* and then as a *capo?*" Yes.

Paul Bergman asks the court for a "continuing objection, so I won't have to keep interrupting Mr. Kennedy."

Kennedy snaps, "Either that . . . or God will have to pull his plug, as He did yesterday." A few jurors laugh.

Kennedy has two final, critical questions, rolled out in ringing tones. Did the Corleonese want to kill Badalamenti? Yes.

Did Mr. Badalamenti know this? Yes . . .

. . . MAY 10, 1981.

PALERMO. A high-powered motorcycle screeched to a halt outside Gioiello Contino in the center of the city. The dramatically spotlit display of diamonds and gold was protected by expensive windows of bulletproof glass. The pillion passenger swung a Kalashnikov around from across his chest and pointed it at the bulletproof windows. The small street rocked to the roar of fully automatic fire. Pieces of masonry and chunks of steel and glass flew into the air. Investigating detectives were amazed to discover no corpses, no missing jewelry, just a riddled storefront and a baffled proprietor.

The following night Salvatore Inzerillo, last major ally of Badalamenti, stepped from the Palermo apartment he maintained for his mistress on fashionable Via Brunelleschi. He checked out the street as he walked toward his new bulletproof Alfa Romeo. Few people ever knew of his movements, and on this night he had been exceptionally careful. Only sixteen days had passed since his close ally and friend Stefano Bontate had been ambushed and murdered.

Inzerillo had not heard of the shooting at the jeweler's shop or he might have been less confident of his new bulletproof toy. As he walked toward his car he failed to notice the men trotting toward him. They opened up with the Kalashnikov. The bullets cut Inzerillo to pieces on the sidewalk of Via Brunelleschi. He never had time to reach his car or even to draw the .357 Magnum revolver he carried in his pocket.

The Corleonese had now cleared all opposition within the Commissione. But they were not satisfied. They intended to carry out a complete reign of terror, and kill not only those who posed a threat, but also those who might offer future assistance to the Losers, and those suspected of having worked with the Losers in the past.

One of the leaders of the Corleonese, Pino Greco, kidnapped the sixteen-year-old son of the murdered Salvatore Inzerillo. The boy had sworn to avenge his father. His captor had him held on a table and sawed his arm off. Greco waved the severed arm at the boy, screaming, "With this arm can you no longer kill Toto Riina." Then Greco shot him.

The slaughter was not confined to Sicily. On a cold January morning in New Jersey, Rosario Gambino, nephew of the notorious New York don Carlo Gambino, emerged from his home to discover that his Cadillac car, stolen days earlier, was now sitting parked outside his door. He called the cops immediately. The young Gambino had emigrated from Sicily, and he knew that in the past his family had been considered allies of the Losers. Someone with such a background knew better than to approach a stolen car.

The police examined the engine compartment, then checked out the interior. Nothing. Finally they gathered around the trunk and forced it open. Jammed inside was the frozen body of Pietro Inzerillo, brother of the murdered Losers' leader, Salvatore. The mouth of the frozen corpse had been forced open. It was packed with dollar bills, as were the murdered man's genitals. . . .

. . . FRIDAY, NOVEMBER 8, 1985. THE COURTROOM. Several lawyers request what has become known as a "Ryan recess," time to visit the men's room. When court resumes, Buscetta says he wishes to amplify one of his previous answers—an ominous moment for the defense. If he changes his testimony, Kennedy's strategy will have backfired.

"Mr. Kennedy asked me if I had ever engaged in drug trafficking." Buscetta had said no. Now he says that he introduced people "for the purpose of having them deal," but received no compensation. He did not participate. "So I should have said yes. But I had to do it. They were both *Mafiosi.*"

"When did this occur?" Perhaps Kennedy can still pull his bacon from the fire.

"1980." Whew. Badalamenti had left Sicily for good in 1978.

But another dangerous question is required. "Was that the only time?" Kennedy asks.

"No. One other time. In 1969, in New York City."

So the bacon is out. At least, it is until Bergman shouts "Objection!"

The sole defense attorney interested in making Buscetta appear truthful is Kennedy. The others would all be happy to see the government's star witness discredited. "The witness is trying to cover that he lied," Bergman says.

Bedlam erupts. Leval pounds his gavel. Kennedy can be heard calling to Bergman, "Cock-sucker! One more question and I'll punch you in the mouth!" Ryan is bawling that this sort of testimony puts his client in double jeopardy regarding pre-1969 transactions. Bergman once more asks for a continuing objection. Fogelnest suddenly announces, "I do *not* object!" The uproar has caused him to rethink his position. "I align myself with the Badalamenti group."

Leval seeks to restore order. "Mr. Buscetta, I have one question to ask you. You spoke just now of a narcotics transaction in 1969. Did it involve any defendant in this trial?"

"No, sir."

This is not enough for Kennedy. "Is it not correct that, after his expulsion, Gaetano Badalamenti became the object of ferocious persecution by the Corleonese, and . . . ?"

Leval interrupts; he will not permit the word *persecution.*

Before Kennedy can rephrase, Buscetta says, "They were looking for him to kill him."

Kennedy, fast: "Do you want to hear the end of the question, your Honor?" Appreciative laughter from other defense lawyers; sometimes one gets lucky. Buscetta has given Kennedy an unexpected gift. A quick, whispered check with the other Badalamenti-group lawyers, and Kennedy says he has no further questions.

Now he must sit silent and watch while others beat up on Buscetta. Will the Kennedy defense survive?

First up is Bergman, who requests a severance for his client, Amato, based on Kennedy's cross-examination. "He did nothing further than advance the prosecution's case." The severance is denied, but Bergman's accusation is almost an open declaration of war between defense counsel. Nonetheless, the day ends with the Badalamenti defense firmly anchored on Buscetta's word: The Old Man did not deal drugs.

The Kennedy camp is jubilant. The back-row lawyers claim the wily Badalamenti has pulled yet another of his Sicilian tricks and induced his old ally Buscetta, after saving his own skin in the U.S. Witness Protection Program, to march into this courtroom and rescue Don Tanino, the old lion of Cinisi. Sicilian games!

... TUESDAY, NOVEMBER 12, 1985.

THE COURTROOM. Another chilly morning. Buscetta enters wearing yet another glossy, black toupee and a new pearl-grey suit. Some of the weight of the invisible burden he carries seems to have been lifted from his sharply tailored shoulders. Badalamenti slowly worms his big, grizzled head around to the left, and his black eyes rake the spectator side of the courtroom. He gives a visitor a warm, benign smile. But it doesn't feel benign; one is rendered weak-kneed and Trilbylike by the dark, malign power of his gaze.

Next to cross-examine is a new lawyer, Lee Ginsberg, substituting for Marvin Segal as counsel to Gaetano Mazzara. Segal has been forced to remove himself from this part of the case because Buscetta is his former client. Segal had represented Buscetta in 1970 at the time of his New York arrest and deportation, and later, after Buscetta's capture in Brazil, Segal represented him again on certain immigration matters.

Mazzara at this juncture urgently needs an advocate. He has just been denounced by Buscetta as the Sicilian Mafia's chosen drug ambassador to the United States. The Badalamenti-group lawyers are apprehensive. They fear that Segal's detailed knowledge of Buscetta's past could be used by his colleague, Ginsberg, to destroy the repentant Mafioso on the stand.

"Mr. Buscetta, you've committed perjury before this trial," Ginsberg snarls. "You've lied under oath, haven't you?"

"I've never been put under oath."

"Were you not put under oath by the Immigration and Naturalization Service in 1966, Mr. Buscetta?" The lawyer hands the witness a document. "You recognize the signature? Is it your own?"

"Yes." The document is signed "Manuel Lopez Cadena," one of Buscetta's aliases.

"You lied to the INS when you said you lived in Mexico, and had never been to the United States?"

"Si."

"You lied about your age. You were born August 21, 1923?"

65

"Si."

"You lied when you said you spoke only Spanish?"

"Si."

"We know you speak Italian and English, as well."

"I speak English to live, but not well enough to get along in this courtroom." A hint of menace, defiance even, has crept into Buscetta's voice.

Ginsberg leads Buscetta through a long series of questions concerning his travels around the world under various aliases. Each time Ginsberg moves on to another border crossed, another false name and false passport, another love affair, another wife, Buscetta is forced, over and over, to admit he lied.

Ginsberg's savage cross-examination continues. "Did your Mafia boss put you into the drug traffic?"

"No."

"Wasn't your family heavily involved in drugs?"

"Yes."

"And didn't you have substantial contacts here in the U.S.?"

"Yes."

"And you were well aware of how to move between Italy, the United States, Canada, Brazil, and so on?"

"Yes."

"And in 1973 weren't you charged with drug-trafficking?"

"Here, yes. Brazil no."

Eleanore Kennedy whispers, "He's trying to sink the whole Badalamenti family! That's why he keeps bringing up Brazil."

. . . 1982.

RIO DE JANEIRO. Tomasso Buscetta was increasingly worried that his friendship with Badalamenti and Bontate would place him and his family in jeopardy. His fears were confirmed when he learned of the murder in Milan of his first wife's brother.

Then in January 1982 Buscetta received a visitor he had been warned to avoid. Gaetano Badalamenti had come to Rio de Janeiro in hopes of persuading Buscetta that together they could rally the opposition to the Corleonese, and return to Sicily to wage war against their enemies and wrest control of the Mafia from their hands. Buscetta would hear none of it. He wanted only to remain in Brazil and be left alone.

Back in Sicily, the Corleonese had lost all sense of restraint and were seemingly determined to terrorize the entire island into submission. Pio La Torre, regional secretary of the Communist Party, traditional enemy of the Mafia, spoke out against the slaughter. He demanded that the Italian prime minister move not only against the gunmen, but also against the shadowy group of businessmen who laundered the heroin money and ran the island's commerce for the Mafia.

On April 30, 1982, La Torre and his driver were murdered in the center of Palermo. The Italian government decided to send one of its most renowned law-enforcement officers, General Carlo Alberto Della Chiesa, to the island. The general had won fame throughout Italy for his leadership in crushing the terrorist Red Brigades. He arrived in Sicily in time to attend the funeral of Pio La Torre.

Della Chiesa set about investigating the secret links between the Sicilian Mafia and major Sicilian and Italian financiers. Within five months he was dead, murdered in his car alongside his young wife. They had driven to a Palermo restaurant for a late-night meal. A powerful motorcycle pulled up beside them, and the pillion passenger raised the Kalashnikov rifle and sprayed the car. Both died instantly. The Kalashnikov bullets were tested. The assassins had used the same weapon that had killed Bontate and Inzerillo.

Buscetta saw the news of the Della Chiesa killing on television at the Regente Hotel in Belém, Brazil, seated beside Gaetano Badalamenti. The exiled old don of Cinisi recognized the slaying of the general as the work of his enemies and fumed about their "supreme arrogance." Badalamenti exhorted Buscetta for the second time to join him in the fight against Leggio, Riina, and the murderous Corleonese. Between the two of them, he argued, they could muster sufficient forces to wipe out their tormentors.

Buscetta still refused. But the intelligence-gathering power of the Corleonese was formidable. Somehow they learned of the quiet meeting in Brazil. The ruling faction of the Mafia viewed mere association with Badalamenti as treachery.

Just eight days after his conversation with Badalamenti, Buscetta telephoned his son Antonio in Palermo. The phone was answered by Antonio's weeping wife. Both of Buscetta's sons, Antonio and Benedetto, had disappeared from the pizzeria they operated in Palermo. They have never been seen again.

        ... **WEDNESDAY, NOVEMBER 13, 1985.**
THE COURTROOM. Under Ginsberg's cross-examination, Buscetta refuses to admit to anything except cigarette smuggling. His testimony mirrors his own image of himself, the last Man of Honor. He denies any contact with drugs.

Next up is Larry Bronson, representing Sal Greco, pizzeria owner of Oakhurst and Neptune City, New Jersey, and a brother of the Sicilian Mafia leader Leonardo Greco. "You were expelled from the Mafia for cheating on your wife?"

"No."

Bronson reviews Buscetta's womanizing in detail, then jumps to his Italian heroin conviction in 1973. Buscetta denies it all. His testimony is more than a tissue of lies; it's an entire Kleenex box full. His evasions are sometimes breath-taking. Known to all the lawyers, indeed to all readers of Italian and Sicilian newspapers, though to none of the jurors, is Buscetta's horrifying family history, which finally forced him to betray *omerta.* By the time Buscetta decided to switch sides, two young sons, a brother, and six other close family members had been butchered in bloody Mafia revenge. Yet when Bronson asks him, "Were your sons convicted of heroin trafficking?" he gets only the laconic reply, "Don't know."

The Buscetta bashing culminates with fiery Joe Ryan, speaking at first in gentle, whispery tones, then letting his voice rise with the temperature of his cross-examination. Soon he is yelling across the space between the podium and Buscetta as though the informer's extensive plastic surgery had somehow damaged his hearing.

"You have a lawyer. Philip Douglas represented you in the United States. How did you get his name?"

From Richard Martin. Buscetta first met the chief prosecutor in March 1985, and when he was ready to discuss a deal, Martin provided a list of possible lawyers to represent him. Most, like Douglas, indeed like Ryan and many defense lawyers in this case, were men who had recently left government service to graze the greener pastures of private practice.

Martin asks for ten minutes' redirect. Since Ryan introduced into evidence a portion of the agreement between the government and Buscetta, Martin asserts his right to introduce the entire document. The defense lawyers are united in their opposition. They know that spelling out the terms will alert the jury to how serious Buscetta's need is to be protected from extremely violent men—men like the defendants.

Several lawyers protest that they never asked to examine Buscetta, but that their clients will be branded as murderers nonetheless because of Ryan's mistaken introduction of the document. This they claim is the curse, the basic injustice of this government catchall conspiracy trial. Some of these twenty-two men face contamination from misdeeds they had no knowledge of, let alone any influence upon.

Leval works out a compromise. The jury will learn that Buscetta has testified, or will testify, against hundreds of people either here or in Italy. Therefore he has some reasonable cause for concern for his safety. They also will be told that he has entered into a detailed financial agreement with the United States government covering his future life in the U.S. Witness Protection Program. The jury is summoned once more.

When Kennedy asked Buscetta if he had any knowledge of Badalamenti's drug dealing, the informer had replied, "Personally, no." The prosecutor takes the word *personally* as his springboard. "Do you have any knowledge as to whether Mr. Badalamenti ever participated in drug trafficking?"

Kennedy and Fisher shout, "Objection!"

Leval sustains. "Asked and answered."

Martin asks, "Did you have a conversation in 1974 with Domenico Coppolla?"

Kennedy demands an immediate bench conference. He already knows from the Buscetta background material that the government will try to use Coppolla to establish a link between Badalamenti and Sicilian drug dealing, and he wants it stopped dead.

In 1971 Customs agents, acting on a tip, searched the Italian liner *Raffaello* and discovered eighty-one kilos of heroin hidden inside a Ford Galaxie car. The agents trailed the drug-laden car around New York and eventually arrested a Sicilian mobster named Frank Rappa. Rappa's arrest caused an accomplice named Domenico Coppolla to flee to Sicily, where he was arrested and jailed.

Buscetta has told U.S. authorities that while he was a prisoner in Ucciardone in 1974, he had a conversation with Coppolla, whom he knows to be a Mafioso, and Coppolla told him that Gaetano Badalamenti—at that time a fellow prisoner—had also been involved in the 1971 car shipment. Coppolla also said he had fled the United States because of his fear that Rappa might be cooperating with American authorities. Rappa had been sentenced to fifteen years for his participation in the heroin scheme, but released after serving only three.

In a separate conversation in Ucciardone, prisoner Badalamenti had told prisoner Buscetta of his distrust of prisoner Rappa.

All this is hearsay of hearsay of hearsay, as several lawyers point out. What's more, Coppolla is now dead, and Buscetta is in the hands of the government.

Leval rules that the alleged Coppolla drug conversation is clearly not in furtherance of this conspiracy, and cannot come into evidence. But the Martin redirect is off to an incendiary start.

Kennedy next suggests that Martin has jogged, even jabbed at, Buscetta's memory, in order to make his testimony more helpful. "Now they have this man [Buscetta] whom they own. They take him into the back room, for God knows what purposes. He comes back out and he is more contrite. It's simply unfair. Not only is it unfair, it smells and it looks bad."

Michael and Eleanore Kennedy have just sent out baby announcements. They have adopted a two-month-old Nicaraguan orphan, whom they have named Anna Rosario. After court today, the happy father hands out Nicaraguan cigars to the lawyers and defendants as each one comes over to congratulate the jubilant parents.

At the elevator, as Pat Burke is leaving, he says he is appalled by the day's events. He has "known Dickie Martin for years," and can judge matters from the government's point of view, having himself spent four years as an assistant U.S. attorney for the Southern District. "But I have never before seen such a prosecutor. I think he's a little crazy."

. . . THURSDAY, NOVEMBER 14, 1985.
THE CAFETERIA. Kennedy has been working on his recross since before dawn. In the coffee line, a lawyer in another trial asks him, "You *still* believe Badalamenti did not deal drugs?" and gets an impassioned affirmative reply.

Martin jumps straight in where he left off yesterday, and rewalks Buscetta through key moments of the Kennedy cross-examination. Buscetta was sure Badalamenti did not deal heroin because it would be fatal for an expelled Mafioso to continue to deal with Mafia members. Martin tries a different approach. "But if you had known that after his expulsion Badalamenti did deal with other Mafiosi, would that have changed your mind?"

The room rings with Kennedy's shout: "Objection!" Leval gavels for order.

Buscetta continues to narrow and hedge his previous testimony. No, he never actually heard Badalamenti say he was against drugs.

"And when you talked about him not doing drugs you were referring specifically to heroin?"

"Yes."

"But not cocaine?"

"Yes."

At each question Kennedy yells "Objection!" louder, but always in vain. Martin switches tack. Was Badalamenti allied with the Mafia chief Sal Inzerillo? Yes. Did you speak with Inzerillo about his alliance with Badalamenti? Yes. Do you know that Inzerillo personally dealt drugs? Yes.

"Objection!" Kennedy roars. "He is deliberately distorting!" Martin is furious at Kennedy's allegation, and unrelenting in his determination to connect Badalamenti to drugs in any way possible. He switches to another Mafia leader. How about Mr. Riccobono? Is he an ally of Badalamenti? Did he deal drugs?

"Objection!" shouts Kennedy. "Again, the time frame. This is the deliberate distortion I was talking about. . . . He is not talking about the time of the alliance, he is talking about the time of the conversation, and deliberately trying to mislead the jury about it. . . ."

Leval interrupts. "Please don't make a speech in front of the jury."

Kennedy goes right on talking. "I have no recourse but to defend my client."

"The jury will disregard comments by counsel," says Leval. "May we have quiet, please!"

Kennedy cuts in sharply. "You're permitting it! You're permitting *his* misconduct."

Just as sharply, Leval says, "The jury will leave the room."

In silence, the twenty-four "triers of the fact" trudge offstage. When the last juror has vanished, Leval says dryly, "We will take a short recess, and I will ask counsel during the recess to think for a few moments about the fact that they are lawyers, and think about conducting themselves as such throughout the balance of this trial." Like a displeased schoolmaster, he gathers his black skirts about him and sweeps offstage.

Eleanore thinks it is worth risking a contempt citation to expose Martin. Several kibitzing defense lawyers agree, and offer cash contributions toward the martyr's possible future fine.

There is no way a juror can understand what he has just heard. Not even Leval yet understands the game going on. Martin has very cleverly created a confusion of time frames. Buscetta had testified that, before 1978, Badalamenti and Inzerillo were more or less aligned on every subject, except drugs. In 1978 the allies went in different directions: Badalamenti into exile, Inzerillo into drugs.

By deliberately confusing and blending two different time frames, Martin appears to be providing himself with a basis to argue, in summation, that Buscetta testified that the two men were allies, and that one partner in the alliance, Inzerillo, told Buscetta he dealt drugs.

This sort of subtle legal gamesmanship, invisible to all but the two dueling players, underlies much of the tedious daily courtroom give-and-take. It emphasizes the necessity for lawyers to keep themselves hyperalert while wallowing through endless seas of apparently meaningless testimony and colloquy.

The recess ends. As befits a judge of his stature, Pierre Leval has several bright young law clerks who assist in running his court. Joe LaMura, his pleasant, mustached court clerk, serves as judicial collie dog. At the start of each day, and again at the end of each recess, he must round up the straying flock of lawyers, defendants and assorted bit players and herd them back into the courtroom.

"Judge is on the bench!" he announces to the cafeteria line, bellows into the dining room, hollers down the stairwell toward the men's room, shouts along the corridors. "Judge is on the bench!"

Kennedy and Martin remain locked in bitter conflict over the question of Badalamenti's alliances in Sicily. For the Badalamenti group, Buscetta's key piece of testimony was that the Sicilian Mafia did not get involved in heroin smuggling until 1978, after Badalamenti was kicked out. Tempers flare. "This man speaks with forked tongue," Kennedy growls, glaring at Martin.

Leval is imperturbable. You are saying that both Inzerillo and Riccobono were *still* allied with Badalamenti in 1980? he asks Martin.

But Kennedy interrupts. "I would like him put under oath to make that proffer! That is an absolute lie! This man has said repeatedly on this stand, and in government documents, that after 1978 and the expulsion, no Man of Honor would have anything to do with Gaetano Badalamenti!"

Ignoring this outburst, Leval reminds Kennedy that he himself, not Martin, brought out the matter of the reason for Badalamenti's expulsion.

"I did not bring out *drug trafficking,* and that's what you're permitting. Don't blame me for what you're letting *him* do. Take responsibility for it yourself."

Dryly, Leval asks Kennedy to control his temper.

Kennedy says, "I am in control. My temper is in control. I am telling you—don't lay the blame on me. Accept the responsibility yourself for what you're permitting him to do!"

Leval is firm. He cites an earlier question put to Buscetta by Kennedy dealing with Badalamenti's expulsion from the Commissione. "Because that question was asked and not objected to by anyone, it seems to me that you are not in a position now to object when Mr. Martin asks . . . whether his opposition to drugs was the reason for his expulsion."

"And I want the record to reflect that you have asked this man Martin repeatedly to state the basis. He stated everything in the world but that. *You* then dive into the record, pull this out to help him, and then blame me for it. Terrific!"

Leval tries again. "Mr. Kennedy, you are unwittingly—I am not saying you are doing it intentionally—but you are misstating the record."

"*You* are misstating the record. I am not."

The collision between Martin and Kennedy has brought to the surface each man's deep dislike and mistrust of the other.

Martin fixes his gaze on the witness and hurls his final question. He does not mind delivering a low blow to his own prize witness when his real target is Michael Kennedy. So Buscetta shares the common fate of informers: All his protestations of honor have brought him to the point where he must dishonor himself.

"Mr. Buscetta, do you believe you were falsely accused by the United States of drug trafficking in 1973?"

The answer, in a hoarse whisper: "No."

"No further questions."

The court recesses for the weekend, the air still vibrating with the acrimony of the day as the jurors file offstage, to be spirited away in hired limousines to take up their anonymous lives. Only they know the impact on an American jury of the most important Mafia informer ever.

. . . MONDAY MORNING, NOVEMBER 18, 1985.
THE COURTHOUSE CORRIDOR.   The Pizza cast has assembled
to start its second month. How will the Badalamenti group handle the
coming last few moments with Buscetta? The Mafia informer has taken
on double importance: He is no longer just the government's star witness; he may be Kennedy's star witness as well.

"We think Buscetta is not going to say anything," says Kennedy.
"His balls are in their hands."

The honored jurors trot in, each to his or her own personal revolving
chair. Buscetta enters, eyes downcast, like a wallflower at a ball. Leval
gets straight down to business. "Mr. Kennedy, will you be cross-examining?"

"I will not, your Honor."

The Buscetta faucet is thus permanently shut—unless one of
Kennedy's co-counsel seeks to reopen it. Leval runs down the list of
lawyers, in the order their clients are named in the indictment. During
this roll call, Tomasso Buscetta continues staring at the floor—a sallow,
painted, weeping Sicilian saint with a new-made, retroussé nose. No one
wants to ask him anything. Departing from the courtroom for the last
time, he looks three feet shorter than when he came in.

When Buscetta finishes, Kennedy also departs, leaving behind his
attractive but overworked-looking stunt lawyer, Joseph Calluori, to sit
in the lead counsel's chair. This is a deliberate ploy to demonstrate
Badalamenti's lack of interest in the coming proceedings. Kennedy
thinks it "particularly important to absent myself for a while after the
Buscetta testimony. For effect. They may not talk about Gaetano
Badalamenti again for months."

Mere mention of the next government witness, one Antonietta Mantora, sets off sparks. Ken Kaplan is first to complain, and Leval dismisses the jury in anticipation of a long lawyerly wrangle. Burke says
it as well as anyone: "This testimony involves a separate, disparate,
distinct and totally discrete conspiracy, and has nothing to do with my
client. . . ."

The source of Kaplan and Burke's distress is a five-year-old heroin
seizure in Milan.

... OCTOBER 1979.
U.S. ATTORNEY'S OFFICE, EASTERN DISTRICT OF NEW YORK. The first break had come when Eastern District prosecutors were able to persuade Frank Rolli, a 300-pound drug-trafficking suspect and former New York City cop, to turn government informant. Rolli worked at John F. Kennedy International Airport as an Alitalia baggage handler. The job provided inside information on Alitalia freight shipments, which he passed along to friends, among them the three Adamita brothers. The Adamitas owned a pizzeria on Worth Street directly across from the courthouse and with the benefit of Rolli's information smuggled heroin on the side. One brother, Emmanuele Adamita, was chauffeur for the New York Mafia don Carlo Gambino.

One day the brothers precipitately invited the fat man to accompany them to Italy as a sort of bodyguard while they arranged the shipment of a consignment of heroin. At the time, Rolli was being shadowed by a couple of FBI agents, and so the brothers, informant, and agents all piled onto the same flight to Milan. Thanks to Rolli, American authorities learned that forty-one kilograms of highest-quality heroin were soon to leave Milan. They intended to bug the shipment so that it could be monitored continuously en route to its final U.S. distribution point, and all middlemen snared.

The Italian police were watching the Adamitas' Milan apartment the night a big lemon truck rolled up. Other police were watching a freight warehouse when the truck arrived there. Jubilant, and impetuous, they swooped down, captured a crate of drugs, arrested everybody in sight— and wrecked the American plan to trace the ultimate receivers of the consignment. Rolli was spirited out of Italy that night, only steps ahead of the Italian police. For some reason, his arrest warrant was issued in the name of Felix the Cat.

Rolli's career as an informer thereafter went into decline, while the forty-one kilos of heroin took on a kind of life of its own, becoming the evidentiary equivalent of Cinderella's glass slipper. The government first sought to fit the heroin into the Eastern District drug trial of Giuseppe Gambino and his associates. But when a juror admitted watching a TV show on drugs and the Mafia, a mistrial was declared. The government tried again, but the second Gambino jury voted for acquittal. The Adamitas' forty-one kilos had also shown up in a San Diego, California, drug case. Now the government was ready to trot out its glass slipper again, in hopes it would fit some of the Pizza defendants. First it would be necessary to sketch in the background for the jury.

. . . TUESDAY, NOVEMBER 19, 1985. THE COURTROOM. Antonietta Mantora, the next witness, a chemist, is head of the Italian Police Chemical Analysis Bureau and chief inspector of the National Science Police in Rome. Her strong Italian profile would not look amiss carved in bas-relief on one of Sicily's ancient stone fountains, but she is a thoroughly modern professional drug expert clad in a sharply tailored plaid suit.

Chief Inspector Mantora has supervised thousands of drug tests on all kinds of suspected illegal substances. Under questioning by Robert Stewart, she identifies the heroin she first saw in her laboratory in 1980.

Ivan Fisher, who has built up a reputation as a topnotch cross-examiner in narcotics cases, uncoils from his seat and strides to the podium. In time-honored manner, he first attacks the records-keeping system of the Italian drug police, seeking to cast doubt on whether this is the same heroin originally tied to Felix the Cat.

"Were the forty-two plastic packets heat-sealed?"

No, but they were kept locked in the safe overnight.

"So it was vulnerable to air, was it not?" Fisher smiles. "Was a thin-layer chromatography performed on each of the forty-two samples?"

Fisher has hit his stride. Like a cabaret artist working the room, he pulls the long microphone cable behind him as he lopes back and forth from podium to witness box to jury rail. Kennedy has stopped in and is standing in the shadows at the back of the room. "I wanted to see how Ivan was relating to this jury. It's perfect. He's got the mike and the pace. All he needs is the violin and he's Henny Youngman incarnate."

Fisher hammers away at Inspector Mantora's system of analysis until he is able to show that the notes on which she is basing her testimony are of very recent origin. This is unacceptable. The law is always finicky about authenticating evidence, especially in drug cases, where opportunities and temptations to tamper are notorious. Knowing full well the difficulty of what he is asking, Fisher insists on seeing her original 1980 lab reports. Prosecutors scramble to place telephone calls to their Italian counterparts. Italian narcotics authorities are reluctant to disturb their original-evidence files, particularly in drug cases; they have precisely the same fears as the Americans.

Despite maximum interruption by defense attorneys, seasoned drug lawyers who have asked these same questions many times, and who are skilled at brewing a primal broth of doubt, murk, and confusion from expert-witness testimony such as Mantora's, the police chemist is finally able to get her information before the jury: Heroin is made from the white latex, or sap, that leaks from the seedpod of the opium poppy. It hardens and turns brown upon exposure to air. Heat and solvents are employed to process the morphine base—this hardened ooze—into heroin. The heroin she first identified in March 1980 ranged from 80% to 100% pure heroin hydrochloride.

Next into the docket steps Warrant Officer Calogero Scarvaci, of the Italian Treasury Police. He testifies that five years ago he photographed defendant Sal Catalano on a sunny Sunday afternoon in the Piazza Politeana, a main square of Palermo. It was Valentine's Day 1980, just weeks before the forty-one kilos of heroin were seized in Milan. The policeman had been tailing Giorgio Muratore, a well-known Sicilian Mafioso and drug trafficker, when into his camera range stepped Catalano and his friend Joe Ganci.

Muratore and the two Americans entered a snack bar and café called the Extrabar. A short time later, the three men emerged and drove off in two cars. The policeman photographed the encounter, and has brought along his pictures.

Fisher is aptly named: a knowing, skilled, and patient angler who, by the time he has finished cross-examining this witness, has brought out that only one photo in the series shows his client, Catalano, and that in the picture Catalano is alone, crossing an Italian street—no Muratore, no Ganci, nobody. Furthermore, the original Italian police report documenting the sequence of photographs fails to mention this photo of Catalano. With a knowing smile toward the jury box and a look that says "Told you so," Fisher flops back into his seat.

Two more Italian police officers tell the jury that, five days after Muratore was seen in the square in Palermo, he met up with an American waiting at the airport to board a flight to Rome. This was the man in the back row, Frank Castronovo. At this, defendant Castronovo leans forward to whisper into the ear of his lawyer, Ken Kaplan.

It has taken Stewart several days to do it, but in laborious, grinding fashion the prosecutor has now connected a well-known Sicilian drug dealer to three Pizza defendants seen in Palermo in mid-February 1980—Catalano, Ganci, and Castronovo. He has talked about heroin seized a few weeks later from the Adamita brothers in Milan. The scenario is building. . . .

. . . TUESDAY, NOVEMBER 26, 1985.

THE COURTROOM.   Despite the knocking of the old steam radiators, a dank chill prevails. The winter weather has left Pierre Leval with a heavy cold and no voice. He seems rather pleased with his homemade substitute—three plain shirt cardboards, one marked with a white *O* for overruled, one emblazoned with a big red *S* for sustained, and a third card for the ubiquitous *Form,* the most common legal sin committed at this podium. Thus equipped, the judge can semaphore his ruling on almost any objection. "See how fast we can move when I don't talk?" he croaks.

Says Kennedy, not inaudibly, "This is the best thing that's happened since Bergman's microphone went out."

Fisher arrives swathed in camelhair and gets his usual cheerful greeting from Filippo Casamento, "Gooda mornin', Meester Feesh."

The next witness is Paolo Netti, a small, brisk man in tinted glasses with a strong voice and an assured manner. He is a captain in the Italian Tax Police who specializes in narcotics traffic. The judge will first hear his evidence out of the presence of the jury, to determine whether it is in furtherance of the government's case. "In furtherance" is the key phrase. Once more, twenty-four people trudge offstage, and Stewart places on the witness stand a cigar box filled with cassette tapes, first among the more than 55,000 telephone conversations overheard and transcribed in this case. These first cassettes contain wiretaps of the conversations of the Sicilian drug dealer Muratore, but Stewart has a hard time formulating the proper questions to permit the tapes to be introduced as evidence.

Leval, normally a man of immense patience, whispers hoarsely, "Frankly, I found it very difficult to follow the examination." He tags Stewart with "flitting around in time," and says his foundation was laid in so "confusing" a fashion that Leval is honestly uncertain whether the necessary steps have been covered or not. "This kind of a foundation should be laid the way you build a house. You start at the bottom and piece by piece you add bricks or uprights or whatever, until it is visible that the house has been constructed." Because tapes are easily altered, the lawyer seeking to admit them in evidence must thoroughly negate the possibility that the tapes *have been* altered. He must also establish that the agent used a device "technologically competent" to the job. To do this, even with Leval's help in framing proper questions, takes Stewart the better part of an hour.

In recess, Dave Lewis says: "This is going so slow, I feel like sucking my thumb and crying."

By the next morning, Leval has recovered his voice and ruled the tapes in. It is time to play them to the jury. A small speaker on the left end of the judge's bench, beside the twinkling map, emits a static-filled crackle of muffled Italian. Yes, Captain Netti recognizes both voices. Muratore, the caller, is speaking to Filippo Ragusa, another known narcotics trafficker. Like all drug dealers, the men converse in language designed to foil eavesdroppers. "Did you get the thing?" "Next week tomatoes."

Leval summons several unhappy attorneys to the side bar to make the usual defense objections to the admission of coded testimony. Other lawyers meanwhile swap old stories about conversations in other Mafia drug cases:

"Sally, about those suits you sold me. One was half a suit short!"

"The price is too high, Luigi. I'll take half a car."

"How many acres is it?" "Fifteen. Very good property." "Bring one over. Let me look."

"Hello. What time is it?" "Twelve-thirty." "Good-bye."

Just before Captain Netti leaves, Stewart manages to elicit the reason that police were watching Palermo's Punta Raisi Airport on February 19, 1980. They had heard a reference in a tapped telephone conversation to a certain Ciccio l'Americano. When they went to look for him, he turned out to be defendant Frank Castronovo.

In the courthouse cafeteria, during a recess, the defense lawyers enjoy a favorite pastime, bitching about the judge. Marvin Segal, attorney for the New Jersey restaurant man, Tommy Mazzara, used to work alongside Pierre Leval when both were Southern District prosecutors in the 1960s. "He lets you talk, and talk, and talk . . . and *then* he says no! He should be able to torture less, and act more quickly."

Lawyers in narcotics cases usually agree on a fixed fee, payable in advance, calculated in part according to the estimated amount of trial time involved. The current court estimate on the Pizza case is six to eight months. In fact, the Pizza trial will drag on for more than sixteen months, making it the longest and most expensive criminal trial in federal judicial history. As time passes, attorneys on both sides will complain that Judge Leval is to blame for the killing pace.

In theory, when a trial runs overlong, the fee can be renegotiated. In fact, the client usually says he has no more money, and the lawyer is stuck. "The system is very unfair to defense attorneys," says Segal. "They get locked in on fees"—he stubs out his half-smoked cigarette—"and then their meter starts running. . . . Well, we'd better get back to the toppling temple." The lawyers head back to the metal detector.

Leval has made another ruling. The government has demonstrated to his satisfaction that it has sufficient evidence connecting some of these defendants to the forty-one kilos. The Milan heroin will be allowed into the case. No longer will the government's all-time mammoth drug conspiracy be embarrassingly lacking in drugs.

Boring little Captain Netti now gives way to the government's second big-time Mafia informant. He is Salvatore Contorno, thirty-seven, an Afro-haired, blue-jowled, sleepy-eyed, big-shouldered man with a sullen manner. He seems a low-level hood type, what Kennedy would call "a real mook," mook being this lawyer's made-up word for someone between a mug and a crook. Contorno answers questions in a monotone, speaking English with a thick Sicilian accent.

It quickly becomes apparent that Contorno is sitting in this witness box, ready to give testimony, only because he could see no other way to stay alive. . . .

. . . 1981.

PALERMO.   The morose-looking Mafioso Salvatore Contorno was a member of the Santa Maria di Gesu Family of the Sicilian Mafia. This was the family headed by Stefano Bontate, the doomed leader of the Losers faction in the Sicilian Mafia war, and a close ally of Gaetano Badalamenti. Contorno had attended the farewell party for Tomasso Buscetta at Bontate's villa. Three weeks later he found himself in the cathedral, attending his boss Bontate's funeral. He was shocked at the sparse turnout. One of the few Mafia leaders to show up was Salvatore Inzerillo. Within weeks Inzerillo, the last don on the Losers' side still in Palermo, was also dead, shot to bits by the killers with the Kalashnikov rifle.

Contorno had remained doggedly loyal to the Losers. The Corleonese tried to lure him out of hiding with an offer of peace, but Contorno would have none of it, and now the Corleonese had put the word out all over Palermo: As soon as Sal Contorno was spotted he was to die.

On a warm summer's evening in June 1981 Contorno broke from hiding to visit his parents. After the visit he left their apartment on Via Ciaculli to return to his safe house. His cousin acted as driver. As they drove along an overpass he spotted a passer-by on foot acting suspiciously. Contorno, alarmed, looked into the rear-view mirror of his Fiat 127. A high-powered motorcycle was roaring up behind them.

Contorno shouted to pull off the road as the motorcycle overtook them. The pillion passenger, the notorious assassin of the Corleonese, Pino Greco, raised the Kalashnikov and let loose with a burst of automatic fire. Contorno's car was riddled with bullets. The driver was hit in the cheek. Contorno was miraculously untouched.

He dragged the driver from the car, took cover behind the front fender, and pulled a .38 revolver from his belt.

The motorcycle had spun around. Greco had slammed another magazine into the rifle, and the machine was bearing down once more on the shattered car.

Contorno took close aim as Greco opened fire. Chunks of glass splintered and flew. Contorno fired five shots in rapid succession. Greco jolted back on the seat, and the Kalashnikov rose in the air. Contorno and his wounded driver ran and escaped just as a car full of Corleonese arrived.

Salvatore Contorno's face was pitted with glass but he had survived a massive ambush. He fled immediately to Rome.

Within days, his wife's uncle was gunned down. The Corleonese had begun systematically murdering his relatives in the hope that Contorno's drive for revenge would force him out into the open. But the Italian police got to him first. He was arrested in Rome and persuaded to turn against the organization that was slaughtering his family.

When he met with fellow informer Tomasso Buscetta in a Rome cell, he wept. Buscetta had consoled him and encouraged him to follow his own example. Now he was ready to finger his former associates.

... MONDAY, DECEMBER 2, 1985.
THE COURTROOM.   Richard Martin's plan is to bring the witness
Contorno on cold, and ask him right off to look around the courtroom,
if necessary to walk around the room, so he makes certain he sees every
person present, and then to identify as many defendants as he can. The
mook climbs down off the stand and begins to stroll about, accompanied by the schoolmarmish madame interpreter.

"In the first row, Gaetano Badalamenti . . . Over there . . . Salvatore
Greco . . . Mr. Gaetano Mazzara, with the brown jacket . . . there is
Mr. Toto Catalano . . . Mr. Castronovo . . ."

Fisher is immediately on his feet. "May the witness be excused so
that matter can be put on the record reflecting the identifications?"

Contorno is escorted out, and Kaplan says that "Mr. Contorno
identified Mr. Polizzi as Mr. Castronovo. Is that correct, Mr. Martin?"

"That's right," says Martin, a surly dog, "and I would also like the
record to reflect that he identified Salvatore Greco as Salvatore Greco,
Gaetano Mazzara as Gaetano Mazzara, Salvatore Catalano as Salvatore Catalano, Gaetano Badalamenti as Gaetano Badalamenti."

Fisher says he's "a bit confused. I thought that the witness identified
my colleague, Mr. Segal, as Mr. Catalano, and then Mr. Segal stood
up."

Martin recalls Contorno, and gets him to identify Catalano correctly.
Then he asks Contorno where he first met defendant Greco.

In the town of Bagheria in the spring of 1980. On that occasion, he
says, five of the defendants were present: Greco, Ganci, Catalano,
Mazzara, and Castronovo. The Bagheria meeting took place at 10:00 or
10:30 on a Sunday morning, in a country farmhouse, and eleven men
were present in all. The meeting lasted about forty-five minutes. Contorno had met Ganci and Catalano previously, in 1978 or 1979, at the
Favarella estate of the wealthy Michele Greco, known among Mafia
members as "The Pope" (and no relation to defendant Sal Greco).
Hundreds of people had been present that day. A huge banquet was
served.

Contorno also knew Badalamenti. He had met him "once at Bontate's place, and once at Michele Greco's place." One of these occasions
was a formal pigeon shoot.

The government's latest informer is much more amenable to placing himself in close proximity to drugs than Buscetta had been. In fact, Contorno is quite willing to admit that he wanted to benefit from the enormous wealth he saw flowing into the pockets of his fellow Mafiosi, and hoped to invest in the narcotics trade. Alas, he could not raise the seed money.

In 1976 Contorno completed serving a prison term for Mafia membership, but he still faced three years of internal exile. (Italian law enforcement relieves prison overcrowding by sentencing certain felons to *soggiorno obbligato*—compulsory exile in a town far removed from the criminal's native haunts. It was Contorno's luck to be condemned to Venice.) However, it proved an easy matter when necessary quietly to leave his assigned place of exile and visit his home city.

In the period 1976 to 1979, Contorno returned often to Palermo. He was bankrupt; his frozen-meat business had failed. In Palermo, he discussed with his fellow Mafioso and cigarette smuggler Salvatore D'Agostino the possibility of entering the drug-trafficking business.

To buy in, Contorno needed to raise at least 40 or 50 million lire, he was told. This would purchase a half-kilo of heroin, which D'Agostino could then export to his contact and friend in New York, Gaetano Mazzara.

At the mention of his name, the hawk-faced, high-colored defendant in sharply tailored olive green shakes his head and leans forward to whisper to his lawyer. Marvin Segal is already getting to his feet. "This is a dress rehearsal, your Honor!" he says. "This should not be a moot court for the government!" The prosecutor has just suggested that Segal's client is involved in yet another heroin conspiracy, totally unrelated to the Milan forty-one kilos.

Leval says wearily, "Mr. Segal, please sit down so that we can accomplish the business of this hearing." But the lawyer's comment evidently rankles. Marvin Segal and Pierre Leval are long-time toilers in the legal vineyards. Although they once worked together as fellow prosecutors, little love now seems lost between them. At the start of this trial, Leval sharply and publicly criticized Segal for discussing the case with the press, and used the episode as the occasion to slap on a gag order forbidding attorneys to speak to reporters while the trial is in progress.

"Let me add a word of comment to the ridiculous charge that was made," Leval says a moment later, interrupting the testimony. "The government doesn't need my presence, or your presence, to have a dress rehearsal," he says, glaring at Segal. "This is not a dress rehearsal. This is a hearing for the purpose of the court determining whether there is foundation for some testimony that we were told the government was going to offer.

"I was not satisfied that there was foundation. It is very difficult to find out whether there is such foundation in the presence of the jury, because in many cases you need to hear the statement made by the person to know whether it is in furtherance or not.

"Therefore, I directed that a hearing be held out of the presence of the jury, so that I could find out, without having the jury present, whether there is foundation for such proof. If there isn't, the proof will be excluded."

"Your Honor," says Segal, just as steely, "my point is that normally the government takes its chances. The government should learn its lessons in school, and not in the courtroom. And the government does not have to have a preview so that the court can make a determination. If the government can't ask questions, or lay a proper foundation, the court will sustain objections and that's it.

"All we are doing now is giving them a road map, and I don't think that is a proper method for this kind of a hearing."

"Your objection is noted," says Leval.

The witness continues his story, detailing his visit to the Bagheria farmhouse in the period of February-March 1980 to watch a test being performed.

. . . THURSDAY, DECEMBER 12, 1985.
THE COURTROOM. Eleanore Kennedy is seated in the visitors' benches, busy writing out thirty place cards for her gala Christmas lunch. The Kennedys are indefatigable hosts, noted even among other lawyers and café-society habitués for the generosity, originality, prodigality, and savvy of their frequent large and small entertainments. The notion of hosting an expensive Christmas lunch for this ragtag collection of strange and uncomfortable legal bedfellows seems just right. The setting too is perfect: a private corner of the New York Athletic Club on Seventh Avenue overlooking Central Park. This is the posh, misanthropic, old New York hangout of Tammany judges and Catholic clergy, and until recently the club admitted no Jews and still does not admit women as members. All those on the defense team, including stunt lawyers, will be invited to the party, but no wives or other outsid-

ers. One unspoken purpose of the gala is to encourage feelings of trust and solidarity among the disparate and suspicious members of the Pizza defense. Mario Malerba has said firmly that he wants his co-counsel, Emanuel Moore, included on the guest list, a power play that means Catalano will have three lawyers at the Kennedys' party.

Eleanore, with an experienced appreciation of the pride, vanity, and sheer ego that mark a gathering of this kind, has decided to place Malerba on Kennedy's left—a bravura gesture toward the Catalano team—and senior attorney Marvin Segal at Kennedy's right. A fanatic about detail, she will take an armful of fresh flowers to the club an hour ahead of time and arrange them herself. At a signal, during the preprandial cocktails, the nanny will arrive to present the newest member of the family, thirteen-week-old Anna Rosario Kennedy, dimpled, winning, and black-eyed, in christening dress and pink hair ribbon.

"Objection!" shouts Ivan Fisher, pushing himself to his feet. Fisher claims Martin has been nodding to Contorno, cuing his answers.

Martin is outraged. "Bullshit," he shouts back. Louis Freeh laughs.

Eleanore Kennedy is busy inking menus onto small gold-rimmed pasteboards: terrine of swordfish; choice of grilled steak or salmon; chocolate eclairs with fudge sauce; choice of cordials; Cuban cigars from Fidel Castro's private stock. This woman knows how to feed lawyers.

Leval has had enough for the day. "Let's go home." His words are greeted with sighs of relief. The lawyers rush to wrap themselves in camelhair and English worsted against the stinging rain that bounces off the courthouse steps.

By now the defense attorneys have formed into several small cocktail clubs. Pat Burke heads off with Moriarty, Lombardino, and Benfante for the warm, crowded bar opposite the courthouse. The place is vibrant with laughs and drunken shouts. The season of Christmas parties is under way, and groups of secretaries are fortifying themselves before heading off to Brooklyn or Bellmore.

. . . 5:00 P.M., MONDAY, DECEMBER 16, 1985. GREENWICH VILLAGE, NEW YORK CITY. Through the bustling, cheery streets of Washington Square, Professor G. Robert Blakey made his way to the Law School auditorium on the nearby campus of New York University. He was about to deliver a lecture. The event had attracted a great many members of the law-enforcement community—federal prosecutors, FBI agents, New York City detectives. They had all gathered to hear Blakey speak about his brainchild, a piece of legislation that had become the federal government's key weapon in its war against the mob.

RICO (the Racketeer-Influenced and Corrupt Organizations Act) sounded like one of the thick-necked, stripe-suited wiseguys it was designed to eliminate. Law Professor Blakey, of the University of Notre Dame, had been chief counsel to the McClellan Committee on Organized Crime, established by President Lyndon Johnson in 1967. Blakey says that the committee "demonstrated beyond serious debate that existing law was inadequate in dealing with the illicit activities of the Mafia." Blakey had firsthand experience of the difficulty of obtaining convictions in organized-crime cases. "When I was a Federal prosecutor, the institutional affiliation of a defendant was beyond the pale," he has said. "If you dropped the word 'Mafia' in the course of a trial you were apt to get a mistrial."

As a result of his McClellan experience, Blakey set about correcting this inadequacy by drafting legislation that would enable prosecutors to attack the business structure of organized crime. Congress passed the RICO statute in October 1970. Its provisions were complex and not at first fully appreciated. Indeed, it took prosecutors a decade to learn the full potential of the statute.

To prove a RICO charge, six elements must be met. The government needs to prove that a criminal enterprise existed; that the criminal activities of this enterprise involved either interstate or foreign business; that the activities had some financial base; that the people charged were involved in the criminal enterprise; that the defendant and at least one other member of the criminal group conspired together to participate in the affairs of the group through a pattern of racketeering activity; and that the defendant committed or conspired to commit two racketeering acts that were part of a pattern of racketeering activity.

Ronald Goldstock, lanky, intense chief of the New York State Organized Crime Strike Force, and Mafia maven *extraordinaire,* had arrived on campus early. He had parked his Buick with its police radio, car phone, and dual set of scanners, to monitor activity on the NYPD and New York State Police wave bands in a lot nearby and walked to the lecture hall. A small cocktail reception was in progress.

Professor Blakey worked the room, chatting with the various

prosecutors, field agents, and fellow law professors who had been invited to share a drink and talk with others about their particular attachment to Blakey's law. . . .

. . . THE SAME EVENING, 5:15 P.M.

MIDTOWN, NEW YORK CITY. "Big Paul" Castellano and his driver, companion, and henchman, Thomas Bilotti, had just left the law offices of Castellano's lawyer, James LaRossa. The sixty-nine-year-old Castellano, head of the Gambino Family, was a tall, robust man, overweight yet conservatively stylish in his dark suit, crisp white shirt, and mohair overcoat. He had a full head of curly black hair and a round, soft face made sterner by a pair of thick, black-framed spectacles. His bearing was that of a prosperous businessman, and his soft-spoken manner successfully masked his power.

Jimmy LaRossa had been hired by Castellano for a fee of several hundred thousand dollars to defend him as one of nine mobsters accused of running a stolen-car ring, one part of the Gambino Family enterprise he headed. The ring was said to be responsible for some twenty-five murders of witnesses and competitors. The trial, which had begun a few weeks before Pizza, in the same courthouse, was the first of what Rudolph Giuliani had promised would be a half-dozen orchestrated attacks on organized crime. They would culminate in the so-called Commission trial, scheduled for the following spring, of the heads of New York's five Mafia families: Tony "Ducks" Corrallo, of the Lucchese Family, Fat Tony Salerno, of the Genovese Family, Carmine Persico, of the Colombo Family, Philip Rastelli, of the Bonanno Family, and Big Paul Castellano. Giuliani had indicated he would prosecute the Commission case personally, and no one doubted that he would create a cannonade of rackets-busting headlines unmatched since the days of Thomas E. Dewey. Meanwhile, the Castellano trial, which was taking place two floors above Judge Leval's courtroom, in the courtroom of Judge Kevin Duffy, was currently causing even more of a sensation than Pizza in the newspapers and on TV.

The Castellano prosecutors were making full use of Professor Blakey's RICO law. But what was getting the big press attention was another surprise turncoat witness. The use of such witnesses had become a feature of Giuliani's headline-grabbing trials. In this instance the attraction was Victor Arena, "the gay hit man." Arena was a ruthless killer who, as part of his deal for testifying against his former contractors, had demanded that his prison lover be moved into the next cell, and that he himself receive a government-paid face-lift to make him better looking. It was all a huge joke around Giuliani's offices, and gorgeous copy for the press.

The wind sweeping around the skyscrapers of Madison Avenue blew the rain in an ice-cold mist as Castellano and Bilotti left LaRossa's office. The lawyer had pronounced himself confident about the outcome of the trial; Castellano need not concern himself about this one. But Big Paul had plenty of other worries. He was facing four future federal and state indictments including the famed Commission case, Giuliani's all-star Mafia spring carnival in which the prosecutor intended to deliver a death blow to organized crime, and propel himself into the political stratosphere.

More trouble for Castellano were the guys in Queens, capos in his own crews, who had begun saying that Big Paul was neglecting family business, too wrapped up in his own legal problems to provide leadership to the Gambino mob.

Castellano had taken over control of what was currently the nation's largest and most lucrative crime organization from his brother-in-law, Carlo Gambino. Big Paul had been Gambino's closest adviser, and when the Gambino sons showed little interest in inheriting their father's position, it naturally fell to his wife's brother, Big Paul.

After Gambino's death, Castellano quickly became the most sophisticated of the New York bosses. He left the everyday work of robbery, loan sharking, hijacking, and extortion to his lieutenants and their own street crews. By 1985 the Gambino Family numbered some 250 soldiers, with double that number of associates, and a huge network of semilegitimate businessmen and small-time hoods.

Big Paul concentrated on the infiltration of the New York trucking and food-distribution industries. He reaped huge amounts of cash in kickbacks from the construction industry. He regulated profit-sharing and disputes within the New York Mafia Commission. He worked to put his gang on a businesslike footing. Castellano was happy talking profit-sharing and contract guarantees, and he sought to insure that risky and nakedly criminal activities such as drug dealing could never be connected to his men. The Gambino Family had issued a strict order to its soldiers: Deal drugs and you die. Leave that to the Zips over on Knickerbocker Avenue.

Castellano and Bilotti arrived at their black Lincoln town car, parked on West 43rd Street, to discover that it had been ticketed for illegal parking. Bilotti snatched the ticket from under the windshield wiper and stuck it in his pocket as he slid behind the wheel.

The cutting rain had snarled rush-hour traffic, and Bilotti was anxious to get to their next appointment, a dinner reservation at Sparks Steakhouse, across town on East 46th between Second and Third Avenues. Sparks was pricey and popular. Only weeks earlier, trendy *New York Magazine* had named it the best steak house in Manhattan. Its expensive menu catered to corporate carnivores with large expense accounts, exactly the kind of company in which Paul Castellano felt most comfortable.

Bilotti edged into East 46th Street and pulled up beside the red canopy with the legend SPARKS stenciled on its side. As Paul Castellano stepped out of the Lincoln, he failed to notice the yellow taxicab pull across the junction of the street and block off the flow of traffic. Thomas Bilotti had just closed the door of the car when he caught a glimpse of two men in tan Burberry raincoats and caps advancing toward Castellano. Both raised their hands at the same instant, and Bilotti was hit in the head with a bullet from a 9 mm Browning automatic pistol. Castellano stood staring at the hit men, frozen, as they shot him twice in the head and once in the chest. He collapsed at the side of the Lincoln as the two gunmen ran to a waiting car at the corner of 46th and Second. . . .

. . . At New York University Law School, the room set aside for Professor Blakey's cocktail reception was comfortably crowded. The gathering was predominantly male, white, mid-thirties to early forties. Conservative suits, quiet sports jackets, and neatly groomed hair were the dress mode. Ron Goldstock sipped a glass of white wine. Then the electronic beeper attached to his waistband started to sound. Next, at random, like popcorn in a skillet, beepers began going off throughout the crowded room, and FBI agents and New York police officials scrambled to get to the phones. News of the Castellano hit had spread like wildfire. Platoons of law-enforcement personnel quietly but rapidly excused themselves and left. Professor Blakey's lecture on dealing with organized crime had been upstaged by organized crime dealing with its own. . . .

**. . . TUESDAY, DECEMBER 17, 1985.
THE COURTHOUSE CORRIDOR.** Tension and nervous energy
are everywhere evident. Some defendants huddle together in small
knots, talking in rapid Sicilian. Catalano, Amato, and Sal Lamberti
pace the seventy-foot length of corridor speaking in low voices, gesticulating extravagantly. Overthrow and succession are on everyone's
mind.

Joe the clerk yells, "Judge is on the bench!" Lawyers queue up and
dump their newspapers on the table alongside the X-ray metal detector.
The judge has imposed a ban on all newspapers in the courtroom lest
a juror catch a glimpse of a headline that might influence his opinion
of the Pizza evidence. Today's papers are stuffed with words and photographs of the Castellano murder.

Inside, Leval sharply raps for order. The jury is not yet present. "The
first thing to talk about is the news of the killing of another defendant
currently on trial in this courthouse."

Bob Fogelnest waves a fistful of front-page clippings from the city's
four major daily newspapers, and asks that they be put into the record.
He adds that the murder has also been widely discussed on TV, and
linked to the Carmine Galante killing. Hence "the potential prejudicial
effect is overwhelming" to the Pizza defendants. The *Post* headline says,
THE MOB ALWAYS CATCHES UP.

The lawyers want all the jurors questioned to see what they know and
what they think about the Castellano killing. Paul Bergman begins,
characteristically: "There are a number of things to be observed about
this." As a partner in the LaRossa firm, which represented Castellano,
he speaks in tones of funereal and almost surreal probity and gravity.

After much posturing by the defense lawyers on the prejudicial
consequences of the Castellano hit, Leval summons the jury. "Some of
you may be aware . . . that yesterday in New York City, a defendant
in another trial in this courthouse was killed on the streets of the city.
There has been so much publicity, it will come to your attention, if it
hasn't already. So now let me repeat something I have said to you many
times before: Do not allow yourselves to be exposed to *any* publicity.
There are certain to be many articles. Do not read or watch TV. Second,
the events of yesterday have absolutely nothing to do with the case

before you. There is no conceivable connection. Anyone have a problem with that? All right. Let's proceed."

The government calls a slight, young bantamweight bakery owner from Queens. Vincenzo Russo bought his one-man bakery from Filippo Ragusa, one of the men involved with the Milan forty-one kilos. Witness Russo first heard that he would be required to appear in court today at 8:30 last evening. He does not know why he is here.

Stewart gets him to identify a photograph of Filippo Ragusa. Russo mingles his answers with his own repeated question, "Why am I here?"

"No further questions, your Honor," says Stewart.

"May I ask a question?" says the witness good-naturedly, with a heavy accent. "Why am I here? I wanna *know*. I lose-a work today."

Leval directs the witness simply to "wait and answer questions that are asked."

It is time for cross-examination. "Mr. Kennedy?"

Kennedy stands. "Just one question, Mr. Russo." Pause. "Why are you here, sir?"

The jury breaks up.

Now the scramble for Christmas planes and trains and limousines. The jurors will all pile into the limos driven by federal marshals, which will take them to drop-off points, after which they can try to become ordinary citizens once more. But the Pizza Connection has started to permeate their existence. It has become the most time-consuming element in their lives. Although the jurors have been cautioned to avoid all exposure to the Castellano killing, the media—not just television, radio, and newspapers, but periodicals, advertising, talk shows, and comedy routines—are saturated with it. Leval would seem to be demanding an unreasonable degree of self-censorship. The defense team is calling it self-delusion on the government's part.

... THURSDAY, JANUARY 2, 1986.

THE COURTROOM. A new year. The most ominous sight in the room is the ribbon of blue-bound transcripts on a shelf behind Judge Leval's chair. Four feet long and growing like a tapeworm, the 4,474-page trial record already fills more than half the shelf. One juror is late; another has problems concerning necessary future medical treatment. Leval has called the juror's doctor and had the schedule readjusted.

"Could you do the same with my dentist?" Bergman asks.

"I'd be glad to . . . do the work myself," snaps Leval. "We will proceed with the witness Contorno, which began before the Christmas break."

The scowling informant has already settled into his seat, all set to tell the jury how he bought his way into the heroin trade, and encountered several of these defendants along the way.

Dick Martin will steer the testimony toward its climax. First, to kick-start the jury's memory, he has Contorno identify three defendants in the back row: Mazzara, Castronovo, and Greco. He had met them at the hillside farmhouse in the middle of a lemon grove outside the little town of Bagheria. On that Sunday morning, Contorno had been driven to Bagheria by his Mafia associate Nuncio LaMattina, who was offering to make Contorno rich through the heroin trade.

It proves damning testimony. The government had used Buscetta for the glitz, to scare the jury with tales of exotic Mafia initiation rites and blood feuds. But this lowly soldier of Bontate's family is doing real damage, placing these harmless-looking American pizza bakers at a sinister drug meeting in a lonely Sicilian farmhouse.

The government believes the Bagheria gathering was a quality-control test. A previous batch of heroin shipped from Palermo had been judged of inferior grade, and had drawn accusations of cheating against the middlemen. In defense of their honor, and future profits, some of the middlemen had come to Sicily to presample the next shipment themselves.

Contorno tells the jury that the five Americans there that morning—Catalano, Ganci, Castronovo, Mazzara, and Greco—were fellow Mafia members, hence the coded phrase *la stessa cosa*—our thing—was used in making introductions.

All the Badalamenti defendants except the nephew Randazzo, who is on hunger strike and refusing to leave his cell, have removed their fancy microwave wireless earphone sets. Some tilt back their heads and close their eyes. They too are Sicilian, masters of gesture, and this wordless bravura shows that such talk of heroin has nothing to do with them.

On a table in the farmhouse, Contorno saw bags filled with white powder, and a thermometer. Like a magician reaching into his top hat, Martin picks up from his table an eight-inch thermometer with a glass pipette attached. "Like this?"

Contorno describes watching a tiny glass vial containing white powder being attached to a thermometer and heated over a flame. "There was a foul acid-y smell." Today's translator is a young Sicilian prince who speaks clipped, elegant English with none of Contorno's extravagant gestures and magnificent eye-rolling. The temperature at which the drug liquifies indicates its purity. But the odor of burning heroin soon grew too noxious for Contorno's nose, and he fled to the lemon grove and sucked a lemon to banish the disgusting stench.

The informer is on a roll. He now gives Martin what any prosecutor would have to consider a series of very high-quality answers. The person who offered to cut Contorno in on the international heroin traffic was Carlo Castronovo, a famed Sicilian drug-runner. The operation would be very smooth, he said, for he worked with an American cousin, one Ciccio l'Americano.

Every Sicilian is named for a saint, and each name has several common nicknames—Toto for Salvatore, Don Tano, or Tanino, for Gaetano, Turiddu for Giuseppe, Ciccio for Francesco. Ciccio l'Americano is Carlo Castronovo's American cousin, the Pizza defendant Francesco "Frank" Castronovo.

Ciccio "had pizza parlors here in America, as a front . . . [and] there were no problems in shipping the goods to America because he was a Man of Honor, such as we."

A numbing silence fills the courtroom. Defendant Castronovo sits in the back row, arms folded across his chest, stone-faced as a library lion.

The atmosphere has heated up, and the man responsible feels the strain. He whispers to the translator, who announces that Mr. Contorno has a severe headache and would like a rest.

The witness is led off, and Martin, reasserting who is really in charge in this case, announces that those defendants who have not yet had an extensive set of finger and palm prints taken must report to FBI headquarters this afternoon.

. . . WEDNESDAY, JANUARY 8, 1986.

THE COURTROOM.   Contorno has now finished his direct testimony. The future pattern of examination is set. A government witness is first led through his testimony by a prosecutor, who elicits the evidence in a series of tightly formulated questions. The defense lawyers may object to these questions if they believe the subject is outside the scope of the witness's knowledge; if the question might produce an answer that is too far-ranging in its implications; or if the form of the question is not clear enough to produce a precise, factual answer, or if it might lead to speculation on the part of the witness.

Following the government's direct examination, each defendant may cross-examine the witness on the topics raised by the government. The lawyers are always called on in the order of the indictment—Kennedy first, Ryan last. This running order, like the seating order, is considered a matter of immense strategic importance, and no changes are made without passionate debate, all of it invisible to the jury. Also invisible is the fact that, since the government drew up the indictment, the government has determined the order of battle.

Cross-examination is followed by redirect, if the government chooses, followed if necessary by recross, then reredirect, and so on until the last drop has been squeezed out. But the pattern of questioning moves in always narrowing circles, ever more tightly focused. The object is to mine truth, not undermine it, and subsequent questions must clarify previous testimony; they may not range into new areas of inquiry. The refereeing of these rules, which are never explained to the jury, is a principal judicial function, and a measure of judicial aptitude. A case like Pizza, wherein twenty-two individual trials are in effect taking place simultaneously, is a supreme test. Pierre Leval ranks very high. His mind is logical, sharp, uncluttered. He never loses the thread. He works effortlessly—a good butcher swiftly, deftly, tirelessly, and almost always good-humoredly sawing up and then filleting the facts. He is at ease in his robes.

Still, a big, multidefendant conspiracy trial like Pizza presents unique problems, especially for the defense. Often—*most* often—the witness is giving evidence about one defendant, or two at most, which has no relation whatsoever to the other twenty or twenty-one men also on trial. Almost always, it is in the best interest of the other defendants to lie low, say nothing, and maintain maximum distance. Yet the rules require that each defense attorney be offered an opportunity to cross-examine, and that is an opportunity few of these egotists can resist. Ego-enlargement is the occupational hazard of the defense bar, the silicosis of the trade. Verbosity is the other lawyer's disease, and many herein are afflicted, including on occasion the judge. As time wears on, the pestilence will spread until chronic, incurable, absolute inability to shut up lengthens this trial by at least one third.

The attorneys who represent the five men fingered as witnesses to the Bagheria drug test have some serious damage control to attend to. The best possible response is to show up Contorno as a habitual liar, and perhaps even suggest some prosecutorial collusion in his story. The lawyers plunge into their work with gusto, and with each foray some of the Contorno veneer peels.

Contorno has already told his story to the Italian authorities. The Pizza defense lawyers have read these documents. They contain a wealth of information pointing to the fact that Contorno is no reformed Robin Hood but a ruthless criminal and, at the least, an accomplice to murder. As a macabre part of his initiation into the Mafia, Contorno was taken to the outskirts of his village, where he watched a man forced to kneel on the ground and shot in the head. "This is how death is," commented one of the Mafia assassins.

Before the jurors can return, the defense lawyers battle out the pros and cons of informing them of the murder ritual. Ken Kaplan, lawyer for Castronovo, is one of several who want the story told, to paint Contorno as the murderous thug he is. Several Badalamenti-group lawyers argue that to introduce a grisly murder scene as an aspect of Mafia membership taints all defendants unfairly, and further prejudices the jury.

Kennedy, ever the defender of Badalamenti's honor, is quick to point out that "the people who would conjure up, let alone acquiesce in that kind of conduct are themselves very base people, and it is that ascription to Mr. Badalamenti that is so severely prejudicial."

Leval thinks Kennedy's point respectable, one that "no doubt you will argue vociferously on appeal."

Kennedy descends on the judge like a hawk dropping from the sky. "I intend to win this case, Judge!"

Leval always appears faintly taken aback by Kennedy's savage ripostes. He decides to restrict Contorno to saying merely that, shortly after he was sworn into the Mafia, he was taken to witness a murder. The jury will be offered this killing as a cold statistic, no blood on the ground, no name of the victim who fell face down on a dark Sicilian hillside while a new Mafioso stood by, silently witnessing the practice of his new trade. Nor will the jury ever be invited to ponder the line of macho Latin philosophy "This is how death is."

. . . WEDNESDAY, JANUARY 22, 1986.

THE COURTROOM. Each jury recess finds Ivan Fisher on his feet repeating the same request: He wants the judge to require the prosecutors to distribute a complete set of documents relating to the original meeting between Contorno, U.S. officials, and Italian investigators. The date was March 1985, in Rome, and the man in charge was Magistrate Giovanni Falcone, the top Mafia hunter in all Italy, newly endowed by his government with special powers to destroy the Mafia for all time. The American delegation consisted of Assistant U.S. Attorney Richard Martin and FBI Special Agent Carmine Russo, the Bureau's chief Sicilian-dialect expert. At this meeting Contorno was asked to identify 147 mug shots of suspected Mafiosi. So where are the records of all this?

Martin is stonewalling. No notes were made, he claims. Fisher refuses to back down, and demands a phone call be placed right now to Judge Falcone to establish whether any of the Italian investigators took notes. Fisher's cat-and-mouse game with Martin has been precipitated by an investigator on Fisher's staff who flew to Rome over Christmas and unearthed at least one document relating to the March meeting.

Armed with this evidence, Fisher stands to voir dire Contorno. The giant lawyer is like a taut spring, ready to hurtle in any direction. Has Contorno spoken to Martin over the past few days? His answer is evasive. How about documents? He cannot recall any documents. Each evasion makes the witness less credible. When Fisher judges he has beat up on him sufficiently, he flatly accuses him of lying. The truth is, is it not, that Contorno *never saw* defendant Catalano in the Bagheria farmhouse?

"Isn't it a fact"—Fisher is shouting now—"that then you had *not the slightest idea* who these men were?"

"If I had not had any idea, I would not have said 'familiar faces.' "

"You couldn't afford *not* to know them."

"What do you mean—afford?"

"I mean your wife . . . your child. . . . The fact is, it was Dick Martin who told you those names."

Martin's objection is sustained, and Leval says quietly, "Come to the side bar, please."

The side bar is the side of his bench farthest from the jury. Judge and lawyers can confer here without risk of being overheard, and it is easier to whisper at the bench than to send twenty-four people out of the room. All lawyers, prosecution and defense, have a right to listen in on sidebars, as such conferences are called. Just now, a large crowd of defense lawyers huddles at the bench like a football team. The critical point to Leval is not that Fisher has caught Contorno making conflicting statements, not that in Italy he said the people in the farmhouse were strangers to him, and today he claims he knows them.

What concerns the judge is a more subtle point, which surely would be lost on this or any jury. Leval is always conscious of the trial record, and the appellate judges who almost certainly will one day be asked to read it. Pierre Leval's high reputation among jurists is based in part on his careful attention to such matters. His point in this instance is that Fisher's last questions could be ambiguous. To prove that a witness is lying, one must prove he has made two inconsistent statements, and the lawyer must make his questions clear.

Fisher says hastily that he was not attempting to pull any funny stuff. "I'm not suggesting you were trying anything," Leval replies. "I am pointing out to you that there was a lack of clarity, and I would suggest that, if you are going to proceed with impeachment . . . you clarify what your question was. . . . [Is it:] Did Mr. Martin ever tell you he was interested in Ganci and Catalano? Or is your question: Did Mr. Martin tell you that the person in the photograph is Ganci or Catalano?"

Although hard to follow, this is Leval at his best, carefully filleting and sorting evidence with the sharpest of knives. "The problem when you go into this," he continues, "is that it has the capacity to impeach him on something that is not necessarily an inconsistent statement. You can't impeach him with this, because it has not yet been demonstrated that it *is* inconsistent."

Cross-examination resumes. Contorno tries to stick to his guns. But by the end of the tumultuous afternoon Fisher is bombarding the Sicilian witness with shouted questions as to what he told prosecutor Martin when. Most of the other lawyers have the aura of circling sharks locked in on the first drops of blood in the water.

Kennedy's concern is more specific. He thinks Fisher could be framing his questions in a yet more deadly way. Fisher should be hammering: Didn't you tell *Martin* this? Didn't you tell *Martin* that? "That way, Martin's ass is in the street."

. . . THURSDAY, JANUARY 23, 1986.

THE COURTROOM. Lawyers quickly take their places, eager for yesterday's battle royale to resume. Fisher is already standing at the podium going over notes. Richard Martin enters through the judge's door, a slight smile on his face. Then he drops a bombshell. The palm print of defendant Salvatore Mazzurco has been found on the tissue paper inside a shirt box that was used to convey a kilo of heroin to an undercover agent.

The bright-eyed little man in the second seat of the second row drops his head to stare at the floor. Mazzurco's lawyer, Joe Benfante, is dumbfounded. He makes several false starts at registering his dismay; the enormity of the damage to his case leaves him only semicoherent.

The damning news against Mazzurco has in no way dampened Fisher's zeal to expose the government witness as a lying scoundrel. While Contorno was in Rome, being interviewed by Richard Martin, was he not shown a number of photographs, including pictures of these defendants? Fisher knows and intends to elicit that Contorno failed, then, to name the several Pizza defendants, including his client, Catalano.

Contorno gloomily corrects the lawyer: He said then only that he was *familiar* with the faces. He saved his identification of them until he was in the United States, and under the shield of the government's Witness Protection Program.

"Sir, at this minute, isn't it accurate you just lied through your teeth to all these people?"

"What is this lie you are talking about?" Contorno has hunkered down in his chair, as if to withstand the withering blasts of scorn from six-foot five-inch Fisher.

The translator cannot keep up. Fisher throws up his hands at the delay. "Isn't it a fact"—Fisher is shouting now—"that then you had *not the slightest idea* who these men were? . . . The fact is, it was Dick Martin who told you those names!"

Fisher keeps up the rapid-fire, truncheon-blow questions. Each time, the defendant withers a little more, stumbles, tries to evade. The pauses for translation slow the pace of Fisher's cross, but not its power.

Kennedy moves in to pick the bones that Fisher has left. Juicy meat for Badalamenti remains in Contorno's cadaver. In the March 1985 statement to Judge Falcone, Contorno had discussed Badalamenti's expulsion from the Mafia. He spoke of how the Corleone Family had fought to seize "complete hegemony concerning international traffic of narcotic substances." He went on to mention that Gaetano Badalamenti did not have sole control of Sicily's Punta Raisi International Airport. This damages the government's contention that Badalamenti, as don of Cinisi, the town outside Palermo near which the airport is located, should be held responsible for drug trafficking in and out of the big new airport—that is to say, all drugs moving by jumbo jet to and from the island of Sicily.

Third, Contorno's original story was that had it been known in the Mafia that a Man of Honor and an outcast—Ganci and Badalamenti—were dealing heroin with one another, it would have meant an automatic death sentence for both men. The document is clearly helpful to Kennedy's client, and he wants Martin's blood for withholding exculpatory material.

"When we have a man of that fundamental lack of integrity who sits in the position of lead counsel, and makes for our government the initial determination of what is or is not Brady [exculpatory matter], and only comes forward with it when he is forced to, I suggest that that man needs to be replaced."

Leval's reply to this rather extreme demand is spoken in tones as calm and unruffled as Kennedy's own. He is not prepared to waste jury time; he will rule on the motion later. For now Kennedy must decide if he wants to examine Contorno as a defense witness.

"Who wants to call Contorno?" Leval asks.

"I do," says Kennedy, adding saucily, "Call him *what,* your Honor?"

The exquisite prospect of being able to use Contorno to dirty up Martin is not lost on the other lawyers. Fisher stops pacing the aisle long enough to bend down to Eleanore Kennedy, in her regular left-hand aisle seat, and murmur, "This . . . is . . . marvelous!"

Robert Koppelman, attorney for Vito Badalamenti, stands and says he "would like to join with Mr. Kennedy in asking that Mr. Martin be excluded from further participation in this trial."

"I don't think Mr. Kennedy's motion went quite that far. Maybe he wants to amend it."

"It did," Kennedy snaps, at once adopting Koppelman's even more militant position. "I should have made myself clearer. . . . My application is to have Mr. Martin, who has now demonstrated his lack of integrity beyond anyone's doubt . . . removed from this case entirely."

Kennedy remains at the podium, deceptively mild-looking, like a hungry leopard on a branch in dappled sunlight. Martin stands up. He is reasonable, and cool. First, the report contains inaccuracies that Contorno himself later corrected to Italian Magistrate Falcone. Second, as to the questions about the activities of Badalamenti, in fact Contorno knew little about him, and says that after a person is expelled from the

Mafia, he is not supposed to talk to other Mafia members about Mafia business. But the witness did not say at any time that a non-Mafia member could not speak to a Mafia member about narcotics. Third, it is his recollection that what the witness said was that the area of Punta Raisi was part of the area under the control of Gaetano Badalamenti.

Leval forestalls any confrontation with a firm ruling: one hour's adjournment, and no further discussion until after lunch.

In the corridor, Fisher is whispering to reporters that he had predicted this entire imbroglio. Fisher's own tension right now is so great it has caused him to gnaw a large paper clip almost in half. One reporter asks if the lawyers often find themselves in such a good position vis-à-vis the government.

Koppelman smiles. "It's rare. We make the accusation all the time, but we can seldom back it up."

"It's not checkmate," warns Fisher. "It's check. He can still move to another square."

In an aside to another lawyer, Fisher says, "There's more evidence against us now than when this case began! *Oi veh,* what they were doing to us while we were waiting for Mr. Badalamenti to get the brains to hire Kennedy!"

Fisher is referring to the time in mid-1985 when the case was ready to go to trial, and the defense begged Judge Leval for a postponement, then another.

By the time the Pizza Connection trial actually began, three months later, in October, the adversarial lineup had changed considerably. For one thing, the government had got itself at least two dynamite new witnesses, Buscetta and Contorno. The latter was a man of far less rank and brains than Buscetta, but he had an impressive amount of blood on his hands.

The second change was that the major heroin dealer among the defendants, Giuseppe "Il Bufalo" Ganci, had become terminally ill, and would never appear in the courtroom. This allowed for certain shifts in emphasis and responsibility among other defendants.

The third change was Badalamenti's lawyer. Ever since his extradition to the United States, the Old Man had been holding court in MCC. Two groups of people came to see him. Incarcerated Mafia members in jails across the country sought transfers to MCC in order personally to pay their respects to the venerated Sicilian Mafia chieftain, and literally to kiss his hand. Badalamenti meanwhile had fired his original lawyer, Charles Carnesi, and in between receiving the kisses of the faithful, he was auditioning the elite of the criminal defense bar. Ace criminal lawyers and hotshot hoods had been stumbling all over each other in the jailhouse corridors.

Less than a month before the twice-postponed trial was to begin, Badalamenti had made his final choice.

. . . MICHAEL JOHN KENNEDY, forty-eight, is a seasoned criminal trial lawyer from San Francisco, now practicing law in New York City with his wife and only partner. Kennedy has financed his extensive political work, which has been almost entirely *pro bono,* by representing a wide variety of criminals, including an occasional cocaine merchant and some very big-time marijuana dealers. He is an active supporter of NORML, the lawyer/citizen lobby to legalize marijuana. But he had never before taken a heroin case. Heroin enslaves the children of the poor and unfortunate he had devoted his life to trying to help. He took the Badalamenti case for several reasons: a fee of $250,000, a guarded relish for the power so conspicuous a case would confer, a firm belief that his client was innocent of the crimes charged and was a victim essentially of political harassment by an overzealous Justice Department eager to ornament its holy war on drugs with a major Mafia scalp.

Kennedy is one of the last of a breed. Criminal trial work is one of the few careers left in America where one can still work alone, single-handedly doing combat against the forces of darkness, single-handedly taking responsibility for victory, or defeat. The really big money is in corporate law work, not here. It is the big risk and the bare stage that attract such a man. A few of these legal Lone Rangers can be found practicing law in every big American city. Several are in this case, most notably Ivan Fisher. But Kennedy is different from most of the others in that his roots are primarily political. He is a left-wing Lone Ranger, a self-styled guerrilla lawyer who has devoted most of his legal career to championing the cause of other single individuals against the mighty power of various governments.

Kennedy invariably believes that any government, because of its vast power, must always be held to a higher standard than is the individual. In lectures to younger lawyers, he always makes the point that it is easy for attorneys to defend people they like; the test of democracy, the test of the merit and health of the American system, "comes when we defend people we despise."

Until he met his wife, Michael Kennedy was almost entirely a self-made man, sent to boarding school at age four, educated by Jesuits, then at the University of California at Berkeley, and its law school, followed by a two-year stint during the Vietnam War handling army courts-martial. He is admitted to practice in front of the United States Supreme Court and most Circuit Courts of Appeals, and has tried cases in thirty-five states.

Here are extracts from a typical Kennedy speech to budding young trial lawyers. He makes several of these each year, before bar associations, judges' conventions, and in law schools throughout the land.

"What I am going to try to do is encourage you to try more cases [rather than negotiate settlements, which is how most trial lawyers spend 85% of their time]. . . . Encourage you to take the worst case, the most disgusting defendant, in front of the most obnoxious judge, with The People being represented by the most killing, bloodless prosecutor you've ever met. . . ."

On choosing clients: "I want to commend you for representing pariahs. Not take pride in who or what they are . . . But how we treat those we most despise, those we most want to kill, is a measure of our society . . . because I know that we will never rise higher than the least of us, we will never be better than the most base of us. . . . So I want to applaud you for representing the depraved and the deprived and the sick and the despised. It is an honor."

On lying: "I am told (nowadays) that if in fact we think a client is going to take the stand and lie, we have a responsibility to do something about it. Well, we do. That's to keep our mouths shut. Other than telling the client, 'You run a big risk, Charlie, because if, in fact, the judge believes you are lying, you will get tried, convicted and sentenced for perjury, in addition to this offense, without the benefit of a grand jury or a petit jury or anything else.' . . . I try very hard not to be cynical, but the experience I've had is that everybody lies in court. The judge lies, the jurors on voir dire lie, the prosecutor lies, the defense attorney lies, and the witnesses lie. You have everybody, the bailiff included, lying. But when the defendant lies, it is thought that there has been some heinous, irreparable breach of morality. . . ."

On defendants: "We begin to lose sight of the fact that the defendant is what it's all about. None of us in the criminal justice system has anything to do with the criminal justice system, other than a vicarious relationship to it through the defendant, through that human being. And it is that human being whose life and liberty we have in our hands. And our loyalties—I don't care how badly we want to be liked—our loyalties lie singularly with the deprived, depraved, despised and accused. And I, for one, consider it an honor. In this great country, notwithstanding all our problems, we do it better than anywhere else in the world."

For a 1971 anthology of essays on law, Kennedy contributed a piece entitled "The Civil Liberties Lie." His youthful words suggest that sometimes a man of principle who knows what he's for, and against, can survive fifteen years' busy practice of criminal law without risk of inappropriate mellowing.

"I'm human first, an anarchist second, and a lawyer last," Kennedy wrote. "The first came about through chance. The second through choice. And the last through chicanery . . .

"As an attorney of some years' practice, I know the law is replete with myths. As a matter of fact, law practice is a methodology of myths. Among the most popular myths of the law are those that tell us that the Bill of Rights, as the highest embodiment of legal principles, applies to all the people. Civil liberties is championed as the essence of the people's rights over all others. . . .

"The civil liberties lie can be exposed by an examination of reality: That, in fact, our political and economic system protects the rich, screws the poor, ignores the majority, and pretends to apply all laws equally to all people. . . .

". . . If the human right to petition for the redress of grievances in the First Amendment has any meaning, it is its recognition of the most fundamental human right of the people to dismember and overthrow an inhuman, unresponsive government.

"Even Lincoln caught this historical imperative. In his inauguration address of March 4, 1861, he said:

> This country, with its institutions, belongs to the people who inhabit it. Whenever they shall grow weary of the existing government, they can exercise their constitutional right to dismember, or overthrow it.

"Well, the people do grow weary. And if this government continues its crimes against humanity, humanity is, by God, going to burn it down."

. . . 1:55 P.M., THURSDAY, JANUARY 23, 1986.
THE COURTROOM. "Judge is on the bench!"

Over lunch, Leval has been considering the defense motion to censure Martin or remove him from the case. As the lawyers take their seats, Leval is already reading his ruling aloud. "There is no suggestion of any motive Mr. Martin would have . . . [and] in any case, I regard the various motions made just before lunch as altogether without basis, and they are denied."

Kennedy is left to wrangle with the slippery Contorno, who wants to do nothing that might help this lawyer. But his halting answers simply lend credence to the fact stated in the Italian document—that Badalamenti could not have had contact with the Mafia after his expulsion.

The lawyer has scarcely finished cross-examination before Martin bounces to his feet, agile as the gymnast he surely is. "Mr. Contorno, so far as you are aware, is it prohibited within the Mafia for a person who has been expelled to talk about drug dealing with a person who is still in the Mafia?"

Once defense objections are overruled, Martin asks the court reporter to read back the question. When he does, Salvatore Contorno's seventeen thorny days on the witness stand culminate in this inscrutable reply:

"One can speak of business, one can speak of drug. What one must not talk about are the facts still taking place within the family. Business is free."

. . . TUESDAY, JANUARY 28, 1986.
THE COURTHOUSE CAFETERIA. As the defense lawyers gather for morning coffee, the news spreads that the space shuttle *Challenger* has exploded, killing all aboard. Groups of defendants and lawyers shake their heads in shocked disbelief.

Inside the courtroom the prosecutors whisper and wait for the crowd to filter in. The next witness is yet another government informant, a cut below the first two. Luigi Ronsisvalle is a man of middle years and height, gross, stout, balding, coarse-faced, dressed for court in a shiny blue suit and red striped tie. He takes his seat and knowingly adjusts the microphone. Luigi Ronsisvalle will turn out to be quite familiar with microphones.

It has been agreed that he will testify in his very heavily accented English, not Sicilian. His interrogator will be Assistant U.S. Attorney Louis Freeh, the number-two man on the government team. Freeh is thirty-five, younger than Richard Martin and less broadly built. He is a pale, serious-looking former FBI agent with a close-cropped head and blue-grey eyes, and is tightly buttoned into a conservative three-piece grey suit. Freeh is from New Jersey, and is said to have spent more time on this case and to know it better than any man in the U.S. Attorney's Office. Richard Martin was brought in over him by Giuliani to head the trial team because Martin had more courtroom experience, and presence, but not more integrity than Freeh. Among the defense attorneys, Freeh is most often characterized as "a gentleman."

Under Freeh's quiet, rather toneless questioning, witness Ronsisvalle tells the court he is forty-five years old, born in Catania, Sicily. On March 16, 1966, he entered the United States for the first time, and has never left it. He was then twenty-five or twenty-six years old, and had a fourth-grade education. In 1979 he pled guilty in New York State to first-degree-manslaughter and obstruction-of-justice charges. Yes, he has an agreement with the prosecutors: Nothing he says here can be used against him in future trial proceedings, provided he tells the truth to this court and jury. The jurors are alert and attentive; they find Mr. Ronsisvalle a more than usually interesting witness.

In 1967 the witness was living in the East New York section of Brooklyn. He visited the Knickerbocker Avenue neighborhood on the Brooklyn-Queens border once or twice a week, and hung out at a Sicilian coffee shop known as Café Dello Sport.

. . . KNICKERBOCKER AVENUE, BROOKLYN,

is a bustling, crowded, manic artery, a New York street. Korean fruit markets spill oranges and kiwi fruit into the doorways of Puerto Rican five-and-dimes with Statue of Liberty T-shirts and straw hats crowding the windows. The cigar stores ring with the clatter of the New York State lottery machines as their Lebanese proprietors stack bundles of the New York edition of *Il Progresso,* the Italian daily newspaper. The sound of salsa music booms from the huge portable radios that the young Puerto Rican teen-agers carry in Knickerbocker Park.

Knickerbocker Avenue, like New York itself, is in a permanent state of flux. Its changing ethnic make-up charts the advent of successive waves of immigrants better than a set of demographic maps. At the turn of the century this avenue was the stronghold of German immigrants, Bavarian Catholics who built solid two- and three-story brick houses with flat roofs and high stoops, buildings designed to house three families, perhaps all related or from the same town or farmland in Bavaria or Saxony. Then, as the German families established themselves as New York's brewers and butchers, they moved up and out of the neighborhood to the semidetached homes and manicured gardens of Ridgewood, Queens.

The neat streets of apartment houses around Knickerbocker Avenue next became the new American homes for thousands of Sicilians fleeing the rural poverty of their native island. On summer nights the high stoops echoed to the sound of kids playing and neighbors chatting in the Sicilian dialect, and on Knickerbocker Avenue the men of the neighborhood drank and gambled in the cafés—the Italian coffee houses where they could sit for hours over a cup of espresso, nibble on pastries, or drink anisette as they talked, while in the back room the card game was in progress.

The game was baccarat, and baccarat was the engine of Knickerbocker Avenue. Whoever controlled the game controlled the street and the neighborhood. The owner of the biggest game in the best café was the "street boss" of Knickerbocker Avenue. And if he was boss of Knickerbocker, then he was also a capo in the Bonanno Family of the New York Mafia. For the Bonnano Family ran Knickerbocker Avenue.

. . . 1924. SICILY.

The influence of the Fascist leader Benito Mussolini had spread throughout Italy. His Blackshirts were a powerful force within the Palermo Naval Institute, where the young Giuseppe Bonanno studied. When Giuseppe refused to wear the Blackshirt uniform, he was forced to flee the college. He soon decided that he had had enough of Fascist politics in Sicily, and emigrated to the United States. His father, Salvatore, had gone to New York years before, fleeing Sicilian prosecutors who sought his arrest for participation in a Mafia murder. Five years later, after the charge was dropped, he had come back to Sicily.

Young Giuseppe settled in Williamsburg, New York, a few miles west of Knickerbocker Avenue, where his father had earned great respect as a tavern owner. These few streets were populated with thousands of immigrants from Bonanno's town, Castellammare del Golfo. The language of trade and conversation was Sicilian. The *salumeria* at the corner of North Fifth and Roebling sold Sicilian cheeses and pastas. The churches heard confessions and said mass in the native tongue of their parishioners.

Giuseppe, now Joe, moved in with his uncle Peter Bonventre, who ran a small Italian bakery. It was the era of Calvin Coolidge, Babe Ruth, and Prohibition. Joe Bonanno had inherited his father's role as a Mafia power broker among these Castellammarese Sicilians. He quickly became involved in bootlegging whiskey and gin to the speakeasies and cafés of Brooklyn.

In 1929 Joe Bonanno wanted to marry Fay Labruzzo. He asked Salvatore Maranzano to be his best man. Maranzano, a fellow native of Castellammare, was Joe's boss in the bootlegging business, and the head of his Mafia family in New York. In the 1920s the Sicilian Mafiosi in New York had consolidated around five families. The most powerful and therefore the most successful in bootlegging was the Masseria Family. The family, headed by Joe "The Boss" Masseria, had among its younger members Charles "Lucky" Luciano and Frank Costello.

The second family, allied to Masseria and with similar interests in Manhattan and the Bronx, was headed by Al Mineo. Among its members were Albert Anastasia and Frank Scalise.

The Bronx was controlled by Tom Reina, who later conceded power to Tommy Lucchese.

Joe Profaci, an importer of olive oil and tomato paste, controlled a part of Brooklyn and Staten Island. His sympathies lay with the fifth family, the Castellammarese, led by Maranzano.

Sal Maranzano asked Joe Bonanno to postpone his plans for marriage. Tensions were running high between the Castellammarese and Joe Masseria over bootlegging revenues. Within weeks, the Castellammarese War had broken out. It raged for three years, until, in April 1931, the weakened and demoralized Masseria was set up by his underboss Lucky Luciano. Lucky was dining with Joe "The Boss," and stepped out to the washroom just in time to avoid the two gunmen who arrived with shotguns to kill Masseria.

For a short period Maranzano assumed total control of the New York Mafia, but his dictatorial style upset the young bloods now moving to the forefront in the five families. Lucky Luciano, with the support of several other leading Mafiosi, had Maranzano, the Boss of Bosses, hit in his red-and-gold office building on Park Avenue. Luciano, with the agreement of the other heads of families, including Joe Bonanno, who had taken control of the Castellammarese, now established a ruling Commission of the New York Mafia. The Commission was composed of the heads of the families, with one man selected as boss of the Commission. He was *capo di tutti capi,* but a chosen leader, not a dictator.

Two months after the death of the friend Bonanno had asked to act as his best man, Joe married Fay Labruzzo in Brooklyn. By 1945 he had become a naturalized American citizen and many times a millionaire. He was the undisputed boss of the Bonanno Family. His cousin John Bonventre had become his closest confidant. A young and tough under-boss, Carmine "Lilo" Galante, handled negotiations with other families.

Galante was a New York native, born in East Harlem in 1910. At the age of eleven, he used to boast, he was serving time for assault and robbery. By 1930 he had aligned himself with the Castellammarese and was robbing delivery trucks on the same Williamsburg streets that Joe's father, Salvatore Bonanno, had ruled years before. On one occasion Galante and his gang were interrupted in the middle of a hijacking by a police officer. In the exchange of gunfire, the policeman's coat was latticed with bullet holes, but despite a leg wound he managed to pounce on Galante and beat him unconscious. Galante was sentenced to twelve and a half years. After nine years, in 1939, he was paroled and was immediately back at his boss's side. A few years later Galante was suspected of murdering the exiled Italian anti-Fascist writer Carlo Tresca. The hit was said to be a Vito Genovese favor for his protector, Benito Mussolini.

The Bonanno Family prospered after the war. All five New York families went through a period of stability, which Joe liked to call "the Pax Bonanno."

In October of 1957 Bonanno took a trip to Sicily. He would later claim this trip was a vacation, a return to his birthplace at the insistence of Fortunato Pope, owner-publisher of *Il Progresso.* However, his trip coincided with trips by Carmine Galante and another Bonanno underboss, Frank Garafalo. On the night of October 12, in the Spano Restaurant in Palermo, Bonanno, Galante, and Garafalo sat down to eat with the exiled Lucky Luciano and most of the major Sicilian Mafia dons, including Gaetano Badalamenti and Tomasso Buscetta. This was the meeting at which Luciano recommended to the Sicilian Mafiosi that they move from the nineteenth to the twentieth century, and set up a ruling Commission like the one in New York, a council to adjudicate disputes in a more modern manner: sensibly, peacefully, and by negotiation, not by slaughter.

The years after Bonanno's return to New York were difficult times for La Cosa Nostra, Commission or no, and by the early 1960s Bonanno and his own family had found it prudent to flee to Tucson, Arizona. By that time the Bonanno underboss Carmine Galante had been put away for twenty years for narcotics trafficking. Gaspar Di Gregorio took control of the New York Bonanno Family.

Galante emerged from jail in 1974 to find that most of the old bosses he had worked with had retired or died. He was ready to assume the role of leader of the Bonanno Family and establish himself as the dominant mobster in New York. To emphasize his return, Galante decided to strike against his hated old rival Frank Costello. The fact that Costello was eleven months dead was no problem for Galante. He ordered the bronze doors of Costello's tomb in Greenwood Cemetery blown to bits with a time bomb.

Galante had taken pains during his 1957 trip to Sicily to spread the word that hungry, ambitious young Mafiosi could form their own crews under his guidance in New York. By the mid-1960s, young Sicilian men were starting to establish themselves in business on Knickerbocker Avenue. Some bought into bakeries or opened pizzerias; others worked in the numerous cafés along the busy thoroughfare.

Knickerbocker Avenue was solid Bonanno turf. Even though the convicted drug trafficker Carmine Galante had assumed control of the family, this area of Brooklyn still remained under the control of Pietro Licata, a Bonanno underboss in the old Mustache Pete style.

Pietro Licata ran his crew and his neighborhood and his several cafés as though he were a combination feudal lord and Catholic priest. He was an easily recognized figure on the street, for he wore nothing but white. Even on the coldest winter day Licata could be seen walking between the cafés in his white suit. Some years earlier, his daughter had become seriously ill with hepatitis, and Don Pietro had prayed in the church that her life might be spared. He swore to the Virgin Mary that if she saved the life of his precious daughter, he would henceforth wear only white in gratitude. The daughter recovered, and Licata kept his vow.

Licata took the title of Man of Honor literally, and sternly enforced the old Mafia ways. If he heard of any of his soldiers or their associates cheating on their wives, he sent for them and chastised them in front of whomever he happened to be meeting with at the time. The Licatas ran a number of cafés. Each day the cafés sold espresso and cannoli and pastries from the bakeries on the street. At night the tables were rearranged, and the game would commence.

The Caffe del Viale, in the middle of a busy block between Hart and Arcadia Streets, had the best game on the street, and it was the flagship of Licata's empire. Its narrow, unimposing front belies the establishment's size and status. Any stranger might wander in and ask for coffee or doughnuts, were he not daunted by the hostile glares from the men behind the food counter and the questioning stares of the few male customers sitting around. But when the Venetian blinds are lowered over the plate-glass windows at night, the Caffe del Viale is transformed. Its long rectangular room has enough floor space for thirty coffee tables. At night it can easily accommodate five poker games and a baccarat game run by the house. The stakes at the tables are set by the players, and they run from one-dollar bets to no limit. The house gets a percentage of each pot. The cafés on Knickerbocker Avenue can turn a $300 daytime business into a $3,000 nighttime profit from the tables. On one night in the Christmas season, the Caffe del Viale took in ·$34,000.

One block up on the opposite side of Knickerbocker Avenue is the Café Dello Sport. Its ice-cream-colored façade is more inviting than the Viale's. The window signs promise Budweiser and fine foods.

Luigi Ronsisvalle, newly arrived from Sicily, could speak no English. He felt out of place, disoriented in the East New York district of Brooklyn. At night the squat, bespectacled man betook himself to the hubbub of Knickerbocker Avenue, where he could speak his native Sicilian and drink Italian wine in the cafés. Occasionally he would gamble part of his meager wages.

Ronsisvalle knew that the owners of the cafés along Knickerbocker Avenue—the Café Dello Sport, the Café Bella Palermo, the Caffe del Viale—were Men of Honor. He knew that although they were now members of the Bonanno Family of New York, many had equally strong ties to the Mafia families of their native towns in Sicily; Castellammare del Golfo, Corleone, Catania, Cinisi, Santa Maria di Gesu.

Ronsisvalle struck up a relationship with Pino d'Aquanno, the owner of the Café Dello Sport (and later one of 283 unindicted co-conspirators named in the Pizza Connection case). They talked about life back in Sicily, about the newcomer's chances of work in New York, and about d'Aquanno's association with Pietro Licata. D'Aquanno said he was a soldier in the Bonanno Family, that Licata was his boss, and that Licata might be able to put Ronsisvalle to work. He should remember to show the proper respect, and show he had guts. If he handled himself right, he might even end up a soldier in Licata's crew.

Pino d'Aquanno was careful to follow the proper protocol when making the introductions to Licata. "This is Luigi Ronsisvalle, a good friend of mine." Licata put Ronsisvalle to work as a debt collector for his loan-sharking operation. Soon Ronsisvalle became a familiar figure on the avenue. On hot summer afternoons he could be found drinking beer under one of the brightly colored Campari umbrellas outside the Café Dello Sport. In the evenings he was learning to drink Scotch whiskey.

As Ronsisvalle moved around among the cafés he noticed several new faces among the made men who hung out in the Caffe del Viale. These new arrivals were all recent immigrants from Sicily, Zips. Their leader was one Salvatore "Toto" Catalano, a bull-necked, slit-eyed native of the Palermo suburb of Cimino. Catalano had arrived from Sicily in 1961 to join his brothers Vito and Dominick in running a successful bakery just off the avenue. Within a few years he had opened up a lucrative Italian gift shop, Coliseum Imports, selling records, Italian newspapers, and other souvenirs of the old country, across the street from the Caffe del Viale.

On the night of November 4, 1976, Pietro Licata was shot dead on the triangular pink brick doorstep of his own Café Licata. The next night Sal Catalano had assumed control of the baccarat game at Licata's Caffe del Viale, and flashy young Sicilians wearing Italian silk shirts and Gucci shoes were collecting the take on Catalano's behalf. Baldo Amato and Cesare Bonventre had been boyhood friends in their native Castellammare del Golfo. Cesare was a nephew of the old Bonanno underboss John Bonventre. When Amato and Bonventre followed others of their family to New York, it had been only natural for them to gravitate toward the Men of Honor and the game on Knickerbocker Avenue.

... **TUESDAY, JANUARY 28, 1986.**
THE COURTROOM. Louis Freeh patiently coaxes out the lines of
testimony he needs from Ronsisvalle. Occasionally this slow, unattrac-
tive man attempts a crude joke or a sassy reply, but his English is so
poor that he sounds only pathetic. His halting speech also for a time
masks the amoral nature of the man.

Ronsisvalle tells the court how he met someone called Felice Puma.
At the time, he needed $5,000, and Puma lent him the money. One
morning in the Café Scoppello he saw Sal Catalano, Puma, and another
man, a friend from the Bronx. At this, the drowsing jurors wake up.
Several are from the Bronx. That evening, in the Castellammare del
Golfo Restaurant, Puma told him, "Luigi, you know the pipe from
Canada, with oil?"

"I say yes. I never seen one, but I knew. He say: Well we got the same
thing, from Sicily, with *heroina.*"

Within weeks of the pipeline conversation, Ronsisvalle had become
a heroin courier, a mule. He delivered heroin by train to Chicago, he
delivered heroin by plane to California, and for each trip he was paid
$5,000.

This information causes Bergman to request a sidebar. The lawyers
know, though the jury does not, that Ronsisvalle already has testified
to most of this, in the 1985 Miami hearings of the President's Commission on Organized Crime, and Bergman has noted that his prior testimony did not mention any California trips. Nor are they mentioned in
the 3500 or Brady materials, the information about the witness that the
government is required to turn over to the defense in advance of testimony. Bergman, now backed hard by Fisher, therefore suspects those
trips were part of a different heroin conspiracy, one the government has
stumbled upon and is now attempting to wedge into Pizza.

Leval asks Freeh what he intends to bring out by mentioning California, and Freeh says, just the fee, the $5,000. The judge suggests Freeh
"go by" the L.A. trips, at least for now. "It seems to me it is the subject
of some confusion whether the Los Angeles trips are this conspiracy's
heroin, or somebody else's heroin." If necessary, they can always return
to the matter.

Freeh moves on, turning the pages of his yellow pad and methodically following his careful sequence of handwritten questions. In late 1977 or early 1978, says Ronsisvalle, he rode with Felice Puma in Puma's red Porsche from Collins Avenue in Miami Beach, Florida, back to Brooklyn. Ronsisvalle could shoot but not drive; he carried a revolver and a shotgun. The car trunk contained a load of heroin. They drove to Knickerbocker Avenue, parked in front of Puma's restaurant, and saw Sal Catalano standing on the corner a block away. Puma got out and went to speak to him, returned to the car, and said, "We have to wait a little."

Ronsisvalle watched Catalano go into the Caffe del Viale across the street, and emerge moments later with one Dominic "Mimmo" Tartamella. They approached the red Porsche, and "Mr. Felice Puma say to me, Okay, Luigi, leave everything in the car. Go home. I see you tomorrow. . . . As I go I hear the noise of the engine—vroom!" The next day Puma gave him another $5,000.

During this testimony, defense lawyers Fisher and Lombardino have taken up front-row positions directly facing the witness box, the better to observe this dangerous witness from as close a vantage point as possible. Fisher's client is now in big trouble. To save him, the lawyer must demolish Ronsisvalle. The threat to Lombardino's man, Joe Lamberti, is not yet apparent, but his lawyer's belligerent appearance recalls the look of a bad-tempered water buffalo preparing to charge.

The young prosecutor leads Ronsisvalle through a catalogue of his numerous drug trips to Chicago and L.A. On the train, he carried forty-pound loads in an ordinary suitcase. On planes, he carried two kilos of heroin taped to his body under his jacket, and he always boarded the plane last, with a garment bag thrown over his arm to conceal the bulk.

Ronsisvalle says his hope was to become a made member of the Bonanno Family. Although he was told his chances were good, he was kept waiting. On one trip to Chicago, he was double-crossed. He sensed something dangerous was about to happen to him, and at the last minute he switched hotel rooms. That night two gunmen burst into the original room and sprayed the bed with gunfire. Ronsisvalle set about tracking down the instigator. But before he could kill the man, Sal Catalano intervened and brought the two together. He told Ronsisvalle to shake hands and forget.

On another occasion, Ronsisvalle became involved in a brawl that arose from a traffic accident on Knickerbocker. The dispute spilled over into one of the cafés, and it involved a godson of an acquaintance of Toto Catalano, one Patsy Conte, a supermarket king. Ronsisvalle decided he had been deeply insulted, and he was about to arm himself and shoot the offending lad when Catalano arrived, this time accompanied by Patsy Conte himself. Catalano told Ronsisvalle that these were good people, "our people." Conte added that Ronsisvalle's own ally in the fight, the driver at the time of the crash, was someone to be avoided. "Don't hang around with him," he told Ronsisvalle. "He no one of us. He's a piece of shit."

. . . WEDNESDAY, JANUARY 29, 1986. THE COURTROOM. It is a dark, cold day in the dead of winter. Outside, snow disfigures the public statues. Inside, the courtroom air is sullen, subdued. Leval announces that, after extensive hearings, he has decided to permit testimony on the California heroin trips. The jury files in, followed by Ronsisvalle, scrape-shaven, jail pale. Leval greets the jury and, as often happens, offers a cautionary word before testimony begins. Yesterday, when he told them that the Badalamenti group was in no way connected to Ronsisvalle's evidence, "I was making no suggestion regarding any other defendant, one way or the other."

Second, although the eight Badalamenti defendants are related by blood or marriage, and their lawyers refer to them as "the Badalamenti group . . . I remind you that in performing your task of declaring verdicts, you must regard each defendant as standing separately.

"There are twenty-two trials going on before you. As to each one separately, you will be required to decide whether or not the evidence shows that defendant's guilt beyond a reasonable doubt." Judge Leval has repeated a key point, perhaps *the* key point in this entire affair. The jurors in effect are watching not one trial but twenty-two, all going forward simultaneously. At the conclusion of argument, they will be asked to render twenty-two separate verdicts—each one based on their evaluation of only the evidence relating to that particular defendant.

But how can this be done? The jury has now been sitting for three months; it has heard only about one fourth of the promised evidence. Yet to disentangle, comb out, and follow only this fraction of the evidence already seems well beyond human capability. Even a panel of wise old judges, accustomed to hearing and sifting evidence, would seem unequal to the task. How can ordinary citizens manage, especially citizens who are not allowed to take notes? Note-taking is a matter of judicial option, and Leval permitted it in the Westmoreland case but has forbidden it in Pizza. In light of the insane complexity of the evidence, and the howling throng of like-sounding Sicilian names and nicknames, his decision is understandable. Notes taken under these circumstances, especially notes made by ordinary citizens, would only increase confusion and the likelihood of error. Much better for the court to maintain tight control of what gets into the jurors' heads.

Like almost every other sitting judge, and most experienced trial lawyers, Pierre Leval has a near-religious belief in the wisdom of the American jury, and in its mystical ability to evaluate evidence, no matter how complicated, or twisted, or arcane, or, for that matter, perjurous it may be, and to reach the correct conclusion as to guilt or innocence more than 99% of the time.

Luigi Ronsisvalle is an unappealing figure, a mook, a street hood. The excuse for putting such a lowlife before the jury is always that the government must use bad guys to catch bad guys. Nonetheless, to minimize the inevitable damage on cross-examination, Freeh wants to tell the jury himself about his man's unsavory past.

"In January 1979, you told us yesterday, you committed a robbery in Queens." Yes, a jewel robbery. He was arrested and, while out on bail, tried to borrow $30,000. Ronsisvalle describes the conversation to the jury. "I needa money," he told an acquaintance. "I'ma facin' trial, an' I no like da face of da judge. Eef I no getta da money by seex o'clock, I'ma turn myse'f eento FBI, an' I'ma takin' you wid me. . . ."

And that is what he did, and that is how the United States came to have the assistance of this crucial witness in this important case.

Louis Freeh sits down at the prosecution table. The jury files out for another recess while the defense lawyers begin to digest the latest batch of government documents.

The background material on Luigi Ronsisvalle is startling. The man admits to murdering thirteen people. Some were killed as contract hits, others because he had some particular grudge against or dislike for them. At least some of his thirteen murders seem to have been done in hopes of being invited to join the Mafia. But it didn't work. Even the Mafia doesn't want Ronsisvalle; only the U.S. government does.

The documents include the psychological profile required by law for persons in the Witness Protection Program. Wading through dense thickets of psychobabble, heavily blue-penciled to protect the subject's confidentiality, one reads, "since being incarcerated he has spent one year in segregation due to his need for protection. . . . [He has] a lengthy history of profit-motivated violence. . . . Failure to achieve success in [emotional] relationships . . . could well lead him to regress to his former lifestyle, which would certainly pose a threat to his community."

Also among the background documents are letters on Ronsisvalle's behalf sent by Rudolph Giuliani, Richard Martin, and other law-enforcement officials to the New York State Parole Board. In stilted, formulaic sentences—but sentences whose real meaning is well known to all who write and read such letters—the federal authorities express their hope that due consideration will be given by state authorities to how helpful this prisoner has been to them. The letters will be effective—they always are—and seasoned defense attorneys know it. Indeed, the letters will put Ronsisvalle back in circulation the weekend after he concludes his testimony.

"Cock-suckers!" Segal is screaming. "They're gonna let this guy out on the *streets!*"

Says Kennedy quietly, "Some witnesses in the Witness Protection Program are asking for protection from this witness."

It will be up to the court to rule, after listening to the lawyers debate the matter outside the presence of the jury, on how much testimony, if any, the jury should hear about Ronsisvalle's murderous past. Some is probably in order; all might properly be considered "prejudicial." The government of course would like as little as possible. The defense lawyers seize the opportunity to give full vent to their opinions, which vary dramatically, and reveal as much about the attorneys as about their clients. Several want the murders kept out entirely. They feel that mere mention of more horrific crimes by a Sicilian against other Sicilians will only further prejudice the jury against people whose names end in vowels.

Bob Koppelman is one who wants no murders mentioned. He renews his routine request for a severance for his young client, Vito Badalamenti; it is routinely denied.

Paul Bergman, who represents an accused murderer, splits hairs—with a cleaver: "There are all different *kinds* of murders. His murders have no relationship to any Mafia disputes." Yet Bergman adds that he wants *"some* murder evidence in, so we can show how cold-blooded he is."

Several lawyers, including Fisher, want all the murders left in. They not only impeach the character and credibility of the witness, but also show that Ronsisvalle was a free-lance hit man, allied with no crime family. "The government has suggested my client has some connection with every crime this guy ever committed, just because he's the boss of Knickerbocker Avenue," Fisher says. Joe Benfante asks full latitude for Fisher on his cross-examination. Anything the artful Fisher can think of to dirty up this witness is bound to help Benfante defend Sal Mazzurco.

DeVardo's lawyer, Jimmy Moriarty, says, "This fellow has tried to kill an Assistant U.S. Attorney!" His words are righteous, but a wicked Irish smile sends another message. Young Moriarty is one of several lawyers who want all the murders in because they feel that one, in particular, impeaches these prosecutors as much as it does Ronsisvalle.

The story is convoluted. In late 1978 Ronsisvalle was asked to assassinate a U.S. attorney, John Kenney. Kenney was then prosecuting Michele Sindona, the renegade Italian financier accused of masterminding the swindle that led to the collapse of Franklin National Bank. (Sindona's lawyer at the time was Ivan Fisher.) The man who proposed the hit was a Sindona accomplice. The plot was held up when Ronsisvalle attempted to extort $30,000 from the accomplice, and threatened to kill his wife and children, saying he needed money to flee a robbery conviction. When he was refused, he flipped, decided he had more to gain as an informer than as a fugitive, and turned himself in to the FBI.

In short, Giuliani and Martin have sought to intervene with state authorities on behalf of this man, even though he had plotted to kill one of their own colleagues. The prosecutors considered their intervention a fair exchange in return for the chance to use Ronsisvalle to convict the Pizza defendants. Certain Pizza defense lawyers now hope to exploit this lapse of delicacy on the government's part to the advantage of their beleaguered clients.

Judge Leval listens to all the arguments, denies the government's request to keep all evidence of Ronsisvalle's murders out of this case, but adds, "I think the particular beastliness of a particular crime has no special bearing. It is inflammatory. It tends to involve prejudice. So I will not allow any extensive inquiry into gory details."

Twenty-four jurors and alternates file in. Even before they are seated Fisher is up on his long legs, pacing, hands on his lapels, microphone enfolded in his right hand. Gesturing with his left, he sets out to do what he does best—cross-examine a hostile witness.

...IVAN S. FISHER,
forty-two, is an engaging man of appealing immodesty. So enormous
as to seem faintly sinister, he today weighs about 330. His physical
condition is atrocious: he chooses a baroque diet, gets little exercise, has
weak knees that require surgery, and sometimes suffers serious fidgets.
He is frank to say he was the class fat boy in every school, and compen-
sated by being very bright, and a cutup. All his life he has gone on crash
diets, and can drop fifty pounds in a few weeks. Fisher thin and tanned
is a handsome dog.

Ivan Fisher grew up in the Riverdale section of the Bronx, the eldest
son of a bookbinder. He is married to his second wife, Diane, a leggy,
lovely, long-haired blonde, and he recently won custody of his seven-
teen-year-old son, Ari, clearly a tender and important event.

In style and substance, Fisher is Kennedy's opposite. Politics is
Kennedy's fundament. Fisher is so entirely apolitical he has never
voted. "Because it doesn't make a bit of difference. I don't want to be
a part of a system in which I don't count."

Whereas Kennedy detests celebrity, and sees it as a trap, Fisher says,
"I love celebrity! I *invite* it. I woo the media. I won Abbott with media.
You must use the energy of the media to create the atmosphere you
want for your client."

Fisher started out as a San Francisco Legal Aid lawyer. Kennedy's
first experience was in military courts-martial, followed by several years
as a personal-injury lawyer.

Despite their differences in background, both men have encyclopedic
knowledge of courtroom technique, learned the hard way. Says Fisher:
"Juries always want you to be straight with them. Don't ever talk fancy
to them, don't get carried away by sheer love of words." He learned this
lesson some years ago. "My guy was running away, from a bank robbery, and hit another car. I told the jury: They had a 'vehicular tête-à-
tête.' I was so in love with the phrase, I lost the case."

Says Fisher: "Lawyering is about being accurate. Juries like me. They
like me because I say to them what is so. Prosecutors often say: All I
want is a jury that can be fair. I never say that. I say: All I want is a
jury that will acquit my client. That's what it's about, and what it's all
about. It's about *winning.*"

Ivan Fisher was brought into the Pizza Connection case early on by Mario Malerba, Giuseppe Ganci's long-time lawyer, because of his skill at trial work and his popularity with juries.

Fisher believes that after four years' investigation of his client, the government was "seriously contemplating dropping this case" when they stumbled upon the mysterious Badalamenti connection. After that, "his capture became the major impetus to go ahead."

But "every bit of evidence" was acquired "after the fact. Buscetta was an addendum. Contorno is a post-addendum. When Badalamenti was indicted in November 1984, they had *nothing*. We blew it!" (His reference is to the defense failure to press for a speedy trial.)

Then Kennedy came into the case. "Mike Kennedy added a quality of elegance, eloquence, refinement" heretofore lacking.

In the Pizza case, Fisher sees "an unusually good team of lawyers. Usually in long, multidefendant cases, you see garbage.

"Segal's interesting. Leval is tough on him because they were once prosecutors together. But Marvin has very, very good credentials. He's regarded as a semi-Brahmin, or quasi-Brahmin. His partner, Bill Hundley, *is* a Brahmin. Yet, this far into the case, he's been horrible. If you get a judge who doesn't respect you, it's a nightmare experience. Marvin Segal has been eviscerated in this case by that experience. That's why he always sounds so shrill. Yet he's one of the most respected people in our profession.

"Gerry Di Chiara's good. He should have been retained as a CJA lawyer, court-appointed, and was not. He's a very decent person.

"Joe Ryan is interesting, a former Queens County prosecutor.

"Men like Benfante in today's courtrooms are anachronisms. Brontosauruses. But characterized by unflinching loyalty."

Among organized-crime lawyers, Mario Malerba is known as "The Prime Minister." Fisher calls him "the lawful version of the *consigliere*. To use a medical comparison, he's like an internist. In this kind of work, you bring in the orthopedist, the surgeon, whatever specialist the case may require. But *he* has something *none* of us has—their trust. He is Sicilian. His instincts are theirs. Without Mario, I don't know how else I could connect with my guy. The government has 142 experts who say it's his signature, it's his fingerprint. He just says: 'I didn't write this. It's not my fingerprint.' He simply denies." In this frustrating situation, "Malerba is like the Tappan Zee Bridge for me. I need him to effectively represent this guy.

"Bronson is a former Hudson County prosecutor. Hudson County,

New Jersey, used to be known as the most corrupt county in the universe.

"Tony Lombardino is a former assistant DA from Queens, and former chief of the U.S. Attorney's Office, Eastern District. I don't like him. Basically because he doesn't like me. But I think this is a man who really knows how to ask questions.

"Pity the jury doesn't like Ken Kaplan. He's a very decent person. Smart. And competent.

"Mike Querques has a superb reputation. The cognoscenti of the criminal bar recognize him as one of our very best. . . .

"Lemme tell you how the courtroom works: In any criminal trial, many layers of distortion occur. The *first layer of reality* is what really happened. The *second layer* is what people like Sal Catalano think happened. So that's the first lens which distorts. Because it's a function of the Sicilian code that no client ever tell any attorney what really happened. The *third layer* is what the cops see. A special cops' lens is applied to the 'evidence.' That lens, which is bifocal, further distorts reality. One part of the lens wants to see the full field, wants to really know what happened. Another part of the lens wants to filter out that which is inconsistent with the cop's preconceptions and/or inconsistent with his evidentiary needs.

"A *fourth layer* is the government prosecutor's level. He wears not bifocals but trifocals. Because the prosecutor has stronger problems. One, he needs to see what *is*. Two, he also has a visceral need to see *guilt*. And his guy can't be just guilty. He's gotta be Big Guilty. Or Big, Bad Guilty. Because this prosecutor must devote the next three or four years of painstaking work to proving that guilt.

"On the government side, you have this enormous need to justify oneself. They *must* win! There *must* be a Mafia. Organized crime *must* exist—that being the entire foundation of their years-long investigation, and also the designated launching pad for Giuliani's immense personal ambition.

"The *fifth layer* is ours. The defense lawyer wears glasses that are the most distorting of all. We want to look least at what really happened. Who except some psychopath can want to look closely at a client who is involved in embedding heroin into the veins of young people? Who's involved with shipping millions of dollars back to Italy to buy more heroin? Who's plotting the murder of Carmine Galante? Who intends to shoot his head into fragments and plaster him all over the walls of some restaurant?

"So we think in terms of the presumption of innocence. We persuade ourselves that we enforce a very important system—the criminal justice system, predicated on every defendant's presumption of innocence, and the prosecution's need to persuade a jury otherwise, beyond a reasonable doubt.

"Also, we defense lawyers operate always off the assumption: *Nothing* the government says about our client is accurate. Because we don't have to accept anything they say as accurate, we can presume our client is innocent—and what a distortion that is!

"So here's our situation: One, we don't know what the reality is. Two, we can't find out from the only person who does know—our client. Three, we operate always from the automatic preconception: Anything bad they say about our client is wrong; anything good they perchance say is right. In the Pizza case, you have the foregoing constraints and distortions operating to the nth degree, much more than in a normal case."

Ask Fisher his opinion of Judge Leval, and his eyes light up. "A plus. Wonderful! He's the most underestimated, unappreciated, insufficiently respected element in this trial. How this man can assume the bench each morning with such unflappable good spirits I cannot imagine.

"Ideally, Pierre Leval should be on the Court of Appeals. He has the perfect temperament. There, you can be even purer than as a district court judge. I have a feeling Leval greatly enjoys his purity. I would too—if I felt that pure. I feel Leval gets up every morning and tells himself: Yesterday I did nothing but good. . . . How else could he get through this horror show? He *enjoys* that feeling, of having done nothing but good, of purity, the way other people enjoy money, or sex."

This leads Fisher back to a favorite topic: great lawyering. Of what does it consist? Its essence, he says, is to be as accurate as you can. "Have the courage to see what really happened, to see your client selling heroin; then go back into the system, and use it to defend him.

"Jurors always love you for being accurate. When you're speaking straight to them, you can tell it by their body language . . . love gushes out to you! And when your questions are *accurate,* and the witness's answers are accurate, you don't need any tricks. They *know.* Because you and they—the jury—then share something. And that's what wins a case for you.

"In the Pizza Connection case, there is an incredible opportunity waiting for whoever has the guts to say it: Yes, Virginia, there is a Mafia. It does do bad things. And these guys are part of it. You've seen a ton of evidence to that effect.

"You can *win* this case with an argument like that. You know why?

Because there's too much bullshit going on. From the government side. And the jury can smell it.

"To be a great lawyer, you have to be willing to live dangerously. You have to go to the edge of the cliff and be willing to jump. 'Never ask a question you don't know the answer to.' They teach you that at Harvard; the First Commandment of good lawyering. And it's wrong. You will never look like a jerk that way. But you'll never soar, either. There's no magic to what you do.

"The best cross is when you allow yourself to range free, and be at the mercy of the witness, as Michael did in his cross of Buscetta. He asked some questions that were truly breath-taking. It didn't even look like Michael was responsible for those answers. He made it look like Buscetta was responsible. Wonderful!"

. . . THE COURTROOM.

Having elicited from Ronsisvalle that he has on numerous occasions identified countless photographs of suspected criminals, Fisher asks him, "Amongst the hundreds of pictures that city and federal police agents and prosecutors have shown you, sir, did you see *any* picture of what you said you saw from Puma's red sports car: Puma talking to Catalano on Knickerbocker Avenue?" No, sir.

"Who paid for the suit you are wearing now?"

The U.S. marshals. It's the only suit he has.

"Are you thinner now than in 1978?"

"Objection!"

"Well how about this way: Were you heavier then?" The jury laughs. Fisher has them with him.

"You told us you attempted to borrow $30,000. Do you think 'borrow' is the right word for that particular effort, sir?"

"No. You're right."

"What is the right word for that, sir?"

"Blackmail."

"And you received $200 for that effort, right?" Yes. "Would it be fair to say, sir, that you come cheap?"

"I was broke."

"With all those trips, sir? At $5000 a clip?"

In 1978, Ronsisvalle admits, he was paid more than $65,000 as a heroin courier. Was that his only crime that year? No.

"Were you murdering anyone in 1978?" No.

"Were you setting anyone's home on fire in 1978?" No.

"Dealing in any stolen property in 1978?" No.

"I give up. What crimes, other than drugs, were you committing in 1978?"

Extortion.

"You got $200 for that, right? What else?"

What else *what?*

(Elaborately abject) "I'm sorry. What other *crimes?*" (Sneering) "Oh, you mean you didn't file tax returns? Mr. Puma didn't *withhold* taxes. . . .

"I direct your attention, sir, to about the time, in late 1978," when the blackmail plot fell through. "You got angry?" Yes. "Is it accurate— that when you get angry with a person, that person is in very grave danger? . . . When you get angry you sometimes kill people—as in *shoot them dead?* . . . He called you a name, you decided to kill him! Right?

"And Mr. Catalano *stopped you,* right?" Yes.

"Another time, in Chicago . . . You switched rooms with a woman, and two guys came and sprayed the room with bullets. . . . You didn't give him a receipt, did you?"

Give him a receipt! He tried to kill me.

"And Catalano *stopped you,* right?"

Fisher's flamboyance notwithstanding, three jurors are asleep. But the performance is masterful: Using no notes, his long arms looped to the curl of his lapels, the lawyer lopes freely around the courtroom, swooping and pacing like an impossibly long-legged, knock-kneed ostrich. His grotesque grace recalls the dancing ostriches which perform Ponchielli's "Dance of the Hours" in Walt Disney's *Fantasia.*

"You know the word murder?" Yes.

"You've done it many times, too." Yes.

"Thirteen separate times, sir. Right?"

"Yessir."

"You intended to kill somebody. . . ."

"It was not personal, sir."

"You did it for money on some occasions?" Yes.

"How many?"

Six separate times.

"Including Brooklyn?"

"No. Conspiracy. I no killa da man. I just talk about to do it."

"Did—you—plead—guilty—to killing someone—in—Brooklyn?"

Yes, but he didn't get paid for that one. "I wanna make sure if I killed a man, or not." At this, several jurors laugh aloud. The two Lambertis and Mazzurco laugh even harder than the jurors.

"He's a death machine," Eleanore Kennedy mutters, and walks up to her husband to warn him to caution his colleagues that death is no laughing matter, at least not in front of the jury. By now Benfante, Lombardino, and Bronson are convulsed with mirth. In the midst of all these ill-advised snickers, Badalamenti turns, perfectly poker-faced, and beams his lawyer's beautiful Italian wife a sober and grave Sicilian smile. He has seen all.

Ronsisvalle did his first murder when he was eighteen years old. He was not paid.

"And the next killing?"

"Was almost nineteen. Not paid."

"Two for free so far, right?"

The next murder was at age twenty, but still no pay.

"On the next occasion, sir, that you murdered someone, how old were you?"

"Twenty-two. Can I explain?"

"Just answer the question, please," says Leval.

The next at twenty-three, no pay. The next at twenty-four, no pay.

"You left one out?" Fisher inquires.

"No. I left two out."

It is time for a coffee break. The other lawyers appear genuinely shocked by the moral squalor of this witness. Says Koppelman: "It's disgusting how they beg and plead for this animal to be put back in the street!"

In the courtroom, Fisher has the killer trying to explain himself. He uses the rationale of all monsters: "That was a job. It had nothing to do with destroying people. . . . If you give me $30,000 to kill a person, *you* kill him, not me."

Fisher turns to Ronsisvalle's extremely dangerous testimony connecting Sal Catalano to the red Porsche, and with great patience and skill he demolishes it. He demonstrates to the jury that Ronsisvalle's description of how he watched Catalano take possession of the heroin-laden Porsche cannot possibly be correct. Fisher has had the foresight to make and bring to court a sequence of two-foot-long, full-color blow-ups of traffic on Knickerbocker Avenue. He props these against the jury rail, compares them to the shopfronts and other landmarks Ronsisvalle says he saw that day as Catalano walked down Knickerbocker Avenue, and shows that he has omitted from his description an entire city block.

But Ronsisvalle finds a way to hold his own. As one o'clock approaches, he turns to Leval and asks him the very question that is uppermost in the jury's mind: "How about lunch, your Honor?" They burst out laughing. In a sentence, he has recaptured the affections of this jury, and at least partially destroyed Fisher's morning's work. The man may have had only a fourth-grade education, but he is very smart.

Bob Koppelman, a former fat man who today has a permanent lean and hungry look, is sharing a cafeteria table with other defense lawyers, too angry to eat. "This guy's evil has been *stroked* by agents. Even the government lawyers and the federal judge are fawning. *He* runs the courtroom!"

"The guy is really pissing all over *both* sides," says Benfante. "Ivan's doing beautiful."

Leval might not agree. Fogelnest had asked Leval to instruct the jury that Ronsisvalle's comment regarding lunch was inappropriate. But the judge replied that Fisher's style of cross-examination invites such behavior.

Eleanore Kennedy's fine-tuned intuition tells her, "This man has a button we haven't pushed yet. If we can find it, we can make him explode on the stand."

Koppelman says, "Catalano is the Invisible Man. In the early IDs, he's never there."

Lewis adds, "Yes, there isn't proof. There's *evidence.* And this jerk Leval doesn't know the difference! Proof is an established fact which *comes from* evidence. Evidence is just what goes in. When Leval uses the word *proof* for *evidence,* like the time he talked about the proof of Catalano's drug involvement, that's what worries me."

In line at the metal detector, Eleanore whispers, "I thought everybody came down on Ivan very hard during lunch," for overacting. Mrs. Kennedy, not normally a Fisher fan, and very much an expert in the flexings of the legal ego, thinks, "This is going beautifully. . . . Then twenty of these idiots are gonna get up and muck it up."

One of the greatest defense hazards in multidefendant trials is the temptation for individual lawyers to grandstand to the jury, and to their clients, at the expense of the whole. Such posturing can be controlled only in a strictly disciplined defense team that meets nightly to redefine strategy and reassert solidarity. The Kennedys know this as veterans of many political trials. Such rigor is impossible in so various a gaggle of mutually hostile, suspicious, ept and inept lawyers as Pizza has brought together. The government's primary objective in its adamant refusal to sever this case into manageable parts may be less to amalgamate incompatible defendants than to impair the effective functioning of their lawyers.

Joe Benfante, a former wrestling champion with an ego as wide as his shoulders, gets up to cross-examine. His client, Sal Mazzurco, has no connection whatever to Ronsisvalle. Yet Fisher's already overdone cross will now be further weakened by repeated attempts at grandstanding by lesser lawyers unable to resist the sound of their own voices, or unable to ignore such a putrid piece of meat as Ronsisvalle.

"One, do you recall using the word 'swag' in 1979 to the agents? Two, do you recall saying Puma was involved in fencing gold, jewelry, gems? Three, did you say Settimo Flavior had a brother-in-law involved in fencing?"

These questions relate in some way to Ronsisvalle's 1979 arrest for attempted jewel robbery. But to experienced ears, the odd questions hint that Mazzurco and his lawyer are not team players. Regardless of *what* other defendants may say when it comes time to explain the thousands of cryptic phone calls, it looks as if Mazzurco intends to say that, yes, he was a smuggler, but not a dope smuggler; he was dealing in stolen gems.

Spectators hear a big crunching sound from the bench: Leval is stapling papers. That's it. No more questions by anyone, and no redirect. The witness is excused. Bergman reserves the right to recall Ronsisvalle on his direct, thereby again having the last word. A recess is declared.

Fifteen minutes later, FBI Special Agent Joseph Pistone enters with a slightly rolling gait, like a champion middleweight approaching the ring. He is in his late forties, a tough, bald, lean, dark cop with a large nose, lowered eyes. His noble Roman head is set squarely on wide shoulders, and, from certain angles, the pale, narrow face suggests an old daguerreotype of an Italian immigrant. He wears a narrow red tie, dark-blue suit—his working clothes when not working undercover. He testifies in the clipped, deadpan style popularized a generation ago by Jack Webb in "Dragnet." *My name's Friday. I'm a cop.*

Pistone will face extensive voir dire before he gets in front of the jury. The evidence that the government proposes he give is so controversial, so heavily contested by the defense, that each part of it must be heard in advance and ruled on by the court. The highlight of the undercover agent's testimony will be his inside knowledge of the murder acted out in front of the jury by Stewart during the government's opening—the killing of Carmine Galante.

Fattish, pink-cheeked Robert Bucknam, fourth and youngest of the assistant U.S. attorneys on the prosecution team, has been chosen to lead the undercover agent through the events of his four years inside the Bonanno Family.

. . . 1977.

NEW YORK CITY. Special Agent Joseph Pistone, a seventeen-year FBI veteran, was assigned to infiltrate a Manhattan organized-crime fencing operation. He posed as "Donny Brasco," an Italian-American professional burglar, and he maintained an apartment, car, and driver's license in that name. Brasco was an appealing character, level-headed, confident in his burglary skills, the kind of man likely to do well in professional criminal circles.

In March 1977 Pistone was introduced to Tony Mirra, a soldier in the Bonanno Family. Mirra owned the Bus Stop Luncheonette at Madison Street in the Little Italy neighborhood of Lower Manhattan, as well as a Midtown nightclub called Cecil's.

Calling himself Brasco, Pistone hung out in Mirra's joints and ingratiated himself with the notoriously violent mobster. Within weeks Mirra had introduced Brasco to Benjamin "Lefty" Ruggiero, a mobster who ran a bookie operation out of a small social club a few doors down Madison Street. Mirra told Lefty that Brasco was "a friend of mine," thus establishing that he was prepared to vouch for Brasco.

The maze of narrow streets that make up Little Italy is honeycombed with hole-in-the-wall clubs, one-room establishments sometimes outfitted with a small coffee bar and an espresso machine. The clubs post large signs reading MEMBERS ONLY, and surly, bored men hang around outside to discourage any who fail to notice the warning. The street crews of the five Mafia families run their loan-sharking and numbers rackets out of these social clubs.

Lefty Ruggiero explained to Donny Brasco that he was a soldier in the family under the control of a capo called Dominick "Sonny Black" Napolitano. Sonny Black worked out of Brooklyn, and they were all part of the Bonanno mob.

A few blocks from Lefty's bookie club was the headquarters of the Bonanno Family underboss Nicholas "Nicky Cigars" Marangello, also known as "Nicky Glasses." He ran his operation out of a small storefront called the Toyland Social Club. Lefty was particularly careful to warn Brasco that Nicky Cigars was a man who needed to be shown utmost respect. "If you have to do business at the Toyland Social, go in, don't speak to Nicky unless you're spoken to, do your business and get out. Don't hang around."

Ruggiero took Brasco to the Toyland Social Club and introduced him to the boss. "This is Donny Brasco and he's a good friend of mine." In Mafiaspeak, Ruggiero had now vouched for and adopted Brasco as an associate of the Bonanno Family.

Lefty promised that he would "school" Brasco in the ways of organized crime: how to become a good earner for the family, and for Lefty; how to treat soldiers and other wiseguys with respect; how to speak Mafia.

Ruggiero grew more and more attached to Donny Brasco, particularly because he seemed to be such a good thief and pulled in lots of money. The prosperous "burglar" supplied Lefty with a car, some diamonds, and a steady flow of government cash, all to win his total confidence. Earning—or stealing—power was all-important for a wiseguy. He was expected to give up half his booty in return for the criminal contacts and influence of the family. A good earner kept all the bosses happy.

As the bond between them grew, Lefty began to school Brasco in some personal canons of Mafia etiquette. Wiseguys should be neat and tidy. He persuaded the undercover agent to shave off his bushy mustache and get his long hair cut. There were also some perks with the job: Mobsters never worked on Mother's Day, said Lefty. Instead, the entire Mafia closed down so that every made guy could take flowers to his mom.

Brasco was now a familiar figure on the streets of Little Italy, though he was also something of a rarity among the mobsters and their associates. He didn't drink, and he didn't chase the women who hung around Mirra's nightclub or the restaurants on Mulberry Street. What's more, he was a physical-fitness fanatic, and people said he had a wife. But so what if he was a little unusual? He was a good earner.

One summer's day, Lefty Ruggiero and Donny Brasco were given a special assignment. They were told to go to the Casa Bella on Mulberry Street and stand guard outside the doors of the smoked-glass-fronted restaurant while a balding man in his late sixties went inside to eat. This was the boss of the Bonanno Family, Carmine Galante, a mean son of a bitch, said Lefty.

When Brasco suggested that they could just as easily guard Galante from inside the restaurant, Lefty told him that the family boss didn't sit down with ordinary soldiers, only capos or above. Galante was famously ill-tempered, and he trusted only the people he had imported from Sicily for assignments within the family. They had no American criminal records, and they were solid Mafia men, steeped in the bloody tradition of *omerta*. They had not gone soft, like their American counterparts. When Brasco visited Nicky Cigars' Toyland Social Club, he could watch the constant flow of traffic in and out of the club. Lefty pointed out which ones were Zips, and said they were the guys who ran drugs for Galante.

In midsummer of 1977 the FBI decided to move Agent Pistone to California so he could use his Little Italy contacts to infiltrate West Coast organized-crime groups. He told Lefty that things were looking bleak on the New York burglary circuit, so he needed to move out west to make a few good scores. Lefty was happy to see his associate so anxious to earn.

Brasco was careful to maintain close contact with his "teacher." He visited New York frequently, and plied Lefty with money and gifts. In return Lefty was eager to keep the undercover agent informed about changing family politics. When they first met, Lefty had told Brasco he could make $30,000 per week with the family. Yet Lefty was always broke. Brasco continually had to give him money. In restaurants he borrowed cash to pay the check. Brasco even had to pay Lefty's phone bill. The FBI could scarcely allow such a hot talker as Lefty to be silenced by a debt to the phone company.

Early in 1979 the FBI decided to move Pistone again, this time to an undercover assignment in Florida. Once again the Brasco contacts on Mulberry Street would be used to smooth the way and make mob introductions in new areas. Brasco told Lefty he was going to open a nightclub in Tampa, and possibly run book out of it. Lefty was delighted, flew down to look over the setup, liked what he saw, and immediately cut himself in. Back in New York, he told his capo, Sonny Black, about Brasco's Tampa setup, and he too flew down for a look, liked what he saw, and cut himself in.

The protective arm of Sonny Black quickly proved useful. The new nightclub had also attracted notice in Miami-based Mafia circles, and the local wiseguys, under Sam Trafficante, were looking to muscle in. Then they heard about Brasco's Sonny Black connection, and the problem disappeared.

Pistone continued to run the nightclub through 1979. In July of that year Lefty Ruggiero called and urged his protégé to look at the newspapers. The story he wanted him to see was all over the front pages. Carmine Galante had been found in a pool of blood on the patio of Joe & Mary's Restaurant.

Lefty told him that Nicky Cigars and Mike Sabella, another underboss, had also been targeted to be hit, but were spared at the last minute. Instead of a rubout, they were merely knocked down in rank from *capo* to *soldato*.

. . . JULY 31, 1979.

BROOKLYN. The Brooklyn district attorney's office is located on the fifth floor of the Municipal Building at Joralemon Street. This hot July day the lobby was jammed with TV cameramen and press photographers. The cameramen pushed and shoved to get the best shots of the two tall, tanned men who had turned up, accompanied by their lawyer, Mario Malerba, to answer questions for the Brooklyn DA. Cesare Bonventre and Baldo Amato had been Carmine Galante's less-than-adequate bodyguards on the day he was shot dead. Thereafter they became the subject of a nationwide police search. Two weeks later Malerba got word to the Brooklyn district attorney's office that Bonventre and Amato were ready to appear to answer questions. It was agreed by both parties that the surrender would be kept from the press. Someone had broken the agreement.

In addition to their lawyer, Bonventre and Amato were accompanied by three other men: Toto Catalano, Giuseppe Ganci, and an auto mechanic and part-time pilot from Brooklyn, Santos Giordano. Amato and Bonventre said they could remember little about the shooting, and showed no sign of any willingness to cooperate. Without that, the DA's office lacked sufficient evidence to connect them with the masked men who had gunned down Carmine Galante, Nardo Coppolla, and Joe Turano, and a few hours later they were released.

The death of Galante had left a power vacuum in the Bonanno Family. Toto Catalano moved up to become street boss of the Zips, a special high post outside the normal Mafia hierarchy of *soldato, capodicine, consigliere,* and *sotocapo.* He now ranked just under the family boss, Philip Rastelli, who was serving a term in federal prison. Bonventre was made a capo, the youngest in the American Mafia.

By early 1980 Donny Brasco's esteem among his peers in the Bonanno Family had grown. He was now a close personal friend and business associate of Sonny Black, and Sonny Black's star was in the ascendance. Deep divisions had split the Bonanno Family into two factions, for and against the leadership of Philip Rastelli. Five capos initially opposed the leadership of the jailed Rastelli. They were Alphonse "Sonny Red" Indelicato, his son Anthony "Bruno" Indelicato, Dominick Trinchera, Philip "Lucky" Giaccone, and Cesare Bonventre. This faction sought to make Giaccone head of the family.

The Rastelli loyalists were led by Donny Brasco's capo and close friend Sonny Black, and his ally Joey Messina. Sonny Black worked hard to strengthen the position of his loyal group within the family, and he reached out to some of the other New York dons to forge alliances. He managed to win the particular support of Carmine Persico, the powerful head of the Colombo Family of Brooklyn. But even more important, he won the support of Toto Catalano and the Zips—and this in turn assured that Bonventre would break his connection to the opposition.

Then, on the night of May 5, 1981, three of the four opposition capos disappeared: Alphonse Indelicato, Dominick Trinchera, and Philip Giaccone. Twenty days later Indelicato's partially decomposed body was found in Queens. He had been shot three times in the head and back. The other two bodies were never found.

Several days after the hit on the three capos, Brasco was summoned from Florida to New York by Sonny Black. He was told that Bruno Indelicato had escaped a hit, and a contract was now out on him. If Brasco was to discover him in Miami, he was to "whack him in the street and let him lie." Sonny Black went on to say that Bruno Indelicato was crazy, that he had a $3,000-a-day cocaine habit, and he needed to be dealt with swiftly.

Sic transit Donny Brasco. The FBI would never ask or permit an undercover agent to involve himself in violent crime. If Brasco might have to perform a hit, the charade was over. The FBI moved in to scoop up the mob figures against whom he could testify. Lefty Ruggiero was hauled out of his house. The Bureau decided to let Sonny Black stew for a while and perhaps turn him into a government witness. Before that could happen, he disappeared. As Pistone drove past the home of his former capo, he noticed that a rooftop pigeon coop which had been Sonny Black's favorite recreation spot was empty. The pigeons had been killed, he realized; nothing else could keep these homing birds away from their nest. The agent knew then that the man who had been his boss for three years was dead. Napolitano's decomposed, mutilated body was found a year later, half buried in the mud of a Staten Island creek.

... FRIDAY, JANUARY 31, 1986.

THE COURTROOM. Prosecutor Bucknam has finished his long Pistone voir dire. One of the lawyers wants to question the agent about another side of the powerful Mafia soldier Lefty Ruggiero. Robert Koppelman, attorney for Vito Badalamenti, represented Ruggiero in the federal case that resulted from Pistone's activities. He wants to show the court and remind the government of the kinds of things Lefty tells people. Lefty Ruggiero is the Mafia's own Walter Mitty. He said he had participated in a cowboy-style shootout on the Manhattan waterfront. He sometimes claimed he had 4,000 men after him. He claimed he had killed two men, been arrested, gone to trial, bribed the judge—a woman—and got off with a sentence for disorderly conduct.

Koppelman has made his point. Special Agent Pistone's carefully cultivated underworld connection is no big, bad Mafioso; he is an idiot, a buffoon.

The judge is smiling, but he has heard more than enough for one day, he says. Tomorrow he will listen to final arguments about the relevance of Pistone's proposed testimony. Outside the courtroom, Kennedy is the first to admit that Pistone is one of the bravest men he has ever heard of. He sometimes wore a wire during his pose as Donny Brasco, and occasionally he was forced to sleep over in Sonny Black's apartment while he still had the body wire on him. On those nights he had to hide it in a jacket pocket, place the jacket in a closet, and hope it remained undiscovered.

... TUESDAY, FEBRUARY 4, 1986.

THE COURTROOM. The Ship of Fools has settled in, and many shipmates appear to be enjoying the voyage. Lawyers, clients, court officials, jurors, and spectators have become a group now, afloat together in mid-ocean. The marshals no longer really bother to scan their metal detectors in the mornings.

There will be no jury today, and no witness, just lawyers on both sides fighting over terms and restrictions on Pistone's coming testimony.

The important question, as Leval defines it, is this: Assuming that these defendants participated in the Galante killing, was the intent of the killing to further the heroin-importation business, or was it a matter of internal Bonanno Family business and Mafia politics?

First, however, Leval has decided even before hearing defense arguments that several parts of Pistone's testimony are prejudicial, and he intends to exclude them. The jury will hear no mention of the importation of Zips to pizza parlors for the purpose of dealing drugs. Nor will the murders of the three capos be mentioned to the jury.

All the defense lawyers make the same basic point: Even in the government's best-case scenario, wherein Catalano arranged the hit, and Amato and Bonventre carried it out, it still has not been demonstrated by the government that this hit was in furtherance of drug trafficking. Whereas Peter Licata opposed drugs, and his shooting resulted in the commencement of the Zip drug trade, the Galante hit was merely to achieve a rise up the ladder within that trade and the Bonanno Family for Catalano.

The arguments are circuitous, legal possibilities are examined from every angle, lawyers expand upon minute points like medieval scholars. Leval sits through it all, chin leaning on hand in classic Thinker pose, occasionally correcting an errant legal argument. He will make his decision overnight.

Next morning Leval tells the lawyers he is deeply troubled that the proffer on the Galante murder made now by the government does not support the papers submitted to him eight months ago, which had argued for the inclusion of the murder as an act in furtherance of the drug conspiracy. He therefore formally rules the Galante killing out, and the Mafia murder of the decade, so carefully restaged by prosecutor

Stewart in his opening statement, is no longer in this case. The jury will have to be told that the most tantalizing part of the government's opening story must be expunged from their minds, wiped out entirely, so that no trace of residual prejudice remains.

Martin registers his disagreement with the ruling, and suggests an alternative. If the jury cannot consider the Galante murder as part of this conspiracy, then how about letting the jury hear the murder evidence against Catalano and Amato after the major verdicts in this case have been reached? Amato and Catalano have also been charged with the murder under a separate RICO charge that does not have to be considered in relation to the overall conspiracy and all twenty-two defendants.

"The possibility that we have a two-stage verdict" is "something we can discuss later," says Leval, and grants a brief recess to give Bucknam a chance to reprepare Pistone, excising the Galante murder from his testimony. Then the jury is called. They have been absent from the courtroom since Wednesday last, a total of four court days. Leval tells them they will be hearing a lot in the next few days about a certain Ruggiero. This person has no connection of any kind with attorney Larry Ruggiero, who appears before them in this case. "All right. Call the next witness."

Special Agent Joseph Pistone walks into the courtroom, ready to give the jury a sanitized version of his life as Donny Brasco. Unaware of all that they are missing, the jurors are nonetheless more attentive than at any time since the early days of Buscetta.

Bucknam takes Pistone once more through his "schooling" by Lefty Ruggiero, and his repeated warnings that "if I made a mistake, we would go bye-bye," meaning they would be killed.

Bucknam gives his witness a handful of brightly colored 3"-by-5" cards, and elicits from him that Lefty said that "boss" was the top position in a Mafia family, a position obtained through power only, and that a boss was absolute ruler of the family. Now the prosecutor asks Pistone to insert the yellow card in a plastic window at the top of a large black chart resting on an easel between witness and jury. This has previously been identified as Government Exhibit #1-A, a diagram of the organizational structure of a Cosa Nostra family. Pistone grimly inserts a card expensively lettered CARMINE GALANTE in the top slot. He next inserts a NICKY MARANGELLO card into the "underboss" slot, explaining that the underboss is the acting boss.

The *consigliere,* or counselor, is an elected position, and his function is "to settle beefs." In 1978 the *consigliere* in their family was Steve

Canone, also known as "Stevie Beef." The next Mafia rank is the *capodecine,* or chief of ten, the crew chief, an appointed position. *"Soldato* is the position you start at."

In the corridor, defense lawyers are charged up, eager for the cross-examination to come. Fisher, who will go first, can scarcely wait to bring to the jury's attention that Lefty Ruggiero has also said that his attorney is the eighty-two-year-old partner of Clarence Darrow; that he had Supreme Court Justice William O. Douglas in his back pocket; and that he intended to take a boat back to New York from Milwaukee, "hugging the shoreline all the way."

"But is it relevant?" asks Fogelnest.

"If I can make the Mafia funny, get the jury to laugh, it's *very* relevant."

One lawyer says Pistone appears close to a nervous breakdown. "He's pissed off," says Kennedy, "because 90% of his testimony was cut out." He spots a *Post* reporter and calls, "Got your next headline— 'Pierre Pissed on Pistone.' "

Back in the courtroom Bucknam is showing Pistone surveillance photos of Nicky Marangello's Toyland Social Club. One picture shows Tony Mirra outside the club embracing and kissing Sal Catalano on the cheek.

"Agent Pistone, were you ever kissed, kissed often in this manner?"

"The whole assignment—till 1981." The jury laughs. They love this witness.

2:30 P.M. The jury is dismissed. Comes now the debate on what and how much Leval should tell the jurors about his ruling on the Galante murder. Fisher wants a jury instruction that they should disregard the government's previous mentions of murder(s). But Bergman says that, at this point, *any* mention of his client only exacerbates "a situation which is bad enough already." Leval tells Bergman and Fisher to "caucus and work something out."

But Kennedy also wishes to be heard. "The opening statement of Mr. Stewart was so prejudicial . . . that I don't want the jury's nose rubbed in it once again. . . . So I agree with Bergman. Yet I feel Mr. Fisher has a right to his request. So if I could have just one request . . ."

Leval interrupts. "Let me guess . . ."

"It begins with an S, and it's called severance," Kennedy says.

Other attorneys join in one by one until Leval asks, "Anyone *not* move for a mistrial, or severance?" Yes. Fisher and Bergman. They prefer to see where the government is trying to go with this thing.

The Kennedy faction is in good spirits. With the murder ruled out, and the assertion of sole control by Badalamenti of Punta Raisi Airport also ruled out, only one thread is left tying the old Mafia chieftain to this drug conspiracy: the telephone calls from Badalamenti in Brazil to defendants Alfano and Mazzurco and the Lambertis. Kennedy is smiling as he heads off arm in arm with Eleanore to their Checker-cab limousine.

. . . THURSDAY, FEBRUARY 6, 1986. THE COURTROOM. Leval wears his most grave judicial expression as he tells the jury, "You are not to consider the death of Carmine Galante as part of this case.

"You may recall it was mentioned in opening statements. As I told you at the time, opening statements are not evidence. There has been no evidence in the trial concerning the death of Carmine Galante . . . and there will be none. Whatever you may have heard in the opening statements you should put out of your minds."

During this, Kennedy stares hard at the jurors; they appear impassive. Then with no further word, as though Leval had taken an eraser to the collective blackboard mind of the jury and wiped it clean, the trial picks up with the defense offered its opportunity to cross-examine the undercover agent. Most think he has been showcased enough. All attorneys except the last, the ever-bellicose Joe Ryan, pass up the opportunity.

Ryan's style is aggressively mocking. He focuses on the ridiculous Lefty Ruggiero. "You remember him telling you . . . he was a good friend of Supreme Court Justice Douglas?"

Bronson and Benfante have begun to giggle. Kennedy, Fisher, and Bergman remain absolutely poker-faced. By the end of his examination, Ryan's voice has risen almost to a scream. Any sense of the pathetic, Mittylike character of Lefty Ruggiero has been lost in the Irish lawyer's excessive histrionics.

In the corridor later, his colleagues are variously glum, mortified, disgusted. Fogelnest is enraged. "Ivan Fisher manipulated that! To make Lefty look like the gang that couldn't shoot straight. He tried to get me to do it. I wouldn't."

Fisher is furious. "We shoulda had the jury rolling in the aisles! But I didn't want to be the one to do it. I wanted Toto's lawyer to be dignified, and just say: No questions. So I made a mistake and let Ryan handle it."

The government too has been caucusing, reassessing, and when court reconvenes they announce that they will have no redirect. They are happy to let matters end with the jury's last impression being the spectacle of a brave, cool undercover agent withstanding a diatribe by a pipsqueak.

. . . WEDNESDAY, FEBRUARY 12, 1986.

THE COURTROOM. Mario Malerba interrupts the routine pre-jury haggle between defense and prosecution. "It's my sad task," he says, "to report to the court the death of Giuseppe Ganci." Il Bufalo has succumbed to the lung cancer that had caused Leval to sever him from the trial. Malerba now wants a guarantee from Martin that the attendance of any defendant at the funeral will not be seen by the government as an act in furtherance of the alleged conspiracy. Martin is willing to go some of the way toward alleviating the defendants' anxiety, but he also wants to anticipate future defense strategy. The government does not know, he says, "of any attempts by law enforcement to observe the wake or funeral, but [attendance] could be relevant if people say they don't know each other but are seen together in a way that suggests that they do."

Malerba, a consummate diplomat, refines this government position by putting a few additional questions, and then accepts Martin's terms. Malerba has arranged for the funeral parlor to stay open late, and he asks the court to adjourn a little early to accommodate the grieving defendants.

4. *The Laundrymen*

... **THURSDAY, FEBRUARY 13, 1986.**
THE COURTROOM. The largest of all the government's charts appears today. Despite vigorous defense protests, it will remain on view at least intermittently throughout the many benumbing, bewildering weeks of financial testimony to come. The chart is an elaborate multicolored schematic of the money flow, as large as two Ping-Pong tables. Its matte black background is entirely covered with multizero numbers, arrows, lines, flags, names of various international banks and brokerage houses, symbols of planes, phones, ships, people talking, and assorted world currencies, all laid out in glossy yellow, red, green, and blue, the whole thing as complex and not unlike a plumbing diagram of the *Queen Mary.*

Earlier this morning, Michael Kennedy has filed with the court a letter objecting on behalf of all members of the Badalamenti group to the forthcoming testimony of all the financial witnesses, on grounds that it is in no way related to the Badalamenti-group defendants, and it prejudices their ability to have a fair trial. Before testimony begins, eight other lawyers whose clients also are unconnected to the forthcoming evidence join in the objection.

The government's new witness, Salvatore Amendolito, fifty-two, born in Taranto, Italy, is just what Pizza's colorful cast of characters has heretofore lacked: a crooked financier. Sleek, fleshy, and heavy-browed, he dresses in various shades of grey silk, nicely chosen to complement his abundant wavy silver-grey hair and thick, silver-metal-framed glasses. He testifies in English, with a luxuriant Italian accent.

His sleazy background and criminal history are just right, too. Amendolito's Italian police record includes a 1969 conviction for fraud, and a later one for tampering with the odometer of a rented car. Later, while he was out of the country, the Italian government found him guilty *in absentia* of "Mafia association" and sentenced him to a four-year prison term.

Amendolito was arrested again in New Orleans, in July 1983, by the Americans, and charged with illegal money moving and possible narcotics conspiracy. He at once agreed to cooperate with the U.S. government in return for immunity. Thus it was that Salvatore Amendolito, crooked financier and professional *spallone* (slang for money launderer), became the unlikely Orpheus chosen to lead this jury through the dark and tangled underworld of international money laundering.

Under extremely well-prepared direct examination by prosecutor Louis Freeh, the witness describes himself to the jury as a "financier" who has for the last nine years played his money games in the United States. He came to this country in 1977 with the intention of developing a rather ingenious business. He would carefully package fresh fish from the teeming waters of the American North Atlantic, then fly his catch overnight to the fish stores of Europe.

Amendolito established three separate businesses to take care of the financial and logistical juggling necessary to put day-old sole and salmon on the tables of Brussels and Milan: Overseas Business Services, Inc., International Fish Services, and International Fish Company. But the financier soon found himself in fiscal deep water, and more than $100,000 in debt. Just then, conveniently, he was approached by two Sicilians, Giorgio Muratore and Mario Di Pasquale, who said they wanted to sell fresh fish from New York direct to the Palermitani.

The jury has heard of Muratore before, though it is doubtful they remember him. He was the known drug trafficker photographed talking to Sal Catalano in Palermo's Piazza Politeana, and later overheard on Italian wiretaps talking about Ciccio l'Americano, a nickname for defendant Castronovo. Now Muratore wanted to work out a fish deal with Amendolito whereby he would take over responsibility for the cargo at a point somewhere near John F. Kennedy International Airport. Amendolito said no; his personal supervision of the icing and loading process on the Manhattan docks was essential to insure freshness on delivery.

To line up customers, Amendolito went to Milan and met with Salvatore Miniati, manager of the local office of Finagest, an international Swiss brokerage firm. On the side, Miniati represented Amendolito's fish businesses. A bit further on the side, Miniati was a practiced money mover, or *spallone.*

Back in the United States, Amendolito heard again from Miniati. This time he said he needed someone to transfer funds from certain pizzeria owners in New York and New Jersey to a construction company in Sicily. Once the hotel or resort under construction was completed, the Americans would get their money back. But they did not intend to charge interest, and they wanted to avoid any contact with the Internal Revenue Service. The money would first be sent to Switzerland, Miniati said. That was the part he wanted to discuss with Amendolito. The Swiss would take care of moving it on from there to Sicily. The amount involved was $9 million.

Miniati said his client was one Oliviero Tognoli, a wealthy Milanese businessman in Sicily. But Tognoli was not the owner of the funds; he was fronting for a shadowy group of "principals" in Italy and, perhaps, the United States. Hearing that cash from pizzerias was being channeled to—of all places—Sicily, Amendolito tells the jury that he of course took steps to assure himself that, except for the IRS angle, the money was "clean." He satisfied himself that it was.

In June 1980 Tognoli gave Amendolito a New Jersey phone number, and he made contact with a man he believed was called Frank Ciccio. (This will turn out to be the same Ciccio l'Americano who so intrigued the Italian police. In short, defendant Castronovo.)

At this point, the silver-haired man on the witness stand pauses in his story. In response to a question from prosecutor Freeh, Amendolito stands up and points to the little crinkle-haired, square-faced defendant in the back row. Yes, Pizza defendant Frank Castronovo, seated between slim and elegant Sal Greco in the aisle seat, and hawk-faced Gaetano Mazzara to his right, is the man Amendolito knew as Frank Ciccio. Castronovo's lawyer, stoop-shouldered, skinny, bright Kenneth Kaplan, watches the jury intently as this identification is made.

Ciccio/Castronovo told Amendolito he wanted to transfer $300,000 abroad. The financier said in that case he intended to buy banker's checks of not more than $10,000 each, then wire the checks to Switzerland. (Federal law requires that checks of more than $10,000 be reported to the government. The regulation is intended mainly to catch tax cheats.) Castronovo said he was not interested in Amendolito's techniques. If Tognoli had recommended him, Amendolito knew what he was doing.

Amendolito kept $28,000 of the first money for himself. The size of his commissions in the future varied somewhat according to the difficulties—and opportunities—of each transfer. But he kept handwritten records of all his transactions, notes that wound up in financial-records storage. Then came the day in June 1983, while the financier was out of the country, that he was tagged for failure to pay his rent. His records were seized and put in storage by a liquidator, and remained impounded until recovered by the FBI.

The mechanics of being a *spallone* were simple at first. Frank Castronovo was co-owner of the Roma Restaurant, in the Menlo Park shopping mall in Menlo Park, New Jersey. Amendolito says that Castronovo normally packed the cash into used liquor boxes. The financier would drive out to the Roma Restaurant, check over the money with Castronovo, then back his station wagon in to a loading bay so that Castronovo could place the boxes in the rear.

On the first occasion, a sort of test run from Amendolito's point of view, Castronovo had given him $100,000 in used fives, tens, and twenties. The normal method of international money transfer would be to take the cash to an international financial house, fill out the required U.S. government registration forms, and deposit the cash with the bank, which would then send a wire representing the cash to the overseas destination. The government would note the sum of $100,000 as taxable holdings of the dealer. In the days previous to receiving Castronovo's cash, Amendolito had opened new accounts at twelve different banks in Lower Manhattan and Brooklyn. The day he received the money he went to ten of these banks and purchased ten separate $10,000 money orders. He then visited four international money houses—Credit Suisse, Swiss Bank Corp., Citibank, and the Lavaro Bank—and at each stop he wired individual money orders to one of three Swiss bank accounts whose names and numbers had been supplied to him by Tognoli and Miniati.

On July 11 and July 14 Amendolito repeated the process with two more $100,000 cash deliveries from Castronovo. A week later, Castronovo contacted Amendolito to say he had still more money to send.

When Amendolito met with him next, in a New Jersey motel room, the restaurateur handed him four suitcases, containing a total of $550,000 in well-worn fives, tens, and twenties. The financier drove home and contacted his superiors in Italy for instructions.

Miniati told Amendolito to call the Manhattan office of Finagest, on Park Avenue, and speak to a Mr. Lanfranchi. Lanfranchi worked in the public relations department, but his function at Finagest seems to have been limited to shopping for office furniture and occasionally calling banks to try to solicit business, with little success. For this he was paid $28,000 per year. Upon receiving the Amendolito call, Lanfranchi contacted his head office in Lugano, and was instructed to take the money to Conti Commodity Services in the World Trade Center.

Lanfranchi made arrangements to meet Amendolito in Midtown. He had hired a limousine to shuttle the money to the World Trade Center. The financier showed up on a Manhattan street with the four suitcases packed with small bills, and this strange pair drove downtown to the Conti office. But the Conti people were not prepared to handle such a large amount of cash, and advised Lanfranchi to try Chase Manhattan, also in the World Trade Center. The two men dragged their four cases to the bank, but had no better luck. They would have to go to Chase Manhattan's main office, they were told.

The men struggled in the 90° heat of a sweltering July day over to the marble edifice at One Chase Manhattan Plaza, at the junction of William and Pine Streets. One of the managers at Chase escorted them to the main counting room, only to discover that all the counting machines were in use. They would have to return the next day.

Twenty-four hours later Lanfranchi and Amendolito were back in the Chase Manhattan money room. The count revealed the money to be $2,500 short of the agreed $550,000 transfer figure. Amendolito personally made up the missing amount on the spot so that Finagest could take control of the money. The suitcases of worn bills would be credited to the Finagest account with Credit Suisse in Lugano, and laundered by declaring it to be part of Finagest's everyday cash transfers of development debts and profits.

Four days later Amendolito met once more with defendant Castronovo, and this time received $500,000 in two suitcases. It was too soon to try the Conti–Chase Manhattan route again, and by now Amendolito knew that his $10,000-check-wiring system could never handle the sheer volume of cash. A more direct method of money movement was essential. So the banker chartered a private jet from World Airways and, suitcases in hand, flew to the Bahamas. As he disembarked and went to pass through customs at Nassau, he was met by an extremely accommodating and knowledgeable local banker, Peter Albisser, manager of the Bahamian branch of Banca Della Svizzera Italiana, or BSI.

Albisser stood within the customs area of the airport and was able to assist Amendolito in by-passing the customs formalities and simply carrying the suitcases to his car. They drove to the BSI office in Norfolk House, an office building on Bay Street in downtown Nassau. Amendolito, following the orders he had received from Miniati, instructed Albisser to wire the money to the BSI branch in Menderisio, Switzerland, for account #27971, registered to Stefania.

Once Amendolito was satisfied that the transfer was under way, he returned to the airport, where his plane waited to take him back to New York. The transaction had taken far less time and wear and tear than hiking to ten New York City banks merely to launder $100,000. Seven days later, on August 6, the financier repeated the Bahamian loop with another $550,000.

By August 1, Amendolito had opened up a Madison Avenue office for his Overseas Business Services. The first days of August 1980 were an extremely active and profitable time for Salvatore Amendolito. Miniati called from Italy to say that he had a new client, someone whose name Miniati did not know but who would call Amendolito at his office soon. The next day the mysterious client called. He would not give his name, but he suggested a rendezvous on a Queens street corner the following afternoon. Amendolito drove to the meeting place and waited as he had been told. Soon two men walked up and introduced themselves as Vito and Sal. Amendolito was uncomfortable about the curbside conference, and invited them to a restaurant or diner to talk. But Sal refused, saying they could talk just as well in the narrow doorway close by.

Sal borrowed a piece of paper from Vito's notebook, scribbled "Sal" and "Vito" and a telephone number he said belonged to Vito. The doorway meeting broke up with the understanding that Amendolito would be contacted again when the money had been gathered.

The financier returned to his office and placed the piece of paper in a plastic envelope section of his Rolodex. He then called Miniati to complain about the clandestine nature of the meeting. Miniati reassured him by saying that these people were very worried about alerting the IRS. Next day Miniati called Amendolito to say that $1.5 million was ready.

Amendolito phoned the number he had been given and asked for Sal.

The person at the other end denied knowing any Sal. When Amendolito then asked for Vito, he was informed that Vito was out. Amendolito hung up, puzzled. Later that same day he received a call from a Sal who said he had learned that Amendolito had been trying to contact him. He would call again the next day with word of the money.

On August 8 Sal called to say they were ready; they should meet at the same Queens street corner. Amendolito first rented a hotel room in the Barbizon Plaza, on Central Park South in Manhattan. He planned to count the money there in the presence of Sal, so that all parties would be satisfied. He drove to the rendezvous and found Sal waiting alone in his car. Amendolito suggested they repair to the hotel room. Sal thought that would not be necessary. He told Amendolito to back his car so that his trunk was close to the trunk of Sal's car. Sal then transferred one large, heavy suitcase and two smaller suitcases into Amendolito's vehicle.

Amendolito was startled. What about the count? Sal slammed the trunk lid, told Amendolito not to worry, jumped into his car, and took off. Amendolito was left parked at a street corner in Long Island City, Queens, with $1.5 million in loose bills in his car.

He drove to the Barbizon, left his car at the curb, and struggled into the lobby with his three cases of cash. The front desk was in its normal midday uproar, arriving guests arguing with bellboys over bags as departing guests with other luggage fought to check out. Amendolito frantically tried to keep his new-found fortune close by him as bellhops sought to take the cases, and tourists pushed past hauling loads of matching luggage. The financier was beginning to panic. At length he staggered into his room with the $1.5 million in tow. But the task of actually counting so much money was too great. He settled for counting the bundles of notes, judged them to be approximately right. He had arranged for his Bahamian banker to come to New York and collect the cash. Albisser, assisted by his deputy manager, soon set off with $1.47 million—Amendolito had removed his commission—for the offices of the International Bank of Boston, the U.S. affiliate of BSI.

Albisser returned to the hotel room somewhat annoyed; the suitcases had contained thousands of dollars more than the $1.47 million Amendolito had estimated. But the transaction had gone through.

Between late June and September, Amendolito laundered some $3.4 million. Then he decided to make a trip to Switzerland and Sicily to meet with the principal figures in the money-moving enterprise: In Lugano, he again saw Salvatore Miniati, who said he was pleased with the operation so far, and introduced him to another "international

financier," Franco Della Torre. He suggested a way to make Amendolito's job even simpler. Professional Swiss money movers could be
made available. They would fly direct to New York on commercial
Swissair flights and take the cash away with them for a fee of 6%
or 6.5%. But Amendolito, getting 3% or 4% himself at this stage, was
unwilling to turn over his one-man gold mine to others who charged
more.

Amendolito drove with Miniati to Milan, then on to Sicily to meet
the principals, Oliviero Tognoli and Leonardo Greco, head of the immensely powerful Ciaculli Family, and second only to Luciano Leggio
in the hierarchy of the Corleonese faction then striving to dominate the
Sicilian Mafia. Leonardo Greco is also the brother of Pizza defendant
Salvatore Greco, the skinny, silver-haired, aristocratic-looking fellow
who occupies the back-row aisle seat, next to Castronovo.

Amendolito returned to New York. In October he received another
call from Miniati. $619,000 was ready to be collected from Castronovo
in New Jersey. This time the pickup was back at Frank's restaurant,
but the instructions were more elaborate than usual: $290,000 of the
total was to be passed to a group of Neapolitan furriers who were
visiting New York City. Amendolito drove with his bodyguard/chauf-
feur to the Roma Restaurant. The money was waiting: $619,000 in cash,
packed into a plastic bag and a cardboard box. As his driver headed
back across the Hudson, Amendolito checked the packaging. Castronovo had told him that the plastic bag contained two smaller packages, one holding $220,000, the other $100,000. Amendolito placed this
money in one side of a large, double-sided Samsonite suitcase. On the
other side he packed the contents of the cardboard box, some $299,000.

They drew up at the Southgate Hotel, near Pennsylvania Station, and
he left the driver to watch the car while he hurried with the suitcase
to the furriers' suite. Four men were waiting, playing poker. Amendolito quickly snapped open the cardboard-box side of the suitcase, and
dumped the contents on the table. Bundles of money spilled out, some
onto the floor. Amendolito took $9,000 from the pile, which left the
$290,000 he had been instructed to pass to the furriers. Back in his car,
he checked the money remaining in the suitcase, and to his horror
discovered it now contained $220,000, not $320,000. He checked the
empty bag and box. Could he possibly have mislaid $100,000?

The panicked financier bolted from the car and phoned Frank Castronovo in New Jersey. "No," Frank said, "you are wrong. I told you
the box contained $399,000 and the plastic bag contained $220,000."
Amendolito tore back up to the furriers' suite and found them grimly

counting his bundles. Had they discovered an extra $100,000 in the pile? Sorry, replied the furriers, and returned to their task.

Amendolito went to his office. He had lost $100,000 as a child on its way to the corner grocer might lose a dollar. He called Miniati and confessed. The industrialist Oliviero Tognoli called him back and said calmly that while Amendolito was responsible for the loss, he should not worry unduly, and should certainly continue to deal with Frank in Jersey.

Salvatore Amendolito could scarcely believe what happened next. He had just lost $100,000 of what he must by then have suspected was Mafia money. Yet within three weeks the same people gave him a further $2 million to handle. Between October and December, Amendolito laundered a total of $6.4 million through BSI Nassau and the British-owned Bank of Butterfield in the Bahamas. To smooth the way further, Peter Albisser introduced him to a Bahamian politician, Dod Maynards, who had a friend, Deighton Edwards, who badly needed a loan of, say, $230,000. Amendolito, recognizing a bagman when he met one, immediately contacted Tognoli, and in a short time Edwards had his money. When asked, months later, by Leonardo Greco, in Sicily, to explain the loan, Amendolito termed it "the cost of doing business in the Bahamas."

Hearing the story now, in Judge Leval's courtroom, it seems strange that these massive, intricate, and well-documented fiscal doings did not lead to a much earlier start of the Pizza case. Did no one report all this cash blowing in the wind? "The cost of doing business in the Bahamas" must have been well worth its price.

By November 1980 new problems had arisen. Tognoli accused Amendolito of hoarding the cash to benefit from the interest. Amendolito blamed the banks. They demanded the cash remain with them, in non-interest-bearing accounts, he said, long enough to make some profit from the enterprise.

In December Amendolito transferred to Bermuda approximately $3 million in cash, all of it from Castronovo. Early in 1981, Tognoli asked for a meeting in Montreal, at the Queen Elizabeth Hotel. Secrecy was imperative. Amendolito must mention this to no one, especially not to Frank. The financier was stunned therefore to see Frank Castronovo at the airport, standing in line to board the same Montreal flight he was on.

At the hotel Amendolito saw other interesting visitors, among them Oliviero Tognoli and Adriano Corti, another well-known Italian money launderer. Giuseppe Ganci was also there. But Amendolito still did not get to meet the principals. Instead, he was told rather sternly that they wanted the money currently resting in the islands transferred immediately to Credit Suisse. Tognoli was now unwilling to write off either the "loan" to Edwards or the missing $100,000 from the furriers' exchange. Even if he had done so, Amendolito was still in trouble. The money Tognoli now wanted transferred to Credit Suisse was short $140,000. Amendolito required a face-to-face meeting, he said, to discuss the $470,000 he now owed the principals.

On May 15, 1981, Amendolito flew to Sicily. A driver picked him up at his Palermo hotel and took him on a circuitous route round and round the sinister back streets of the city. At one point he pulled to a halt and turned Amendolito over to a second driver, who then drove him to a rendezvous with a third driver. The third car headed out into the Sicilian countryside, and finally pulled up in front of an abandoned villa. Just then, Oliviero Tognoli pulled up and led the financier inside.

If the jury finds any of this hard to believe, they give no sign. They sit calmly listening to these carefully choreographed reminiscences of a life in big-time crime by a man who says he owed the Mafia $470,000; that he was driven round in circles and found himself alone in an old mansion in the Sicilian mountains, all in a tone of voice that suggests he had been attending a board meeting of a Fortune 500 company. Soon after the two men entered the abandoned house, they were joined by Leonardo Greco and another elderly man. Greco said Amendolito should make every attempt to call in the Edwards loan, but he was willing to write off the loss of the furriers' $100,000. This left Amendolito in the position of owing the principals $370,000, on which note the meeting broke up.

Thus ended Amendolito's activities on behalf of Tognoli and the "principals." Within weeks the new man, Franco Della Torre, had moved into a suite in the Waldorf-Astoria Hotel in New York City. Soon a steady stream of visitors was arriving lugging bulging suitcases of cash.

Amendolito struggled on with various financial maneuvers until July 1983, when he found himself in New Orleans, working on a deal to persuade a group of Arab oil sheiks to lend $50 million or $100 million to the government of Costa Rica. One morning the failing financier was awakened in his hotel room by the FBI, arrested for illegal money laundering, and flung into a New Orleans jail. Within days he had agreed to cooperate with his captors and inform on his prior associates. He was shipped back to a quiet motel room in New Rochelle, New

York, which put him closer to the center of the Pizza investigation shaping up at the FBI office in Manhattan.

By November Amendolito was sufficiently certain of his value to his new employers to draft a new agreement that changed his status from undercover informant to paid undercover agent. His new fee: $3,000 per month, plus expenses. By that time, the United States government had already paid him some $70,000 in wages, plus expense money.

. . . TUESDAY, FEBRUARY 25, 1986.
THE COURTROOM. Judge Leval takes a moment to say a bit more to the jury on a subtle but important matter: Government Exhibit #4700, the huge money chart. Back on February 18, the day he had admitted the chart into evidence, he had told them, "This is an exhibit that falls into a somewhat unusual category. . . . It is not really evidence in itself. What it is is a summarization of the witness's testimony.

"The witness has testified before you that putting together as to certain items his memory; his recollection of events according to his testimony; notes that he wrote in Exhibit #4100, which he identifies as his notebook, or memorandum, of these matters; bank records of which he received copies, and other bank records that have been received in evidence: Putting together all those things, a chart has been prepared which is a kind of summary, according to the witness, of the information that he says can be gathered from these sources."

Could anyone but a federal judge have composed in his head and then ad-libbed a sentence of this stunning complexity? Could anyone hearing it, but a federal judge, have understood it?

Nodding then to Louis Freeh, he had ordered, "All right. You may proceed."

But perhaps it was not entirely all right. The chart had been officially received into evidence, but five court days later, Judge Leval is again taking time to remind them that "received in evidence" does not mean the same thing as "is evidence," and in fact this looming chart, big enough in a storm to roof over the entire twenty-four-person jury, is *not* evidence.

"The chart is nothing more than a summary offered by the government. . . . Whether you accept or reject what is depicted on the chart is up to you."

What does this really mean? The point is hard to grasp and hold, as mercurial as Amendolito's silver hair. Leval's instruction seems to give the jury total freedom to do something it is de facto unable to do: comprehend the chart, then decide which parts, if any, to accept, which to reject. It would be as easy to chew up the chart and swallow it as to act upon this "freedom" they have been granted.

Now a nice vignette. Amendolito is at JFK, en route to Bermuda on a commercial flight, when he is stopped by a female security guard who notes that the large, soft suitcase he carries seems to be full of paper. She demands he open it, sees the wads of dough, and calls the cops, who say one must fill out currency forms in order to leave the country with so large a cargo of cash. What forms? Amendolito claims he needs the cash only for his Bermuda fish biz, but eventually agrees to fill out the forms, declares $220,000, though the actual amount is $400,000, and by that time has missed his plane and jauntily walks out unimpeded. A few days later, he portages the mother lode to Bermuda on another commercial flight. But this time he has arranged that an armored car, rather than a taxi, convey him from the airport to the bank.

. . . WEDNESDAY, FEBRUARY 26, 1986.
THE COURTROOM. Louis Freeh now focuses on a Brooklyn phone number listed in Amendolito's 1980 address book as "Vito Parrucchiere" (wigmaker, or hairdresser). It is the number of the beauty salon owned by Sal Catalano's brother Vito. It also turns out to be the same phone number as the one written on the scrap of paper recovered from Amendolito's Rolodex, the scrap he was given in the Queens doorway by a man who called himself Sal, the scrap that bears the names "Vito" and "Sal." With this dramatic and devastating bit of evidence, Freeh ends his direct examination.

Castronovo's lawyer, Ken Kaplan, is first to cross-examine, and at once sets out to nail the witness as the crooked financier he surely is. Amendolito was convicted of passing bad checks in Italy in 1968 and was also convicted of fraud. In 1981 he was arrested in New York for passing a bad $4,000 check. He admits with a silvery smile that he has passed in excess of 100 bad checks.

Kaplan's cross-examination worms along. Amendolito has been struck by amnesia; he cannot remember whom he was dealing with in Canada, or in Zurich. Yes, he did some money brokering in Costa Rica, for Arab clients, and he acknowledges a "London connection."

The financier is proving a slippery witness. Kaplan struggles to pin him down. Didn't he say that at Christmas 1980 he counted money in liquor boxes in his apartment? No, he said that, while he was driving a hatch-back convertible through Manhattan, other people were counting bundles of money in three liquor boxes in the back seat.

The jurors have begun laughing at the scene. They are in high spirits as Leval declares the week's proceedings at an end.

. . . TUESDAY, MARCH 4, 1986.

THE COURTROOM.　No trial today. A bizarre dispute has broken out backstage. An alternate juror appears to have gone bonkers, fighting, sobbing, making accusations, breaking windows. Leval is now interviewing the woman. About 11:00 A.M. he appears and reports, "Apparently a family situation . . . husband suffering stress as result of Vietnam service . . . admitted to military hospital . . ."

It happened in the car-pool limousine. The juror became so convinced the driver was taking a wrong route that she got out of the car and slammed the door hard enough to break a window, a marshal said. Over the past two days, she has been involved in an escalating series of fights, with one other juror in particular; racial epithets have been hurled. But the juror wants to stay, downplays the marshal's story, and denies that yesterday she tried to walk out. The marshal reports, however, that she grabbed her coat and bag, yelled, "I'm going to fucking leave! *You* explain it to the judge," and marched off.

What do the lawyers think Leval should do? "I asked her if she found this trial a strain," Leval reports. "She said no. She found it relaxing." The lawyers manage to remain poker-faced.

The loss of this woman would be serious to the defense. Marvin Segal says it could well be only a temporary aberration. "A lot is colored by what the marshal has said, and my experience is that marshals sometimes overstate. This seems less a fight with other jurors than something in the marshal's mind. I'd suggest, keep going; then, if this continues, we look again."

Fisher is "in disagreement with Mr. Segal. The marshal's report seems persuasive to me. Racial epithets cannot be countenanced."

Leval has more. "Let me add that she said a racial remark in the car had been made to her."

"We represent an ethnic group, many of us here," says Ruggiero. "It would be good if the jury saw swift, clear action by us."

Leval says the outburst was "triggered by some dispute over the car route," but that it indicated "great hostility."

The discussion has begun to sound like a conference call among psychiatrists. Young Joe Calluori stops it. "This has been a lengthy proceeding. If she feels she can continue, can sit here and listen to evidence, that's the most important thing."

"I think we should keep her on," Genay Leitman says firmly. But Leval completely ignores her, and rules that the trial will continue with further Amendolito cross-examination. He will decide about the juror overnight.

The next morning the jury box has an empty chair. Leval has exercised his prerogative. A lengthy parade of supporting witnesses begins. A few interesting facts emerge, among them that $1.45 million in mostly $100 bills takes three and a half hours to count. But for the next few weeks the jurors mostly snooze, and the lawyers mostly coast.

Then tragedy strikes. Beloved Judge Henry T. Friendly, of the Second Circuit, has been despondent since the death of his wife a year earlier. On the morning of March 11, the seventy-nine-year-old judge throws himself out of the window of his Park Avenue apartment. When word reaches Leval, he announces the suicide to the courtroom in a choked voice, and adjourns the trial. Leval's first job after Harvard Law School was clerking for Judge Friendly, who has been his idol since. Later Leval will memorialize his mentor: "As long as scholars, lawyers and judges go on citing Hand, Brandeis and Cardozo, so also will they cite Friendly." In all areas of the law he dealt with from the federal bench, "Henry T. Friendly's opinions served as the signposts, maps and direction markers. He had made himself the master and guide for almost every territory. In some areas it is difficult to write an opinion without reference to his decisions."

Michael Kennedy caucuses with no one, trusts no one, except his wife. That same night he tells her, "The crazy juror, it's good she's gone. I know the others disagree. But we want discord on that jury, random discord, and she polarized it. She coagulated the hate. We now have space for divisiveness to proceed."

Kennedy's quiet strategy has secretly shifted entirely. He believes he can strike a very attractive deal for the lesser members of the Badalamenti group. This would leave him free to concentrate on the Old Man's defense. As lead counsel, he has already begun very private meetings with Louis Freeh to work out the best possible deals, not only for the Badalamenti family, but perhaps for others as well. In such a big case, it is good strategy to get as many defendants to plead as possible. In theory this makes juries less apt to do what they so often do in complex, multidefendant cases: focus on one or two "heavies," throw the book at them, and let the little fish go. Leval too has been quietly urging Kennedy to start dealing. This is the best way to break up the administrative logjam the case is causing.

Segal is desperate to get out. Although Kennedy would never say so, he too is probably desperate, and so are the other men who practice alone. No fee short of Fisher's $500,000 is sufficient to sustain a solo practitioner in a case of this length. A very long case does more than prevent a lawyer from courting future work. If it goes on long enough, a feeling gets around that the lawyer is permanently out of action, and referrals from other lawyers tend to dry up. The only lawyers who do not want out are the CJA lawyers, characterized by some of the non-CJA lawyers as "happily snuffling at the public trough."

The timing is ripe for another reason. Inevitably, the character of this trial is about to change radically. "The jurors see Martin as a ferocious prosecutor," Kennedy points out. But sooner or later the prosecution will cease, the defense will begin, and jurors will see something quite different. What they will begin to see, Kennedy believes, "is that this whole system is ass-deep in hypocrisy."

Michael Kennedy is never one to mince words, not even out of the courtroom. "That fundamental hypocrisy is the basis of our adversary system," he says in his careful, perfect diction. "And no system is better. But it is as funda-mentally flawed as—although no more flawed than—the human condition generally."

5. *The Great Gobi Desert*

No announcement is made. Dick Martin does not stand up and read a stipulation. Joe the clerk does not alter his ritual cry. But in the spring, the Pizza caravan slowly wanders out of the lush forest of superinformers and dashing undercover agents into a legal wilderness, a waterless, treeless, featureless expanse of dry fact which becomes known in defense circles as the Great Gobi Desert.

It is an endless sandscape of official FBI surveillance logs and incomprehensible telephone conversations. The desert silence is marked by the mumblings of a hundred Sicilians speaking an arcane language where nuance is all. One syllable can suggest a joke or a death threat, depending on inflection. But nuance is lost in the Gobi, for every word has been flattened and sanitized by the fact of its translation. Read aloud, in English, the vivid Sicilian patois sounds like the computerized voice in a new sports car announcing a flat tire. As for content, the messages are like snippets from some Alzheimer's soap opera wherein the daytime lovers forget the last word of each punch line but deliver the sentiment anyway. "Is Pinuzzo . . . ah . . . can come . . . with the fresh flowers . . . the ones that bloomed just . . . good-bye, many beautiful things."

To cross the dry Gobi will require 115 court days and the testimony of hundreds of witnesses, most of whom are government agents, and all of whom are subject to cross-examination by any defense lawyer so inclined. Occasionally, and then—as time wears on—more frequently, exhausted defense lawyers will waive their right to cross-examine. These waivers will be the only winds to blow across the burning Gobi sands.

Some of the drudgery is unavoidable. The difficult, lengthy, formal procedure for putting materials into evidence is tedious but essential to assure the integrity of the evidence. When the evidence consists of tapes, logs, and wiretaps, so readily tampered with, the rules get stricter still. The volume of evidence amassed for Pizza was colossal. The 55,000 conversations taped over five years by teams of agents in Italy, the United States, Brazil, Switzerland, Sicily, Mexico, and perhaps elsewhere were winnowed down to a mere 900, translated into English, and bound into nine-volume sets. In addition, the evidence included seventy-seven volumes of computer printouts of U.S., Sicilian, Swiss, and Brazilian telephone-toll records and subscriber records, all backed up by an equal amount of pen-register tape. (A pen register is a device attached to a phone line, without the subscriber's knowledge, that keeps a record of every number dialed.)

On top of all that, there were voluminous bank records; motor-vehicle records from Albany to Palermo; drug-analysis records, fire-arms records, and God knows what else, all of which the government was compelled by law to make available to the defense. Accordingly, the government provided a huge room in the Federal Building, across Foley Square from the courthouse, which contained wall-to-wall, floor-to-ceiling materials on the case. There was *so much* material, the lawyers complained, it was difficult to find anything. There was no librarian, and no facilities for copying documents. Also, the rules stipulated that an agent must be present at all times, and lawyers were often told that all agents were busy. Too often, "the good stuff" was not there. The prosecution already had withdrawn it from the "evidence library" in order to "work on it." Further, with such an oceanic amount of evidence "available," it was almost impossible to know which evidence was relevant.

Colossal too were the rampant opportunities for error, and perhaps for subtle improvement by the government of its position. Colossal was the determination of the defense lawyers not to let the government get away with anything. Defense zeal in some cases was enhanced by the absolute necessity to dirty up or at least raise doubts, or if not doubts, then confusions, about the government's evidence; no other defense was available.

These factors combined to transform the midsection of the Pizza trial into a benumbing expanse of absolutely bewildering testimony. Intermingled with the phone calls was a procession of live agents. Without them, it might well have seemed as if AT&T, rather than the FBI, had rounded up what the government called the world's most dangerous drug cartel.

The Great Gobi Desert broke the backs of spring and fall and wiped out a complete summer. Between the months of March and October it featured 194 witnesses making some 346 separate appearances. The 152 who made dual or multiple appearances were all federal agents, men who had spent nights outside Sal Mazzurco's big house in Baldwin, Long Island, and days sitting down the street from Joe Ganci's garage; men who had rotated, and reported; men who had frozen on the Southern State Parkway, or Queens Boulevard, watching three Zips hovering over a public phone that was the hottest wired item from Florida to Maine. Now it was time for the agents to be heard.

Behind it all was a story of men making phone calls and meeting and exchanging packages, and of calls leading to other calls, which led to new encounters with new Sicilians who had other onions sprouting or had 100% acrylic shirts that cost more than 80% acrylic.

The government lawyers of course understood it all. Indeed, they at times deliberately increased the confusion, stirred up sandstorms by presenting evidence out of sequence, separating facts that belonged together, and insisting upon putting in seemingly irrelevant evidence now, knowing that its significance would not become apparent for months.

Leval understood very nearly all, and when he didn't, he stopped the trial, recessed the jury, and demanded a government proffer—a dry run of testimony to come. Then he ruled on the admissibility of the evidence: Was it relevant? Was it fair or prejudicial? Was it inclined to be inflammatory? And so on.

The defense lawyers understood much but not all. They read the voluminous materials the government was compelled to provide. But they protested continually that the prosecution was holding back or misrepresenting vital bits. Some of their complaint was mere posturing; some was probably correct.

In any trial, both sides play dangerous games. All the time the boring witnesses were parading past the jury, the dangerous games that lawyers play were going on backstage. In a trial of this size and nature and political sensitivity, the danger level may have been a bit higher than usual. But the games are essentially the same. They are trial lawyers' games, the long-range strategies and short-term tactics of courtroom combat. More than the whopping fees, more even than the headlines and TV spotlights that feed the trial lawyer's ravenous ego, it is the thrill and fun and danger of playing these games that keep trial lawyers doing what they do. The hazards of the profession are well known: cynicism, alcoholism, greed, and the withering of personal and family life. The burnout rate is high. But like the athlete, the gambler, the flyer, the artist—the trial lawyer does what he does because he finds therein a high he cannot match elsewhere.

How much of the evidence the jury understood will never be known. Only their verdict will be public. Although many studies have been made of juries in action, the mystery of how juries reach their verdicts remains a dismal swamp of mythology and mystique within the swept and tidy premises of the law. The mystique universally proclaimed by lawyers and judges is that the jury almost always arrives at the correct verdict. Even if they do not understand, cannot understand, the evidence; even if they are inattentive, or ignorant, or lazy, or inept, they still almost always come to the correct conclusion. This belief, piously proclaimed, religiously clung to, underlies the oft-repeated assertion that the jury system under Anglo-Saxon law is the best means devisable by man for arriving at truth and justice. No one has come up with a better system, lawyers say, and they are right. No one has.

Most likely it will never be known what the jurors made of the Gobi Desert evidence. Three things, however, can be stated for certain: Some jurors—like some attorneys, and even, though very rarely, the judge— slept or appeared asleep through some of the Gobi. Some jurors slept through most of it. And not a single juror or alternate stayed awake through all of it.

. . . FRIDAY, MARCH 14, 1986. CHAMBERS OF JUDGE LEVAL. After the close of court on the last day of the week of Judge Friendly's death, Pierre Leval convenes a private, off-the-record meeting of all Pizza attorneys, prosecution and defense. Ways simply must be found to break the legal gridlock and move the case along faster. All the Southern District judges are concerned, he tells them, not just himself; so too is the appellate court. It is desirable that negotiations begin immediately to encourage as many defendants as possible to change their pleas; to plead guilty to reduced charges in return for lighter sentences, and certain considerations on forfeiture of property.

Leval stresses his own liberal sentencing philosophy: The heaviest sentence he has ever handed out was fifteen years, in a major drug-conspiracy case. Hence, some defense lawyers conclude, fifteen years is the heaviest sentence even being suggested for this case. If that is true, probation would not be out of the question for the lesser defendants.

These thoughts are of course unspoken. Aloud the defense lawyers take the position: It is not our policy to plead for deals; if the government wants deals, let them make us an offer. The prosecution's response is equally starchy: It is not our policy to make offers; if they want deals, let them come to us. Judge Leval encourages both sides to start talking, and says he will expect to hear something within thirty days.

Also unspoken is a statistic well known to all lawyers, prosecutors, judges, and others who ply their trade in the federal courts: In the Southern District of New York, the government has a conviction rate approaching 90%.

Informal caucusing begins at once, and continues in corridors, elevators, men's rooms, barrooms, and late-night phone calls throughout the month. Various defense lawyers hear privately from various members of the prosecution. Proposition and innuendo swirl; the backstage maneuvering for advantageous deal-making is soon in high gear. Says one participant, "Here's the bottom line. Some lawyers are CJA. They don't want it to end. Some lawyers are in a rut; they like to have a place to go every day. Some lawyers are having a ball just being part of this juggernaut. The result of all this is, the clients' best interests are not coming forth."

The prosecutors privately acknowledge that they too have been terribly unhappy with the way the trial is going. The glacial pace has made Martin and Freeh, in particular, tense, tired, keyed up, edgy, and frustrated because they feel unable to do their best. They worry that the jury will grow bored, fidgety, and weary, and will forget the beginnings of the story long before the end comes. They fret that four or five months' work has produced only 9,000 pages of transcript. "We should have 20,000," they say. "Pierre isn't moving it along. He should know better. He's a former prosecutor himself."

The defense in its free time talks about little else than deals. The New York and New Jersey lawyers are aware by now that Kennedy has been meeting with Freeh, and they are mulling over an alternative strategy: Instead of a package deal for the Badalamenti group, what would happen if one or more of the "big guys"—the more obviously guilty— could be persuaded to plead? With these heavyweights gone, the jury would be inclined toward leniency for the *schnooks.* Also the *schnooks*—men like Trupiano, Vitale, Palazzolo, perhaps DeVardo— are suffering great economic and emotional hardship, are living on salami and cheese in fleabag hotels away from their families, and by now might prefer probation, or even a brief jail sentence, to six months' more time in Leval's courtroom.

In truth, many defense lawyers are not sure what their clients want. They complain that their clients won't talk to them, probably don't trust them, and certainly don't confide in them.

Michael Kennedy has a different problem. Gaetano Badalamenti has made it clear to him from the beginning that he himself would not consider, would not even discuss, a deal. *Mai!* He sees this as both a matter of principle—no Man of Honor would plea-bargain with his captors—and sheer pragmatism. Whatever the outcome of this case, he faces even more serious charges in the so-called maxi-trial in Palermo. Those extraordinary proceedings, taking place daily in a newly built, concrete underground bunker, represent Italy's all-out, all-time assault on the Mafia. For security reasons, the 466 defendants appear together in court behind ceiling-high steel bars. Their grotesque cages are connected by underground tunnels directly to the cells where the men live between court appearances. On TV, the mob of howling, gesticulating men are like lions waiting to get into the arena. Gaetano Badalamenti is in no particular hurry to join them.

Furthermore, in Italy there is no such thing as a deal, or plea-bargaining. The very notion of reaching a compromise with the prosecution is regarded as a deep dishonor. Since this is Badalamenti's code and background, Kennedy anticipates considerable difficulty in convincing his client to urge any of his family members to make deals with the U.S. government.

As for the fourteen non-Badalamenti defendants, the common wisdom in multidefendant cases is: If some plead guilty, the jury is apt to go easier on the remainder. But who should plead, and to what? Not surprisingly, mistrust is rampant. When Fisher buttonholes Fogelnest and urges him to plead, for example, the lesser lawyer immediately asks himself: *Why my guy? Ivan may have a hidden agenda. He usually does.*

My guy's name is Sal. His guy's name is Sal, too. Maybe if I'm out, he figures he can dump on me. Fogelnest knows that certain incriminating notes have "Sal" written on them—the one in Amendolito's Rolodex, for example. Perhaps, with Sal Salamone out, Fisher can see a way of convincing some jurors that the government has switched Sals on them. Similar thoughts may be occurring to lawyers Benfante, Schechter, and Bronson, who represent Sal Mazzurco, Sal Lamberti, and Sal Greco.

"The little guys can only benefit if the big guys plead," Lewis urges. One strategy would be to negotiate individual pleas for the big guys first. But some little-guy lawyers want to stay in; proximity to the big guys could increase their chances of drawing lighter sentences. Big-guy lawyers think differently. Says one, "What I think is: We gotta go en masse to the prosecution and say: We're talkin' package. You give me my deal, and if you make it sweet enough, I'll bring seven guys with me."

The weekend after Leval's meeting, U.S. Attorney Giuliani appears on television to talk about New York City's latest corruption scandal. He is beautifully dressed for TV in a beige suit of subtle plaid, blending haberdashery. The masklike face barely moves, but the eyes glitter with vitality. The TV interviewer is interested in the deal-making process. Will the latest politician to be arrested be offered a chance to deal?

Persons accused of corruption can make the best deal if they "decide to cooperate before we catch them," says the famed prosecutor, lisping slightly. "Next best is to cooperate before we indict them." Third best is a decision to cooperate before we convict them. Lowest level, worst deal, is not to decide to cooperate until *after* we convict them.

In the courthouse, silent messages are circulating in several directions. Kennedy sends a message to Leval: Hurry up the pace of this trial, or you damage your chances of getting into the Second Circuit. Martin sends word to Kennedy that he wants to discuss a bench trial for all members of the Badalamenti group. A bench trial, without a jury, would greatly speed things up. Much of the evidence could be stipulated to. Leval, knowing the issues, the case, the law, would move things along much faster.

"A bench trial would go like lightning," Kennedy agrees. But what would the jury make of it if several defendants suddenly disappeared? As for the holdouts, Badalamenti and his son and nephew: "They don't want it, because when this ends, they fold up their tents and costumes and move on to Palermo. So they figure—why hurry?"

Other lawyers are discussing the possibility of a bench trial for everybody. Marvin Segal is strongly opposed. "We cannot dismiss the jury.

This case uniquely has to have a jury," he says, because it will never be fairly decided by Leval. "This judge has already made up his mind. That's partly why he is being very careful not to make mistakes. Why he's prescreening witnesses. Because he's watching his ass."

... TUESDAY, MARCH 18, 1985.

THE COURTROOM.   A new money-laundering chart has appeared, and the day's argument begins with the defense objecting to a box at the top which reads, "Castronovo/Ganci/O. Catalano/Tognoli/Cavalleri/Corti channel." Kaplan argues that the government has, not for the first time, linked names in a box that it has been unable to link on the chart itself. The box is argument as well as summary, he says, and it is "inflammatory." Leval agrees. Freeh removes the box.

Mario Malerba, supremely courteous as always, requests that Leval remind the jury at the time of his charge that the chart is not itself evidence, only a summary. Leval, equally courteous, asks only that "Mr. Malerba be sure and remind me."

"Certainly," says Malerba, and gives Catalano a thumbs-up sign.

One of the names in the banished box is Antonio Cavalleri, a friendly Swiss banker from Breganzona, in the Italian Alps. Through his big-shot-banker friend Sergio Dafond, at the huge financial institution Credit Suisse, Cavalleri opened a Credit Suisse account called "Traex," and used it to receive funds wired from New York to his small bank in Breganzona. When a new laundryman was needed, Amendolito and his helpers having outlived their usefulness, it was Cavalleri who recruited a Swissair employee, telling him that certain Swiss businessmen wanted to take their profits home in cash, no questions asked. The man was happy to oblige.

One of the cash pickup points for the Swissair man was a Brooklyn parking lot. There the FBI watched him receive a Samsonite suitcase from a man driving a red Chevy Blazer truck with Pennsylvania plates. This man turned out to be Filippo Salamone, a brother of front-row defendant Sal. Together the brothers Salamone owned two pizzerias in the small town of Bloomsburg, Pennsylvania: Two Guys from Italy and Sal's Place.

The next witnesses are not actually present in court. They are a couple of low-level *spalloni* who happened to be holed up in Manhattan's elegant Plaza Hotel in August 1982. Their phone chat was recorded by the FBI, and has since been typed out in notebooks. Prosecutor Martin wheels over to the jury box a metal evidence trolley, like a hospital instruments cart, and from it hands each juror a heavy, two-and-one-half-inch-thick black loose-leaf binder. "Please turn to Conversation 2," he says. The jurors oblige. They do not know that these volumes contain 900 extremely fragmentary, mostly incomprehensible Sicilian-vernacular conversations translated into English, and that they are fated to hear nearly every word.

The defense has stipulated that these voices are indeed the voices of the Plaza *spalloni.* Now Martin himself reads one voice, and an agent in the witness box reads the other. The jurors follow along, and so do the defense lawyers and the judge, and the turning of so many pages in unison is like the rustle of pigeons. Undisturbed, Baldo Amato sleeps soundly, his head tilted backward and resting on the foot-high stack of transcript on Mike Querques's desk behind him, as if reclining on a Japanese wood pillow.

... TUESDAY, APRIL 1, 1986.

THE COURTROOM. Today Anna Rosario Kennedy is nine months old, and her parents have decided it's time for her day in court. Dressed in her Easter frock and Paris bonnet, she is in the corridor, on her mother's lap, dimpled and adorable, waiting for the next jury recess. "I'm willing to take cheap shots, but not with my baby," says Eleanore.

As soon as the jury leaves, Kennedy carries his daughter up to the bench. Judge Leval comes down to coo and gurgle with the infant. He had been urging the Kennedys to bring her in ever since he heard about her adoption last November. Martin, Freeh, and Stewart all come over to admire the child. "It was a very, very special moment," Eleanore said later. "Michael hoped she would give the judge her raspberry. But she was a perfect lady. And Leval was genuinely, genuinely charmed by her. . . . Oh, if only he was a law professor! Or on the Court of Appeals!"

Sandy Fox, the tough but motherly chief marshal, has given her permission for Badalamenti to walk to the rear of the courtroom, where Kennedy now hands him the baby. He smiles and tells the Kennedys, through a translator, that he will remember this day for the rest of his life. "You can get anything in jail: drugs, liquor, food. Anything but two things: flowers, and a baby."

The baby leaves, the jury returns, and the prosecutors push two trolleys into the courtroom, one heaped with tapes, the other with transcriptions. The witness is a DEA agent-translator who gives the provenance of the tapes. Staring at the two trolleys, the jury looks stunned. Smote.

Lena Pecosi, the chic Roman woman who translates for the Badalamenti group, has worked for years with Sicilian suspects as an official court interpreter, and she has become something like a legal paramedic. She may lack a formal law degree, but she has had plenty of hands-on experience, in courtrooms and in MCC, interpreting the mysterious Sicilian speech patterns and attitudes. "It's not that they don't exactly know what they're saying," she explains. "It's that they don't exactly say what they know."

Today Lena spreads the word that members of the Badalamenti group are very negative on pleas. "It always happens like this with Sicilians." If they are *found* guilty, that's one thing; they can blame the lawyers, blame the judge, blame the jury. But if they are asked to *plead* guilty, and they are Men of Honor, "Well, they feel honor goes down the drain."

Lunchtime. The government has continued quietly reaching out for pleas. Last night an approach was made to Fogelnest, who, with his poor, spindly, jailbird client Salamone, certainly represents the soft underbelly of this case. Now he buttonholes Kennedy in the cafeteria. "They're talking plea with me. What do I do? Ivan and Mario are dogging me to take it." But that might make him look chicken. "I don't want to be the first guy to plead out. I'm a new kid in New York."

"If you think you've got a winner, that would be a totally different situation." Kennedy's meaning is clear.

But Fogelnest keeps telling himself: Stay in, and you can probably get your guy off. "If there's an ounce of mercy on that jury, I can explain away the money," he says, and then he reminds Kennedy of a speech he once heard the older man give to a Washington lawyers' group. Most trial lawyers spend most of their time not trying cases but negotiating pleas. Eighty or 90% of all cases are settled that way. Were they not, the already overloaded courts would collapse utterly. But Kennedy had exhorted his listeners not always to take the easy way out. "*Try* it—you'll like it!" had been his theme. Fogelnest never forgot.

Kennedy tells Fogelnest now, "Either take 'em down the line all the way, or see *what else* you can find out they have on him. Use the plea discussions to your own advantage. Try to penetrate the counsels of the government." His advice reflects his overarching conviction that, for the system to work, the government must always be held to higher standards than any defendant, without exception.

"Judge is on the bench!"

Next witness is a two-dollar-an-hour pizzeria waitress. In midsummer 1982 her boss, Sal Salamone, asked her for a favor. He needed some money changed, small denominations into large. He took the young woman into the kitchen, removed $10,000 from a suitcase packed with money, and placed it in a white plastic bag. Several other employees were present, and the alert waitress noticed that five of them also had white bags. Sal told them to visit different tellers at three or four banks in the Bloomsburg area, and to change no more than $2,000 or $3,000 each time. The waitress eventually managed to change $30,000. In the restaurant, she watched Salamone pack the hundreds and fifties into the Samsonite suitcase.

Across the Atlantic, in Lugano, the receivers of the Samsonites were busy dividing up the fortune. Key figures in the distribution were two truly terrible Turks: a certain Paul Waridel and an even more shadowy figure, Yasar Musullulu. Both were men of "good family." Waridel's brother is director of Swiss Social Security. Neither man considers himself a drug dealer. Each describes himself rather grandly as an importer of morphine base.

Waridel's evidence is especially important, key to establishing the existence of the conspiracy. He *is* the Pizza Connection. He provides the vital link between the Middle East shippers of morphine base and the Sicilian exporters of refined *heroina*. But the jury will hear his knotty, spotty, incredible story only by fragmented deposition; his Swiss lawyers have been able to protect their client from extradition to the United States.

. . . PAUL WARIDEL

had lived in Switzerland since 1954. He owned Swiss computer companies, and was in the real estate business and used-boat business in Spain, Mexico, and elsewhere. Waridel is fluent in Turkish, Greek, French, English, German, Italian, and Spanish.

In 1972, in Izmir, Turkey, Waridel got to know another Swiss-based

Turkish businessman, Yasar Musullulu, also known as Avni Karadur-
mus, also known as Attila Oksuz. Both men were dealers in, or posing
as dealers in, archaeological artifacts.

In late 1976, in Zurich, the terrible Turks ran into one another again
in a restaurant that featured Turkish home cooking. This time Musullulu told Waridel he was a drug dealer. He obtained large quantities of
morphine base from corrupt Bulgarian border officials who confiscated
the contraband as it was being smuggled to Europe for refinement from
the poppy fields of Afghanistan. Originally Musullulu had been hired
by Bulgarian officials, he said, to resell the captured narcotics on commission. And of course he dealt a bit on his own. Waridel understood.
He had certain foggy connections with Greek authorities.

Not long after, Waridel moved to Rome, and there met a man eager
to buy heroin. Lo and behold, Musullulu soon turned up in the Eternal
City. Waridel set up the deal. His first venture into the world of drugs
proved a disaster, at least in the short term. The Italian police had been
tipped off, most likely by Musullulu, and Waridel spent the next three
years in Rome's Regina Coeli Prison, where he got to know several
important Mafia leaders and some big-time heroin dealers.

When he got out of prison, in 1980, Waridel made friends with a close
associate of Tomasso Buscetta, one Nuncio LaMattina, a major Mafia
tobacco smuggler who recently had switched from cigarettes to morphine base. One of his major suppliers was Musullulu, and they were
embroiled in a dispute over some $11 million, which Musullulu claimed
he was owed. LaMattina hired Waridel to negotiate for him. When he
failed to reduce the debt, LaMattina figured Waridel had sold him out
and instead tied up with his brother Turk. Waridel, aware of LaMattina's powerful Mafia rank, figured it was a good idea to leave Italy as
soon as possible and moved back to Zurich. It was 1981.

The following year, in a Turkish nightclub, he again ran into Musullulu, who asked him to act as a translator in his dealings with a group
of Sicilians. One of them turned out to be the son of LaMattina, who
was again buying morphine base from Musullulu, having negotiated the
Mafia's $11-million debt down to $1.5 million. Musullulu complained to
the Mafia that he still had not been paid. LaMattina's excuse was that
his courier had been robbed while en route to Switzerland with the
money. The Mafia did not believe LaMattina, and he was murdered.

Waridel now became the courier between the Sicilians and Musullulu. He sat in on huge cash-counting sessions in Credit Suisse and other
Swiss banks. He drove suitcases containing millions of dollars, and he
met a new set of Mafia leaders, including Leonardo Greco and Franco

Della Torre, Vito Roberto Palazzolo, and Antonio Rotolo, the man who had replaced LaMattina.

Waridel learned that Musullulu operated a fleet of tramp steamers, which loaded morphine base in Lebanon, made their way across the Mediterranean, and rendezvoused with fast Mafia speedboats off the coast of Sicily. If Musullulu was threatened with discovery, his practice was to scuttle his ship and all aboard.

Musullulu had no monopoly on the morphine trade in the Mediterranean. A rival smuggler was Giuseppe Ferrara, whom Waridel also knew from prison. Then Waridel discovered that Musullulu had sold a steamer to his pal Ferrara, received $466,000 in advance, and refused to turn over the ship. The next time Waridel ran into Musullulu, in Bulgaria, he stole all three of his passports, called him a "cockroach," poured gasoline over him, and set him on fire.

Again it was time to find new friends. Waridel sought out the representative in Switzerland of the United States Drug Enforcement Administration and offered to cooperate. It was 1985.

Musullulu survived his burns, and was reported to have escaped Bulgaria with another $6 million in Mafia money. But Waridel understandably refused to leave Switzerland—which is how, the summer before Pizza went to trial, lawyers Fisher, Bronson, Lombardino, Burke, Benfante, Moriarty, and Kaplan, along with U.S. attorneys Martin and Freeh and an American judge, Edmund Palmieri, found themselves spending a sunshiny week in a five-star lakeside hotel in the resort city of Lugano, Switzerland, at American taxpayer expense.

. . . **KENNETH KAPLAN,** thirty-nine, is savvy, lean, frustrated, talkative, and easy with himself as a capable attorney. One of the original Pizza lawyers, he represents the New Jersey restaurant owner Frank Castronovo, and is the man most knowledgeable about the money-laundering phase of the case. He maintains that the Pizza prosecutors and jurors are getting on well because the jury has begun to suffer from the Stockholm Syndrome, a state of psychological dependency on one's guards or captors, named for a famous Swedish bank robbery during which bank employees held hostage in the vault swiftly fell in love with their captors.

Kaplan was chief defense strategist during the Swiss depositions.

"The purpose of the expedition to Lugano was to cross-examine witnesses who could not be extradited to the U.S.," in particular, the Italian industrialist Tognoli, the Turk Waridel, and Amendolito's successor, Franco Della Torre. The proceedings were conducted in Italian, under Swiss law, in a courtroom in Bellinzona, capital of Ticino canton, where Lugano is located. The American judge, Edmund Palmieri, seventy-eight, had been appointed by the Southern District as a special magistrate. Swiss magistrates presided, and punishing time constraints were imposed. Two hours for the United States, two hours for defense cross-examination.

Fisher was set to go first. "Ivan's very good. But very erratic," Kaplan said later. "He knows that. On the last night, we had finally got a very important witness." Only Waridel's testimony could connect the Levantine dealers smuggling morphine base into Sicily to the money from America flowing back through Switzerland.

It was 6:30 P.M. by the time the government finished. "Ivan wants to go ahead, though he's completely jet-lagged, and exhausted to the point where he's making no sense," Kaplan said later. "He uses up all but twenty minutes of our total time. We then *refuse* to cross-examine under such constraints. So we never *did* get to cross-examine these most important witnesses!"

Kaplan has faced Martin across the courtroom floor in a previous heroin-trafficking case, and considers the chief prosecutor "somewhat schizophrenic." One day Kaplan meets Martin in the corridor and says, "Hey, Dick, got that material for me?" and Martin replies, "Fuck you." The next day, Martin says, "How ya doin'?" So Kaplan deals only with Freeh, whom he finds "straight and responsible."

Having spent eight years as a federal prosecutor, Kaplan prides himself on his knowledge of how prosecutors think and work. "Prosecutors are Pirandello," he says. "They put together a prosecution—construct a story—any way they think it will play best."

Kaplan can also speak with authority about prosecutorial ambition. In the mid-1970s he tried some of the Knapp Commission cases against corrupt undercover cops on which the book and the movie *Prince of the City* were based. DA Thomas Puccio, later, in private practice, the savior of, among others, Claus von Bülow, was Kaplan's boss. The crooked police officers they prosecuted "were basically cops. But a mystique was created. And look how many careers came out of that series of cases! Not just Puccio. Giuliani! It was all based on the SIU [Special Investigations Unit] of the New York Police Department, an elite unit, and thoroughly corrupt. By building up their targets, the

prosecutors built up themselves. And police corruption became roman-
ticized to the degree that prosecutors were able to create for themselves" that snug, invigorating ambiance that facilitates the forced,
hothouse blooming of the sincerely ambitious man.

Kaplan believes he understands the prosecutors' overview of the
Pizza case: "This is an international drug conspiracy and money-laundering case." Therefore, *"any* phone conversations among these people,
known criminals, are likely to involve illegalities. So they assume *all*
their conversations are about narcotics, which they ain't.

"I'm not saying my client is innocent. Far from it. But they have
hundreds of intercepts of Castronovo conversations." One has to do
with "cutting cheese," which the government contends is a reference
to drug cutting. When Kaplan heard it, he thought, Boy, this one is
really damaging! But when he talked to his client, who is in the grocery
business, he learned that when cheese is soft, it sticks to the mechanical-
slicer blade. One worker had in fact cut off the tip of a finger. In the
wiretap, the bosses were joking that now they could really make a
meat-and-cheese sandwich.

Kaplan, like many other Pizza lawyers, has been amazed by the
old-country morality of his client. Castronovo lives in a modest house,
eats hero sandwiches, drives a middle-priced Audi. He has five sons,
one a college graduate who has helped Kaplan as a paralegal. This lad
has a long-time girlfriend, and the lawyer was amazed to discover from
his client that the girl had never been to the Castronovo home. When
Kaplan commented on the oddity of this, his client said, "What am I
running, a whorehouse? I got five sons!"

... MONDAY, APRIL 7, 1986.
METROPOLITAN CORRECTIONAL CENTER. No court today.
Judge Leval will be busy hearing testimony on another case, the seizure
by the United States of the assets of deposed Philippines president
Ferdinand Marcos. Late-night plea discussions between Kennedy and
Freeh have now been going on for some weeks. A few days ago, at a
quiet MCC meeting of the Badalamenti group and their lawyers,
Kennedy had spelled out what he knew from Freeh about the deals that
might be available to each man. Individual lawyers had received private
offers as well, so Kennedy had then gone back to Freeh and got him

to write everything out, saying he hoped to work out some sort of package. The lawyers had then explained to their clients that they were obliged to inform them of the individual offers. But Badalamenti had stood firm: no deals for anyone. And no family member had dared disagree with the Old Man, at least not openly.

Today Kennedy has called a follow-up meeting, and the Badalamenti lawyers and clients spend four hours with Lena Pecosi in a metal-walled, windowless MCC room in what feels like 110° heat. They parcel out the transcribed phone conversations and, by the time they break up, each attorney knows which of the conversations he will be responsible for. The meeting has been a psychological success, forging a new feeling of cohesion among the seven attorneys. Before the meeting, they had felt pulled apart by the struggle to reconcile the attitudes of their diverse clients to the various pleas being discussed.

... 1983. BROOKLYN. U.S.
ATTORNEY'S OFFICE, EASTERN DISTRICT OF NEW YORK.
A government wiretap order is not easy to get. The rules for maintaining the protections of the Fourth Amendment are, understandably, finicky. Before applying to a court for a wiretap authorization, the government must demonstrate a good-faith basis to believe that illegal activities will be overheard. It also must demonstrate a continuing good-faith effort not to listen to other kinds of conversations occurring on the same line—chats with wives, doctors, girlfriends, and legitimate business calls of varying kinds. The process of protecting the speaker's privacy and other Constitutional rights is called "minimization." As the agents do this, what the government calls "patterns of innocence" emerge.

If the agents fail to obey the rules, the judge can suppress the tape. If the tap is productive, however, the government in recent years has become much more adroit in using wiretaps to show probable cause that a crime has been committed.

The 1970 Title III wiretap statute requires FBI agents and federal prosecutors to work much more closely together than ever before, and the task is extremely manpower-intensive. Each tap must be manned round the clock by teams of agents working eight-hour shifts. Each court order must be renewed monthly, after filing supporting affidavits that demonstrate the value of the previous month's harvest. The network of bugs increases exponentially: One suspect may be talking to three or four other likely suspects, each of whom justifies an additional tap. What's more, each wiretap application must be triply signed—by the U.S. attorney, by the individual FBI agent, and by the attorney general's office in Washington—and reviewed by a federal judge.

Early in 1983, two years into the money-laundering investigation, the government felt it had enough on Joe Ganci to seek a court-ordered wiretap. By March 1983 taps were also in place on the Roma Restaurant, Catalano Brothers Bakery, Pronto Demolition, and the Mazzurco and Lamberti phones. Eventually the Pizza investigation would have six-agent teams listening round the clock on forty-seven different phones.

. . . MONDAY, APRIL 14, 1986. FEDERAL PLAZA, NEW YORK. The Kennedy Checker limo pulls up, not at the federal courthouse, but at the modern, metal-sheathed Federal Building on the opposite side of Foley Square. Today the United States Congress is due to vote more aid to the Nicaraguan Contras. Anti-Contra demonstrators are picketing the CIA offices in the Federal Building, and forcing mass arrests by crossing police barricades. Kennedy is taking part of a morning off from Pizza to get himself arrested. As a long-time political activist, he doesn't feel right, he says, unless he disturbs the peace at least once a year.

He strides through the police barrier, and a couple of bored cops lead him to a waiting police van. When it pulls away, Eleanore runs alongside with her camera, recording Kennedy's smiling face and clenched-fist salute through the wire-glass. The picture will go into baby Anna Rosario's scrapbook, along with last month's photograph of her parents marching up Fifth Avenue in the St. Patrick's Day parade alongside their eighty-six-year-old former client Michael Flannery. In 1983 Flannery had been chosen grand marshal of the parade after Kennedy won the old patriot an acquittal on charges of running guns to Northern Ireland.

In the parade pictures, the Kennedy baby is wearing a green bonnet and sweater knitted for her in prison by another *pro bono* Kennedy client, the former boarding-school headmistress Jean Harris. The scrapbook is being compiled as a record for the child of her parents' serious political commitments, and their long-held belief in the value of integrating family, politics, and private lives.

. . . 10:04 A.M.

THE COURTROOM. Special Agent Carmine Russo is the chief government language expert on the Pizza wiretaps. He has a round face, small mustache, precisely groomed black hair, silver-rimmed spectacles. His shirt collar is uncomfortably tight. The FBI veteran tells the yawning jury his credentials. Russo and his wife are both Sicilian, and speak only Sicilian or Italian at home. He is the FBI expert who first listened to the wiretapped conversations and analyzed the cryptic references. He also sat in on interrogations of Mafia informers in Italy and the United States. The actual translation into English of most of the 900 or so conversations in the nine volumes on file in the official-evidence library was done by a genial retired DEA agent, Anthony Mangiaracina, who, over the past two years, has earned $200,000 in translation fees.

The prosecutor asks Russo to translate the Sicilian phrase *"Semu, pedi, pedi."* The agent says hesitantly, "I'm on the street. I'll be around." This provokes animated response from the defendants. Catalano leans forward to whisper to Fisher, and his chair collapses, dumping him on the floor. The unexpected slapstick jolts the jurors and a few lawyers awake.

Moments earlier, Kennedy arrived, smiling, after his release from Central Booking. He has no interest in questioning this witness now, he says, but wants the agent subject to recall during the reading of the telephone conversations to the jury. Badalamenti's five or six calls from Brazil, all in Sicilian, are the entire case against him. If Kennedy can challenge, or even throw doubt on the English translations, he might seriously damage the government's case.

This evening, an observer of the MCC plea negotiations sums up what has really been happening within the Badalamenti group. The American Mafia don Carmine "The Snake" Persico is imprisoned in MCC awaiting trial in Giuliani's big Commission case, scheduled to begin in four or five weeks. Persico and Badalamenti are long-time friends. For a year prior to the start of Pizza, they occupied neighboring cells. The Old Man holds his American counterpart in great esteem. Sicilians listen first to Sicilians. Badalamenti listens first to Carmine Persico. Before Kennedy ever discussed with his client the deals he was discussing with Freeh, Persico was already warning Badalamenti: Watch out for Kennedy. Don't trust him. He will try to sell your guys out.

Some of the Badalamenti attorneys have their own reasons for wishing to stay in the case, and they too have quietly been warning their clients to stand firm, no matter what blandishments Freeh or Kennedy may offer. When Badalamenti began to hear from members of his own family the same story he was getting from Persico, he made up his stubborn Sicilian mind: no deals, not for any of them. Not even for his son Vito. Not even though Freeh had promised that, in return for certain other considerations, Vito would walk away, completely free.

Although Badalamenti himself had no incentive or intention to deal, there was a compelling strategic reason for him to counsel his family members to deal out, even though he mulishly refused to see it. Surrounded by his loyal family group, Badalamenti looks like a dangerous Mafia patriarch. Take away the retinue, and the jury is more likely to see him as a burned-out, has-been warlord.

When it became clear to Kennedy that not one member of his client's family was going to accept the deals he had worked out, he called the other Badalamenti attorneys together. Get your clients to put it in writing, he said: This is the deal that was offered; we declined to accept it. "Otherwise," he warned, "it will come back to haunt you if your guy is convicted."

Personally, some Badalamenti defendants would very much like to take the deals. But they would not dare do so without the Old Man's consent. They are too family-minded, too Sicilian, too Mafia to challenge the boss. He does not even have to say anything. They interpret his silence, his "no comment" stance, as a negative, and they would never appear to question the wisdom of the capo.

"This whole thing has become a tragedy of Italian noncomprehension," says Eleanore. "Result? Everybody is losing."

. . . 1981.

BLOOMSBURG, PENNSYLVANIA. Defendant Sal Salamone had begun buying guns, not a difficult undertaking in Pennsylvania, though

Salamone seemed unaware that legal arms dealers maintain close ties with government agents. After telling the clerks in Bloomsburg's Renco Gun Shop that he needed to purchase protection because he moved large sums of cash, he bought an AR-15 rifle, the civilian version of the M-16, the standard infantry rifle of U.S. forces, as well as a MAC II machine pistol, and the salesman filled out the required purchase form for each weapon, and sent it to the Bureau of Alcohol, Tobacco and Firearms. One year later Salamone returned to the same gun shop with his brother. Filippo Salamone bought seven AR-15 rifles, as well as seven MAC II machine pistols, and three Uzi machine guns. When ATF ran a check on these forms, they discovered that the names on some of them were fictitious.

. . . 6:00 A.M., **SUNDAY MORNING, APRIL 9, 1984. CLIFTON, NEW JERSEY.** One target of the coordinated mass FBI arrests was a new luxury-condominium complex, Patricia Village, on River Road in Clifton, New Jersey. Inside apartment 46, the agents found two of the AR-15s and one MAC II machine pistol purchased by Filippo Salamone at the gun shop in Bloomsburg, Pennsylvania. The owner of the apartment was Joe Ganci.

Giuseppe Ganci had been born in the small village of San Giuseppe Iato, in the province of Palermo, Sicily, and had become a respected *soldato* in the Santa Maria di Gesu Family. In 1965, when one of the Sicilian Mafia wars was at its height, Ganci decided to emigrate to the United States.

"Il Bufalo" was a small, rotund man of five feet six inches, with a fleshy, cheerful face haloed by a plenitude of curly grey hair. His nickname denoted his ample belly, a testament to Ganci's love of good living, especially of fine food. At the Villa Maria Restaurant, on Fresh Pond Road in Queens, near his home, he had a special back-room table perpetually reserved in front of the blazing log fire. In Little Italy, he enjoyed a similar fireside table at the Ruggiero Restaurant, on Grand Street, a favorite hangout for the Zips. When the Buffalo was feeling especially good, his choice was often Il Valetto, a chic East Side dining spot favored by expense-account eaters and UN diplomats. He thought nothing of running up a $400 bill.

Ganci conducted much of his business out of his home, on 68th Road in Middle Village, Queens, where he lived with his wife and two daughters. He could walk to his pizzeria, the Al Dente, on Queens Boulevard, the main artery of the bustling neighborhood, or stroll over to nearby Catalano Brothers Bakery. He was a partner in Pronto Demolition, which had offices on Provost Street, Brooklyn, but the partners preferred to hold board meetings at Ganci's house.

Afternoons, Ganci almost always visited his New Jersey apartment. The Patricia Village complex had been built by Polizzi Builders, the construction company owned by Ganci's *compare* from San Giuseppe Iato, defendant Frank Polizzi. It was at his old friend's restaurant, Casa Polizzi, that Ganci had first met his young mistress, Carol Giuliano. She was an attractive brunette in her early thirties, and Ganci loved to give her presents—fur coats, a car, rings, diamonds. He bought the apartment in Patricia Village for her. After spending the afternoon there, Ganci and Carol went out to eat, usually at Polizzi's restaurant, then headed back to their love nest. A nice, quiet life.

. . . TUESDAY, APRIL 29, 1986.

THE COURTHOUSE.   In the spring light the sunwashed marble and granite of the building glows like limestone in Luxor's Valley of the Kings. This place too seems a mausoleum, a storehouse of buried pharaohs, writings, curious hieroglyphics half understood and obscured by drifting sands. The trial seems becalmed here in some trackless, timeless place, the hapless, somnolent jurors condemned to wander forever amid this rubble of inscrutable "evidence." Evidence of *what*, evidence meaning what? The jurors are never told. Meaning will come later, in the summing up, when all the facts have been laid out, and the time is at hand for the two sets of lawyers to offer two conflicting explanations of what it all may mean.

Today's testimony shifts to the April 9, 1984, arrest of New Jersey defendant Sal Greco, the pencil-slim man seated in the rear row on the aisle. Although he looks as dapper as Mr. Coffee Nerves, Greco is said to be the compulsively hard-working owner-operator of a small family-style pizzeria in Neptune City, New Jersey. Fifteen federal agents took part in the 6:00 A.M. raid on Greco's modest home on that Sunday morning two years ago, and details of the Greco search will occupy more than four court days. Similar catalogues of evidence must be endured for each defendant. The cumulative effect of twenty-two detailed accounts of searches and seizures will become stunningly soporific. Prelunch naps are now commonplace in the jury box and visitors' benches. By afternoon, one or two defense lawyers are often asleep. Their clients snooze—as they do everything else—professionally. They nod off for reasons of image—to indicate lack of interest and involvement.

The lawyers, normally the slickest of talkers, struggle for words to describe what it feels like to be part of this trial. In the morning coffee break, Michael Kennedy comes up with the *mot juste*. It feels, he says, exactly like being overtaken by a glacier.

Tony Lombardino looks up from his pastry. "It's the fuckin' *Titanic.* Without the band."

Special Agent Michael Lee, the third witness to testify about the Greco search, is handsome, slim, natty, black. He describes for Robert Stewart how Greco gave the agents the keys to his pizzeria, and Greco's son Antonio accompanied them to Neptune City. There, hidden in the dropped ceiling, Lee and his partner found an Uzi semiautomatic rifle. At this, several drowsing jurors awaken. The arms cache also included a MAC II machine pistol, with magazine installed and loaded; a 9 mm German Luger pistol with fully loaded magazine; boxes of 9 mm and .38-caliber ammunition; a silencer for the Uzi; and another bag containing 140 loose rounds of .223 mm ammunition.

On a cart in front of the jury box Stewart has placed a giant yellow shopping bag. He extracts the Styrofoam case containing the Uzi and places it in front of the witness. This causes nine defense attorneys and two prosecutors to hurry to the side bar. This is the first of an arsenal of weapons found in the April 9 raids on the defendants' homes, and the defense lawyers want to lodge objections to what they see as inflammatory waving of "ugly items."

Yes, the agent recognizes Government Exhibit #603D-63. It is the Uzi's case, now covered with evidence tape and dusting powder. He removes the small, powerful, dull-grey weapon. The young men on the jury lean forward.

Stewart continues producing guns and ammunition from his big rumpled bag as if it were Santa's sack. Out comes a rifle. Yes, says the witness, this is an AR-15.

Fogelnest objects. Witness not qualified as a gun expert, he blurts. So saying, he inadvertently breaks the lawyer's First Commandment: Never raise a question to which you do not already know the answer. Agent Lee now ticks off his two years with the Bureau of Alcohol,

Tobacco and Firearms; his five years as a SWAT-team member; his two more years as an expert firearms instructor with the FBI.

Stewart asks the agent to pull back the slide on the Luger pistol. Inadvertently, it knocks into the microphone, causing a loud *thwock!* Several jurors and the court reporter jump. Defense attorneys are shouting, furious.

Segal calls hoarsely for a mistrial. "None of us," he fumes, "with years of experience in this courthouse, have *ever* seen a demonstration with live ammunition in front of a jury! It has no purpose but to inflame. . . . There has been fear instilled here! . . . a dog and pony show."

He is drowned out by other shouts of protest. Leval says, "I think live ammunition should not be brought in. . . ."

"Judge, the damage has already been done. . . ."

Martin is cool. Photographs alone are "inadequate to show the kinds of things these defendants had. . . . I've been here six years, and have brought in live ammunition dozens of times."

"We will talk about it later," says Leval.

Before cross-examination, Leval issues an instruction to the jury: "No defendant is charged here with illegal possession of firearms. The fact that any defendant possessed firearms—if you so find—is not in itself a crime. But you can give it any weight you wish. As you recall, the charges here are illegal drug dealing, and trafficking in money."

Fogelnest crosses first, emphasizing that it is legal for a civilian with a firearms license to buy a MAC ii machine pistol, provided it has not been adapted for fully automatic fire. The lawyer is restrained, polite.

In the corridor later, someone praises the tone of his cross. "Man, you don't ever beat up on a soft-voiced black guy!" he says. But Bronson is enraged, almost ready to slug Fogelnest. By asking if the guns were legal, he has opened up the issue of the silencer being *illegal.* Fortunately, the prosecutor did not catch on.

. . . LARRY BRONSON,
fifty, attorney for Salvatore Greco, is a cheerful, smart, hard-working son of New Jersey retailers. One day, age fourteen, he saw a movie about a glamorous trial lawyer, and his future was decided. He never wavered. Before going into private practice, Bronson served three years as a Hudson County prosecutor.

Like that of many of the Pizza attorneys, Bronson's personal life is more sybaritic than solid. His children live in Florida. For six years he has lived on Park Avenue in winter, and in Tuscany and Monte Carlo in summer, with a good-looking doll named Jill, whom he treats with great deference and respect.

This is not Bronson's first multidefendant case. He was in a forty-four-defendant cocaine case in New Jersey, was active in the big New Jersey toxic-waste cases, and was in the Serpico case. He got his present client in the usual way, "either through another attorney or a prior client. That's always how it happens."

The Pizza Connection is "a very difficult case, because of the scope. And it keeps getting larger." Yes, like the Blob. "They're throwing everything in. And after eight months, many of the lawyers are close to sheer exhaustion."

Bronson drives Segal and Kaplan to court each morning, and notes how both men have begun literally to waste away from fatigue. Between them, they appear to have lost thirty or forty pounds. Bronson himself continues chunky, cheery, unflappable.

Of the prosecutors, Bronson says, "Louis Freeh is a wonderful guy. He'd do anything for you he could. Dick Martin is different. He's not honest. He's not a gentleman."

Of the twenty-two-man defense team, he says, "We have a problem in this case—a lot of dead wood. Five guys have done all the heavy work. Kaplan, Fisher, and Bergman and me have carried the whole show. Michael Kennedy certainly did not help us initially. . . . In the Badalamenti group, only David Lewis is helpful. Everybody else has fallen down."

What's more, "some guys really take advantage." The government footed the bill for the Swiss trip, but "some guys just enjoyed Lugano. They didn't even show up for the hearings."

One of the hardest workers is Paul Bergman, "who shouldn't even be in this case," since Judge Leval has thrown out the Galante murder evidence. "But he has done a marvelous thing. He's cultivated the judge, and to such an extent that the judge believes everything he says!" Bergman is another former Southern District prosecutor, and at the beginning of the case, says Bronson, he caught Leval's attention by giving the judge a fair consideration and interpretation of the law on each point. "He always argued *the law,*" always said, *that's* why you should rule. "His argument was not always as favorable as possible to the defendants, but it resulted in tremendous respect by the judge to anything Paul Bergman says." Other lawyers send Bergman up to argue their points for them, "because they know the judge listens to Bergman. Paul is our designated objector."

In the Pizza case, Sal Greco may be a small-time pizza-maker, but Larry Bronson can still say with great satisfaction, "I have a good fee arrangement. Some guys don't." Some mob clients don't pay, no matter what the fee arrangement, and if one "agrees to pay you X dollars, and then he only gives you half X, of course you're upset!"

Bronson and Mike Querques—"a very fine lawyer"—once were partners. But like Pizza's other solo practitioners, Bronson is proud now to be a one-man law firm, an entrepreneur who "goes from one big case to the next." Upcoming on his calendar are a death-penalty case in New Jersey—in his book, a rare and desirable find—and an armored-car robbery.

. . . TUESDAY, APRIL 29, 1986.

THE COURTHOUSE.   Another day over at last, Kennedy and Benfante wait for the elevator. Kennedy says Badalamenti and his family will not even consider pleas. "The concept of cutting his losses is simply inconceivable to him." He describes some of his client's background. Mussolini had clipped the Mafia's wings. After World War II, "the Harvard liberal types in the OSS put Badalamenti and the other Mafia leaders back in power, because they sought the indigenous leaders. We backed the wrong leaders in Southeast Asia for the same reason. It's a policy that seems pragmatic, but it has consistently put us on the wrong side."

Benfante, who has no interest in politics, but a great interest in ferreting out what Badalamenti's defense will be, mentions that the Italian newspaper coverage of the Palermo maxi-trial, where Buscetta is now testifying, "exculpates Badalamenti even more than Buscetta." What exactly is he charged with there?

"He had faced charges of Mafia association." But when the U.S. government sought to extradite him from Spain, the Italians tried to get him first "by adopting all the American charges *en bloc* and dumping them on him. Then they severed the Old Man and his family out of the maxi-trial." But all the charges are still pending.

Mere "Mafia association" is a crime in Italy, Kennedy explains, though not in the United States. But a statement by his lawyer that Badalamenti is a member of the Mafia would be useless to the Italian prosecutors. Kennedy nonetheless had been careful in his opening to refer to his client only as a "Man of Honor." However, if Badalamenti himself said here that he was a Mafia member, the statement could be used against him there.

Kennedy knows that Benfante already knows Italian law. He understands the game now going on: Benfante, like the other Pizza lawyers, is eager to learn Badalamenti's intended defense. But Kennedy will not satisfy their curiosity. He cannot risk it, he says privately. Most would readily trade the information to the prosecution in return for some favor. The truth may also be that Kennedy himself does not yet know what he plans to do.

. . . MARCH 1983. THE FBI SURVEILLANCE. For over a year, from March 7, 1983, until the big roundup on April 9, 1984, the FBI carried out massive, ongoing visual and electronic surveillance of the defendants. Each sighting, and each wiretap, was but one portion in the huge mosaic the government was assembling to put before a jury. When the time came, each piece of surveillance was described to the jury by one or more agent participants. These vignettes were rarely complete, and were presented in erratic sequence. Nonetheless, as the months passed, a sort of picture began to emerge, a very sketchy picture of a huge and complex enterprise. The prosecutors reasoned like paleontologists: From two vertebrae and a fragment of cheekbone, they sought to infer an entire dinosaur.

One of the first wiretaps picked up Filippo Salamone, brother of defendant Sal, calling Tommy Mazzara in New Jersey to say he had four bags of onions, ready to sprout. The FBI interpreted this as code for bags of money ready to go. The Bureau decided to stir the pot a little.

On June 1, 1983, FBI agents dropped in on Sal's Place and questioned some of the pizzeria employees about their recent money-changing activities. The shock waves of this visit were instantaneous. Early the next morning defendant Salamone was overheard urgently warning his wife that great problems had developed, and she should contact his brother Filippo, but only from a public phone.

The FBI's visit to the brothers' pizzeria drove Filippo Salamone into a flurry of activity that in turn exposed still another Sicilian business contact, the wealthy defendant Frank Polizzi. On the hot and clammy night of June 8, the FBI watched Filippo jump into his car and drive for three hours to Polizzi's Belleville Motor Lodge in New Jersey. At 11:00 P.M., in the motel parking lot, they saw him hand Polizzi a brown paper bag, then head right back to Pennsylvania.

. . . MONDAY, MAY 5, 1986.

THE COURTROOM.   The FBI surveillance is crammed with sightings of brown bags, white bags, and cardboard boxes. Today FBI Special Agent Alfred Genkinger—broad shoulders, square face, standard white shirt—describes his stakeout of the parking lot of Polizzi's Belleville Motor Lodge. When the time comes to cross-examine, Polizzi's lawyer, Mike Querques, walks up to the podium carrying a stack of ordinary brown grocery bags, about eight inches wide and twice as high. He asks the witness to fold and close an empty bag so that it resembles as closely as possible the full bag he saw Salamone hand to Polizzi in the dark parking lot. The agent becomes slightly agitated, his voice flutters, but he manages to fold the bag. The lawyer takes it from him and, with a great flourish, thumps his hand on a stapler to preserve its fold. "This the same as the bag you saw that night?" Yes.

"This bag is in evidence!" he cries. It is a welcome touch of Perry Mason, and the jury is paying attention. Querques lifts another full brown bag from the defense table and folds it in a similar manner. He holds the bag aloft and shouts at the agent, "Know what's inside?"

Furious objections from the prosecution. Leval calls the lawyer to the side bar, where Querques reveals that his brown bag, identical to the one the agent has seen, is full of sardines. He wants to show the contents of his bag to the jury. Leval stops him. "The agent never saw what was in the bag on the night in question" so the judge is not going to let the jury see the contents of Querques's bag. His fish story will have to wait.

. . . JUNE 1983. THE FBI SURVEILLANCE.
So far as the agents can tell, Filippo Salamone and family have vanished in the night. The front door of the family home in Jackson, New Jersey, is locked, the red truck has disappeared. Other agents, listening in on defendant Sal Greco's Neptune City pizzeria phone, hear him tell a caller that Salamone's wife has left for Italy, and he thinks Filippo is with her. Greco, it turns out, is in a position to know. Overnight, he had bought both the Salamone family house and red Chevy Blazer truck for a total price of one dollar.

. . . TUESDAY, MAY 6, 1986.
THE COURTROOM.   The trial is entering a new phase. For the first time since Pizza began, in October, the proceedings will develop what lawyers call "meat." The evidence that the government is about to present will deal with the only substantial amount of drugs captured in all of Pizza. Two years after Attorney General William French Smith's exuberant news conference, at which thousands of pounds of heroin were spoken of as though it lay piled in a huge mound on the blue carpet, the total haul of Pizza Connection heroin is contained in three plastic bags now lying on the prosecutors' long table: two and a half kilos of heroin, obtained in three separate buys, all from the same source, all bought by the same undercover agent, and all of it paid for with more than $600,000 in marked money supplied by the U.S. government.

Four new charts have appeared, loaded with new numbers and symbols and headed CHRONOLOGY OF EVENTS. The prosecutor today is apple-cheeked Robert Bucknam, nicknamed by the defense "The Pillsbury Dough Boy," but now almost fit-looking at twenty or so pounds less than his usual weight. Perhaps he looks smaller by contrast to his witness, who is six feet and balding, with a lineman's build, watermelon-sized head, large horn-rims, and a Fu Manchu mustache tapering to a neatly trimmed beard. Stephen Hopson is an ace DEA agent in his late thirties, and he is more comfortable in the witness box than any previous occupant. He looks downright happy to be there. Attorneys Benfante, Segal, Lombardino, and Kaplan know that by the time this mild-looking hulk completes his testimony, their clients will be seriously unhappy.

After an impressive flourish of the agent's credentials—over 100 drug busts, 100 weapons searches—the jury hears for the first time the name Benito Zito. He was the co-proprietor of a Philadelphia pizzeria called "Mimmo's," regarded by the government as a hangout for shady characters.

In the spring of 1983, the government had an informant working at Mimmo's, and he introduced Agent Hopson to Benny Zito. The jury does not hear this preamble. Bucknam picks up the story at 2:30 A.M. on June 11, 1983, in the casino of Caesar's Palace in Atlantic City. Hopson and the informant are shooting craps with a tall, dark Sicilian in his late thirties. Benny Zito's bankroll is over $5,000, in hundreds and fifties. The three new friends gambled and ate and drank for several more hours, Hopson says.

By the time the party broke up at dawn, Zito had confided that he was clearing $200,000 a year as a pizza franchiser, and he offered his new buddy Hopson a chance to buy in. They agreed to meet later in the day at one of the restaurants owned by Zito's friend Dominick Minino, boss of the pizzeria chain. Hopson arranged for DEA surveillance of the meeting.

The new friends met again the next day at Mimmo's, again covertly watched by other DEA agents. Zito suggested he and Hopson go partners in a tavern. Hopson said that, frankly, the restaurant business did not interest him, and confessed that his real work was dealing heroin. He imported up to fifteen kilos at a time from Bangkok, but his sources of supply had temporarily dried up. Could Zito supply him with kilogram quantities of heroin, he wondered, on a temporary basis, just until he could reestablish his Thai connections. For the jury's benefit, Bucknam elicits that one kilo equals 2.2 pounds.

Zito at first was evasive; heroin is a very risky business, he said. A deep mutual responsibility exists between all members of a drug conspiracy. Hopson understood. He said he had asked to start with a half-kilo only to assure himself the quality was sufficiently high. Bigger future deals were implied. The jury is paying close attention.

Hopson says Zito always spoke to him in guarded and cryptic language: "Have you got that thing for me?"

Hopson has negotiated more than 100 heroin buys on the telephone, and he says all drug dealers speak this way. They never utter the words *heroin, cocaine,* or *amphetamine;* they use only coded terms.

"Do they often use pay phones?"

Benfante objects violently. "No pay phones in the Zito transactions!" His frenzy makes no sense now. The importance to this case of pay phones, the prejudice to certain defendants of any mention of pay phones, will not become evident for many weeks. Leval overrules, and cautions him not to make speeches in front of the jury. A moment later Benfante again loudly objects. This time Leval ignores him, and the government glides forward with the imperturbability of an ice skater.

Bucknam puts more pay-telephone questions. Defense objections chorus like frogs in spring. Leval overrules.

Drug dealers have told the agent it is safer to do business on pay phones, he says. This brings a half-dozen shouts of "Object!" "Mistrial!"

"I think the jury understands that Agent Hopson is speaking out of his vast past experience," Leval intones.

Bucknam wheels the supermarket basket up to the jury box and again hands out telephone-transcript notebooks, one to each juror and alternate. The lawyers already have copies.

Bucknam asks the jurors to turn to the conversation headed "1:00 PM, JUNE 20, 1983," and he invites "the readers to come out." Two men and two women enter from behind the translators' booth. These "readers" are professional actors, already known as "The Pizza Players," whom the government has hired to read the translated conversations aloud to the jury. The women, a blonde and a redhead, are in their mid-thirties, perfectly coiffed, and wear false eyelashes. The men are lean and trim, one nearly bald, the other graced with a luxuriant grey Afro. All four are spiffily dressed, and look like daytime soap-opera performers, which in a way they are.

At their debut courtroom appearance, about a month ago, the Pizza Players read their lines in organ-grinder Chico Marx Italian accents— and sounded more or less like the defendants. But some of their lawyers took umbrage and implied anti-Italian bias, so Leval ordered the actors henceforth to cease "acting" and just read the lines. The Pizza Players sit at their own little table, just beneath the escarpment of the bench, facing the prosecutors' table, and they speak into microphones hooked up to a bulky wire-recording device. This became necessary when Joe Lamberti's lawyer, Tony Lombardino, demanded the right to make a record of what the actors actually say—as opposed to the words written in the books they read from—"so that, for appellate purposes, down the road, we can demonstrate what really happened here." At this, Dave Lewis had said that if the government could use actors, the defense reserved the right to use hand puppets.

In the translators' booth, two court interpreters sit ready to translate the actors' English words back into Italian and Sicilian. Almost everyone in the courtroom is now equipped with notebooks and earphones. Leval's large round black ones, askew on his blond curls, suggest a judicial Mouseketeer.

Following the court's protocol, the pink-faced bald man says, "I will read the part of Benito Zito." The man with grey curls says, "I will read the part of Giuseppe Ganci." "I will read the part of Margarita Ganci," says the redhead.

Bald man (in deep voice): "Hello?"

Redhead (warm, friendly): "Hello."

Bald man (inquiring voice): "Pinuzzo home?"

Redhead (mistrustful, nervous): "Who is calling?"

Bald man (matter-of-fact): "Toto."

Redhead (relieved): "No, not here."

Bald man (comforting): "Thank you. Many beautiful things."

A half-dozen similar conversations are read, all of them leading up to the undercover agent's first heroin buy. Hopson waiting quietly in the witness box looks like Clark Kent in the telephone booth.

Hopson tells the jury how he packed $120,000 in hundreds and fifties into a green box; how he took it to Mimmo's Pizza, handed the box across the counter to Benny Zito, and said, "This is for the half."

Now the jury, through the actors, hears Zito immediately call Ganci and say, "I have the how do you say it . . . I have that young fellow here . . . if it can be done . . . I'll take a run late tonight?" They hear Ganci call the Roma Restaurant and ask for Mazzara. He is not there, so Ganci calls Mazzara at home. Not there. He calls Castronovo at home. A son answers; Dad is out. Ganci calls Zito back. "It will have to be tomorrow."

It is lunchtime in the courthouse. The Zito evidence is deadly. Hopson is formidable. The lawyers straggle into the cafeteria. "Days like this," says Segal bitterly, "you want to give the money back." His comment is the more ironic because Mazzara has not paid him, or not paid him enough, and this lawyer has been most outspoken in his resentment at being trapped in a case that is eroding his earning capacity.

Genay Leitman worries that the court will not grant summer vacations.

"How come nobody [in the mob] picked up on Hopson?" Lombardino growls. "He took an Italian alias, but he doesn't speak Italian. And he looks like a cop in the surveillance pictures."

"Judge is on the bench!"

A few more phone calls, and then Bucknam holds aloft Government Exhibit #500: a clear plastic bag of what looks like light-brown sugar—the half-kilo of heroin.

Hopson says he received this heroin on June 30. Five days later, he again met Zito in Mimmo's by appointment. This time his buddy did not shake his hand; instead, he stroked his back, front, and sides. "He was feeling for a body transmitter, a wire." The agent had worn a wire before, he says, but this time, fortunately, he was clean. Zito told him to move to the rear of the restaurant. As he walked, "Zito watched me very closely, scanning my body from shoulders to shoes."

They sat down, and Hopson said he was satisfied with the first buy; could he get more?

Zito replied by nodding his head. He refused to speak.

"Is there some problem?" asked Hopson.

"I'm uncomfortable. . . ."

"I just paid you $120,000," said the brazen agent. "If I was a cop, I'd be arresting you now." The strategy worked, and soon buyer and seller were discussing a one-kilo buy.

Bucknam stops his narrative at this suspenseful moment to hand the heroin to the jury. They seem to enjoy handling $120,000 worth of narcotics. The women giggle; the men flip it hand to hand. The package crackles. A woman in the back row drops it, and the others laugh nervously.

At Hopson's next meeting with Zito, the pizza maker complained he had made too little profit on the half-kilo, considering that the heroin was "untouched"—a common term, Hopson explains, for "very high quality." During this meeting Zito divulged that his supplier "is an older gentleman, experienced in the Sicilian heroin traffic, who sells out of his garage, not his home," and who is also the owner of a pizzeria.

By the end of the conversation, Hopson had agreed to sweeten the new deal with an extra $5,000 for Zito, making the total price $245,000. That night Zito called Ganci and said he wants to visit.

The government would now like to supply each juror with a booklet of charts, to supplement the notebooks of conversations. The defense objects that the real charts already are in evidence, and that "a booklet of charts would be a *written* index of guilt, and would *have* an index!" Leval rules out the booklet, for now.

By July 16 Hopson had obtained $245,000 in hundreds and passed it on to Zito, who said he would receive the merchandise the following day. When Ganci called Zito at 6:44 P.M., Zito said he had "twenty-one and a half little chocolates." Zito had decided to pocket the $30,000 difference.

That same day agents saw Tommy Mazzara drive from the Roma Restaurant in New Jersey to Ganci's house in Queens. The two men drove around the block together; then Mazzara returned home.

At 2:17 A.M. on July 17, 1983, agents watched Zito take a box from his car and enter the Ganci house in Queens. Fifty-two minutes later he emerged carrying a brown paper bag.

That night Hopson picked up the heroin that had been left for him in the closet of his informant's apartment. The drugs were packed in clear plastic, inside aluminum wrapping, inside a brown paper bag.

Not until two and a half years later, on November 27, 1985, while Tomasso Buscetta was on the witness stand, did Marvin Segal, lawyer for Tommy Mazzara, learn from the government that his client's palm print had been found on this same brown bag.

Agent Hopson is totally relaxed. During sidebars, he jokes with the court reporter and grins at the women jurors when he catches them flirting. But his once-exciting talk of heroin and big money has become routine, and several jurors are again asleep.

The following week Ganci called Zito and said, "That guy has two ovens." Zito then told Hopson his two kilos were ready. Hopson said he was on the verge of reconnecting with his Thailand source.

Recess. Manny Moore, a tough, sharply dressed black man who is an experienced drug lawyer and an associate of Mario Malerba, joins the kaffee klatsch. "Watch out for Steve Hopson. He's prime. Notice that big gold Rolex he's wearing? Probably lifted off some drug dealer. He's a minefield for cross-examination. He can hurt you bad. And there's no way to be sure he can help you. One good question is: Are you an instructor in the government school where they teach agents how to testify?"

"Judge is on the bench!"

Bucknam struts up and down the jury rail, holding aloft the second buy, a kilo of pure heroin, ivory-colored and floury-looking, sealed in a plastic pouch about the size of a hot-water bottle.

Hopson begins describing the third buy. He withdrew another $250,000 in government funds, the extra $10,000 being the bonus Zito had demanded for the high quality of his merchandise. This time, after the agent photographed the cash and copied the serial numbers, he packed the bills into a box wrapped with distinctive panda-print paper, certain to show up well in surveillance photos. On August 2, in the parking lot of the Tiffany Diner in Philadelphia, he handed the panda box to Zito through the window of his Volkswagen, and was told he would "have the package the following day."

Zito made another trip to the Ganci garage in Queens. The FBI filmed the visit with a concealed video camera. The following day, Zito handed Hopson one kilo of heroin packed in a blue shirt box and told him, "Enjoy the shirts."

The third heroin buy was "very high quality." The agent performed a melt test. This testimony produces more shouts of "Objection!" Hopson lacks expertise to perform drug tests. At this, Hopson's hairy face creases into a truly scary grin. Looking at him head on is like gazing into the open mouth of a moray eel.

The next meeting was between Zito and Hopson and another DEA agent, at the Hilton Inn. Zito—swept up into the high rollers' game, just as he had been in Atlantic City—said he and his associates would take all the Asian heroin Hopson could supply. They owned a demolition company in Brooklyn, he added, which gave them facilities to transport and store the commodity. And they trusted Benny Zito implicitly.

They began discussing a ten-kilo buy, at a reduced bulk rate of $900,000. Hopson said he would first need to see some front money, and he wanted to meet personally with these associates, to assure himself they were good for the balance. Zito said he would check. The agents walked him back to his Volkswagen, and in the parking lot Zito asked for an additional $10,000, for himself. The agents paid him on the spot.

When Zito called Ganci, Il Bufalo told him to handle it himself. Ganci wasn't going to meet with anybody. This response scarcely surprised the agents. A real drug dealer never cares to become personally involved, Hopson explains. He leaves that dangerous work to his mules—men like Zito, and Ronsisvalle. That is part of what makes catching and convicting drug dealers so difficult: *Lack* of hands-on connection to drugs, in the proper circumstances, tends to prove guilt, not innocence.

The defense wants the jurors to hear the actual wiretap of Ganci telling Zito to handle it himself. The conversation, blasting out of speakers on either side of the courtroom, is scratchy, static-filled, virtually unintelligible. Yet those jurors who are not sleeping are following intently in their black notebooks.

On August 21, Zito called Hopson to put the Bangkok deal on hold, but in the interim he offered to provide Hopson with money-laundering services from the same source.

Bucknam elicits that the agent has bought heroin at all levels, "from wholesalers to street addicts," and the heroin Zito sold to Hopson was 73% to 87% pure, "the highest I've ever purchased."

Bucknam now brandishes Government Exhibit #502-A, the third buy, and Hopson says it is approximately 78% pure.

"Your Honor!" Benfante shouts. "Object to da wavin' around of da heroin!"

Leval ignores him, and Hopson coolly estimates the street value of this lot at "up to $4 million." The witness has stopped troubling to conceal his vested interest. He is a government agent. He has risked his life to nail some defendants in this room. Every time that Leval rebuffs a defense attorney, Hopson permits himself a satisfied little smile.

. . . TUESDAY, MAY 13, 1986.

THE COURTROOM. The Ship of Fools has hit real doldrums today. Kennedy, Fisher, and Malerba are absent. Some lawyers keep themselves and others awake during these dull stretches by elaborate kidding around. Not long ago, Kennedy moved for a mistrial on grounds "that this jury has been irreparably benumbed." Pat Burke had arrived one day with T-shirts for the nonexistent Pizza defense softball team. In red, green, and white, the colors of the Italian flag, they pictured a half-eaten pizza captioned *Porca Miseria!*

Dave Lewis sometimes passes around mock cross-examinations, which sound extremely authentic, and he always gets a copy to Leval, who crimsons with suppressed mirth. Yesterday's read:

Q. Agent Hopson, were you taught law enforcement techniques?

A. No, I was assigned to the New Bedford office where I was taught to spot and monitor whales sent to our shores by Russian atheist monsters.

Q. What about truck hijacking?

A. It wasn't something I was involved in.

Q. But you were involved in other hijackings?

A. Me, I, hijacking.

Q. Airplane hijacking.

A. Airplane hijacking.

Q. You admit airplane hijacking.

A. No, no. I just repeated what you said.

Q. Repeated what I said.

A. Repeated, yes, repeated.

Q. Repeated.

A. Yes.

Q. No further questions.

Today Joe Calluori circulates a mock memo from Judge Leval, which turns into a mock *Playbill* describing the Pizza Connection cast of characters:

TO: The Jury

FROM: Judge Leval

I believe it appropriate, at this juncture, to advise you that this trial has been an experiment in behavioral psychology. All of the lawyers, the witnesses and, indeed, myself as well are professional actors. You will recall the "witness" Ronsisvalle. Mr. Ronsisvalle's real name is Geoffrey Bishop. Mr. Bishop has for many years been a member of the Royal Shakespeare Company of London, England. . . .

Salvatore Contorno in fact speaks no Italian. He is a Portuguese fisherman specializing in man-of-wars. As a result of a work-related accident, he is paralyzed from the neck down. . . . Mr. Contorno has appeared in such films as *My Man of War Godfrey, A Man of War for All Seasons,* and *The Old Man of War and The Sea.* On Broadway, he appeared in the underwater version of *The Life of Jelly Fish Roll Morton,* entitled *Jelly Fish Roll Morton: A Life.*

Salvatore Amendolito is unfortunately a mental patient recently released who believes he is a Swiss financier. In reality he is Frank Castronovo's downstairs neighbor, and whittles professionally. . . .

As to the defendants, some of you may have recognized Mr. Badalamenti as the "cut man" who appeared in the movie *Raging Bull.* His stage name is Frederick Schwartz, although his real name is Bonario B. Bonario. He is known to his friends as "Lucy."

Vito Badalamenti, who, in this trial, plays Gaetano Badalamenti's son, has numerous acting credits, mostly on late afternoon soap operas on Japanese TV. . . .

Salvatore Salamone began his professional career as a lecturer at Oxford in Greek antiquities. He soon realized that his true love was the stage. At 23, he appeared in his first amateur production, playing Nathan Detroit in *Guys and Dolls*. . . .

Baldo Amato, contrary to popular belief, has no hits to his credit.

Joe Benfante launches into his cross-examination of Agent Hopson, an experience the lawyer later would liken to "trying to work a screwdriver in water." Benfante, highly intelligent but somewhat dyslexic, is ill-matched with the cool, glib DEA agent. He sometimes does not seem to know whether the subject of his question is Ganci or Zito. The judge cannot tell either. But Benfante has no false pride, and when he becomes too tongue-tied he is quick to say, "Sorry, your Honor. I messed up." Though primitive, and occasionally near-inarticulate, Benfante has a Flintstone charm that reaches everyone.

"Do you know, Agent Hopson, whether or not Benny Zito on July 16, 1983, met with anybody other than Joseph Ganci at Joseph Ganci's house when he went to pick up the heroin?"

Segal objects. Leval sustains.

Benfante asks, "May I approach? I would like to figure out how to get the question in."

"I don't think you will," says Leval.

"That is why I want to approach."

At the side bar, Leval says he can think of one person who could answer the question in the form Benfante put it—but Benny Zito, alas, is not here.

Most of the lawyers believe Zito got tipped off that arrests were coming down and managed to flee to Sicily.

"He's in Russia, your Honor," Benfante tells Leval. "Running the nuclear reactor at Chernobyl."

It's too much for Bucknam, who sniffs, "I object to the continued laughing at the podium . . . this is a very serious proceeding."

. . . GOOD-NATURED JOSEPH BENFANTE,

thirty-seven, was born in Brooklyn, of Sicilian parents, and grew up in Bensonhurst, a heavily Sicilian-Italian neighborhood. A boyhood friend is fellow Pizza lawyer Gerry Di Chiara. Benfante graduated from New York Law School in 1973 and went directly into private practice. A year later, he married Maria Di Domenico, his neighborhood sweetheart. They live today with their young son and daughter a few miles from Bensonhurst, among the plush detached homes of Dyker Heights.

Benfante has an uncanny ability to get his clients acquitted of drug and murder charges in New York State criminal courts. As a result, he has one of the largest criminal-law practices in the city, and worked many organized-crime cases before Pizza. Only weeks before the Pizza Connection trial began, he won an acquittal for two New York Transit Authority workers caught in their hotel room with a kilo of cocaine.

One Pizza colleague attributes Benfante's seeming courtroom clumsiness to inexperience with the federal courts, especially in the starchy Southern District. "You should see him in the spit and sawdust of the state courts! Joe's up there with the best."

Benfante cherishes the good life. He dines and vacations well. He and his wife each drive a Mercedes. Maria's is a big, roomy 300 SEL, all white. Benfante treated himself to his red two-seater convertible after he won an acquittal for the district president of the New Jersey Teamsters, who was accused of robbing the union dental fund.

Benfante loves to joke with the jury, and his most irate objection is often tinged with a last-minute smile toward the jury box. He was a college wrestler, and he moves and dresses like James Caan's portrait of Sonny in the movie *The Godfather*. He speaks fondly of the old mobsters who were legend in his boyhood neighborhood, men like Meyer Lansky, who controlled Cuba, and seventy-year-old Carmine Lombardosi, who once worked with Lansky and now drives a Rolls-Royce but still gets into bar brawls, after which his wife patches up his wounds.

Benfante wishes to play for the jury a surveillance videotape made during the final Zito deal. The room darkens. Hopson turns to watch the TV screen mounted behind Leval's head. The agent's back is to the jury, his profile to the spectators; his dark beard and pale features make him look old-fashioned, an obscure notable on a postage stamp.

The tape misses nothing. The jury sees Mazzurco and Joe Lamberti get out of a tan Mercedes and enter Ganci's neat white garage through the ground-floor door. Zito arrives in his Volkswagen and saunters up the front steps to the main door. He is young and chubby, smoking a cigarette. His polo shirt is stretched tight across a muscular chest and slight belly. He disappears inside the house. Moments later Lamberti and Mazzurco emerge from the garage and return to their Mercedes. Soon after, Zito walks to his car and retrieves the panda-wrapped box containing 250,000 government dollars. He wedges this tight under his left arm, climbs back up the front steps, goes in. When he reappears, he is carrying the dark-blue shirt box that contains the kilo of heroin, the same box the jurors have already seen in court when an FBI agent testified that he had witnessed Mazzurco carry this very box into Ganci's house.

It is apparent that Benfante has studied this tape many times. But he is unable to formulate coherent questions, and each time Leval sustains a government objection, Hopson's face twists into a small sneer.

"Is this the sum and substance of your testimony: That my client Mr. Mazzurco brought a box to you and . . ."

He tries again. "On July 31, 1983 . . ." And again. "Last week you told this jury you recognized a certain box. In a black-and-white photo. You said you recognized the box, and it appeared to be blue . . ."

Hopson will help him out. "I recognized certain markings on the box. Plus it had your client's fingerprints on the tissue paper," he blurts. Benfante is furious. The jurors do not yet know about the prints. Judge Leval sends them out. The lawyer demands a mistrial. "The agent is in bad faith," he says, not perhaps incorrectly. "The palm print on the tissue paper was a deliberate blurt. . . ." He repeats his demand for a mistrial.

"Denied," says the judge. He cannot resist telling Benfante, "Your question was so broad, the agent had ample chance to put anything in."

Benfante's cross has been awful. His brother defense lawyers acknowledge diplomatically that the performance was, as one put it, "somewhat inartful." Yet the lawyer's Archie Bunker appeal has won sympathetic glances from the jury box.

Good news arrives in the late afternoon. Departing Pizza lawyers encounter TV crews staked out on the courthouse steps. Another Giuliani Mafia prosecution, the trial of Matty "The Horse" Ianello on garbage-racketeering charges, has been running concurrently with Pizza, and that jury has just come in with acquittals on all counts.

... WEDNESDAY, MAY 14, 1986.
THE COURTROOM.   This morning Tony Lombardino redeems his
friend Benfante's poor showing. The jury marches in looking spring-
time fresh, and the Christ-bearded, devil-mouthed witness resumes the
stand. Yes, the agent first met Zito in late May 1983. At that time he
was unaware of FBI case agent Charles J. Rooney and the developing
Pizza investigation, but he soon learned that an investigation roughly
parallel to his work in Pennsylvania was under way in New Jersey and
New York.

Lombardino's structured cross dispels the brown fog of the past few
days and replaces it with the sweet air of logic. He skillfully elicits that
Zito, as a middleman, was in a position to make money from both ends.

"Did . . . you . . . get . . . from . . . Zito . . . the name of *any* defendants
in this case, over a six or seven month period?" No.

"Ever talk to Joe Lamberti? Know what business he's in?" No.

"No further questions."

Counsel for Mazzara follows. Marvin Segal accompanied by a wil-
lowy, chic, fortyish assistant, Harriet Rosen, lugs to the podium an
immense armload of notebooks, transcript, and legal pads. Hopson has
stopped yawning and recovered his anticipatory moray smile.

In a low and weary voice, Segal asks, "On June 28, did you deliver
a package to Mr. Zito?" Yes.

"Why are you looking to the side, agent?" Segal snaps, implying that
Hopson seeks coaching from the prosecution table.

"We have no hand signals," Hopson snarls back.

Hopson's voice is hard and tough. He is wary, his adrenaline is
pumping, but he is not at bay. Both these men are seasoned profession-
als. Segal is better prepared than most of his colleagues. He questions
certain prior remarks by the agent, who bristles, "I testified under oath.
And I would never lie."

"Because the truth is sacred, Agent Hopson?"

"For a number of reasons."

When the government team thinks Segal is being especially unpleasant, six faces like a string of grim-faced paper dolls turn back to gaze
contemptuously at the slim man at the rostrum. Martin, Freeh, Stewart, and Bucknam have been joined by a freshman prosecutor, Andrew

McCarthy, and, as often happens, Agent Rooney sits at the end of the prosecution table.

In the lunch recess, the lawyers compare Segal to the hapless Benfante. "Juries would much rather see a nice guy screwing up than a smart guy being nasty."

Today Baldo Amato has dashed out to Dean & DeLuca's gourmet import shop near Little Italy for some of his favorite delicacies, and now he passes through the cafeteria with brown bag and foil-covered tray, gravely offering to all lawyers and defendants salty shavings of a rare and expensive pâté of tuna roe made only in Sardinia and some very sweet almond cakes. The combination is unusual, and delicious.

Jay Goldberg, lawyer for Matty "The Horse" Ianello, stops by to receive kudos for yesterday's extraordinary win. "To hear 156 'not guilty's' in a row—what an arpeggio of beautiful sounds!"

... FRIDAY, MAY 16, 1986.

THE COURTROOM.   The government's next witness is a veteran FBI fingerprint expert who has given evidence in twenty-seven states. On August 23, 1983, the agent was asked to examine a brown paper bag and discovered a partial palm print. More than two years later, in November 1985, he was given full sets of prints of all the Pizza defendants. He found that Tommy Mazzara's palm print displayed twenty-seven identical characteristics to the print on the bag. Only fourteen identical characteristics are necessary for an official identification.

Attorney Segal is forced to go the no-hope route of eliciting that no fingerprint expert is infallible, and that it is possible to lift a fingerprint with tape and place it on another surface.

The next agent watched both Mazzara and Castronovo visit the Ganci residence seven days before the first Zito/Ganci drug deal. Ken Kaplan, Castronovo's tall, stoop-shouldered lawyer, crosses first. He elicits that this was the first occasion the agent had seen either Castronovo or Mazzara. Yet he did not take pictures, or describe them in his log. He also brings out that the agent was assigned exclusively to the Pizza case for a year and a half, one of five men and five cars carrying out surveillance five days a week, and working eight, sometimes twelve, and occasionally twenty-four hours a day.

Next to cross is the attractive Harriet Rosen. Her boss, Marvin Segal, is about to disappear from the courtroom, pleading financial hardship. She is clear and crisp, and when the agent appears to be weakening, she cleverly underlines his weak points by asking, "Could you repeat that?" or "I'm not quite sure what you're saying." But even good lawyering can hold the jury's attention only so long. Then backsides slide down on soft leather chairs, elbows are wedged on padded armrests, chins are cupped in hands, eyelids close, and Leval says loudly, "Recess!"

. . . AUGUST 25, 1983. THE FBI SURVEILLANCE, MIDDLE VILLAGE, QUEENS.   The continuous traffic in and out of the ground-floor garage of Joe Ganci's house was being faithfully recorded by the revolving teams of FBI agents staked out in five vehicles around the dwelling. As the hours passed, the teams rotated the "eye" position—the car or van best situated to witness any action at the garage. On this warm summer day, the eye team did not have long to wait before Mazzurco and Sal Lamberti pulled up in Mazzurco's brown Mercury. They opened the trunk and portaged a cardboard liquor box into the garage. When they emerged thirty-six minutes later, Lamberti carried a white package. A few days later Mazzurco was back, and this time left with a white plastic bag. Ninety minutes later, other agents staked out at Mazzurco's home in the affluent suburb of Baldwin, Long Island, observed his return. When his garage door opened, they glimpsed several more plastic bags similar to the one he carried out of Ganci's garage. That evening Ganci called Mazzurco and asked, "Did that guy come down from up there?"

Not yet, Mazzurco replied, but he expected him to call.

The FBI considered this answer sufficient reason to place Mazzurco's home under twenty-four-hour surveillance. Two days later their vigilance paid off. At 6:46 P.M. a car pulled up at Mazzurco's house and the driver went inside. Half an hour later he came out, accompanied by his host. Mazzurco took a brown shopping bag out of his car and gave it to his visitor.

When the man drove off, he was followed at a discreet distance by the FBI. Thirty minutes later the surveillance car, backed up by other FBI teams, pulled in front of the stranger's vehicle and cut him off. He said his name was Di Bartolo. The agents frisked him and found a small amount of white powder. The shopping bag Mazzurco had given him contained $40,000 in well-worn bills. "Di Bartolo" was placed under arrest.

Fingerprints soon established that the prisoner was a convicted felon, Giuseppe Baldinucci, a known associate of the Bonanno Family who had jumped bail after being found guilty of larceny and fraud. The white powder he had claimed was recreational cocaine turned out to be 89.2% pure heroin.

. . . 9:30 A.M., WEDNESDAY, JUNE 4, 1986.
THE COURTROOM.   A beautiful, sunny day. The Old Man is in his seat, looking wan. The corridor, as usual, is filled with smoking Zips. At the far end of the hallway, Kennedy is talking quietly with Martin.

9:40 A.M. Leval has instituted a lawyers' roll call. "Off the record: Mr. Di Chiara? Mr. Kaplan? Mr. Segal? Mr. Bronson?" Kaplan enters, scuttles to his seat. "Mr. Kaplan, shall I go to the cafeteria and look for your colleagues? . . . Off the record, it's a scandal. It's just incomprehensible why counsel cannot get themselves here on time. It shows a disrespect to the jury, to the defendants, to the court; it's just extraordinary." The judge says he wants to see the defense lawyers later, in chambers, adding: "It's pointless, I suppose, to lecture, to act like a schoolmaster with a hickory stick . . ." to persons who are not here.

Special Agent William H. Lynch, Jr., large and balding, was on the team which searched the Mazzurco residence on April 9, 1984. Assistant U.S. Attorney Bucknam elicits that the contraption Lynch now holds is the electric money-counting machine he seized from Mazzurco's bedroom closet. In the bedside table he found a fully loaded Smith & Wesson 9 mm semiautomatic pistol with the serial number scratched off.

What else? "In a hidden trap door in the bedroom closet . . ."

"I object to the words 'hidden trap door.' . . ."

"Overruled, Mr. Benfante."

The trap door, covered by the wall-to-wall carpeting, was found by a drug-sniffing dog. Inside a secret compartment was a torn cigarette box holding several rounds of 9 mm hollow-point ammunition. The compartment also held $38,000 in cash and a spiral notebook with a red cover containing a series of tables, initials, figures, and dates.

Throughout this testimony the small, tanned, portly Salvatore Maz-zurco, comfortably tieless, his Palm Beach jacket open, thoughtfully fingers his chin. His face is serene; he appears to be contemplating a long, calm, seamless future. Nothing in his demeanor would tell an observer that this red notebook, a detailed, dated, initialed record of what the government contends are drug transactions, is possibly the most damning piece of evidence against any defendant in this court-room.

Nor has the jury the slightest notion of the crucial importance of the red notebook. Part of the Gobi trek's maddening confusion may be grasped when one understands that three more months of government testimony on scores of other subjects will pass before Arthur Eberhart, an FBI documents analyst, gives his expert opinion: The red notebook is a ledger that reflects payments for a particular commodity. It con-tains notations dating from January 13, 1982, until March 12, 1982, which show entries for 13.8 items. The names or initials Sal, Joe, J. G., or Leo appear alongside each entry. The total of items comes to $1,100,000. In August 1982 five more items are noted at $165,000; in September there are four more items, again at $165,000. On another page, a running inventory shows "41.4 items with a total of $6,623,000."

It is time for Benfante to cross-examine. "Now, Agent Lynch, can you define for me what your definition of a trap door is? . . . Your testimony stated that a sniff-dog led you to that spot. Did you *report* a sniff dog?"

"I did not."

"What's the sniff dog's name?"

. . . TUESDAY, JUNE 10, 1986.

THE COURTROOM. The stress of this trial is reaching everybody. Today Gaetano Badalamenti is ill, red, and blotchy; he spends his lunch hour lying on a bench, waiting for the courthouse nurse to examine him. The jurors are growing restless. One has sent Leval a note: He can no longer afford to live on the thirty-five-dollars-a-day federal jury pay. A second juror has indicated she is growing reluctant to serve for the same reason. In the courtroom colloquy, Martin wonders aloud if there isn't some way of finding additional federal funds to beef up jury salaries during this exceptionally long trial. The defense attorneys are outraged at the prospect. Bergman proposes that Pierre Leval give the jurors a pep talk.

"You have any proposed text?" the judge asks, raising an eyebrow.

. . . THURSDAY, JUNE 19, 1986.

THE COURTROOM. The first break in the monolithic defense occurs at 11:00 A.M. today when Badalamenti's nephew Vincenzo "Enzo" Randazzo pleads guilty before Judge Leval to one count of illegal entry into the United States, and walks out of the courtroom a free man.

"God help the women of New York," says Kennedy on hearing the news.

In August 1983 Enzo had been spotted in the company of Alfano and others at a diner in Queens. The INS had no record of his having entered the United States. Attorney Larry Schoenbach has persuaded the government to drop its narcotics-conspiracy charges in return for a plea of guilty to immigration violations. The maximum penalty is five years, and the agreement Randazzo has just signed with the government lets him off with time served.

When Assistant U.S. Attorney Charles Rose, chief of Narcotics in the Eastern District, heard about Enzo's deal, he was "frankly appalled." Randazzo originally had been tagged as a big shot in the drug ring. The government had gone to the great trouble and expense of extraditing him from Switzerland and had charged him with major crimes.

"To take that plea was an embarrassment! Personally, I'd rather go down the tubes," said Rose. Normally, he added, Martin would "never have agreed" to such a deal. "It was an act of desperation on his part.

"Martin must be figuring: I may not win this thing. So let's get this guy out. This guy is so obviously *not guilty* that the jury may think: What's the government trying to do, charging him? If they're pulling *that* stuff, then what else are they trying to pull off?"

If personal embitterment motivates Rose's remarks, he conceals it well. Rose is cheerful by nature, informal, savvy, stocky, brave, and unabashedly enthusiastic about his job. His outgoing, energetic, amused take on life makes him seem as different from the sedate lawyers in the Southern District as Brooklyn is from Manhattan. Some of Rose's criticism of Martin may arise from the fact that he initiated, then had to give up, the Pizza case. Rose is the man who first traveled to Brazil to negotiate with and bring in Tomasso Buscetta. Rose is the man who was in charge of the Pizza investigation before it was abruptly transferred by Giuliani from the Eastern to the Southern District.

Badalamenti's reaction to Enzo's deal was cold fury. The Old Man had long ago reminded Schoenbach of the ancient adage of the fist: "Take one finger away and it is no longer a strong weapon, merely an appendage." He had warned his nephew, in front of the lawyer, "If you take this plea, you're out of the family."

Schoenbach had assumed that was the end of it. But some weeks later, Enzo phoned him and exclaimed, "Get me the hell out of here!"

The following Sunday, Badalamenti had summoned lawyer and client back to MCC. "What's going on?" he asked point blank. "Didn't we agree, no plea bargains?"

"I look at my client. He is sitting there as quiet as muck," Schoenbach said later. "Badalamenti understands English well enough to handle all this without a translator. So I say, 'Look, I realize that was the agreement at that meeting. But since then my client is telling me something else.' " A lengthy, heated discussion in Sicilian ensued. "I surmise that the Old Man is telling my client he is out of the family, and Enzo is countering by pointing out that at forty-five he feels capable of making his own decisions."

The government's decision, says Schoenbach, was made because "they are afraid of losing this jury. They have been going on for ten months, with maybe another six to go. They needed movement. Enzo was the loss leader. They sacrificed him to break the ice."

Kennedy had immediately called Martin to congratulate him, and say he thought the arrangement was in Enzo's best interest. He did not add that it was also in his own best interest, and might have solved another of his problems. Kennedy had felt for a long time that Genay Leitman was too unschooled to be capable of trying this case. Now he could use this development to urge the court that she be replaced by the nimble-minded Larry Schoenbach.

Kennedy is betting that Enzo will be sitting grinning among the back-row spectators when court resumes next Tuesday morning. What will the jury make of this, and of the empty chair next to Badalamenti? Almost certainly they read about the case in the papers and watch TV, despite Leval's frequent admonishments. If so, they will know what has happened.

On balance, Kennedy feels that, despite Badalamenti's certain displeasure—the Old Man believes Schoenbach personally betrayed him—

events have taken a positive turn. "This will create motion in what has become a stagnant legal pond." And that is likely to precipitate further motion. Mazzurco, who is fifty, may plead next. The case would then lose Benfante, which would be all right with Kennedy. "I think I have learned all I can from his cross-examinations," he says dryly.

If Mazzurco pleads, the logjam will begin breaking up. Pleas from DeVardo and Cangialosi could be expected fairly quickly after that. Their lawyers are ready to make the deals.

Sal Mazzurco is in perhaps the deepest trouble of any defendant, and Benfante is looking hard for the best deal. He figures that might be ten to twelve years, and the opportunity to keep some of his property. Mazzurco is well heeled. In addition to the big Long Island house, the Mercedes, and the bank accounts, he owns part of Pronto Demolition, and most of Upskate, a roller-skating rink in New Windsor, New York. Mazzurco has substantial investments in the Hudson River town. Besides the popular roller rink, he and his brother-in-law Joe Lamberti own a neighboring women's clothing boutique, Pino Europa.

Gossip is that Mazzurco's deal is all ironed out except for the size of the forfeitures on the 848 charges. These could be substantial. As Charlie Rose has put it, "The money the government takes in these days in forfeitures and seizures is so immense that I would be more than happy to run it as a profit-making enterprise. Hell, I'd do it on a commission basis!"

Benfante knows that in the Southern District there are no guarantees. Plea-bargaining is not formally recognized; deals are struck on the delicate understanding by defense lawyers that a judge's encouragement is a reasonable indicator that the client will get fair treatment. Benfante will rely on Leval's expressed desire to stimulate movement. Other lawyers think that, if Benfante is lucky, he and his client will be out next week.

He is not lucky. Mazzurco refuses the deal Benfante works out: keep his house, plus $300,000, plus half his business. Some lawyers say Mazzurco's reason is sheer greed: He would rather do the time than forfeit his property. But others believe Mazzurco has come under strong pressure not to deal from his courtroom neighbor, Sal Lamberti, the silent, ashen-colored man who sits just to Mazzurco's right.

Gaetano Badalamenti has always maintained a formally polite but entirely aloof stance toward all codefendants who are not members of his own family. He has never had anything to do with them, never even met most of them until he found himself chained to this ragbag of strangers in this bitch of a case. The sole exception is Sal Lamberti.

Lamberti is from the next village to Badalamenti's. He is closest to Badalamenti in age. As young men, they knew each other. Sal Lamberti has the most recent ties of any defendant to the old-world Sicilian Mafia; he had emigrated to the United States just three years before the arrests.

Now Badalamenti has stopped trying to conceal his mistrust. He has begun quietly letting it be known that he considers Lamberti dangerous. On occasion he has referred to him as "the second-highest-ranking Mafioso in the world," leaving little doubt as to whom he considers number one.

If Badalamenti seems somewhat paranoid, that is understandable. He has been on the run from the Corleonese faction in Sicily since 1978, moving silently from Italy to Paris to Nice to Brazil, possibly back and forth to Spain, perhaps to other places. His lawyer estimates that as many as seventeen members of his family have by now been murdered by the Corleonese and their allies.

In this courtroom, Badalamenti sits surrounded by Sicilian Mafiosi, some of them surely aligned with his persecutors. He views almost every move by the other lawyers as possible evidence of a plot against him. Most often, although not always, Badalamenti implies that the man behind these shadowy conspiracies is Salvatore Lamberti.

Lamberti's position is that Badalamenti has orchestrated the defense being put forth by his lawyer, Kennedy, in order to ambush the other defendants, or at least paint them as ruthless Mafia killers. He does not openly say this much. The hostility on both sides, being Sicilian, is implacable but invisible. Courtroom encounters between the players are conducted with unerring courtesy. A growing cloud of distrust hangs over the courtroom nonetheless.

. . . OCTOBER 1983. THE FBI SURVEILLANCE, THE BRONX.   One day the FBI overheard Sal Mazzurco receive a call from New Windsor. Franco Marchese, his business partner in Upskate, was telephoning to arrange a meeting in the city. "That friend of mine would like another one today."

A few hours later Mazzurco met Marchese on a corner of Sedgwick Avenue, in a mostly Hispanic neighborhood of the Bronx. Mazzurco took a shoe box from the trunk of his Mercedes and gave it to Marchese, who drove a few blocks, to Webb Avenue. He pulled up in front of 2723, an aging apartment house, and delivered the shoe box to a man called Mike Crespo.

One month later, on November 16, Marchese phoned again. Crespo had something for Mazzurco's brother-in-law Joe Lamberti, he said. Mazzurco returned to the same neighborhood in the Bronx. Crespo was parked, waiting, in his Lincoln Continental. A scruffy, mustached Hispanic man, Sadid Torres, got into Mazzurco's Mercedes for a brief chat. Then Mazzurco got out and talked to Crespo, Torres climbed into Crespo's car, and the two men took off. Mazzurco followed.

At 2723 Webb Avenue, where Torres had an apartment, Crespo pulled up, entered the building, came out four minutes later with a paper package, and handed it to Mazzurco, who drove away.

On November 25, Marchese phoned Mazzurco a third time. "Your brother-in-law said that thing . . . you have it?" Mazzurco said he did, and next day he was back at Fordham Road in the Bronx. He met Crespo's brother Nelson and gave him a brown paper bag. Nelson Crespo took the bag to the apartment house on Webb Avenue. Next day Marchese phoned Mazzurco, who told him, "His brother came. . . . He took that shirt."

. . . APRIL 9, 1984. THE FBI ROUNDUP.

When federal agents stormed into apartment 3K at 2723 Webb Avenue, they found a sawed-off shotgun, $17,400 in cash, 1.25 ounces of cocaine, 1.1 pounds of lactose powder, plastic bags, glassine envelopes and—the trademark of the dope dealer—a Canadian-made Ohaus triple-beam balance scale. This is an inexpensive, precision weighing instrument manufactured for pharmacies and chemical laboratories. Sadid Torres was placed under arrest and taken off to jail.

The government's interpretation of the Bronx trips was a simple one: Sal Mazzurco and his brother-in-law Joe Lamberti were supplying cocaine to a drug ring in the Bronx. On the first trip, Mazzurco took coke to middleman Marchese. On the next trip Mazzurco picked up the money for the first supply of coke. The money was short, hence the movement in and out of cars. The third trip was another delivery of coke, this time to a coke ring run out of the apartment containing the Ohaus scale and the sawed-off shotgun.

If the Zips were dealing coke as well as heroin, another question arose. Heroin comes from Sicily, as amply illustrated by the Adamita brothers, and Bagheria, and Waridel. But where was the cocaine coming from?

. . . **TUESDAY, JULY 1, 1986.**

THE COURTROOM. This burning midsummer day marks the start of the eleventh month of trial. By now, so much information has been put forth that even a man with a photographic memory is in trouble. Says Dave Lewis, "I'm having a problem just retaining. Sometimes I am totally lost, and want to shout, *'Which* Lamberti?' "

The retention problem is causing lawyers' strategy conferences to degenerate into squabbles about what happened, and when. The jurors deal differently with the problem: They appear to have become resigned to it. Those who are not asleep often look inattentive, at least to the court proceedings. A few take off their shoes, or giggle and flirt and carry on whispered conversations, or wigwag signals about the ongoing jury-room bridge game. One cannot blame them. The notion that anyone can follow—let alone come to rational conclusions about—what they are hearing in the Gobi trek has become preposterous.

Today's witness is a DEA toxicologist and forensic chemist. She is young and modishly dressed, and in a breathless voice is describing the four chemical tests she performed to determine that the residue of white powder on another Ohaus scale, seized from the garage of defendant DeVardo, is indeed heroin. Who is defendant DeVardo? The name has not been mentioned here for ten months. Oh, yes, he is the badger-faced client of the freckled Irish lawyer, James Moriarty.

"I proceeded to do a thin layer chromotography of the residue."

"The residue contain heroin?" Yes.

Law-enforcement agencies employ hundreds of thousands of narrow-gauge experts like this young woman. They are the drug bureaucracy. Were drugs ever to be legalized in the United States, on grounds that drug abuse is a "victimless crime," which harms no one but the user, these hundreds of thousands of people would become unemployed. On the other hand, such legislation would also put thousands, perhaps tens of thousands of dangerous drug dealers out of work.

Her soft voice drones on. All the back-row defendants are asleep now, except for the ever-agonized Ligammari, propped against the wall. Even Paul Bergman's eyes have closed.

"He's not really asleep," jokes Eleanore Kennedy. "He's just trying to get a sense of what the jury is feeling, and signal them that he feels the same. Nothing is pure in this room—except the heroin."

This Tuesday is a big day for Jimmy Moriarty and his client, Lorenzo DeVardo. Ten months is a long time to sit still and silent if one is innocent; worse, perhaps, if one is not. The search of the DeVardo house, in Long Island City, Queens, is so insignificant that the prosecution lets the new kid, Andy McCarthy, handle the direct. He brings out the discovery in DeVardo's garage of the scale and, in a bedroom closet, on a top shelf, hidden under a crumpled wedding gown, a .22 semi-automatic, modified to accommodate a silencer, its serial number obliterated. McCarthy marches the length of the jury box like a Balinese stick puppet, holding aloft the wicked-looking weapon.

The day's high point comes when a U.S. Customs agent testifies that he participated in this search, along with his drug-sniffing dog. Leval immediately calls a bench conference, and no more mention is made of the dog. After the jurors have left for the day, Leval explains that the government had wanted to offer hearsay evidence—that is, evidence provided by the dog—that narcotics were in DeVardo's car. Leval has disallowed this. He makes the distinction that if the dog leads the agents to the narcotics, that's one thing; but if they lead the dog, it is an insufficient offer of proof.

At this, Kennedy silently lifts his leg. Behind him, Badalamenti doubles over in guffaws. Ignoring the vulgarity, Leval says he wants to make it clear that "no questions regarding dogs are to be asked in front of the jury until I rule." Several defense attorneys, led by Benfante and Lombardino, break into subdued barking.

. . . SATURDAY, JULY 5, 1986. SAG HARBOR, LONG ISLAND. To escape the grinding tedium of the trial, forty-year-old Bob Fogelnest has rented a small summer cottage, a place he can take his seven-year-old son on weekends. This Saturday night Fogelnest begins to feel extremely uncomfortable, but he does nothing about it. On Monday, in court, friends will say he looks unwell and urge him to see a doctor. The next night he will learn from his doctor that he suffered a heart attack over the weekend, and must have complete rest immediately.

. . . WEDNESDAY, JULY 9, 1986.

No court today. Fogelnest has taken his doctor's advice. He has sent word to Judge Leval asking for a continuance—a two-week trial postponement—something nobody else wants. This development sets off a whole new series of moves. The Badalamenti group opposes a continuance. Pierre Leval then suggests that Larry Schoenbach could replace Fogelnest. The Badalamenti lawyers also oppose this. They are still trying to use Schoenbach to force the inexperienced Leitman out of the case. Leitman, lawyer for the spaniel-eyed Palazzolo, has been resisting. Martin also opposes losing Leitman.

The news puts Leval into a particularly awkward position. He has been stalling for two weeks on the proposal that Leitman be replaced by Schoenbach. Today, at word of Fogelnest's latest collapse, Leval says, "Well, Fogelnest has local counsel." Fogelnest is a member of the Pennsylvania bar. To appear in the Southern District of New York, the rules say he must be affiliated with local counsel, in case of an emergency, and Merrill Rubin, Fogelnest's local counsel, has been forced to hotfoot it down to Leval's courtroom. But Rubin is most uneasy about substituting for Fogelnest. He knows nothing of the case, and has no intention of being stranded in Pizza for the rest of the trial. The client, Sal Salamone, feels equally strongly about being represented by someone who does not know the case. But Leval is insisting that normal protocol prevail, and that Rubin step in as Salamone's attorney. Salamone counters by having another lawyer, Gus Reichbach, file papers asserting that Salamone will not accept Rubin as his lawyer.

When Schoenbach approaches Leval about replacing Leitman, the judge tells him that the government has informed the court of secret evidence that would prohibit Schoenbach from representing any other client in the Badalamenti group.

"I had a conversation later with Freeh about it," says Schoenbach. "He said the evidence was something that won't be made public even on appeal. Leval did say that it was a major conflict of interest which could lead to a mistrial, and jeopardize the position of Palazzolo."

Mistrial is the dreaded word. As Joe Calluori puts it, "Sure Leval did good in Westmoreland. But Westmoreland was a civil case. There were a lot of ways out. But not this case. In this one there is no option of getting out. If he feels he has to declare a mistrial, it's suicideville for him. He'd be pilloried, not only by the press, but by the entire judicial community. He will do *anything* to avoid a mistrial."

Vito Badalamenti's lawyer, Bob Koppelman, speculates on what the hidden conflict might be: "The government could have tapes, or other evidence, of something Enzo said which could be inculpatory to Palazzolo. Or vice versa. Here or abroad. But most likely it's just bullshit; they didn't want Schoenbach back in."

With Rubin still adamant that he won't represent Salamone, and the government opposing Schoenbach, Leval finally nominates a lawyer from the CJA panel, Susan Kellman, and she sets about reading the 21,000 pages of transcript now in the blue binders. The alternative would have been for Fogelnest to stonewall, to insist upon shutting down the trial, as Kennedy had urged him. A quirk of fate, a missed heartbeat, has given this insignificant lawyer, with a near-to-irrelevant client, an opportunity denied to any other trial participant. Single-handedly, Fogelnest can blow the whistle, fold the circus tents, halt the train, stop the glacier. But Fogelnest does not want to buck Leval.

He lets it be known that he intends to return as Salamone's lawyer. Leitman elects to remain as Palazzolo's lawyer, though aware that several of her fellow Badalamenti-group counsel have maneuvered for weeks to have her replaced.

. . . WEDNESDAY, JULY 30, 1986.
THE COURTROOM. Enzo Randazzo is scheduled to be sentenced today, after the jury goes home at 4:00. At 3:40 P.M. he reappears in the courtroom for the first time, accompanied by lawyer Schoenbach, and they take seats in the back row of the visitors' section. The sight causes an immediate flurry of recognition among the jurors. After they are dismissed, Dick Martin goes into a long harangue on the record objecting to Randazzo's early arrival in court, and stalks out, refusing even to talk to Schoenbach.

Leval officially sentences Randazzo to time served, and lawyer and client leave. They are accosted on the courthouse steps by a TV news crew. Randazzo tells the world he never had anything to do with drugs. "You don't have to believe me. Tomasso Buscetta said so."

The reporter asks the lawyer to comment, and Schoenbach says he thinks the deal constitutes a tacit admission by the government that his client had committed a passport violation, nothing more. Told that Rudolph Giuliani had said "No comment," Schoenbach adds that he finds it remarkable that Giuliani, always the first to run to the press with news of an indictment, has nothing to say when an indictment is withdrawn.

Schoenbach does not know until the next morning that this TV team works for the evening news show anchored by Donna Hanover, Giuliani's wife. He finds out when Giuliani, furious, instructs Louis Freeh to tell the defense lawyers that all deal-making is over. As far as Giuliani is concerned, the lawyers can fight their cases through to the end, and see what sort of evidence the government has.

Enzo Randazzo is out of the Pizza case, but not yet out of hot water. Two crucial matters must still be settled. Must the United States return him to Italy to face prosecution, or is he free to go elsewhere? Two, will he get credit in Italy for the fourteen months he has been imprisoned in the United States? These matters are important because Italy has no bail. Without credit for time served, Enzo might languish three years in an Italian jail awaiting trial on the parallel Pizza charges in Italy.

Martin has told Schoenbach that if Randazzo does not show up for the designated plane to Italy, "we will arrest him and take him to JFK."

. . . MARCH-NOVEMBER 1983.

THE FBI SURVEILLANCE. In March, Joe Ganci received a telephone call from a niece who ran a travel agency in Belleville, New Jersey. She needed her uncle to come visit her, and she had made an appointment with "the other gentleman" to come as well. The other gentleman was another of her uncles, defendant Frank Polizzi, the Belleville motel and construction-company owner.

Five days later Ganci visited the travel agency, met with Polizzi, then walked to a nearby public phone. Polizzi watched him make a call. So did an FBI surveillance team.

Almost a month later, on April 4, the niece called Ganci again and asked him to come see her. She wanted him to "speak with that guy."

She added that there was a five-hour difference now, but Ganci said no, seven hours. The next day agents watched Ganci and Polizzi standing at the same phone booth they had used a month earlier. No one called. Daylight-saving time begins a month earlier in Sicily than in the United States, and they had miscalculated.

A few days later the two men met at a different pay phone, several blocks away, one on which the government had not installed a tap. But agents watched Ganci arrive in his Mercedes, and Polizzi drive up in his big Lincoln, and when the phone rang, at 10:00 A.M., they saw Ganci answer it and speak for eleven minutes. The FBI surmised that Ganci and his builder friend were receiving calls from a contact in Sicily.

A month later, on an early-summer afternoon, the two Lambertis arrived at Ganci's Queens house in Joe Lamberti's silver Mercedes. A third person was with them. He was Giuseppe Soresi, a Palermo hospital porter who was paying a brief visit to the United States. Soresi was a native of Borghetto, the same Sicilian town the Lambertis are from. Italian police had tipped off the FBI that Soresi had drug connections.

A short time later Sal Catalano came sauntering along the street to Ganci's house. The agents watched the five men—Catalano, the Lambertis, Ganci, and Soresi—stroll up and down the sidewalk, smoking and chatting. Then the Lambertis and Soresi drove off in the silver Mercedes.

Four months later Sal Mazzurco made a phone call from his Long Island home to Giuseppe Soresi at his home in Sicily. Mazzurco asked Soresi to meet him in Rome. He said he needed "a doctor," and thought Soresi's expertise as a hospital porter would be helpful. Soresi said he thought Mazzurco's chances of finding a doctor would be better if he came to Borghetto, rather than Rome.

Three days later Mazzurco arrived in Rome. When he called home to his wife, he reported he had seen the person he came to meet. Two weeks later he was back home when someone called him from Sicily. The caller had lost the phone number Mazzurco had left with him, and Mazzurco had to scramble to find it. The lost number was that of the street-corner pay phone outside Joe Ganci's Al Dente Pizzeria, on Queens Boulevard.

At 11:00 A.M. the next morning, Ganci and Mazzurco were waiting by this phone, now bugged by the FBI and staked out by at least five agents. Ganci and Mazzurco waited fifteen minutes. Mazzurco was nervous about passers-by who might demand to use the phone, so he took the receiver off the hook and pretended to talk, while holding down the hook with his other hand so that it could still ring.

Soresi finally called from Sicily, and Mazzurco gave the phone to Ganci. Their conversation was long and sometimes acrimonious. Soresi insisted that someone fly to Sicily right away. Problems had developed "in construction."

Six days later Joe Lamberti flew to Palermo, and was picked up at Punta Raisi Airport by Soresi's son, Natale. The next day the senior Soresi drove Lamberti to a hilltop shrine outside Borghetto, where they met briefly with a third man, then took off. Three days later Lamberti was back in New York.

. . . TUESDAY, AUGUST 5, 1986.

THE COURTROOM. Five months have passed since this exhausting Gobi trek began. Rarely in sequence, but always in immense detail, the government has laid out the evidence; the money laundering; the Zito drug deals; the alleged Bronx cocaine deals. Judge Leval manages to keep track of it all by means of an elaborate system of notebooks, with indexes, color-coded as to defense and prosecution, and kept up-to-date by his clerks. Notebook I is a concordance by defendant; anything regarding that defendant is indexed under his name. Notebook II is a witness concordance containing one-sentence summations of what each witness said. The judge's notebooks by now run to seventeen volumes. Without them, keeping track would seem a hopeless task.

But Gobi is far from over. The government evidence will become staggering in its bulk and detail. Federal agents will be able to produce Brazilian phone records relating to a row of pay phones at busy Galeão International Airport in Rio de Janeiro for March 1983, and show that at 11:05 A.M. on March 10, someone made a call from one of those pay phones to an obscure pizzeria in the little town of Oregon, Illinois.

The prosecutors will display a phenomenal ability, not only to link two telephones through two sets of phone records, but to match this to the movements of the defendants, and enable the jury to conclude that these defendants could be the only people at each end of the line. The FBI and the DEA worked for years in a kind of criminal-investigative haystack, and combed through a mind-boggling number of possible calls and phone boxes until they found the needle: the tie between a Brazilian public call box and an Illinois pay phone.

If the government was able to do this, it meant that a standard criminal method of maintaining secrecy was blown, and blown in the most spectacular way. Talking pay-phone-to-pay-phone was no longer safe. More amazing, talking pay-phone-to-pay-phone in two countries more than 5,000 miles apart was not safe either.

So far, all the evidence has dealt with the New York and New Jersey defendants, and all the action has revolved around the late Joe Ganci, "Il Bufalo." Michael Kennedy and the other Badalamenti-group lawyers have sat silent while the government told the jury of an ever-expanding web of calls and car trips, brown bags and boxes, all of it allegedly connecting a complex network of drug wholesalers and retailers, drug buyers, investors, runners, and mules.

But as the Gobi march trudged on, one could almost feel the anger building in the Old Man. Here was a Sicilian Mafia veteran, a man tested and steeled in a land where paranoia, self-insured security, and vigilance were second nature. He spoke in many codes. For long stretches, he spoke in *nothing but* codes. Parable and fable and allegory had become a natural language to him; ambiguity was the name of his game. Additionally, he had moved for years from country to country and abode to abode with the stealth and camouflage of a serpent. Over the years he had arranged for cartons of false documents and phony identities for himself and members of his family. It was not enough. The very precautions that had become second nature to Badalamenti were now about to betray him. In the old days, back in Sicily, no one could hear his untraceable public-phone conversations. But here, because of the FBI's astounding surveillance capacity, the jury can listen in on each cryptic conversation at each lonely parkway rest stop, and, no matter what the real subject of the double-talk might be, each meticulously tape-recorded and translated conversation will make this old don seem a bit more sinister.

The government lays it out in a relentless series of phone conversations read by actors, bolstered by telephone-toll records, airline passenger seat lists, ticket stubs, hotel registers, and agent surveillance logs. In the haze of mid-August, almost imperceptibly at first, the prosecutors begin to spin out the first strands of the web that will enmesh Badalamenti and his American relatives.

The evidence comes in disjointed, random clusters, beginning with faint contacts in late 1982 and early 1983, when Joe Lamberti was overheard saying to Ganci, in the course of a conversation about something else, "That appointment with The Doctor . . . He told you they will go over there. . . . He says, 'I'll send my nephew.' "

On December 2, 1982, Joe Lamberti was issued a new American

passport. On December 17 he flew on Varig airlines to Galeão airport in Rio de Janeiro and returned a short time later. In February of 1983 he repeated the trip, this time staying only three days.

Through the spring and summer of 1983 there were scores of cryptic telephone references to "down there," "over there," and "the Uncle."

At the beginning of June 1983 there was a flurry of phone calls between Brazil and the Midwest, and there were calls in the same period between the Midwest, Sal Mazzurco's Pino Europa Boutique, in New Windsor, New York, and Pronto Demolition in Brooklyn.

At the end of June the pay phone in Alfano's pizzeria in Oregon, Illinois, showed a call to a public-phone booth close to Mazzurco's home on Long Island. Moments later the agents heard Mazzurco call Ganci to say "that guy from there is coming tomorrow." Next morning Mazzurco drove to Ganci's house in Queens and picked up a box and a brown bag. An American Airlines flight from Chicago to New York showed a Mr. P. Alano (*sic*) as a passenger. The government claimed that Mazzurco and Alfano met that day in New York.

In mid-July came another flurry of calls between Alfano's pizzeria and Pronto Demolition, punctuated by several calls to and from Brazil. Again at the end of July came the same rapid burst of calls.

On August 7, there was a breakthrough. Mazzurco called Ganci and told him that "Enzo . . . the nephew of that gentleman . . . the guy from down there . . . he's here in New York. . . ." The reference was clearly to Enzo Randazzo. As for the "guy from down there," he was almost certainly Enzo's notorious uncle in Brazil, the old, dishonored Mafia chieftain Gaetano Badalamenti. The call also made it clear that Ganci was being kept informed of every move in this new relationship that Sal Mazzurco was forging with people in the Midwest and in Brazil.

Not until September 26, 1983, however, did Pizza really connect. On that day the investigators got their first opportunity to match faces to the mysterious phone calls. The FBI had trailed Mazzurco to the Charcoal Grill diner in Queens. There he met four UMs, "unknown males" in FBI parlance, whom the FBI was later able to identify as Pietro Alfano, the owner of a pizzeria in Oregon, Illinois; his brother-in-law Emmanuele Palazzolo, another pizzeria owner, from Milton, Wisconsin; and two Sicilian visitors—Faro Lupo and Lupo's uncle, defendant Enzo Randazzo. Later that day Mazzurco met again with Lupo and Randazzo, and this time he gave them a brown bag. Randazzo and Lupo then joined Alfano and Palazzolo, who were waiting at the Hotel Roosevelt, in Manhattan.

The September 26 meeting in the Queens diner widened the New

York drug investigation across state and international borders. The FBI's vast investigative machine focused on the strangers, particularly Alfano. They studied the telephone-toll records for the pay phone in the Alfano pizzeria in Oregon, Illinois, and discovered the Brazil and New York links.

The next important contact was October 10. That morning Mazzurco received a call from Brazil; the speaker was Enzo Randazzo. The two men talked at considerable length about sweat shirts, dresses, cotton fabric, sizes. The conversation seemed perfectly in keeping with Mazzurco's boutique business. The FBI switched off their telephone tap after nine pages of chitchat about clothes.

That night Mazzurco reported to his brother-in-law Joe Lamberti that Enzo had sent his regards, and that while nothing had been said about "the Old Man," Mazzurco was doing all he could to keep close, and that, as Lamberti well knew, the Old Man was "worse than a snake." Apparently Mazzurco's contact with Randazzo did have another purpose besides the selling of sweat shirts and dresses.

. . . WEDNESDAY, AUGUST 6, 1986.
THE COURTROOM. "Will the readers come forth," says Robert Stewart. The actors are beautifully costumed today, a bright yellow shirt on the bald man, a big pink hair bow on the blonde woman. The prosecutor asks them to read Exhibit #7599, a call made Monday, October 10, 1983, at 6:22 P.M., in which "the Old Man" is mentioned, a call "which the government contends was between Sal Mazzurco and Enzo Randazzo."

Kennedy, in a cold fury, says, "Your Honor, the Badalamenti group also *contends*"—he draws out the word, in scornful mockery of Stewart—"it was Enzo Randazzo."

The actors read a long conversation about shipments of sweat suits. Kennedy requests a sidebar, and as a result the actual tape, in Sicilian, is played for the jury. It is virtually unintelligible. Catalano, Lombardino, Benfante, and Lena Pecosi, the interpreter, appear stunned by its poor, scratchy quality. Even the actors lift quizzical eyebrows toward prosecutor Stewart, who stands propped against the spectator railing, arms folded across his chest, as the gibberish stutters on.

... NOVEMBER-DECEMBER 1983.
THE FBI SURVEILLANCE.   The FBI listened to numerous conversations between Alfano and Mazzurco in which Mazzurco seemed to be pressing Alfano for "new parts." Alfano replied that "the factory still hasn't made them." The failure to come up with new parts led to a need for the New Yorkers to talk to "the Old Man" directly. Mazzurco then gave Alfano the telephone number of the pay phone outside Ganci's Al Dente Pizzeria in Queens to pass along to Gaetano Badalamenti in Brazil.

Next day Mazzurco told Sal Lamberti that a call from the Old Man was coming. On December 14, at 11:58 A.M., the pay phone outside Al Dente rang. The agents watched in dismay as an unidentified man picked up the phone and said no one was there. Lamberti and Mazzurco showed up six minutes later and waited by the phone in freezing weather for twenty minutes.

It was January 20, 1984, when Gaetano Badalamenti finally connected directly with the New York Zips.

... WEDNESDAY, AUGUST 13, 1986.
THE COURTROOM.   An FBI agent with bouffant grey hair and aviator glasses is describing how on January 20, 1984, he saw the two Lambertis emerge from Ganci's Al Dente Pizzeria and go to the pay phone a few yards away at the corner of 68th Road and Queens Boulevard. The agent even has a video. The lights darken. The jurors watch on the large, wall-mounted TV monitor above Judge Leval's head. Leval has his own small monitor on his bench.

The two men in the picture wear their coat collars up and have their shoulders hunched; it is very cold. Joe Lamberti leans forward in his aisle seat. He appears to appreciate seeing such a good-quality image of himself.

"Freeze that frame!" Bucknam commands.

"Your Honor," Kennedy quickly interjects, "Gaetano Badalamenti agrees this is his voice on this call."

The poor-quality voice tape, in Sicilian, is played for the jury nonetheless. At this point in the video, Joe Lamberti is talking on the phone while Sal stands guard outside.

In the front row, Gaetano Badalamenti has removed his earphones. His waxen face is impassive; he fingers his chin. Bucknam orders another frame frozen, and the actors now read the conversation in English.

Joe Lamberti speaks first. "Has there been a problem?"

Badalamenti: "No. Nothing."

Lamberti: "Oh. Beautiful. Right now once in a while I am being followed."

Lamberti and Badalamenti speak cryptically of "the thing of four, five years ago" and "the modern one."

Joe Lamberti turns the phone over to his cousin Sal, and Badalamenti tells Sal, "Let's be careful. Ignazio is waiting for you."

Sal laughs. "What do you want?"

Badalamenti replies, "In March we can go collect a bunch of asparagus . . . do you feel up to it in March?"

Kennedy is on his feet to cross-examine the agent. He has not approached the podium in many months. His strategy had been to convey disinterest. Now his walk to the podium is intended to act as an alert sign to the jury: *Remember this conversation. It is important.*

"When was this phone booth first bugged?" The agent does not know. When was the video set up? He cannot remember. Kennedy is hoping to find a way to suggest that the two Lambertis deliberately lured Badalamenti into talking on a tapped phone. But this strategy is neatly defeated by the nonresponsiveness of the witness. Kennedy sits.

Martin is about to read three stipulations—statements of fact agreed to by government and defense—which the Badalamenti-group lawyers have okayed, but which Paul Bergman now refuses to accept.

Kennedy accuses Bergman of acting in bad faith. The "stips" were intended as a device to save time. To refuse to accept them wastes even more time.

Leval agrees. "The idea is not to waste *hours* of the time of sixty or seventy people in order to prove the authenticity of such obvious documents." In any event, the documents are in no way related to Bergman's client, Amato.

In fact, Bergman has objected on principle: The prosecution has abrogated so many of its past agreements on large-scale stipulations, he asserts, that the government simply cannot be trusted.

. . . PAUL BERGMAN, forty-two, attorney for Baldassare Amato, is highly intelligent, often pompous, and at times insufferable. His problem is a lack of awareness of his effect on people, an insensitivity to his own insensitivity. This oddity of character results in a curious man, a hard-shell, hard-back lawyer. He reminds one sometimes of the ever-vigilant quill-headed secretary bird of Africa, eternally pecking at each cracked kernel of legal dogma.

Bergman's father was also a lawyer, and Paul hopes his fifteen-year-old son will follow the family tradition. Paul Bergman was graduated from Brooklyn Law School, worked six months in Washington for the Federal Aviation Administration, and then spent two years clerking for Judge George Beldock—"a pompous ass." He spent the next two years in private practice, followed by two years in the Eastern District as chief of the Appeals Division.

Bergman came aboard this Ship of Fools early, representing two of the lesser figures scooped up in the FBI's wide-sweeping net. His present client had originally been represented by James LaRossa, the senior partner at Bergman's law firm, and perhaps the top-ranked criminal trial lawyer in New York. When LaRossa opted to defend "Big Paul" Castellano in the Mafia Commission trial, Bergman inherited the suave, menacing Amato.

In the Pizza case, Bergman has stamped one indelible impression: He never shuts up. In any discussion, about any topic, affecting any client, a Bergman objection or point of clarification can be anticipated.

He has also scored the biggest personal victory of any lawyer in the case—the ruling throwing out the Galante murder charge. Now his client is tied to the Pizza drug charges only by a few cryptic phone calls and a series of contested sightings by FBI agents. Yet Bergman continues to argue more than any lawyer in the room, in language always tinged with fawning admiration for the judge.

Bergman sees in Pierre Leval a mirror image. "Leval and I both have the same professional background. We were both chief of the Appeals

Division in the same period. We talk on the same wavelength. At heart, we're both academics. We *enjoy* it."

Another reason for his admiration is that "Pierre Leval takes himself seriously, yet he is never a *pompous* man."

Bergman has a clear view of the complex case. "It's taken the government the last five months to enter that part of the case which was supposed to be *the case.* All that came before was prologue, or afterthought." By putting Buscetta on first, the government did grab the attention of the jury. It got the jury focused on the Mafia, not drugs, and has kept it there since, "though there has been a little dollop of heroin here and there."

... FEBRUARY 1984. THE FBI SURVEILLANCE.

On February 4 Alfano and his brother-in-law Palazzolo drove to Temperance, Michigan, home of Sam Evola, husband of Gaetano Badalamenti's favorite niece, Christine. There Palazzolo rented a car, and he and Alfano drove on to New York. At a Burger King restaurant on Queens Boulevard they met Sal Mazzurco and gave him a brown bag. Then they drove to La Guardia Airport, turned in the rental car, and flew back to Chicago.

The FBI believed they were watching the delivery of "the modern one," a sizable quantity of cocaine, which Badalamenti had somehow contrived to smuggle from South America to his relatives in the Midwest.

On February 6 Alfano was back in New York, this time to stand in the cold with Joe Lamberti at the Al Dente pay phone and wait for another call from the Old Man. No call came. Alfano and Sal Mazzurco drove off in the direction of Manhattan, and the FBI lost track of them on the bridge crossing the East River. Eventually Alfano flew back to the Midwest.

On February 8, Mazzurco and the two Lambertis for the third time took up positions at the Al Dente pay phone. Badalamenti called, and spoke first to Sal Lamberti. They greeted each other cordially. The Old Man was angry at "the little guy"—presumably Mazzurco—for offering him some snub. Badalamenti expressed the formal hope that he and Sal Lamberti might be together soon. Lamberti handed the phone to Mazzurco, and Badalamenti asked if he knew where Fort Lauderdale was. He said yes, and Badalamenti said, "I think that by the beginning of next week . . . they will come with twenty-two parcels or with eleven parcels, whatever you guys prefer."

Badalamenti added, "I met the guy with the shirts of four years ago . . . but there's a little problem. But there is another guy here that has, there's ten per cent acrylic. I understand little about this."

Mazzurco said, "Ten per cent is not bad."

Badalamenti answered, "The cost over here is about forty-five cents. And over there it will cost about sixty cents."

The conversation ended with Mazzurco saying that he was not sure he could handle twenty-two, and asking for a day to think it over.

. . . WEDNESDAY, AUGUST 27, 1986.

THE COURTROOM. Today's main witness is the government's expert on Mafia codes. Kennedy is hunched over his fat volume of phone conversations, indexing them with yellow Post-it stickers until they resemble strings of signal pennants on a yacht. From the back, all one sees of Kennedy is the expensive beige summer suit, straw-colored hair, high color, and glimpses of thin, gold-rimmed glasses. But the image is one of contained concentration and readiness. One can imagine small pointed ears going back—like a wolf preparing to fight—under the thick straw thatch of hair. The message on the signal flags is clear: BATTEN DOWN HATCHES. BIG STORM APPROACHING.

Leval reappears after lunch without the golden curls that would break a mother's heart. He has had a shower or swim, and the damp hair plastered to his scalp makes him look like Abe Fortas.

Teresa Badalamenti, Gaetano's wife and Vito's mother, is in the courtroom today for the first time, having slipped in during a recess, accompanied by Christine Evola and Mrs. Alfano. She is a small, surprisingly young-looking woman, perhaps forty-five, with lovely auburn hair, gold-rimmed glasses, a sad face, wearing a simple brown linen dress and "good" jewelry. She speaks no English. Mrs. Badalamenti has not seen her husband or her son for more than two years. When the men turn and see her, a warm Italian current seems to gush forth between them. The boy lunges toward his mother, and the husband flashes a warm, open smile—something one would not have thought possible to see in that visage of bleached lava.

"Call Frank Tarallo."

A well-built man appears in blue-black suit, pale-mauve shirt, plain purple-and-black tie, a full head of dark hair with widow's peak, narrow silver-black mustache—an impressive figure.

"Your Honor, I have a motion regarding this witness." Kennedy walks completely around the witness box so that he can smile down briefly on this handsome dog before handing the papers up to the judge. Tarallo looks like an Italian tenor, with a tenor's ego, and a small, simpering mouth. He is very cocky. A good duel lies ahead.

Martin elicits that his witness has been a top DEA agent for two decades. He has an engineering degree, speaks Italian and Sicilian, has worked undercover, worked Hollywood vice, worked Palermo, Rome, Milan, spent four years as the DEA agent assigned to disrupt traffic in morphine base coming into Italy via Yugoslavia, and another four, in 1970–1974, as chief U.S. agent in charge of all Italian operations. He sits with chin cupped in left hand, big gold watch gleaming, telling his story in a very soft voice, but his body language shouts—bored and arrogant!

Kennedy objects that the time of his expertise makes him irrelevant to this conspiracy. Overruled.

Tarallo's drug knowledge is not at all out of date. He can cite all drug prices, at all periods, wholesale and retail. Current price of morphine base runs $10,000 to $15,000 per kilo; heroin, $140,000 to $190,000 per kilo, depending on its purity; cocaine, $75,000.

In 1977 Tarallo was assigned to a two-year hitch undercover in Pakistan, charged with tracing the westward movement of opium, morphine base, and heroin. Then he was transferred to Philadelphia, where he supervised investigations of major narcotics cases, purchased quantities of cocaine, amphetamines, PCB, and heroin. By 1982 Tarallo was the top DEA agent in New York, supervising a force of eighty-five men. He helped prepare the Pizza case; he assisted agent Hopson in Philadelphia. On August 16, 1983, he met Benny Zito with Hopson and spoke to him in Italian, posing as the dealer who had Thailand heroin for sale at $100,000 per "key," delivered. The government even has pictures of the conversation.

When Tarallo said he would "need some guarantees"—a ploy to get the hapless Zito to introduce him to his associates—Zito said he would "guarantee it with his blood."

Martin produces fifty copies of this conversation, hands them out to attorneys and jurors, turns on his tape, and Joe Ganci's rough, gargling voice rattles through the courtroom. "No, I'm not interested to meet him . . . he has to talk with you [Zito]."

Martin then leads Tarallo into an analysis of drug dealers' codes. Tarallo says "one dollar" means $100,000; "twelve miles" means a sale price of $120,000, and so on. "So you used ambiguous words . . ." prompts Martin.

"The place . . . the thing . . ." The agent has heard such codes "well over 500 times."

Still other common code words for drugs are *shirts, suits, pants, shoes, stuff.* Martin uncovers a chart of such words, set up on an easel. As his examination progresses, the prosecutor writes more words: *sweaters, ovens, pieces, clothes, cars.*

Code words for prices are arrived at by shrinking the value; 100,000 is called "one," for example. With a smile, Martin flips the paper over; underneath is a new chart, with code words for money: 60¢, 90¢, $1. Tarallo says these numbers mean $60,000, $90,000, $100,000. It sounds not just simple-minded but arbitrary. Does 60¢ *always* mean $60,000? Couldn't it mean $600,000 just as readily?

Drug dealers' nicknames are also simple. A person with red hair is called "Red." Place names are commonly referred to as "up there . . . down here. . . . It depends on the context." Martin moves on to the matter of wholesale prices.

Throughout this testimony, the more vocal, less subtle attorneys—Lewis, Benfante, Lombardino, Bergman, and others—yip "Objection!" "Form!" "Leading!" "Irrelevant!" like blasts from a whistling teakettle, and equally ineffectual. But there are several lengthy, well-attended bench conferences, which suggests that substantial legal points are involved. At one moment, Leval reaches for the first time in this trial for a thick blue paperback, *The Federal Rules of Evidence.*

The sidebars do nothing to halt the forward progress of Martin, who now elicits that from 1974 to 1979 the wholesale price of heroin in Italy varied between a low of $60,000 to $90,000 to a high of $140,000 to $190,000. "Transportation costs"—an elegant way to describe the work of the mules—ranged from $5,000 to $15,000 per kilo.

"Are written records common among drug dealers?" Martin asks.

"What is most distinctive about drug records is that they are hidden."

The cumulative effect of this testimony is devastating. Several defendants were caught with $5,000 or $10,000; mule pay, the prosecution can now assert. At least one, Mazzurco, has a book that reads very much like hidden drug records.

The rest of the morning is given over to a clump of lawyers muttering at the side bar, while across the room a boxful of jurors mutter and giggle to one another, and a silent Frank Tarallo sits tipped back in his chair, staring into the middle distance. Progress is numbingly slow. The reason, in Dave Lewis's opinion, is that "Leval is on very thin ice here, and he knows it."

Tarallo is being presented by the government as an expert witness. Leval has stated that it is "appropriate for the expert witness . . . to give evidence . . . that clarifies the drawing of inferences on matters that might otherwise be confusing." In other words, this witness can make sweeping pronouncements within his field of expertise—drug dealing. The defense lawyers are fighting frantically to gag him, or at least to narrow the field. Leval is responsible for defining the limits of inquiry; he can make them very broad, or very narrow.

Kennedy rises to cross-examine. His tone is crisply courteous. "Good morning, Mr. Tarallo. Have you met Gaetano Badalamenti? Vito Badalamenti? Mrs. Badalamenti?" As he speaks, he motions each one to stand. The agent has never met any of them.

Has the agent heard the Pizza Players read the conversations? Yes.

Leval admonishes Kennedy not to use the jocular term again.

Are there any words that cannot be used in a code? No.

So *any* word can be used as code? Yes.

In his vast experience, did he find some carefully planned codes and find ad-hoc, made-up-as-you-go-along codes too?

"Equally common."

Do they change words?

"If he's found out, he changes it . . . but no, in my twenty-four years, they go to jail, they come out, and they use the same expressions," over and over, even if they suspect their phones are being tapped.

"How do dealers get away with this!"

"They act in secret. They have a lot of money to protect themselves."

"Are Sicilians the same as us?" Kennedy asks.

"Sure."

"Have you any idea how many conversations were overheard? Would the number 55,000 surprise you?"

"Dunno." Tarallo has listened to fewer than 1% of the total. And of those, he has heard only one or two a second time. He listened to one Badalamenti conversation more than once.

Who directed your attention to Badalamenti's conversations?

"Hopson, and the Italian-speaking agents."

"How did you decide, sir, out of this incredible mass of material, to focus on Mr. Badalamenti's conversations?"

The answer comes like a first tennis serve. "Because I know the gentleman's reputation."

But Kennedy returns it. "It would be true to say that your opinion of Mr. Badalamenti is based in part on the input that you have gotten from your colleagues, including Mr. Martin?"

"I form them on the basis of the evidence."

"Have you any other evidence?" The question is a tumbling curve ball, with only two possible results: Either you strike him out, or he hits you out of the park. Several lawyers grimace. So traveled and experienced an agent might dig up anything from twenty-four years of undercover work. Once again it is Kennedy who has violated the first rule of lawyering: Never ask a question to which you don't know the answer. But this is the Kennedy style. He already has the top informant, Buscetta, exonerating his client. Now he is looking for the daddy of all undercover agents to say he knows of no evidence except the phone calls.

"No."

In the afternoon, the duelers go one more round. This time Kennedy shows himself a master at eliciting a "no" that conveys a "yes."

"You have put your life on the line, haven't you, for duty? For your job? You did not risk your life for money, for salary, did you? Five hundred times you have played a role. Five hundred times you had to convince others you were not a DEA agent, but a drug dealer. . . . So you think you have an ability to convince people you're something you're not, don't you? You have to be able to con the con man, don't you, to play your role?

"Have you had any special training in lying, Mr. Tarallo? Or are you a natural?"

The witness is momentarily at a loss for words. Then Tarallo fires back, "It is like an actor. . . . Do actors lie, counselor?"

Kennedy knows Leval will not permit him to answer the question, and so he asks, "May I be permitted to answer the question, your Honor?"

"No."

Kennedy presses on, perhaps too hard. "Do you want the prosecution to be successful here, or not?"

"Yes." The face mottles red. "With this group of people, *yes!*"

Dave Lewis, who cross-examines next, prides himself on being an aggressive investigator. During the IRA gunrunning trial, he had flown to Paraguay over a weekend, dug up a key witness—a master gunsmith living there in deliberate obscurity—and persuaded the man to return to New York to testify. This time he believes he has struck gold in Camden, New Jersey. At the recess he is gleeful. "I've a little surprise for Mr. Tarallo. I'm gonna punch him in the throat."

Lewis is at the podium waiting when the jury is led in. Tarallo takes the stand, and Lewis races to his point. "Agent Tarallo, didn't you and Agent Hopson and another agent commit assault, battery, harassment, and trespass and false imprisonment in Camden, New Jersey, in a bar on November 19, 1979?"

"No, sir."

Martin shouts, "Objection! I would like to have this stricken."

Lewis is sparking with nervous energy. He turns to the prosecutor. "Sorry, Mr. Martin. I don't think you will have the opportunity to do that."

Leval permits the question to be broken down. You were drunk? No.

Did you assault or commit battery on or trespass on or falsely imprison anyone? No.

Were you accused of having $300,000 worth of drugs in your car? No.

Do you know whether you were charged with anything that night, agent?

There were some charges, yes.

Were you drinking in that bar?

No, I was not.

The government has not objected, but Leval raps briskly and sends the jury out. The judge speaks to the young lawyer like an angry father. Your questions, "you know perfectly well, are not proper impeaching questions."

Lewis cites his evidence. Frank Tarallo was demoted in grade. He was told by the DEA that he had acted unprofessionally. He claimed that the government was out to get him. It is a clumsy performance by Lewis. "Pat Burke could have slid it in," whispers Fisher. "But David wanted to do it, because he had uncovered it."

Leval is angry, and Lewis is blustering to the point of incoherence. Why is the government grinning?

The jurors return, and Leval instructs them to disregard the improper questions they just heard regarding a bar fight. Frank Tarallo, back in his witness box, looks as if his handsome face has begun to melt. His habitual hand-to-face gesture now makes him look like a man with a toothache.

Lewis next suggests that, while chasing heroin smugglers in Islamabad, the agent allowed an informant to transport $300,000 worth of heroin in Tarallo's U.S. Embassy car, and that Tarallo failed for six weeks to file a report on the same heroin.

Why is the government so quiet? Has Martin just been hoping all would blow over?

Once again the jury is sent out. *Now* Dick Martin is ready to talk. Leval asks if the prosecutor is familiar with the matters Lewis has raised.

"I'm familiar with the Camden incident, which I know resulted in not only no charges, but in Agent Tarallo and Agent Hopson recovering in a civil suit."

Lewis is startled. "I'm not familiar with that. Against who?"

Leval has had enough of this debacle. His face is an Old Testament mask of disapproval. He sees no reason why the fact that fabricated charges were dropped should have been turned over ahead of time to the defense. Certainly the discredited charges are an improper basis for cross-examination.

The rebuke is stinging. Lewis affects not to have noticed. "No further questions," he says. A little detective work, not properly followed up on, has made him look a fool. Kennedy had tried to muzzle Lewis, at least until he knew the full story, but the younger man would not be restrained. As Kennedy tells his students at law clinics and seminars, the hardest thing to learn in trial work is not to talk. Lewis has not learned, and as Kennedy is about to discover, to his sorrow, neither has the next cross-examiner, Tony Lombardino.

Tarallo versus Lombardino becomes a clash of two old bulls. *Clothing* and *shoes* are narcotics terms, you said. Would that still be true if the speaker was in the clothing or shoe business? Yes.

Tarallo got involved in Pizza in late 1982. Did the prosecutors give you the transcript to read? Lombardino booms.

"Counselor, I'd appreciate it if you'd lower your voice."

"I'm sorry." Lombardino takes a deep breath, and bellows, "WASN'T THERE A REASON FOR THEM TO GIVE YOU THE TRANSCRIPT?"

Now, another prickly exchange. "You're asking two or three questions at a time."

"You can't handle that, huh?"

"I can handle anything you got!"

Lombardino loses control. He tries a wild shot. "What was Joe Lamberti doing in this case?"

The agent fires back, "He was dealing heroin."

"Do you know who Joe Lamberti is? . . . Can you identify him?"

"No."

Attorney Michael Kennedy and his wife, Eleanore

Attorney Ivan Fisher

Attorney Patrick Burke

Attorney Mario Malerba

Attorneys Paul Bergman and his late father, Sigmund

Attorney Harriet Rosen

Attorney Joseph Benfante

Attorney Richard Martin

Attorney Louis Freeh

Attorney Lawrence Bronson

Attorney Kenneth Kaplan

United States Attorney
Rudolph Giuliani

Judge Pierre N. Leval

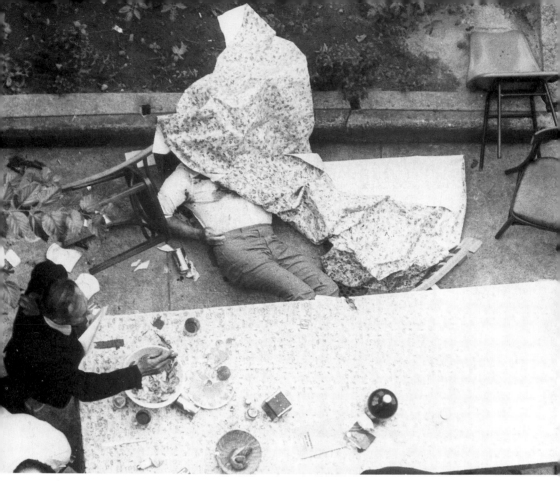

July 12, 1979: the bullet-riddled body of Bonanno Family boss Carmine Galante, covered with tablecloth, on the patio of Joe & Mary's Restaurant, Knickerbocker Avenue, Brooklyn

October 1, 1984: Mafia kingpin Tomasso Buscetta (center) escorted from plane at Rome airport after his extradition from Brazil

April 10, 1984: United States Attorney General William French Smith announces the results of the April 9 FBI roundup of Pizza Connection suspects

Left to right: Rudolph Giuliani, Benjamin Baer, chairman of U.S. Parole Commission, and Senator Alfonse D'Amato display an undercover drug buy in New York

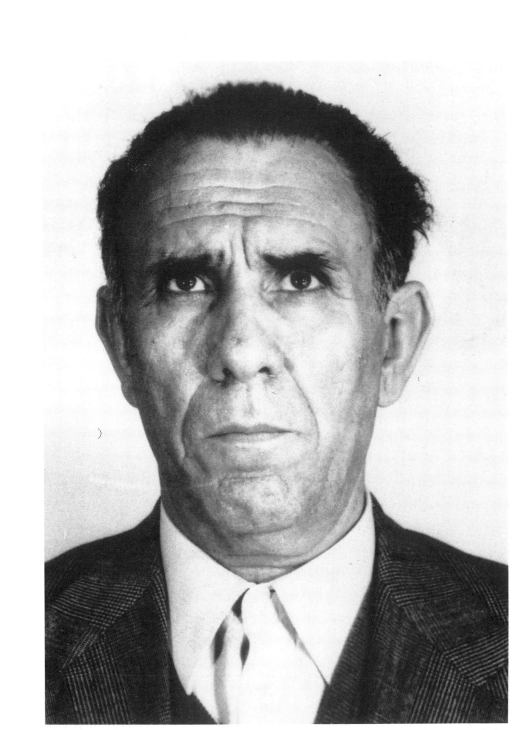

Gaetano Badalamenti, former head of the Sicilian Mafia Commissione and don of the Cinisi Family

July 10, 1983: Salvatore Catalano outside Joe Ganci's home in Queens, New York

July 10, 1983: youngest Mafia capo, Cesare Bonventre, outside Joe Ganci's home; in April 1984 his dismembered body was found stuffed in oil drums in New Jersey

October 2, 1984: Salvatore Lamberti leaves the Brooklyn federal courthouse after being freed on bail

Hit man Luigi Ronsisvalle (seated), surrounded by government agents, testifies before President Reagan's Commission on Organized Crime

Salvatore Mazzurco talks on pay phone on Metropolitan Avenue, Brooklyn

April 5, 1983: Joe Ganci (left) and Frank Polizzi wait for twenty minutes beside a Belleville, New Jersey, pay phone; no call came through

Left to right: Frank Polizzi (partially visible), Cesare Bonventre (facing camera), Joe Ganci (right), and Baldo Amato (back to camera) meet in parking lot of Polizzi's restaurant, Belleville, New Jersey

Joe Ganci (right) and Filippo Casamento load boxes into Ganci's Audi outside Casamento Salumeria, Brooklyn

Joe Ganci with his mistress, Carol Giuliano

Salvatore Lamberti leads Sicilian visitor Giovanni Cangialosi to Lamberti's Mercedes

December 2, 1986: the body of Gaetano "Tommy" Mazzara dumped on a Brooklyn street

Patsy Conte, Sr. (wearing glasses), with attorney Emanuel Moore (left), leaves federal courthouse after posting $3-million bail in Alfano shooting case

David Lewis, attorney for Sam Evola, comments to the press after the verdict

Unknowingly, Lombardino is on the edge of a precipice. He now tries the Kennedy curve ball. "Tell me what first-hand information do you have that Joseph Lamberti was dealing drugs?"

The agent belts it straight out of the park. *"The conversations that he had with Mr. Badalamenti."*

"Objection!" Kennedy immediately demands a mistrial.

"Objection sustained. Mistrial denied."

Recess. Kennedy is furious. Because an "expert" has given his opinion that these were drug conversations, what had heretofore been circumstantial may now be taken as proved beyond reasonable doubt.

"This line of questioning *allows* jurors who want to convict to have the evidence to do it on. That's why so-called expert testimony of this nature is often not allowed," says Kennedy. "The jury believes in an 'expertise' that does not really exist." In this instance, the damage has been so severe that Freeh stops by to offer condolences. He understands that Lombardino has put Kennedy's client into the worst possible company, and that there is now no way to extricate him.

Paul Bergman now conducts an endless-seeming cross about heroin terms and heroin prices. Yes, *blouses, shoes, collars* are code. *Soft collars* are cocaine; *hard collars* are heroin. Why does Bergman do this? None of it has anything to do with Amato, and it only makes the expert seem increasingly credible.

But at lunch the Kennedys thank Bergman. He has been trying painstakingly to show that *none* of Tarallo's heroin-price figures match the figures in the conversations. They don't, but after Lombardino lost his head, pointing this out scarcely matters. Kennedy had objected at the very beginning, in his written motion, that because Frank Tarallo has intimate knowledge of this case, the jury would infer that he knew what he was talking about in regard to Pizza specifically. That he had been debarred from discussing or interpreting the meaning of specific code words would not make any difference. One of Judge Friendly's most important rulings on appeal had been that, although the law says you cannot create your own witness, in fact you can. Martin has done it very skillfully with Tarallo. Kennedy's motion has been denied.

Now, because this agent has testified as to the meaning of *shirts* to him, these defendants will be compelled to testify as to what *they* meant by *shirts.*

"This," says Kennedy, "is where Leval has most clearly shown that he's on the government side."

When, hours later, Bergman's cross finally ends, Martin does a tough, effective redirect. "You recall when Mr. Kennedy asked you if you knew Mr. Badalamenti, and knew his reputation?" Yes.

"I never asked such a question," Kennedy snaps. "I have no interest in his opinion of Mr. Badalamenti's reputation."

You know of his reputation through your colleagues in Italian law enforcement? Yes.

You remember Mr. Kennedy asking you questions about cryptology? Yes. When you spoke of drug codes, were you referring to cryptology? No. Have you ever encountered drug dealers who use no codes? No.

On the Camden bar fight, Martin brings out that the bar manager was a suspect cop, the target of a DEA investigation. At his own departmental trial, Tarallo was completely exonerated and given a promotion. He then sued the city of Camden and recovered $100,000 in civil damages. His current position? He is in overall charge of DEA security.

"We'll take a break now," says Judge Leval.

Matters could hardly have gone worse. Someone stops to commiserate with Eleanore Kennedy. "It just proves the system works," she says bravely. "Michael should now, but won't, ask the cheap question: Isn't it possible, agent, that just as you were falsely accused and acquitted, the same thing could be true of my client?"

Later, the senior defense attorney speaks up for the youngest. Segal is back in the courtroom after some weeks' absence, having left stunt lawyer Harriet Rosen in his chair, and he is struck by how much the proceedings have deteriorated. The sheer length of the trial, now starting its twelfth month, has dulled the normal reaction times of the defense lawyers. The attorneys have grown sluggish, and are not nearly as quick on their feet as they should be.

But he is most angry about the humiliation of Dave Lewis. "This is misuse of Brady! Brady says the defense must have use of *all* relevant information, so it can make tactical decisions as to whether and how to proceed. If the defense doesn't get it, that means the guys in the back"—he nods contemptuously toward the bench and behind—"are controlling what happens in front. Dave had three quarters of the story on Frank Tarallo; he didn't have the expungement. So he was not properly armed and caparisoned to go into battle. *He* should have had first choice on whether to decide to go into the agent's past. By holding back information, the government deprived him of his rightful choice."

As the lawyers file out of the courtroom, Larry Ruggiero, attorney for Giuseppe Vitale and Giuseppe Trupiano, shakes his head in dismay. He mistrusts *any* agent on the witness stand, especially an experienced one. He knows the breed too well. He knows that they rarely answer a question simply, or directly. He knows they are "too eager to serve their masters," that they "always try to put a little spin on the ball."

. . . LAWRENCE RUGGIERO, forty-five, is a passionate man who has worked every side of the criminal justice system but the bench. He is a dedicated defense lawyer, formerly a dedicated prosecutor, and before that, an honest agent, for the IRS, who used to play the dangerous game of exposing crooked agents—the people he considers "the baseline cause of evil in the criminal justice system." The Pizza defendants know Ruggiero's background, and despise him for it. To them, he is a simple snitch.

In 1979 and 1980, when Ruggiero was a senior prosecutor with the Narcotics Division of the Southern District, one of the bright, aggressive lawyers in the office was Richard Martin. Ruggiero used to admire the younger man, and regard him with considerable affection. "At first he's guarded; later he opens up. Basically, he's a very nice guy. Lovely family.

"But in the Pizza case, we're seeing a new breed of prosecutor. Martin & Co. don't care what they do to people's lives. My guy Vitale sits there seven months—his name is not even mentioned!" Then the jury is told of a phone call by Alfano to Vitale. "But no one says to the jury that the two women, Mrs. Alfano and Mrs. Vitale, are sisters!" Needless to say, Ruggiero intends to mention this when it is time to put on his defense.

Ruggiero was raised by an aunt and uncle, immigrant Neapolitans with a surpassing belief in the American system. After law school at St. John's, he started in law enforcement in 1965 as an IRS agent, in the Yonkers office. Because he had a background in public accounting as well as a law degree, he was assigned to investigate Mafia efforts to evade taxes.

"I began making cases on organized-crime guys." The mob sent an attorney to see the young agent and attempt to bribe him. "He also suggested I lighten up on my *paisans.*" The approach rang both the bells that rule Ruggiero's professional life: his abhorrence of corruption, and his sensitivity to anti-Italian slurs. Astonished, and stung, Ruggiero immediately reported the encounter to his superiors.

Six months later Ruggiero was stopped on the Cross County Parkway by the same lawyer. He asked, "Why are you doing this to your own people? If you give 'em a break, they'll pay you money. Join the team. We're paying off."

It was 1967. Ruggiero again reported the encounter to his superiors. They flew him to Washington, took him to the office of the commissioner of the Internal Revenue Service, along with the chief of the Intelligence Division, and asked him if he'd be willing to work undercover. "Absolutely not!"

A few months later, in a Westchester diner, the mob lawyer appeared for the third time and told Ruggiero in greater detail about the number of IRS agents already on the organized-crime payroll. Ruggiero was again appalled, again flown to Washington, and again declined undercover work. But the idea was beginning to eat into him, and soon he could not sleep. "I'm in an office full of corrupt agents," he told his wife. "I'm convinced these cases are being bought and sold wholesale." A few weeks later, he recalls, "I heard myself telling my wife, 'Well, I'm going to do it.' "

"You do and you'll get killed," she said. "I don't want to live that way. You do it, and I'm leaving." He did, and she kept her word.

For the next two years he worked undercover, wearing a wire, "and I began to see *how much* corruption was involved." Soon he noticed that he was getting a lot better treatment by the senior special agents, the IRS executive-level personnel. One said with a wink, "Hey, I hear you know Billy" (the mob lawyer). "I said to myself, Holy Christ! This thing goes way up!"

By that time Ruggiero had evidence on tape of seventeen corrupt IRS agents dealing with organized-crime figures. His next move was to tell Billy, "Hey, I'm a businessman, and you and I are in business together. We're partners. I should know what's going on, in case you're out of town or something." He handed Billy a directory of IRS personnel and said: "I want you to put an X next to the name of every person you personally saw getting paid off." This was the start of a four-hour conversation.

"Now I want you to put a question mark next to those agents who you *believe* are getting paid off."

"And, for each question mark, he gives me the case history of why he believes this."

Then Ruggiero asked for a zero against every name who had refused payoffs. The Xs and the question marks added up to over 35% of the names in a directory of perhaps 200 names of both agents and supervisors.

Billy had told him, "Larry, just get into the Appellate Division, and you'll be rich," so the lawyer decided next to look into corruption in the IRS Appellate Division, "where the real horse-trading goes on." By that time he needed two full-time assistants, "because the o.c. guys are always asking favors—look into this case, that case. . . ." One day an organized-crime guy said they mistrusted one of his assistants and were going to kill him that night. Ruggiero swiftly shut down his operations and ended his undercover career.

By then he had made cases on fourteen agents. From 1970 to mid-1973 he testified as chief witness in sixteen trials in the Southern District, against both corrupt agents and organized-crime figures. During that period he was in the U.S. Witness Protection Program. Gradually he evolved into a sort of general expert on government and agent corruption—IRS, FBI, Customs, state troopers, mayor's office, City Council, and others. "That became the thing I did." He got called in, as a specialist, wherever corruption was suspected.

"Result: As a prosecutor, and as a defense attorney, I'm incredibly suspicious of *all* agents, and especially FBI. When the FBI took over DEA, I said, Sayonara! I think the FBI might be the greatest threat that exists to this republic—and that's from someone who's been in law enforcement seventeen years!"

Ruggiero knows it is the savvy agents who really run the show. "You've got to realize how great the pressure is on the agents to make the case. Because you don't go anywhere in a bureaucracy if you lose cases. No way a young, wet-behind-the-ears prosecutor, after three years' experience in some white-shoe law firm, can deal with these long-experienced agents. Not only deal—*supervise* them. You must have federal prosecutors who are *strong* enough to be honest. You cannot expect sheltered kids to deal with street-wise agents. They all wind up the same way—getting conned like crazy."

Ruggiero has several times told Martin, "Get out of that office. You must do it to save your soul. The pressure to make cases is too great. So is the temptation to rabid self-righteousness. Do anything. Drive a bus if you have to." His point is that under Giuliani, "who is incredibly ambitious, and *steeped* in self-righteousness," Martin, who is also ambitious, will not be able to take the pressure. As a colleague has said, "Dick Martin lies. He would never take money to get someone off. But he will tell lies to put someone away."

Says Ruggiero, "I never saw the system go so wrong before as it has in this case. I'm talking about the abuse of the system by the government. As a prosecutor, I could always control situations. If it looked like the agents were cutting corners, bending truth, getting too slick, I could get the case dismissed, and I did." He recalls an eight-defendant cocaine case. The agents didn't like the quality of one of their wiretaps; the speaker's voice was too difficult to identify. So, after the indictment, to "improve" their evidence, an agent called the defendant, pretended to be his parole officer, and thereby got him to speak out, loud and clear, into a tapped phone.

"It's the agents who control what really happens in the courtroom. As a prosecutor, you can supervise the agents. This means that you can hold them to the highest standards." But that is not being done in this overzealously prosecuted, elephantine case. And the agents are without qualms. They believe in "taking care of his"; they feel they are "doing the right thing." So, really, the tail wags the dog.

"Pizza shows what the system can do to people, how far it can go." Ruggiero was outraged to see Giuliani on the "20/20" TV show, before the Pizza trial had even begun, telling the public: The Mafia has moles, just like the CIA has moles, and Trupiano and Vitale are Mafia spies sent over from Sicily to penetrate the heartland of America.

"Before they were even indicted, Rudi was comparing Trupiano and Vitale to foreign espionage agents! He did this *knowing* that the two suspects came from Bible Belt towns; knowing his remarks would ruin two men, and two families, for at least two and a half years before the case could be decided."

What has really upset Ruggiero was seeing his client Trupiano cry. The man had burst into tears when Ruggiero asked him, out of the presence of the jury, to tell Judge Leval what the case was costing him in suffering and money. Trupiano and Vitale are almost indigent. Ruggiero is one of the CJA lawyers.

"I can't explain this thing to Trupiano any longer," his attorney says. "I can't stand to watch what's happening to my guys and their families." Both men live in small Illinois towns of about 6,000 population. "Vitale is forty-four years old, has four teen-age kids, speaks with a very heavy accent. But the kids are Pepsi Generation types, just regular Midwestern teen-agers. Trupiano has three kids, a few years younger than Vitale's, and they too are suffering, are ostracized and taunted at school. And this needless torture and torment has now been inflicted on these two families for more than two years—and the men have not even been found guilty of anything!

"My clients are ruined. The townspeople heard the publicity and now scorn them. Their little restaurants are empty. The more educated townspeople, a few doctors and lawyers, stick by them. But mostly their kids in school hear from other kids, 'Your father kills people!'

"Now banks have begun recalling their loans. First they lost their businesses. Then they lost their cars. Now one of them is about to lose his house!

"I really care about my clients. Other attorneys say I care too much. But I can't efficiently, effectively represent them *unless* I care about them. So: you die with them."

Ruggiero believes that Martin's strategy, from the outset, has been to set all the defense attorneys against each other, like sharks in a feeding frenzy, "and let them all destroy each other, and it's working . . . it's working. . . .

"*All* the attorneys are losing faith in the system. And these are people who could fix the system. From the inside.

"This case has sickened me from Day One—when I saw the government trying to pick the most ignorant possible jurors for one of the most complex cases ever prosecuted."

. . . FEBRUARY 14, 1983.

THE FBI SURVEILLANCE.   By Valentine's Day, Alfano was back in New York again. It snowed that day, and his flight was diverted to JFK. But by 3:55 P.M. he stood once more beside the pay phone near Al Dente.

The Old Man called and talked first to Alfano. He wanted someone to "go to a town in the sun." A reference to Fort Lauderdale, Florida, had been made in the previous call. "They should bring one hundred." Alfano then handed the phone to Mazzurco. Badalamenti asked why "the boss" wouldn't come. Mazzurco said it was because he "had a tail."

After the call, Mazzurco drove Alfano straight to La Guardia, where he caught a flight to Chicago.

By February 18 Pete Alfano seemed to be having considerable difficulty in his dealings with the New York group. When Badalamenti called, Alfano reported, "Those guys over there are as dry as a rock" (no money). This did not satisfy the Old Man. He told Alfano to "go and get it" because somebody "was down there walking around."

The next day Badalamenti again called the Al Dente pay phone. Sal Lamberti answered, and Badalamenti told him that Alfano should be "given the eighty." Otherwise the Old Man would be embarrassed because "that guy is on the street with twenty-two." The government interpreted this to mean that Badalamenti had not been paid and wanted his money quickly.

Two days later Mazzurco called Joe Ganci, who told him, "That thing" (the money) was very difficult for that day. He would have it in two days. The next few days produced a flurry of phone calls to pay booths and private phones. Money was the problem. In New York the FBI watched defendants Catalano, Ganci, Mazzurco, both Lambertis, and Ligammari enter a social club above the Rutledge Deli on Rutledge Avenue, in Queens.

In the Midwest, Alfano and Evola also seemed desperate to collect money owed to them and were hounding an associate named Giralamo Vito Palazzolo, a relative of defendant Palazzolo. Alfano repeatedly called the man's home, and finally told Evola, "As soon as you see him, kill him with a hammer . . . take his money and bring it."

On February 27 Alfano drove to a liquor-store pay phone in Oregon, Illinois, to receive a call from Mazzurco. This phone too had been tapped, and agents heard Alfano instruct Mazzurco to go see a Mrs. Anna Alvarado, and to ask for the Duke account. The next day, other agents watched Mazzurco carry a briefcase into the offices of Manfra, Tordella & Brookes, a foreign-money brokerage in New York's World Trade Center. Anna Alvarado was a vice-president.

Two hours after Mazzurco's visit, he was back on the phone to Alfano, now hollering, "Where the hell do you send me! Do you know what they were looking for? Passports, documents, they have to *report* it!"

Alfano was weighed down with problems. Badalamenti called him again to say he had forgotten one phone number, but would give him another. He spelled out U-R-E-R-M-E-S and promised that, in another twenty minutes he would be there.

Martin recalls Special Agent Carmine Russo, the FBI's chief translator. The Badalamenti-group lawyers are restless; there is much moving about, and study of notebooks. Lena Pecosi, the translator, stands beside the stooped figure of Kennedy towering over the Old Man.

Martin announces that he will write a series of letters on a blank easel page. He writes: T E R M I N U S A.

Russo says he does not recognize the word.

Next Martin writes:

I M R S U R R
S T E U R E R M E S
ERMES PEP SROARET
STEANAETM

Russo says the letters bear no resemblance to any Italian or Sicilian words. Martin sits down. The jury looks perplexed.

Kennedy is first to cross. The jury sits up—a Pavlovian response. Kennedy equals *action*.

"Agent, have you been told that the word TERMINUSA is actually a code?" Yes.

Kennedy goes to the chart and writes the letters vertically:

$$T = 1$$
$$E = 2$$
$$R = 3$$
$$M = 4$$
$$I = 5$$
$$N = 6$$
$$U = 7$$
$$S = 8$$
$$A = 9$$

"Agent, is this the key to the code?" Yes.

The lawyer goes on to write the letters IMRSURR, which translate to 543-8733, the telephone number at the Badalamenti apartment in São Paulo, Brazil. Kennedy sits down.

Recess. Smiles in the corridor. Kennedy feels his strategy has worked. Martin, he says, was foolish to introduce the codes without putting a cryptologist on the stand. What Kennedy has done is acknowledge that these mysterious letters are codes, and put the jury on notice that they will be explained in the fullness of time. Martin wanted to be able to scream "drug dealing" as every cryptic word was presented. Kennedy has at least muted the scream.

At the revelation of the TERMINUSA code, Dave Lewis had turned to stare at his client. Evola had told everybody, including his lawyers, that Terminusa was the name of his uncle's favorite cow. Glancing at the code written on the easel, Evola gave a Sicilian shrug and told Lewis, "It can mean that too."

. . . **WEDNESDAY, SEPTEMBER 10, 1986.**
THE COURTROOM.   Bad luck had first struck the Evola camp a couple of weekends ago, when Sam decided to do some home repairs, fell off his scaffold, and broke his leg in two places. Arrangements were made temporarily to proceed without him. Now he is back in the courtroom, on crutches, grey-faced and still in considerable pain. The Badalamenti-group lawyers are thinking of putting the blond, rugged-looking former construction worker on the stand, as the family's most attractive and articulate member. This would also afford an opportunity to point out to the jury his loyal, lovely wife, and perhaps one of his strapping sons, the one in medical school.

These hopes are dashed with the appearance on the witness stand of Special Agent Delmar Ward, of the Ann Arbor, Michigan, FBI office. When Evola was arrested and read his Miranda rights, he said, "You can't prove nothing on me." The government takes this as an acknowledgment that there was something to be proved. In Evola's wallet, agents found a cryptic scrap of paper on which were inscribed the words TERMINUSA and IMRSURR. Later, after Evola had been escorted to the Detroit FBI office, he waived his Miranda right to have a lawyer present before answering any questions, and when shown the scrap of paper told the agents about his uncle's cow.

Toward the end of the FBI interview, Evola was asked about twenty-seven grams of white powder found at his home. Was it heroin? No, he said: cocaine. Asked if he had any more, he said he once had a kilogram, had kept this bit "as a sample," and sold the rest. Evola refused to say where he got the drug.

No one cares to cross-examine. Agent Ward's testimony has been a crushing blow to Evola and to the Badalamenti group.

. . . **MARCH 1984.**
THE FBI SURVEILLANCE.   The relationship between Alfano's Midwest group and Mazzurco's people in New York did not improve.

Joe Lamberti told Mazzurco that Alfano kept insisting upon receiving "that thing." At the same time, Alfano was telling the Old Man in Brazil that the New York people were "six shirts short."

Baldo Amato was busy building Café Biffi, a slick new Italian coffeehouse and bar on Manhattan's Upper East Side. When the FBI saw Amato and Bonventre, as well as defendants Catalano, Ganci, Polizzi, and Joe Lamberti, gather at the building site, they concluded that the purpose of the meeting was to try to solve the money problem between the New Yorkers and the Badalamenti group—the same matter that was causing Mazzurco to be "six shirts short."

A dispute had also erupted between New York and the Midwest over who was going to go "there." Alfano had called his brother-in-law Palazzolo and told him to be ready to take a car ride. He had called another brother-in-law, Trupiano, and talked more about a long automobile trip, a trip made necessary because "the guy over there [Mazzurco] won't go," but did agree to meet "two or three hundred miles before."

The FBI's reading on the call was that Mazzurco was unwilling to go to Florida and pick up the twenty-two parcels himself, but would rendezvous with someone 200 or 300 miles outside New York City. Alfano then tried to recruit someone to make the long drive. The plan was to fly to Fort Lauderdale from Chicago, then rent a car and drive back along the East Coast.

. . . THURSDAY, SEPTEMBER 11, 1986.

THE COURTHOUSE. The government's case is nearly finished. The defense will begin soon. But the defense for weeks has been in increasing offstage disarray. In multidefendant cases, it is always best to go last. Last place gives a lawyer an opportunity to repair damage to his client by fellow lawyers, and provides the only sure protection against a stab in the back. A deadly first-and-last game has been quietly in progress for some weeks among the defense lawyers.

The game becomes more sinister when word gets out about Kennedy's medical problem. The lawyer has known for some time that he must go into the hospital for delicate facial surgery, followed by two weeks of bed rest while he regains equilibrium and doctors check for bleeding. During a diving vacation last year, Kennedy came up with his mask full of blood, and doctors later found a tumor in his nose. It is benign but growing, and must be removed before it invades the cartilage. Otherwise a cartilage transplant could be necessary, probably from a rib, and that would mean major surgery. Kennedy had been hoping to put off the whole business until the trial is over, and Eleanore has joked that she might consider contributing the tip of her splendid Italian nose. But now Kennedy has begun to experience some bleeding and hearing loss, and the doctors say they dare not wait much longer.

Kennedy has put all this in a letter to the court, and has suggested to Leval that a convenient time for him to take off would be at the end of the prosecution case.

In multidefendant cases, it is customary for lawyers who wish to cross-examine to be called upon in the order of the indictment. In Pizza, it has been Kennedy first, Ryan last. When it comes time to put in the defense case, the order is often reversed, to equalize matters. Sometimes the judge makes this decision; in other instances, he leaves it up to the lawyers to work out, as Leval has done. Kennedy in his letter to Leval has proposed that if the defense case were indeed presented to the jury in reverse order—Ryan first, Kennedy last—there would be sufficient time for him to have his surgery and convalesce without slowing down or shutting down the trial.

Unfortunately, Kennedy did not send copies of the letter to his brother attorneys. Such by now is the level of mutual mistrust that when the others do hear about it, they do not believe it. They suspect Kennedy and/or his client of pulling a fast one. For once, some prosecution lawyers agree with the defense. Martin writes to Leval that Kennedy's emergency is "not life-threatening."

As for the clients, none of them trust Kennedy to go last, and nobody trusts the Old Man. They think he is the one who wants to go last, and that he has forced his lawyer to make up a phony story about needing an operation.

Ivan Fisher has made plain from Day One that he wants in all matters to stick as close to Kennedy as possible. Before the trial, he fought to have Badalamenti and Catalano seated side by side, and might have won had not the marshals insisted that the four incarcerated defendants sit together for security reasons. Fisher has grown increasingly insistent that his own defense follow Kennedy's, rather than precede it. Other lawyers fall in behind Fisher. Their clients agree. Nobody but Kennedy, it seems, trusts Kennedy's client.

The corridor talk is that all the made men expect Badalamenti to stab them in the back if he can. Sal Lamberti is a Mafia member; so, too, are Castronovo, Greco, Mazzara, and Catalano. Of the five, only Mazzara is not pushing for Kennedy to go first.

Another reason everyone wants Kennedy to go first is to find out what his defense will be, and give themselves maximum time to oppose it, or work out alternative strategies. Kennedy is adamant: he will not disclose his defense to anyone. His reason, though he still refrains from saying so, is his belief that to disclose it would guarantee a leak to the prosecution.

. . . FRIDAY, SEPTEMBER 12, 1986.
THE COURTROOM.   The actors take their places. The wiretaps they read now sound particularly damaging to Badalamenti. He and Alfano are talking about "Things . . . little shirts . . . one driver." The actor who plays Alfano telling Evola to go see someone and "kill him with a hammer" happens to be wearing a black shirt and white tie, and somewhat resembles an actor playing Nathan Detroit in *Guys and Dolls.* Marvin Schechter objects to this "dressing for the part." Bergman says if the actor isn't careful, he could find himself indicted.

Coffee break. In the cafeteria line, handsome Baldo Amato, former Galante bodyguard, is approaching the cheerful, plump young woman who works the cash desk. He carries a carton of milk. As he draws level with the woman he whips back his jacket, pulls a banana from his belt, and points it at her. "Dees ees a steekup!" he says. The woman giggles.

. . . WEDNESDAY, SEPTEMBER 17, 1986.
THE COURTROOM.   At the end of today's session, the courtroom will be cleared to permit the defense lawyers to caucus and resolve once and for all the raging debate over who goes last.

"A lot of lawyers are upset about the way this is turning out," says Schechter. "My client, Sal Lamberti, and Joe Lamberti, and Mazzurco all need to know if this is going to be a collective defense or not. The whole thing revolves around whether Kennedy will reveal his strategy."

The judge has left the bench. The marshals have gone home. The defense lawyers sprawl on the visitors' benches. Kennedy puts his case plainly. Badalamenti wants to go last. Kennedy intends to mount an aggressive defense to explain the phone calls. He cannot tell the other lawyers what that defense will be, but he can assure them that they'll like it.

This is not enough for Benfante or Lombardino, the two lawyers, besides Schechter, who have to deal most with the damning Al Dente pay-phone calls. Does Kennedy even *know* what Badalamenti's defense will be? Yes, he does. Many lawyers are not satisfied. Benfante says, "What am I supposed to do, go to my client and tell him, I don't know what the defense is—but you'll like it?"

Lombardino is more direct. "Tell Badalamenti to stuff it."

The meeting breaks up. Kennedy will have to go first, and postpone his surgery until after he explains his client to the court and jury.

. . . MONDAY, SEPTEMBER 22, 1986.

AFTER COURT.   Every night now the Badalamenti-group lawyers hold brainstorming sessions with their clients, and each other. Kennedy has spent long hours at MCC huddling with the Old Man. The Badalamenti-group attorneys have divided up sections of the evidence to be studied and rebutted. Tensions are high. The family members are silent and sheeplike, taking every cue from Badalamenti. The usually soft-spoken Pat Burke is angry about the lack of feedback the lawyers are getting from the Sicilians in return for their efforts. Today, for example, Burke had worked out an elaborate cross-examination of one of the government's witnesses, one that developed a reasonable explanation for a particularly damaging Brazilian phone call. Burke wrote it all out, and "went and had an audience with the Pope at MCC.

"He shot it down," says Burke with some bitterness. "Those guys are blockheads. Dumb shits. There's a lot of animosity now from him to me. I can't do my job. It's stupid."

. . . PATRICK BURKE,

forty-two, practices out of the small New York State town of Suffern, some forty miles northwest of Manhattan. He was born in Scranton,

Pennsylvania, to Irish-American parents who later moved to the Bronx. He was graduated from Fordham Law School in 1966, married Jane Kennedy, and soon thereafter joined the Marine Corps as a military lawyer with the Judge Advocate's Office in Quantico, Virginia. When he was discharged three years later, he had reached the rank of lieutenant colonel. In 1969 he joined the U.S. Attorney's Office for the Southern District of New York. In 1975 he settled in the quiet suburb of Suffern and teamed up in practice with a local lawyer, Joe McGlinn.

The law offices of Burke & McGlinn look no different from the other two-story shingle houses on Washington Avenue, except for the painted sign fixed to the front porch. Burke and his partner have built up a busy and lucrative practice handling an unending flow of drunk driving, assault, and negligence cases.

In 1983 Burke was asked by a fellow lawyer if he would be interested in trying a heroin case in the Eastern District that involved Sicilians accused of smuggling heroin in crates of Italian marble. Burke got his man off, and word spread around MCC that the lawyer had handled himself well. Soon Burke was getting inquiries from some of the Pizza defendants.

In June of 1984, six weeks after the arrests, Burke received a call from Pete Alfano's wife. She was waiting for her husband to be extradited from Spain and needed an American lawyer to deal with the Spanish authorities. Eventually the three men were moved from Madrid to New York, and Burke was asked to meet with Gaetano Badalamenti in MCC. The Old Man was interviewing prospective attorneys. Burke strongly disliked him. Badalamenti's peasant cunning put him off. He tested Burke with sly questions that seemed designed to measure his comprehension of the indictment, and the lawyer found the process demeaning. Next, Pete Alfano asked Burke to defend him, and after much haggling a fee was set.

The length of the case has taken its toll on Burke's law practice and his family life. His military background taught him to work at keeping fit in order to win the fight to remain awake and alert in the courtroom. He drives into Manhattan early each morning and jogs several miles in Central Park before changing clothes in the New York Athletic Club and hopping the subway to court. Burke is a keen athlete, and his four teen-age sons, athletes all, play on teams that require a lot of coaching and support. Now he finds he must sacrifice Saturday mornings and Sunday nights to Pizza. His wife, Jane, the nurse at the boys' high school, has been forced to take over as basketball-team driver.

Burke thinks the government has assembled a forceful case, but one with major contradictions. "Look at the tapes. The New York people are running about in 1984 trying to raise $80,000. That was walk-around change to these guys!" When the government introduced the money-laundering evidence, millions of dollars were being exchanged in liquor boxes. What happened to all that money?

"Then you have all the phone talk between Mazzurco and the Lambertis about staying close to Enzo, about the Old Man being 'over there,' and how Mazzurco should not probe too closely into his whereabouts, lest the Midwest people back off. They're clearly trying to discover where Badalamenti is."

. . . MARCH 1984.

THE FBI SURVEILLANCE. Mazzurco still seemed to be having problems raising money, and called Alfano to ask that he postpone his trip to New York a few more days. On March 7 Mazzurco called Soresi in Borghetto, Sicily, and said a man was coming who "had to be examined at the hospital . . . quickly."

Defendant Lorenzo DeVardo, the Queens painter who the FBI believed was Soresi's American contact, flew to Sicily, and Italian agents reported that he was attempting to make contact with Soresi. Four days later DeVardo returned to the United States and on March 14 met with Joe Lamberti. That same night Lamberti told Ganci he had met with the guy who was "over there," and everything was prepared. "But the weather got bad and everybody took cover." The FBI interpreted this as a reference to heavy police surveillance of Soresi and his Sicilian contacts. Lamberti added that "the guy from over there," Soresi, had called him and had "sent his cousin."

The next day Mazzurco drove to JFK to meet a flight from Rome. He picked up a Sicilian truck driver, defendant Giovanni Cangialosi, who is Soresi's wife's cousin. This quiet, thirty-five-year-old man who looks like a smaller Harpo Marx without the wig has been sitting silently for twelve months at the far end of the middle row.

The following day, Cangialosi and Joe Lamberti were observed meeting with DeVardo in the parking lot of a Long Island shopping mall. Four days later, March 20, Mazzurco and Cangialosi were waiting at a pay phone on Long Island's Southern State Parkway when Soresi called from Sicily. The FBI had bugged this phone after noticing Mazzurco hanging around it.

Soresi first said it was "sleeting," a reference to heavy Italian police surveillance. The early-spring weather in Sicily in fact was glorious and mild. Soresi told Cangialosi to "wait for an answer before returning."

Six days later the same three people were back talking on the same pay phone. Soresi reported that the weather was still bad, and Cangialosi would have to remain in the United States for now. That night Cangialosi again met with DeVardo.

In the Midwest, Alfano was growing anxious. Nothing had been heard from Badalamenti in eighteen days. When the Uncle finally called, on March 28, Alfano told him, "You are making me die." Badalamenti ordered Alfano to go to the prickly pears, another pay phone, the next day.

In anticipation of Badalamenti's call, Alfano had made a call to Mazzurco, and Mazzurco then had a very strange conversation with Joe Lamberti. Mazzurco said he wanted to "shrug shoulders" to Alfano. But Lamberti warned, "No. Because if he sees that we will be rid of him, then we will have to go after him. . . ." The harmony of 1983 appeared to have vanished. Now the conspirators speak of "going after" people.

On the prickly pears phone Badalamenti also sounded troubled. "Words slip out," he cautioned. Then he told Alfano, "I'm not coming over there . . . you should talk with them. . . ."

Later that night, Mazzurco called Joe Lamberti and said, "I have to meet the nephew in the morning."

On March 30 Alfano, under the name Joe Musso, flew to La Guardia Airport and was picked up by Mazzurco and Cangialosi. They drove him to Pronto Demolition in Brooklyn, where Joe and Sal Lamberti were waiting. Forty minutes later Alfano was driven back to La Guardia, and boarded a return flight to Chicago.

On April 5 Badalamenti again called Alfano at the prickly pears. "Do you want to come?" he asked. "Make it for Madrid. Put some money in your pocket . . . not a lot."

"Five?"

"About ten."

Alfano bought an open-return round-trip ticket on a KLM flight from Chicago to Madrid. That night he called Sam Evola, told him his travel plans, and described the meeting at Pronto. The tone of their conversation was mysterious. "I was there with all three. . . . I told them: Friends of mine, if you all say you love him, we have to show him how we love him. . . . What can I tell him? . . . They love you but they want to stay home?"

When Alfano departed from Chicago on the KLM flight, a team of DEA and FBI agents was also on board. At Madrid's Barajas Airport, Alfano was warmly greeted by Badalamenti's son Vito. They took a cab to an apartment building at 11 Santa Virgilia Street. The next morning, Sunday, April 8, at 11:30 A.M., the Spanish police, working in conjunction with the FBI and Interpol, arrested Gaetano Badalamenti and Pietro Alfano just as they were strolling by the municipal police station. Then they raided the apartment and picked up Vito.

The three men were taken to a police station and searched. Gaetano and Vito Badalamenti gave false names and false addresses. Alfano at first admitted his identity but denied knowing Badalamenti. By 7:00 P.M. he had signed a statement saying he had received an invitation to visit Madrid from Badalamenti, who was his wife's uncle. He also identified a picture of the uncle.

Badalamenti and his son spent the next seven months in Spanish prisons, insisting on their phony identities. Badalamenti did not acknowledge that he *was* Badalamenti until he was aboard the U.S. military plane that took him to the United States on November 15, 1984.

When the Old Man was first searched after his arrest, the Spanish police had found a tiny ball of paper rolled up inside his eyeglass case. They unrolled it, and read the words ERMES PEP SROARET. Using the TERMINUSA code, SROARET becomes 830-9321, and 830-9321 is the number of the pay telephone outside Joe Ganci's Al Dente Pizzeria.

. . . APRIL 5-9, 1984. THE PIZZA ROUNDUP.
Law-enforcement agencies in three countries cooperated in the arrests of the Pizza conspirators: Randazzo in Zurich on April 5; the two Badalamentis and Alfano in Madrid on April 8; defendant Cangialosi at JFK International Airport also on April 8; and the U.S. defendants in their homes on April 9. Raiding parties in Spain, Switzerland, and the United States thereafter combed through the various residences and businesses.

In Zurich, the Swiss police seized Vincenzo Randazzo's passport and saw that in 1983 he had entered and exited Brazil ten times.

In Badalamenti's Madrid apartment, the Spanish police discovered $10,000 in U.S. hundred-dollar bills, held by a rubber band and hidden in a woman's shoe. The FBI believed this was the "ten" Badalamenti had told Alfano to bring.

The Spanish police seized Alfano's U.S. passport and saw that in 1982 he had visited Brazil four times. On two of those occasions he had entered and left on the same day.

Giovanni Cangialosi was arrested just as he was boarding an Alitalia flight to Rome. In his pockets were $6,000 in cash, a sheet of hotel stationery bearing the numbers of eight Long Island pay phones, a passport, a holy picture, and a torn scrap of paper with a mysterious scribbled note: *Dottore a Nice, Francia, nipote Zurich, nipoti Americana.* Loosely translated, this reads, "Doctor in Nice, France, one close relative in Zurich, several close relatives in America."

In the raids across the United States, government agents seized nineteen pistols, two of which were fitted with silencers; nine high-powered rifles, five shotguns, one sawed-off shotgun, four machine guns, two of which had silencers, a veterinarian's hypodermic dart gun, two suits of body armor, and three Ohaus triple-beam scales.

Along with this primary evidence, the agents also uncovered a wealth of documents: telephone books, wedding-photo albums, canceled checks, credit stubs, used airline tickets, hotel bills. Large stashes of cash were discovered. Mazzurco had over $67,000 in assorted currencies; Mazzara had $63,000; Joe Lamberti had $7,800.

Only a few men escaped the net. When the FBI knocked on the doors of Baldassare Amato and Cesare Bonventre, neither man was home. A month later Amato surrendered to government authorities.

Cesare Bonventre had disappeared shortly before the arrests. Ganci and others were worried. The FBI overheard Ganci's mistress talking to her mother about it. Theresa Bonventre was pregnant with their first child and about to give birth.

The newest Bonventre, a son, was born April 10, one day after the mass arrests. It was just three weeks later that his father's dismembered corpse turned up in the three barrels of glue in New Jersey.

6. *The Defense*

. . . THURSDAY, OCTOBER 9, 1986.
THE COURTROOM.   After presenting 236 witnesses and more than
a year of evidence, the government is finally concluding its case in chief.
Now comes the defense. What will it be? Rumors are flying. Dangerous
games are in high gear.

The government had at first said it would finish last week. Then Leval
granted a defense motion for a three-day adjournment to prepare its
case. Since then, last-minute bits of government evidence—more guns,
more agents, more documents—have kept straggling in.

Ivan Fisher called Eleanore at 7:00 A.M. last Monday morning to
report that Freeh had been phoning defense attorneys all weekend
trying to check out the rumor that Kennedy intended to put Badalamenti on the witness stand. Before daybreak, said Fisher, Paul Bergman
had called him to ask the same question.

Eleanore believed "Ivan was fishing me," but she was not sure for
what. "At this point, no one trusts anyone," she said.

Freeh still longs to know if Kennedy really intends to put on Badalamenti—a very audacious move—or, more likely, is trying to bluff the

government into using its undisclosed, ace-in-the-hole evidence. Almost certainly the prosecutors are holding back some juicy piece of evidence, should they decide to put on a rebuttal case.

The bluff game goes thus, says Eleanore. "If the government holds back evidence, in order to sandbag us, and then we rest, without putting on Mr. B.," the government will have saved its heavyweight final evidence in vain. Should Kennedy rest, relying on the weakness of the government's evidence, and his client's presumption of innocence, to argue in summation that the government has not proved its case beyond a reasonable doubt, then the government gets no opportunity to put on a rebuttal case. If Kennedy rests, the government must also rest. If Kennedy does put on a defense case, the government wants to be holding a solid punch in reserve.

"And our problem is: Where do *we* use *our* good stuff? If they hold back, to sandbag, and then we rest—we don't get to put on Mr. B., but we also prevent the government from putting on its best evidence. You know what I really think? I think the government is setting us up."

Eleanore had ventured a guess that the prosecution would not rest until noon Thursday, thereby giving Kennedy Thursday afternoon and Friday morning to begin his case, after which the government would be assured three and a half days—Friday afternoon, Saturday, Sunday, and the Monday holiday—to prepare to rebut whatever Kennedy might put on.

Eleanore has figured it on the nose. At 10:21 A.M., Louis Freeh says quietly, "The government rests."

Two jurors look stunned, a few others react faintly, the rest are totally blank. The lawyers take this as confirmation that someone, probably a marshal, has a pipeline in to the jury.

Kennedy leaps to the podium. He says he has three options: Put on no defense and simply say the government's charges are not proved; put on a defense without his client; or put Badalamenti on the witness stand. "I prefer the latter." But there are problems.

Lawyer and client have been talking to Italian attorneys about how his testimony here would affect his standing in Italian courts. Kennedy asks Leval to compel the government to state *what* drug Badalamenti is accused of trafficking in.

They have told me both, says Leval, and Martin nods assent. How about the twenty-two containers, Kennedy continues suavely. What does the government suppose them to be?

Leval asks Martin if he has an answer. When he says no, Kennedy recommends they be taken out of the case. This is admittedly an "unusual application," but not an idle one. There are no cocaine charges in Italy.

"You raise very reasonable . . . very real" concerns, says Leval, equally suave. But the government is charging *conspiracy,* so the court sees no legal obligation to specify which drug. In sum, the law, that most precise, hair-splitting of disciplines, does not require the government to name the drug it accuses these men of conspiring to deal in.

If the government is saying it doesn't really know, that's fine, says Kennedy. But if Martin is just being "coy"—if he does know, but for tactical reasons chooses not to reveal his hand—the court should please reconsider.

A long pause while the prosecutors confer, and Kennedy paces. In fact, everybody is being coy: Kennedy as well as the judge knows perfectly well by now that the government will charge cocaine as well as heroin. Everybody, except the jurors, knows there are no cocaine charges in Italy. No one needs an Italian attorney to advise him of that. Martin says the government has evidence in furtherance of the conspiracy, and he does not think there is any obligation to disclose in advance what it is. Everybody but the jury knows this too. Both sides are essentially "posturing," equivalent to pawing the ground before the charge.

Kennedy moves to his next point. He asks the government to specify "who it is precisely Mr. Badalamenti is accused of having managed, controlled and supervised." He is asking about the 848 count, known as "the kingpin statute," which charges a conspiracy defendant with being a part of a continuing criminal enterprise in which he supervises, manages, or controls five or more other people. Since Badalamenti and his son and his nephew Alfano are the only defendants not charged with RICO, the 848 is the major charge against them. Conviction means an automatic ten years to life.

At the start of the trial, Freeh had given Kennedy a letter naming fifteen persons the government accuses his client of supervising, managing, or controlling. Kennedy wants the list whittled down, because "the jury must focus." This argument, like the previous one, is really intended to let the lawyer focus his defense on the main charges, and restrict the government from wandering all over the place in its summation.

Six of the fifteen are codefendants: Alfano, Vito Badalamenti, both Lambertis, Sal Mazzurco, and the departed nephew Randazzo. Kennedy would like the other nine to be dropped for lack of evidence. Three are persons who have never been mentioned. Three are "unknown males" referred to in the phone conversations: the "guy from five years ago," the "guy with ten per cent acrylic," and "Boss." Three are figures allegedly involved in funneling funds to Brazil.

Kennedy, "focusing" ever tighter, now says he does not want to have to refute charges individually against the six codefendants, because it would be irresponsible to his client's future in Italy, and the government has not made out a single overt act. . . .

Motion denied.

Kennedy suggests the interpreter spend some time over the weekend with his client. "It will speed things up a lot if he does take the stand."

"Very good idea."

Finally, the cruncher: It is Thursday morning, and there is no way Kennedy can proceed before next Tuesday. "I am simply not ready."

Then put on another defendant, says Leval. But no other defendant is willing to precede Badalamenti.

It was very difficult, says Leval, to justify three days off last week. Ever since he did this, he has been telling himself it was a mistake. Ergo: *We're going ahead now.*

I *cannot* be ready before Tuesday, says Kennedy. I have sat here for twelve months with Mr. Badalamenti, and he has sat in prison two and a half years!

Leval's eyes remain resolutely cast down.

Think of all the half-days off given to men with a toothache! What about a man whose life is on the line?

Leval is coldly furious. "You spring this on me at the very *moment* I am expecting your defense. . . ." He grants Kennedy only a brief recess in order to caucus with his colleagues and choose a substitute. As the lawyer turns to leave, one can see him faintly smiling. Other lawyers spill into the aisle, joining him.

"What'll we do?" Dave Lewis whispers. As the defense construes it, Leval has just demanded the judicial equivalent of a human sacrifice. Refusal would invite a contempt-of-court charge.

"Have a meeting," says Kennedy. "Pull 'em together somehow, Dave."

"I reserve my right to go last," says Ryan, not yet even out the door.

"I refuse to go first. I have no defense anyhow," says Fogelnest.

"I have no witnesses," says Schechter.

"I'm not ready," growls Lombardino.

Then how about Joe Benfante? This caucus is taking place just outside the courtroom door.

Lombardino shakes his head. "We're together. Joined at the hip. I have never before had a judge squeeze so hard," he adds. "I think he's got a jury problem."

Certainly the defense has "a judge problem." It's a stand-off; someone must yield.

If somebody has to be held in contempt, Fisher says, he is willing to volunteer. Yom Kippur is coming up, and "I have to fast anyway. I can do it in jail. I can give my cash to Mario and go right now."

Kennedy turns to try to recruit someone else, and Eleanore whispers, "What can we give Pierre to save face?"

Benfante lowers his voice and mutters, "I think Michael Kennedy is under tremendous pressure because he was not told until yesterday by *El Exigente* what his problems were."

The brief recess is over. "I *cannot* go now," Kennedy tells the court. "I could do filler. I could read all the Badalamentis in the Rio de Janeiro phone book." But that is not his style. Ivan Fisher is not ready either. "I have tried to persuade others to go ahead, with other stuff. I was not successful."

Leval's face seems to get narrower. He scratches his hair with a blue pencil. A very tense minute passes. Leval keeps his face averted, tugs at his curls, feels his chin. Kennedy, Fisher, and Martin also stare down. Silence.

Then: "Nature abhors a vacuum, and I abhor silence, so . . ." It's Bergman, of course.

"I'd rather stick to this problem," Leval says. More silence. His mouth opens, fishlike, three or four times, but no sound comes out. Then: "What puzzles me about the application is, it's being made, without any prior notice, at the moment of the government's resting."

Kennedy had expected the decision by Badalamenti and the Italian lawyer last week, he now says, as to what his client can say in self-defense in this trial without putting himself in double jeopardy as regards Italy. He promises it will come no later than tonight or tomorrow, and then he will know his client's intentions.

Had he told this in time to the court, or other lawyers, they could have been ready, says Leval.

Kennedy didn't know when the government was going to rest. "I had hoped, but I didn't know."

"I will allow you until tomorrow morning. . . . I think that is an exercise in generosity."

Kennedy and client disappear into Leval's chambers to call Palermo to find out what is holding things up. Leval sends for the jury and dismisses them for the day.

Kennedy returns and reports that the Italian lawyer's arrival is being delayed by the failure of the U.S. government so far to respond to his questions regarding obligations under the new treaty relationship.

Straggling out, Fogelnest sums up the day. "The single most despicable act by this judge was permitting the government to rest so suddenly, and forcing Michael to go ahead—when he is not ready, and when he will be forced to show his hand on Badalamenti—and then giving the government the long weekend to regroup."

... FRIDAY, OCTOBER 10, 1986.

THE COURTHOUSE.   The morning is clear, crisp, cold. The courtroom is icy. Court will adjourn at lunchtime for the three-day Yom Kippur and Columbus Day holiday weekend. The heavy traffic has begun.

"We need to fill three and a half hours, and we only have two," whispers Eleanore. "We are praying for a subway tie-up, a late juror, anything. . . ." Like many of the lawyers, she is jauntily dressed in new clothes to honor the importance of the day.

Now that the defense team is finally coming to bat, Bergman asks that the government's enormous money-laundering chart be removed. Burke says the *New York Times* has this morning labeled Gaetano Badalamenti an "admitted Mafia chief," and directly linked him to Catalano.

Leval agrees to ask the jury if anybody saw it. "Mr. Kennedy, what will your position be?"

"Erect."

The jurors enter. Their number over recent months has dwindled to nineteen, four more having been dismissed for various causes. They look solemn and newly attentive. Nobody saw the *Times.* Leval cautions them to "keep an open mind," and remember that no defendant has an obligation to put on any defense. The burden of proof remains on the government.

Kennedy will begin with a read-back of some year-old testimony by Badalamenti and Contorno. The government demands, and is granted, time to find, inspect, and check the appropriate pages. Kennedy by allowing the government and bench "to play into their own compulsiveness" has maneuvered another recess and used up another thirty to forty minutes.

"What a productive day this will be!" Koppelman says sarcastically. "Just because that asshole wouldn't give us four hours off."

Twelve months of vapidity and frustration have goaded silent Mike Querques into speech. What he says recalls Spencer Tracy's description of Katharine Hepburn: "Not much meat on her. But what there is, is choice."

"The most remarkable aspect of this case," says Querques, gazing moodily into his coffee cup, "is: How do you as defense counsel overcome eleven months of government testimony? This includes all the spillover, and rub-off, of one defendant on another. It also includes our concern over the provocative and venal nature of the testimony—homicides, witnesses like Contorno and Ronsisvalle.

"And what about the capacity of the jury? Their task would be impossible even if they were mental giants. Even if they were twelve Phi Beta Kappas, how can they remember these intricacies—the conspiracy, the RICO, the 848—and then see where they fit, in what is undoubtedly the most complex combined case ever put together?

"Even the most intellectually honest judges, who study and apply it daily, tell us they don't really understand 'conspiracy' in its legal meaning." As for the RICO and the 848, they are relatively new charges; Leval has no experience with either.

And what does this lawyer think of Pierre Leval? "A brilliant dope. He knows the law. He's very methodical. But sometimes being this way means you lose sight of the practical. A judge who was less brilliant—and more realistic—would have severed. He would have heard three or four cases that would have really accomplished what the courts say is necessary in these huge cases: first, fairness, and second, judicial economy. Do you know the cost of that last chart? $17,000! I checked.

"This is a trial where the system has broken down. It's too much for anybody. Take any individual—wealthy, middle-income, or poor—how can he afford it? How does a citizen *handle* being thrust into this kind of case? Losing a whole year from his job. Losing his emotional health. His family.

"And *why?* When there is another way to do it? A better way? When this thing ends, I'd like to ask Leval just one question: If he had it to do over, would he sever?"

Of Richard Martin, Querques says, "They say he's overzealous. He's not! It's *intentional.* A lie, to me, cannot be accidental. He's thought it out. These people know this case inside out. There's no *room* for lies."

11:06 A.M. The jury is back. Pat Burke takes the stand. He will read the witness's testimony. Moving as slowly as they dare, he and Kennedy read back portions of year-old testimony. Jurors #7, 12, and 14 are asleep; #12 has completely turned his chair around to the wall. Kennedy reads on, his precise enunciation cutting like a laser through the stale courtroom air. When he gets to the moment in 1978 when Badalamenti is expelled from the ruling Mafia Commissione, jurors #1 and 2 glance sharply at Kennedy, as if they had forgotten this fact. But moments later, despite the crisp elocution, jurors #4, 5, 6, 7, 9, and 10 all appear to be asleep. They do not hear Kennedy read, "Was the attitude of the Corleonese to Gaetano Badalamenti one of ferocious persecution?"

They do not hear Buscetta's answer: "They were trying to kill him."

Kennedy manages to drag out the read-back until 12:17. The jury is sent out. He then summons his first witness. It is Enzo Randazzo, Badalamenti's number-one nephew, the man who used to sit here beside his uncle until, last summer, he negotiated a plea bargain and disappeared from the jury's sight. His lawyer, Larry Schoenbach, too is back, and permitted by the court to stand beside Randazzo to coach his replies. Buxom Mme Interpreter sits on his other side. The narrow-faced witness, here under Kennedy's subpoena, looks very unhappy.

Leval warns Randazzo, cautioning him and his lawyer to "be sure you and your attorney are aware of the legal implications. If you answer any questions, the government may take the position that you have violated your plea agreement, and may become a defendant once again, charged with trafficking and conspiracy. I'm not saying I have a view. . . . I simply want to be sure, *for your protection . . .* "

During this speech, Badalamenti's black-eyed glare of fury, so malevolent he might be a creature in a sci-fi movie, burns into his nephew, seated not fifteen feet away.

The jury returns.

"Are you the same Enzo Randazzo who was a defendant in this case?"

Enzo takes the Fifth. Kennedy asks the court for a ruling. Martin says he does not object to Enzo replying. Schoenbach does. Leval asks to hear more questions, so he can know where the examination is going.

Kennedy offers to give all his questions.

Schoenbach says he takes the same position in regard to *any* questions.

Manny Moore passes by, and Kennedy whispers, "Don't worry about what's going on here, because I don't know myself."

"I love this!" whispers Ken Kaplan.

"I want to see this judge squirm," says Ruggiero.

Leval is pulling out eyebrows hair by hair.

"What was the nature of the business?" asks Kennedy, referring to the Italian sportswear Randazzo wholesaled in the United States.

"Refuse to answer on the grounds that it may tend . . ."

After several refusals to answer Kennedy's questions, Leval invites Martin to cross-examine. Schoenbach says he takes the same position on government questions.

Kennedy turns away with a tiny smile. Is he simply playing time-killing games with his bright young friend Schoenbach, the bearded choirboy? Or has he done this just for the fun of watching Martin twisting in the wind? The man the government once went to so much expense to capture, and then made a tactical decision to release, has now been subpoenaed here to testify against the government. What's more, his refusals to answer are firmly based on his fear of abrogating the very plea bargain Martin and Schoenbach worked out. Or is some other delectable game under way?

Martin says, "You were here in the United States to collect narcotics money, correct?"

"I refuse to answer. . . ."

Kennedy is giggling.

Kaplan shouts out, "How can you impeach someone who isn't testifying?"

"This is *theater,* Kenny," says Kennedy sotto voce.

Randazzo rolls his eyes heavenward until only the whites show.

"How much cocaine did you ship to the U.S. in the last five years?" barks Martin.

Kennedy objects. "Assumes a fact not in evidence."

Martin persists. "And you were arranging to ship a large amount of heroin?"

Koppelman is on his feet. "It has become clear that Dick Martin is asking these questions in hopes there's a reporter here in the courtroom who would put in the paper that witness Randazzo took the Fifth to all these questions. . . ."

Leval (pointing his finger and almost shouting): "Mr. Koppelman. *Sit down!*"

". . . but he is not taking the Fifth," Koppelman continues. "He is saying that because of the plea, he cannot respond."

During this, Kennedy has taken a seat in the empty jury box, and is lolling back with a diabolical smile. He has thought of a good question to ask on redirect. "Mr. Randazzo, if you're such a big, bad drug dealer, why did the government let you plead to only one immigration count?"

The furious objection is, of course, sustained.

Koppelman formally asks that the records of today's proceedings be sealed, to keep them from the press. Leval says, "You did everything possible to exacerbate that problem . . . but okay, they'll be sealed, at least for now."

The reluctant witness and his lawyer leave the courtroom, each wearing a crooked smile as he walks down the center aisle. Judge Leval has ordered Randazzo deported. He must board a flight to Rome on Sunday night. Kennedy and the interpreter head for Badalamenti at MCC.

. . . TUESDAY, OCTOBER 14, 1986.

THE COURTROOM.   The long weekend has passed. Enzo Randazzo failed to board his flight to Rome. Government agents raided his last address, an apartment in Greenwich Village. He was not there.

The players have reassembled for the next act.

"Call the jury, please."

Kennedy and his client exchange gentle smiles. Sounds of offstage laughter, then the jury marches in. The leader of the parade, #8, enters whistling.

Kennedy rises. "I call Gaetano Badalamenti to the stand."

The whole court seems for a moment to hold its breath. The little man crosses stiffly to the box. He looks like a beetle-browed Jimmy Durante with a smaller nose and none of the sweetness.

You are Gaetano Badalamenti? Si.

Then straight in. "At any time in your lifetime, Mr. Badalamenti, have you had anything whatsoever to do with drugs, or drug trafficking?"

"Mai!" The voice is strong, defiant.

"Never," chirps the interpreter, smiling.

The lawyer's second question states the dangerous context in which all his client's forthcoming answers must be understood. "You are facing charges in . . . Palermo, are you not? . . . Can the testimony that you give here in court be used against you in the Italian proceedings?" Yes.

Leval looks acutely uncomfortable.

"You do speak a little English, do you not, Mr. Badalamenti?"

Yes. He learned in prison. Two and a half years. By now he understands a good deal of English, and the translation time chiefly provides extra moments to consider his answers. But the intervention of the interpreter also has a negative effect: It skims off immediacy, cancels flavor, and removes all possibility of direct communication from witness to jury before Freeh, or Leval, can challenge and halt the message.

Kennedy asks Teresa Badalamenti to stand. He introduces the ever-faithful Christine Evola, and then other family members, and elicits the relationship. Palazzolo? "His mother is my cousin." Alfano? "His wife is my cousin's daughter." The Old Man's voice is rough and gravelly. Trupiano? "My cousin's son." Vitale? "He is married to one of my cousin's children." The questioning establishes the defendant as patriarch of a tight-knit, loyal family.

Badalamenti describes his capture in Madrid. When arrested, he insisted he was Paolo Alves Barbosa. "*Why* did you insist?"

"When they arrested me, that was the passport I had in my possession," says the sprightly voice of Mme Interpreter. It is an odd reply, not precisely responsive, but Kennedy moves smoothly ahead. If he feels his man just barely beginning to resist, a tugging as light as a trout's first nibble, he betrays no sign.

"*Why* did you have a passport reflecting an assumed identity?"

Badalamenti resists a fraction harder. ". . . I cannot answer with one word. . . ."

"I am sure the court will permit your explanation, Mr. Badalamenti."

Kennedy's questions seem designed to get the Old Man to say he was in fear of losing his life at the hands of the Corleonese. But he will not say it. "Throughout my life, I have undergone all kinds of travail. . . . I felt that I was being persecuted. . . . I had thought about changing my own and my family's name. . . . I changed the name. The documents were not false."

Kennedy tries again. "What were the reasons, Mr. Badalamenti, for using an assumed name?"

"I have already stated why. However, if my reply was not clear, I can repeat it."

Kennedy must try still harder. "What does *persecution* have to do with it?"

"It is not only one instance of persecution. . . . It is a lifetime."

Kennedy tries several more times. Finally he elicits the only reply

Badalamenti seems willing to give: "In 1981 a charge against me was removed. Four days later I wanted to . . . break away from Sicily," and the first thing he needed was a different name. "What concerned me was [not to] leave that legacy to my sons. I thought of changing country, name, everything, to keep from leaving such a legacy. . . ."

Badalamenti will give Kennedy nothing else. What *is* the evil legacy? Is it his Mafia past? Or is it his present Mafia enemies, the Corleonese and their allies, the people who have been trying to kill him ever since they ran him out of Sicily? Or is it the Italian police? Or something else? No way to judge. His hedged and obscure vagueness could even be deliberate, part of the defense game plan.

Kennedy turns to Badalamenti's plane trip from Spain to New York in the custody of three FBI agents. This is a chance to show the jury that, even out of Sicily, Badalamenti lived under constant danger of Mafia vengeance. Kennedy tries to bring out the threat through the words of the agents themselves. But again Badalamenti will not give his lawyer the return lines. Kennedy is waiting to hear that the agents reminded him, "The opposition is going to kill you. You will be dead if you don't cooperate." But it doesn't come. Instead, the jury hears the incredible statement, "I told them that . . . I had no enemies in Sicily, nor in Italy. That I only had friends [and] no enemies in the United States . . . no one to fear."

If he has no enemies, why is he fleeing?

Kennedy switches subjects. "Let me ask you about some other people, Mr. Badalamenti. Vincenzo Randazzo?"

"Enzo is the son of my sister, Rosa." One has a sense of the inevitable track of this man's life. He is a patriarch *born into* the Mafia. Kennedy is again attempting to humanize his man's heritage, and show him as a courageous relic of an outmoded, Robin Hood world. But nothing can be done about Badalamenti's appearance. His ferocious and glowering face communicates resentment, suspicion, and cunning.

The lawyer leads the Old Man through his life story: born in Cinisi, 1923, one of nine children in a moderately well-off farming family. "And you are the baby of the family?"

"I took a long time coming, but I had a good time doing it," a peasant witticism repeated daily in a thousand Sicilian cafés.

He had four years' schooling and at ten was put to work in the fields. At eighteen he was drafted, but deserted before the Americans landed. "We thought of ourselves as partisans. Really we were only deserters." After the war, hard times came to Cinisi. In 1947 his brother Emmanuele urged him to come to America and try to improve his lot.

Leval declares a recess. The corridor consensus is that this is not going too well. Badalamenti seems often to be giving his own answers, not the ones his lawyer wants. If he has no enemies, who is persecuting him?

Trial resumes, and the witness tells how in 1947 he stowed away and jumped ship in, he thinks, Baltimore, and joined his brother in Monroe, Michigan, where he worked three years in the family grocery before being arrested and deported by the Immigration and Naturalization Service. Upon his return to Sicily he met and married his wife, and set up his successful business as a rancher and lemon grower.

In 1960 Palermo began building a new jet airport. The Badalamenti family owned an adjacent mountain, the nearest source of rock, gravel, and sand. Gaetano soon owned two construction companies, a concrete plant, and a fleet of trucks.

"It sounds as if you made a lot of money off the construction of Punta Raisi airport." Kennedy is trying to position his client as a legitimate businessman. But to Badalamenti, his business is as private a matter as his family.

"I paid all my taxes," is all he will say.

Over lunch, Martin asks Leval to issue a bench warrant for Enzo Randazzo's arrest.

In the corridor, Kennedy is explaining his client. "To him, it is a point of honor to say, 'I have no enemies in Palermo.' He would say it in front of a firing squad." The lawyer acknowledges that much of what his client does say eludes him. "A lot does not make sense. Some answers are traps he has set for the government. Others are the result of his own recalcitrance. Sometimes I cannot move him." But Kennedy has a fall-back strategy. If his client becomes "too Sicilian, I can always get myself in deliberate trouble with Leval, so the old warrior will come to my rescue."

After lunch, it is time to go into Badalamenti's Italian police record. Kennedy takes a bold, direct approach. You have been arrested? Yes, more than once. He has had two convictions, the first in 1968 for tobacco smuggling, the second for "Mafia-style conspiracy" in 1976.

Was he charged with being a Mafia capo?

"That was the charge, but that was not what I was convicted of." The penalty for Mafia leadership is up to twenty-one years. Badalamenti was convicted of Mafia membership, and spent two years in prison.

He was also charged with drug offenses. Were the drug charges separate from the Mafia charges, or part of the same charge? Badalamenti does not want to answer this question, and finds several ways to evade it before admitting that he was arrested for narcotics trafficking, but "was immediately released. If you'd like me to, I'll tell you why."

Object! Sustained.

Kennedy seems astonished. "Your Honor is not permitting him to say *why* the charges were dismissed?"

That's right.

Kennedy has mapped out today's examination in the predawn hours, as usual, on 5″-by-8″ index cards, with Mont Blanc pen and black ink, in his strong Jesuit-trained hand. He has planned to end at 3:00 P.M. so as not to unduly tire his witness, and can time himself to do this. It is 2:26 when he tells his client: I want you to focus on the events in Madrid in April 1984. What was your understanding then of the present Italian charges?

"Nothing had been told to me in Spain, because in Spain I said my name was . . . Barbosa . . . [later] I was told that Gaetano Badalamenti had been charged with narcotics traffic in the United States, in Italy, in Switzerland, in Spain, in Canada, in Brazil and in Venezuela." The basis of all these charges was the same—the investigation conducted by the FBI.

On August 7, 1981, in Italy, were drug charges pending against you dismissed?

Yes. Four days later he left Italy voluntarily, accompanied by his wife and sons and several in-laws, and went to Paris.

How long did you stay in Paris?

This question produces a strange answer; the mulish resistance is back. "It was a matter of months. However, I will be grateful, Mr. Kennedy, if you would like to leave this subject aside."

The family moved on to Nice. There the Old Man received a message from Brazil. "Can you tell us from whom the message was?"

Utter silence.

Kennedy tries it another way: How did he respond to the message? "I went to Brazil."

He did not travel under his own name. Why?

"I didn't want to leave any clues behind. I was leaving my family behind in Nice . . . and I wanted to leave no traces. . . ."

Again: Why?

The question is an open invitation to mention Mafia war, the persecution, the death threats, being chased out of Sicily, the mortal danger to his family. But Badalamenti is reluctant to speak. Finally, this oblique reply: "How shall I tell you? I didn't want my family's whereabouts to be known. I didn't want to have my own whereabouts known. I did it for their security, safety, peace of mind." He will say nothing more.

Kennedy moves on to a more productive area, getting his client to talk about business transactions with Randazzo and others, in Brazil and elsewhere, in leather goods, clothing, lumber, "mines, gold, and precious stones." Yes, he had samples of precious stones with him when arrested in Madrid. This hints that Kennedy may put on a defense that will explain the phone calls about shirts, containers, and so on.

In 1982 Alfano and Evola visited him in Brazil, but the visits "had nothing to do with drugs." He also saw other relatives, and they joined forces in some commercial enterprises: buying small lots and building on them; investing and lending money. In 1983 he and his family returned to Italy to see his dying brother. His wife was ill and run-down; he left her in Spain, to rest. Any mention of Teresa Badalamenti makes her husband extremely ill-at-ease.

On his return to Brazil, he visited Paraguay, and became a dealer in crocodile skins. In October 1983 his son Leonardo was arrested and jailed two months for having false papers. When he was released, his father asked him to visit his mother in Madrid.

"Did Leonardo Badalamenti travel from Brazil to Spain after he was released from jail?"

The innocuous question triggers an extraordinary reaction. The Old Man huffs and puffs and gasps for breath before saying, "But I thought I said that I wanted to leave my family out of . . ." He does not complete the sentence. Kennedy glides on.

The reason for his own visit to Madrid was to bring his wife back to Brazil, he says. Pete Alfano joined them on April 7. He brought with him $10,000 in cash, found by the police in an armoire. The money had nothing to do with drugs.

Did his presence in Madrid, or Alfano's, have anything to do with drugs? No.

Kennedy's ringing voice now asks: Do you know, or have you had anything to do with, an individual named Giuseppe Ganci? Never seen him. Cesare Bonventre? Never. He denies knowing any of the dozens of Sicilians named by the government as the conspiracy's money laun- derers, investors, mules. Finally Leval calls a halt for the day.

Kennedy confesses later, "That was the most difficult examination I have ever had to conduct in a courtroom." He has had to fight three battles: one with the prosecutor, another with the bench, and the third with his client. The day before, he had spent seven hours preparing Badalamenti in MCC. "It took all that time for me to get the answer 'to protect my family'—and then today he didn't give it to me! I went back in the recess and raised hell. 'You broke your word! You have no honor!'

"I . . . am . . . wrung . . . out."

. . . WEDNESDAY, OCTOBER 15, 1986. **THE COURTROOM.** There is no court in the morning. The prosecutors need time off to attend the funeral of a colleague. When the jury and Mr. Badalamenti enter the courtroom after lunch, four men in the back row, dressed in black, perhaps pallbearers from the funeral, hastily exit.

Kennedy must now lead his client through a delicate minefield. He walks along the back row and stops in turn behind Ligammari, Casamento, Polizzi, Mazzara, and Greco. One by one, he asks them to stand. Each time, Badalamenti says: "I did not know him. . . . I never had anything to do with him. . . . I only met him at MCC. . . ." Castronovo affects a chin-outthrust, Napoleonic stance. Mazzara smiles, Greco pouts like Charles Laughton, Amato sulks.

Badalamenti acknowledges that he knew Sal Lamberti more than forty years ago. Lamberti dealt in motor vehicles and had once sold him a tractor. Their family lands adjoined. "I own property between Cinisi and Borghetto, and he worked the land for me." It develops that Badalamenti made only partial payment for the tractor, 8 million lire out of 11 million owed, "because he never turned over the deed, and spare parts." Is it possible, among these strange archaic people, that an old unpaid tractor bill, or a long-ago border skirmish, could be the source of so much animosity?

Now Sal Mazzurco stands. "I do know him. Sal Lamberti introduced us in 1977 or '78." It is Lamberti's turn to look uncomfortable. The Old Man says he then introduced Mazzurco to Randazzo. Both were importing Italian sportswear, and they did some business together.

Joe Lamberti stands. "Yes, I also know him."

Sal Salamone stands next. "I met him at MCC, and . . ." The translator falters. The other defendants laugh. "No! Don't translate that!" Badalamenti blurts. But Martin, fluent in Italian, has heard the slip and demands a full translation.

"And in the morning we share the same set of handcuffs."

One juror guffaws.

The jury is not supposed to know about the cuffs. Salamone's lawyer, Bob Fogelnest, is arguing furiously at the side bar. Leval instructs the jury in the strongest possible terms that they are to "draw no inference" from the remark.

Fogelnest is persuaded to sit down, for now, and Badalamenti ends his tour of his codefendants with the shark-faced Catalano. "I've seen him here. I never had anything to do with him."

Now a crunch question: "We have heard tapes of you and Sal Lamberti. Did your conversations have anything to do with drugs, or drug trafficking?" The jury is closely watching the Old Man.

"Yes, we spoke. But never of drugs."

How about the conversations with Mazzurco?

"I did speak to him. But not about drugs." He gives the same answer in reference to the others with whom he spoke: Joe Lamberti, Pete Alfano, and Sam Evola.

"Are you personally opposed to drug trafficking?" The jury stares at the man in the box.

"I believe people who use it don't know what they are doing."

Have you ever encouraged anyone to deal drugs?

"If I had had the power, I would have done the opposite." All these replies, heard through the lipsticked mouth of the jolly matron interpreter, have an unreal quality. They sound like dialogue in a Sicilian Punch-and-Judy show, not remotely like a man enunciating his life's principles.

Did Badalamenti have anything to do with the ounce of cocaine found in Sam Evola's house? This question brings an emphatic *No!* The first time he even heard of the coke was in this courtroom, and he does not believe it. Kennedy then elicits that Evola has four sons, aged sixteen to twenty-six, and all live at home.

A pattern has emerged in these questions: Badalamenti owes Sal Lamberti money, and Mazzurco deals in clothes with Randazzo. This can be used to explain the phone calls. As for Evola's cocaine, that belonged to the sons.

Kennedy walks to the easel and turns to the TERMINUSA code. "Why, Mr. Badalamenti, did you feel a code was necessary?"

"I have always felt it was better if other people did not know my affairs, my business." But he never used the code for drug dealing.

"Then what *did* the conversations have to do with?"

A pause, then, bold as brass: "Mr. Kennedy, I will not explain."

This is a shocker. A dozen lawyers rush to the side bar. Leval dismisses the jury so that the coming arguments can be held in open court.

Kennedy asks again: "What are the reasons that you refuse to tell us what your conversations on tape are about?"

"There are two reasons. One is that I have never betrayed and I will never betray my secrets. The other is that it would cause me harm in Italy."

Kennedy wants to ask a leading question. Freeh objects. Leval sustains, but tells Kennedy he may whisper to his client.

Kennedy bridles. "There is no jury here! I don't want to whisper to him. That is an insinuation I resent!"

"Then ask proper questions," snaps Leval.

What does he mean when he says his answers here would harm him in Italy?

". . . in Italy, the Mafia trial is worse. I would be harmed during that trial."

If your conversations "do not involve drugs, how . . ."

"Objection!"

"Wait until you hear it! You might like it," Kennedy snaps. "How could your answers here hurt you in Italy?"

"I feel . . . there are Italian magistrates listening here, in this courtroom."

But if the conversations are not about drugs, how could the answers hurt you in the Italian trial?

"In Italy there is waiting for me not only trial for drugs. . . . It is a dreadful matter. . . ."

Bucknam is grinning, McCarthy wears a schoolboy smirk, Freeh and Martin smile.

"What charges are you facing in Italy, other than drugs?"

". . . I am facing a trial in Italy in which I am defined as—as the Capo of the Losers." Badalamenti thrusts out his chin. This insulting appellation is the unkindest cut of all. The charges there are of criminal association, Mafia style, and of Mafia warfare.

Then you fear your answers here would hurt you in reference to the Mafia charges?

"I am sure of it."

"Is that the reason you refuse to answer what these conversations are about?" Yes. Does his refusal have anything to do with drug charges, either in Italy or the United States? No.

Kennedy wants to ask the same questions in front of the jury. Freeh objects. "Either he answers or he doesn't. Or he takes the Fifth Amendment. I don't think he can give a speech before the jury."

Leval asks for Kennedy's position on the matter. The defense lawyer articulates a critical point of law that will occupy this court for seven more days. Badalamenti has, according to Kennedy, taken the Fifth Amendment with reference to the Mafia charges, but not the drug charges. The government will argue that his refusal to answer impeaches his credibility, and that he refuses to answer because the conversations will implicate him in drug trafficking.

"That is an inference that the government knows is false," says Kennedy. "That is an inference that they should not be permitted to make to the jury. We should permit the *jury* to hear, and decide, the question of the credibility of Mr. Badalamenti.

"It is clear that it is not the drug charges here in the United States, or the drug charges in Italy, which [bother him]. It is the Mafia association, and Mafia war charges that he feels his answers, with reference to the phone conversations, would tend to incriminate. And the jury ought to be able to weigh that."

Leval sustains Freeh's objection. Kennedy mentions a couple of prior cases, and Leval declares a half-hour recess to give time to look up the two citations. Kennedy exits beaming. "I've got Pierre Leval where I want him," he tells his wife. "I'm gonna straighten his hair."

Badalamenti's refusal to explain the calls could be taken as paranoia. Except it will turn out that the four black-suited, back-row "pallbearers" were, in fact, four visiting Italian magistrates, in town to confer with some of the government agents.

The half-hour recess stretches to an hour as stunt lawyers research the record. In the cafeteria, redecorated with the same cardboard pumpkins, witches, and broomsticks displayed one year ago, the respected senior court reporter for the *New York Times,* Arnold Lubasch, approaches Eleanore to discuss Badalamenti's curious speech patterns. Lubasch says he understands them. "He does not lie. But his mind is obscure."

Over coffee, Mario Malerba amplifies the point. "Sicilians do not speak like other people. When a Sicilian is asked a question, his answer is calculated to discover where the conversation is headed. If you get a nice [i.e., superficial, pleasant] answer, we part friends. If you get a penetrating answer—well, we'll see. You tailor your answer to elicit the next question."

Why do Sicilians talk this way? It is a response bred into them by the harsh history of their island. "If you're suspicious by nature, if there's no government authority you can rely on, any answer might hurt you." One becomes exceptionally cautious, guarded. Sicilians have a very wary, cynical nature, with good reason. Why pay taxes? The tax collectors will only steal it. Why comply with rulings of the local baron? He may soon be overthrown. In such an atmosphere, some people, some families, do not speak, and may have been killing one another for generations. Yet, when family members meet on the village street, or in church, they exchange meaningless formal pleasantries.

"There is only answer by parable, and by innuendo." That habit makes very difficult the relationship between lawyer and client. Most of the Pizza lawyers have complained to Malerba that their Sicilian clients won't tell them anything, making it almost impossible to prepare a defense. Certainly Kennedy, though he does not complain, seems to be suffering from this ingrained suspicion. The degree that Badalamenti does trust Kennedy is probably based largely on the fact that Kennedy has an Italian wife.

The lawyer illustrates his point with a story about his client Catalano's mistrust of his $500,000 lawyer, Ivan Fisher. Catalano owes Fisher a few hundred dollars, to reimburse him for cash outlays, and the lawyer has been pressing for payment. Malerba pulls out of his pocket a baseball-size wad of bills held with red rubber bands. Fisher was in court all day yesterday, but Catalano would not give the money to him directly. He waited until Malerba showed up this morning and asked him to turn over the cash to Fisher, who now is not here.

This suspicious nature makes it very difficult to prepare witnesses. Malerba has been trying to conduct mock direct examinations in the office, "and even with *me* they start playing games. I gotta drill them: Give me the answer in one sentence! You *can't* prepare these guys!"

As soon as court reconvenes, Joe Benfante requests a mistrial, or severance, on behalf of Mazzurco, the two Lambertis, and Cangialosi. One by one, every other non-Badalamenti lawyer joins in the request. Benfante states the grounds: The refusal to explain the substance of the conversations places the defendants with whom Badalamenti was speaking in a position where *their* right not to take the stand has been impaired or abridged. Badalamenti's refusal to explain virtually compels them to testify. Otherwise the jury could infer that the conversations refer to even more heinous crimes than those charged.

Kennedy would welcome an instruction from the court that the jury is to infer nothing from Badalamenti's refusal to answer.

No, says Freeh, the defendant cannot have it both ways. He cannot make a speech to the jury. Badalamenti has told the jury what these conversations are *not* about, but he refuses to say what they *are* about. "Hence, I think he *must* take the Fifth."

Leval says that fear of foreign prosecution is realistic, not fanciful, in Badalamenti's case.

True, says Sal Lamberti's lawyer, Marvin Schechter, but it may also be that Badalamenti is refusing to answer in order to improve his tactical position in *this* prosecution, and to hell with all the other defendants.

Leval says wearily, "Mr. Kennedy, I thought we might be able to avoid this. But why don't you conduct a further examination of your client. . . ." Sensing that this will take some time, Leval sends word to the jury that they may go home for the day.

He now permits Kennedy to ask the one leading question he had tried to put earlier. Is Badalamenti's refusal to answer based on the pending Mafia-war and Mafia-association charges in Italy?

Yes. The Old Man now betrays a surpassing understanding of English. The interpreter translates his words as ". . . because I have to be tried in Italy on a charge that alleges there is a Mafia war on, and that I am a *Mafioso.*"

Badalamenti interjects, "Madame! I said the word *alleged Mafioso.* I am *not* a Mafioso. I said *alleged.*"

Leval rules in favor of the government. "The defendant is asking to have it both ways. . . . That would be an altogether unreasonable position." It would deny the government an opportunity to cross-examine.

Freeh asks to think overnight about whether to ask the judge to strike the last series of questions.

Leval agrees. This has been "a complete surprise! . . . I don't know of any other instance in which it happened that a defendant takes the stand, testifies to his innocence, and then claims the Fifth as to the central evidence against him."

Kennedy turns his head away from the bench, smiles, turns back, and says, in even tones, "It was exactly a year ago this week, during jury selection," that in Badalamenti's written motion asking for severance, "we raised the strong possibility of antagonistic and inconsistent defenses being put forward, and we offered to, in camera, [make a proffer on] this very dilemma. And the court . . . overruled our motion."

Leval passes on to the matter of the handcuffs translation. Fogelnest asserts Martin knew the comment was "inadmissible, inappropriate, prejudicial," but insisted it be translated nonetheless. The lawyer demands a formal inquiry; he wants Martin under oath. Fogelnest is raging, and Martin is laughing as he is sworn and takes his seat in the box.

Fogelnest asks about his "proficiency in Italian."

Silence.

Fogelnest demands that the judge instruct Martin to answer, "and not play games with me."

Leval says, "He said he didn't understand your question."

"I call him a liar!" the lawyer shouts. Martin snickers. They decide to hold a formal hearing, with Malerba representing Fogelnest, and Freeh representing Martin.

Martin takes the position that he did not hear what Badalamenti actually said; he heard only his request that the interpreter not translate it. Therefore he properly asked that it *be* translated.

"What do we do now?" Fogelnest shouts. Thanks to Martin, the jurors now know that Salamone "comes to court every day handcuffed to the lead defendant, the chief of the Sicilian Mafia, who refuses to explain what his cryptic telephone conversations were. . . . I don't think a man can get a fair trial under these circumstances!"

The lawyer is raving now, raising fears of another heart attack. But he won't be silenced. "Judge! I don't care if I drop dead in this courtroom. I want that to be my eulogy, and you and Dick Martin can live with it, and I don't give a rat's ass. . . . I'll take 15 minutes to compose myself."

"Take a half hour," says Leval.

. . . THURSDAY, OCTOBER 16, 1986.

THE COURTROOM.   Kennedy renews his request that his client be allowed to tell the jury about the phone calls in his own words so that the jury, not the court, can determine whether Badalamenti's refusal has credibility. Leval says he thinks such a ruling would be "extraordinarily unfair," and sends for the jury.

"Mr. Kennedy, you may proceed."

". . . in light of your Honor's ruling, I have no further questions for Mr. Badalamenti at this time."

Kennedy's case has taken a sudden bad turn. Perhaps if the matter were up to the jury, he could make some headway, find some way of making the jurors understand his client's intolerable position: To tell the truth here would be to condemn himself to certain death in an Italian jail. Death could come there of old age, since he faces a twenty-one-year sentence. Murder is far more likely. It is doubtful he could survive even twenty-one months in a prison swarming with his blood enemies, allies of the same faction that has been trying to find him and kill him since 1978. If assassins got to Michele Sindona, in his isolated, closely guarded, country-club cell in Voghera, what chance would Badalamenti have in the dread medieval fortress of Ucciardone? What's more, the Old Man doesn't like and usually even refuses to speak of his mortal peril. A Man of Honor does not show fear. Not ever, to anyone. Not even to save his own skin in an American courtroom. With the jury, such arguments, artfully presented, might fly. They haven't a chance with Leval.

Louis Freeh advances on the podium with a fat loose-leaf notebook spilling over with inserted documents. He carries a grocery carton full of documents to a low table beside him, moving in a stiff-legged, penguin waddle; an old injury, perhaps. He is trim, of medium stature, with a long, closely shaven jaw and a tense, grave demeanor. All his questions will be framed to suggest that the lead defendant has been committing nonstop perjury for the past two days.

"Didn't you attend a meeting of Cosa Nostra in Palermo in 1957 with Tomasso Buscetta and Joe Bonanno?" No.

"Have you ever become a member of La Cosa Nostra?"

The jury for once looks extremely alert. "I have never *said* it. And if I were [a member], I would not say it! If I were, I would not tell you. . . . Because I would respect the oath."

"Are you now, or have you ever been, a member of La Cosa Nostra?"

Badalamenti replies. But before the translator can repeat his answer in English, Martin once again objects, and Leval sustains. This has happened before. The defense lawyers protest that, in a trial being conducted of necessity in translation, Martin's command of Italian means that he, not the judge, is really in charge. Martin controls the flow of questions. Martin controls what the jury hears and does not hear.

What Badalamenti had said was, "You know well, Mr. Freeh, that if I were to answer your question, I would be in very serious trouble in Italy." Martin has been able to prevent the jury from hearing this answer.

Freeh turns to Badalamenti's role in World War II. "Did you, Gaetano Badalamenti, personally fight the Fascists?" Yes.

"You're very proud of that, aren't you?"

"Not proud. I did it."

Freeh has carefully studied the Allies' Italian campaign. He seeks to show that Badalamenti played no part in it, and is trying to pass off his dead brother's war record as his own. Freeh asks the witness to look at the map and show the jurors where he deserted and became a *partigiano.* The Old Man puts on heavy horn-rims, stands, turns around, tilts back his head to stare up at the map. His balding old pate gleams dully in the flat overhead light. He points to an area east of Palermo.

Freeh says the Allied forces made two landings in Sicily, one led by General Patton, the other by Field Marshal Montgomery.

"I never said I was at the point where the Allies landed. What I said was—I was one of those who cleared the area."

Freeh is scornful. "What area did you clear?"

"We arranged it so that when the Americans landed, no Germans would be there."

The Old Man is parrying, not answering; he may be lying or he may just be trying to get Freeh's goat. One cannot tell. The tone of voice—be it forceful, insolent, or satirical—and any other vocal nuance that normally might help a juror evaluate a witness's credibility are completely absent here. Every sentence comes out like every other in the brisk voice of the flirtatious, middle-aged translator.

"Can you name any of your comrades-in-arms?"

"There were so many."

"Give us a couple of names. Please."

He gives a name.

"Where was he from?"

Badalamenti cannot answer, and is unable to give any other names of wartime comrades. Freeh's voice rises in frustration, a failing of which this witness is quick to take advantage.

"But why are you getting angry? What is the matter?"

Freeh moves to the next subject. "Did you hear your lawyer's opening statement? . . . Is it true, as your lawyer said, that you were contacted by the Americans at the time of the Anzio invasion. Is that *true?*"

"Anzio is not in Sicily," Badalamenti replies in a by now characteristic *non sequitur.*

Freeh repeats his question, his voice again rising. "Were you contacted by operatives of the United States government with respect to *any* invasion of Italy anywhere? . . . [Yelling] *Who* supplied you with arms?"

265

In a stage whisper, Badalamenti says, "I didn't hear him. Perhaps he should speak louder." He says he received arms from a Professor Cartinelli, and remains absolutely serene throughout this increasingly unbelievable testimony. The jury cannot know that, in Italy, it is form to lie on the stand; that lying is considered by many the only honorable course.

Freeh is openly contemptuous. "And he contacted *you,* a twenty-year-old deserter, to assist General Patton in the invasion of Sicily! Is that your testimony?"

Freeh now turns to Kennedy's opening statement and asks, quoting, "Did you, sir, receive: 'a credit from the United States government, a commendation . . . thanking you for the role you played in assisting the Allies against the Fascists in 1943'?" Freeh intends to make a liar out of lawyer as well as client.

"Thank God I didn't. . . . The people who received that are dead."

Freeh changes the subject. "Do you remember where you were on April 26, 1950?"

"I think, the United States."

"Do you remember a sworn statement you made at that time?"

"No. I made no sworn statement."

Freeh hands Kennedy a document. It is apparent he has dropped a prosecution grenade in the lawyer's lap. An immediate sidebar is called. Kennedy's face is flushed; he is clearly furious. Freeh tries to resume questioning.

"Do not answer!" Kennedy shouts. "I instruct you not to answer." His roar startles the whole courtroom.

"Mr. Kennedy, you are in contempt!"

"Mr. Badalamenti, *don't answer,* until I finish reading this document withheld from me by the government."

In a voice trembling with fury, Leval orders the government to proceed. Freeh puts a question.

The witness: "I am not answering . . ."

Leval asks, "Mr. Badalamenti, do you refuse to answer . . . ?"

"I am waiting for my attorney. . . . I am not refusing. . . ."

"Mr. Badalamenti, were you asked 36 years ago, and did you give this answer . . . ?"

Juror #1, the balding sanitation man who is foreman, turns clean around in his seat to grin up at #10, the fat concrete repairman from the South Bronx. The grin says, "They got him cold!"

It is one of the trial's crucial moments. Badalamenti's answers on this matter will become increasingly hard to credit. A juror who admires

Kennedy will side with him now. But a juror who dislikes him will have been further put off by his outburst. A Leval-minded juror will be horrified. One thing is certain: After twelve months in their green leather swivel chairs, each juror has a strong sense of his or her own importance in these proceedings. How many jurors now think that contempt of court means contempt of *them?*

Kennedy begins to read from the old document, two sheets of ancient flimsy paper fished by the government from Badalamenti's immigration file. The file is thirty-six years old. Its recovery from the dusty records of the Immigration and Naturalization Service is a feat of bureaucratic archaeology, a reminder that federal prosecutors have instant access to the complete tax records, health records, vital statistics, and other documents on any individual who interests them.

At the next admonishment from Leval, Kennedy throws his microphone on the table and instructs his client in a loud, clear voice, "When this document is translated for you, you can answer any questions. Before, you don't have to!" The jury has seen this happen before. When Kennedy gets angry, he just plain defies Leval. Surprisingly, the judge takes it.

Another sidebar is called, followed by a ten-minute recess.

Defense lawyers caucus in the corridor. The Badalamenti-group lawyers reveal an astounding ability to psych themselves out. "The jury loves Badalamenti," says Koppelman. "Imagine Freeh wasting a whole morning on Anzio and Montecatini!" sniffs Calluori. They seem unaware that this morning has been spent—very successfully—in fatally impeaching the main defendant.

Across the corridor, Kaplan speaks for all the non-Badalamenti lawyers when he says, "Badalamenti is a catastrophic witness. The worst I've ever seen! Fifth Amendment pleas are always disastrous. You can pull that stuff with a grand jury, or in a Senate hearing. But no petit jury gives a damn about the Fifth. They don't understand it. When a witness refuses to answer a question, they get one message only—guilt! And that guilt spills over to all the little guys in Badalamenti's family."

Down the hall, Kennedy is saying that the INS file took him completely by surprise. He had asked about it many months ago. "Freeh lied. He lied with an explanation, which is worse than just plain lying. He said he did not have the file, and was not sure it even existed any longer. He added that Greg Byrne [a young Kennedy assistant] had told him I didn't want it, and that if I changed my mind, I would subpoena it."

Then Kennedy grins. "But I don't mind. I just got the best appeals point in the case: Leval would not allow a witness to look at the papers he was being examined on!"

Court reconvenes, and before the jury returns, Kennedy moves for a mistrial on grounds that a document has been unreasonably withheld from the defense.

If Judge Leval is still furious, he conceals it, and says with sweet reason, "If you had asked for that . . . there is no question it would have been granted."

"I asked . . . for . . . that," Kennedy thunders. "The way you're handling this courtroom is an embarrassment to . . . the bar!"

"I could care less what your opinion of *me* is, but don't . . ."

Kennedy interrupts with a snarl, "As long as it's clear to you what my opinion of you is."

Leval is imperturbable. ". . . but don't speak of things that you are not entitled to in the presence of the jury.

"Now, let's proceed." Judge Leval sends for the jury.

Freeh asks the interpreter to review with the witness the 1950 INS proceedings against him. Badalamenti's response is absurd. "This document should be cancelled. . . . At the time I was stupid. . . . Not knowing what was going on . . . At that time, I didn't even remember the date of my birth. Stupid . . . I didn't even know my name was Gaetano. I wrote: Gaeto." Is he speaking ironically? One cannot tell. The translator's cheery monotone flattens out all nuances.

Are you saying you didn't sign it?

"No. I am saying that in the event I did sign such paper, I must have been beside myself. My brain must have been not functioning. I cannot claim that it is functioning now. . . ."

"You deny that's your signature?"

"Yes."

This testimony is disastrous. How can Kennedy have put this unbelievable, unlikable old mountebank on the stand?

"If you deserted in July, how long had you been fighting as a *partigiano?*" Freeh looks incredulous. "You don't know how long it took General Patton to get from the beachhead to Palermo?"

Badalamenti says he did not "even know there *was* a General Patton. Until you mentioned him today . . . Never heard of Field Marshal Montgomery either . . ."

This testimony sounds so brazen, it's weird. Unless of course it happens to be true.

"Isn't it a fact that you *never* were a *partigiano?* That you made it up? Isn't that a lie?"

"It is not a lie."

"Isn't it a fact that you made it up because you want this jury to believe . . ."

"I don't want them to believe. I want them to judge." To judge *me,* he means, and this would seem to be the heart of the matter. This former *capo di tutti capi* seeks nothing less than a referendum on his moral character. "My main objective is to speak of my reputation. To refute one who said he did not know me, but he knew my [bad] reputation."

Amazing! What galls this old man most is the testimony of Agent Tarallo, the man who besmirched his honor by saying he didn't know Badalamenti, but "I know his reputation." On this bizarre note, court adjourns for lunch.

The only working elevator is crammed with Pizza lawyers. They agree the Old Man is a dreadful witness, and is sinking everybody. Fogelnest says, "Let's go for *veal partigiano.*"

After lunch, Badalamenti denies that he fled to the United States in 1947 because he knew the police were looking for him in Sicily. Freeh tells the court, "This was not a normal case of an alien stowaway. Diplomatic notes were sent. The Italian ambassador was involved." The Italian government was seeking the return of a renowned criminal wanted for conspiracy and kidnapping. Murder and robbery were also mentioned in the diplomatic notes.

The jury returns, and Freeh reads an Interpol document reporting a March 23, 1946, arrest warrant for Gaetano Badalamenti. "Your testimony is that you did not know of the warrant, and were not fleeing the police?" Si.

For the third time: "At what port, city, or beach did you first come to these great United States? . . . Is it your testimony that, coming to the United States as an immigrant, for the first time, you don't *remember . . .* you don't remember whether you saw the Statue of Liberty in the harbor!"

I was just looking for what train to get on, he says.

To look a liar in the face is difficult over long stretches. No one in the room looks at Badalamenti now except for Kennedy, the prosecutors, and certain fellow defendants. Gradually one senses that Badalamenti is not playing to the jury, or the spectators, or to his family: He is playing to a select audience of defendants: the Catalano faction, the Lamberti-Mazzurco faction, and the back-row New Jersey contingent—the very people who, on direct examination, he had said he had never, or hardly ever, met. And behind them, going all the way back to Sicily, back indeed to his boyhood in the village of Cinisi, stretches a much bigger audience. He is playing to the Mafia.

Kennedy moves to keep out the entire INS file.

The defendant has taken the Fifth on the most important evidence in this case, says Leval. The government is entitled to question him on less important matters. "Come to side bar."

In the corridor, the lawyers are buzzing. If Badalamenti had only said, "Of course I lied. Every illegal alien lies to the INS," he would have been so much more believable.

When court resumes, without a jury, it appears Leval has yet again backed down in a clash with Kennedy. "I may have misunderstood what Mr. Kennedy wanted. . . ."

The lawyer says he wants the jury to hear directly from Mr. Badalamenti: I refuse to answer the question on grounds it might tend to incriminate me in Italy with reference to Mafia charges.

Leval asks, You do not wish to add anything in reference to the drug charges?

"I do not."

Freeh objects. "I still won't be able to get any answers from him regarding the calls."

Kennedy reminds the court of this morning's questioning, "Are you or are you not a member of La Cosa Nostra?" And the answer: "You know that would hurt me in Italy. . . . That door has not only been opened. It's been knocked down!"

Benfante is on his feet. "It would not be in our client's interest, it would be highly prejudicial—if he takes the Fifth on drug charges." Kennedy will later point out that Benfante in his puppylike zeal has jumped the gun and asked the question prematurely, before the judge has ruled.

Lombardino weighs in, growling, "If you're going to permit Badalamenti to take the Fifth, we ask for a severance!"

Leval rules that he will permit the foregoing statement before the jury, provided Kennedy agrees not to argue "the other side of the coin" in summation—argue that having taken the Fifth indicates that the coded calls *did not* refer to drugs.

Kennedy says, "Mr. Badalamenti will answer any questions about drugs, but not questions about phone calls. Because in his own mind— which *you* won't permit us to bring out—such answers would tend to incriminate him with reference to the Mafia . . . charges in Italy."

Kennedy has told friends that he believes and hopes to bring out that the phone calls were mostly about murders, past and future; Mafiamotivated killings that are part of the ongoing Sicilian Mafia wars. The pending Italian charges hold Badalamenti ultimately responsible for as many as 100 murders, mostly of magistrates and judges. For the Old Man to recover his former power, and lose the degrading title "Capo of the Losers," certain assassinations must occur. But it appears that the old scoundrel is now refusing, except very obliquely, to say as much. Unless the refusal is part of some master strategy that has not yet come to light.

The jury returns, and Badalamenti resumes his former style, parrying prosecution questions with questions of his own. But there is a new, firmer tone to his voice.

You told us you were convicted in Italy for contraband cigarettes.

"I've already told you . . . I don't remember the names of the people . . . who assisted me. . . ."

"*Were you* . . . head of the Mafia Cosa Nostra *Commissione* in Sicily for many years?"

"If you need this for the Italian trial, I'm sorry. You will not succeed. Because I will not say it."

"Did you hear Tomasso Buscetta testify to that?"

"Yes. But he said it. Not I."

"You knew he was a member of La Cosa Nostra for thirty-five years, didn't you?"

"Did I say that to you, Mr. Freeh? I don't remember it."

"I'm asking you now. Was Tomasso Buscetta . . . a member?"

"*You* know that to be true. . . ."

Shouting: "Do *you* know?"

Badalamenti shoots Freeh a terror-inspiring glare. "Please don't raise your voice. Because you don't frighten me." In fact, it is Badalamenti who is the frightening presence in this courtroom.

After a year, court and jury have now seen this man up close, seen more than the back of his balding head, seen him frontally, and seen that he is an ogre. He is Kennedy's ogre, and he may also be out of Kennedy's control. This puts everything one has been hearing for a year, both in the courtroom and privately from the lawyers, in a different and scary light.

That evening, Ivan Fisher talks about Badalamenti's performance and the Kennedy strategy. "Bad as Badalamenti was before the break, he was great for the last twenty minutes. He was great because he told them the truth . . . that he had been lying through his teeth. It was absolutely gorgeous!"

But, taking a longer view, "Michael's strategy has backfired. Pierre

Leval hates him. The other defendants and their lawyers feel screwed.

"Those phone calls are the worst! Those conversations are so bad on their face that if Cardinal Cooke were talking, not Badalamenti, the conversations could make you doubt that the cardinal was not a drug dealer. Then, with Sal Mazzurco on the other end—there's no doubt!

"That's why Kennedy's defense, hiding behind the bullshit claim of honor, that his guy is a Man of Honor, won't work. It's too slick. The 'twenty-two' could be anything—twenty-two gold bars, twenty-two tons of timber, twenty-two cows, twenty-two sheep; it could be twenty-two fingers, maybe he was a fingers freak. Except that he was *talking to Mazzurco,* and *he* doesn't deal in cows. He deals heroin.

"Kennedy is in a very, very bad position. He made the jury a lot of promises in his opening, and now he's not able to keep them, because the Old Man did not come through on his own promises to Michael.

"I think he did not anticipate the impact on the jury of the Mazzurco heroin dealings. Mazzurco's conversations, especially with Badalamenti, are *key* to this case. I don't think Michael Kennedy had any idea of the hammerlock those conversations would have. He opened grandly—wrapping Badalamenti's old, guilty arms around the entire family group. I don't know why. But I suspect that the *idea* of a family very much appealed to Michael."

Was Badalamenti a drug dealer? Fisher says, "I think the Old Man did not want to deal heroin. But then, he wanted something else, wanted it so much that he was in fact gathering a war chest to get it. That something else was probably to regain his power in the Mafia. He did not want to die and leave his family with the legacy, the reputation: 'Capo of the Losers.' That took a lot of money. And he was willing to deal drugs—heroin and perhaps cocaine—to get it."

There is no court the next day, Friday, but the lawyers talk on phones. One of the most vocal is Joe Benfante. "It was terrible, the worst testimony of any witness I've ever heard; all arrogance, defiance, and ego."

"Terrible would be a godsend," says his friend Dave Lewis. "His real problem is an almost Chinese inability to lose face."

"It's disastrous!" says the taciturn Mike Querques. "That man has ice cubes for blood. He sat there and made only two gestures all afternoon. Once he eased his collar on the left, once on the right. The rest of the time he sat absolutely motionless, arms folded, not even sweating.

"I felt sorry for Michael Kennedy. I've been racking my brains all day, trying to think of ways to help him."

No question Kennedy handles his difficult client well. "One of the reasons Badalamenti chose Kennedy," says Lewis, "is that Michael gives Badalamenti the respect he believes he deserves." His previous lawyer, the experienced Charles Carnesi, had been perceived by his client as insufficiently deferential. "The Old Man thought Charlie treated him like someone from midget wrestling."

No codefendant suffers as much damage from yesterday's testimony as Sal Mazzurco. Until now, says his lawyer, Benfante, he had felt confident that Kennedy's prediction was correct and "there was going to be *something*, something really colorful, that was going to blow their minds." He blames the letdown not on the lawyer but on his client.

"He is a very power-hungry, strong-willed, nasty guy. All he wants to do is look good, and have people write that he refused to name names," says Benfante.

Indeed, this morning's papers have all said exactly this. "That's what *he* wanted. But as far as the jury's concerned, it was totally devastating! They didn't like Kennedy's outburst against Leval. The judge is wrong. But you can make *yourself* wrong by attacking the judge. They like Leval, and they felt sorry for him.

"I felt sorry for Kennedy. There's a great possibility that Badalamenti tried to outfox his own lawyer. I think the Old Man, months ago, decided he was not going to admit anything that could hurt him in the Italian trial; that is, admit the real truth—that he was trying to raise money for the Mafia. I met him two years ago at MCC, and he was irrational then. I thought he had lost his marbles. I would meet with him, and try to explain the truth about these phone calls. He didn't want to hear the truth, so he would glare at me until I left. He wanted a lawyer who was going to treat him with respect. He doesn't deserve respect. He's an asshole."

Lawyers affiliated with the Badalamenti group are understandably more guarded, and willing to talk only off the record. Says one who knows the situation well, "You must understand that Badalamenti is impossible to talk to. He thinks he's smarter than anyone else in the world. He won't take direction. He won't suffer to be corrected. And he's a little nuts. At one point he said to me, 'You know, I could stop this trial if I wanted. I could agree to go back to Italy.' The Old Man is not hitting on all pistons.

"The problem is that Michael *wanted* to believe Badalamenti. I kept telling him, 'Don't believe the old fuck,' but he wouldn't listen."

Perhaps. But the problem could also be that Kennedy *needed* to believe Badalamenti. Many months after the trial ended, both the Kennedys continued to maintain their unshakable belief that Gaetano Badalamenti was never a drug dealer. But by then Kennedy was also willing to say, "I need to believe. If I don't believe, I cannot advocate."

. . . MONDAY, OCTOBER 20, 1986.

THE COURTROOM. On his second day of cross-examination, Louis Freeh methodically takes the witness through his flight to Paris and Nice, thence to Brazil. He examines his finances, and goes into the matter of his illegal visas and passports. Although Badalamenti seems evasive and tricky as ever, he is no longer the all-time disaster witness of Thursday last. He now comes across as a seasoned old crook, holding up fine.

Over the weekend, Kennedy has intensively coached his client in a new type of behavior. By the end of today's testimony, the lawyer has concluded, "We've moved it from the mechanistic to the human level. We're not talking about phone calls any longer. That jury is looking at a man's life, his character. He's no choirboy. He's an old Mafioso chieftain. But he has a kind of honor. Some jurors now are going to say, 'That old guy has balls.' "

Kennedy needs to convince only one juror. That one will convert one or two others, and the jury will then be tied up, and his client will have a chance. "Without this, we had *no* chance."

The next day's cross-examination deals with the Buscetta testimony, the flight to Spain, and more about money and false documents.

Ever tell Buscetta you were opposed to drugs?

He was aware. . . . Don't remember if I told him. But I believe he knew.

Ever express your opposition to drugs at a La Cosa Nostra meeting?

But *I* never told you I knew members of La Cosa Nostra.

Did you?

I've never said I did.

This is stonewalling on an epic scale, comparable to the Great Wall of China.

His answers about a trip to the Copacabana Hotel in Rio seem especially preposterous. The government had presented several hotel employees who saw him. He says he never went there. Yes, he heard the two women hotel clerks give sworn testimony that Badalamenti had registered under the name Marco Ruffino. He heard the evidence that his son's fingerprint was found on one of the registration cards. And *still* he denies. It's embarrassing.

Vito Badalamenti, watching his father on the witness stand, has gone ashy pale.

In the break, Larry Bronson offers his opinion. "This testimony makes it absolutely certain he will be convicted. I cannot understand why he is doing it—unless his master plan is to stay in jail in the U.S. rather than go to Italy. But the whole tone of the courtroom is now very bad for all the defendants. There *is no* up side to what's going on. The only question remaining is: Who is the author of this strategy?"

Back in the courtroom Freeh has returned to the central question of his cross-examination: What were you speaking about in the phone calls?

"Our business . . . It could be we were speaking of business; it could be we were speaking of other matters."

It could be you were speaking about drugs, too?

The Old Man now makes his first salient point. "If it had been drugs, you would have waited a few days before arresting me." That is, you would have waited to catch me with the drugs, red-handed. The fact that you moved so fast proves that you knew it was *not* drugs.

Freeh volleys fast. He cannot risk letting this difficult but good point sink in. You mean, we arrested you before you had a chance to ship the drugs out of the country, right?

No. You did it because you knew it was not drugs.

Louis Freeh is now ready to review the Old Man's taped conversations. He has reprinted about twenty in special brown notebooks, which he distributes to court and counsel, jurors and interpreters.

Marvin Schechter, counsel to Sal Lamberti, objects that all the proposed questioning violates his client's Fifth and Sixth Amendment rights, as well as a half-dozen Supreme Court decisions. He files a strong, continuing objection to every question: By taking the stand and then refusing to answer questions, Badalamenti has impaired the Fifth Amendment right *not* to testify of all other defendants. They now must speak, to neutralize the highly prejudicial effect of Badalamenti's remarks.

. . . **WEDNESDAY, OCTOBER 22, 1986.**
THE COURTROOM. Freeh has barely begun his cross-examination when Judge Leval, very stern, interrupts to declare an immediate recess. He sends out the jury, and summons Freeh and Koppelman. Vito Badalamenti is seriously ill. He has been taken to the hospital with severe stomach pains and is hemorrhaging badly. Kennedy is backstage with his client. Mrs. Badalamenti is in the courtroom, with Christine Evola, but as yet knows nothing. Kennedy goes down the aisle to the two women. "Please explain to Mrs. Badalamenti that the hospital has done tests; that Vito is run down, but they don't think it's serious."

Koppelman had warned Leval yesterday that Vito was ill. But what much upset the judge just now was a call from Beekman Downtown Hospital that Vito has lost nearly half his blood.

Badalamenti has become so upset that Kennedy seeks to have court adjourn for the day. But the Old Man insists on continuing. Genay Leitman volunteers to escort Mrs. Badalamenti and Mrs. Evola to the hospital, to be certain they're admitted. As they leave, Freeh goes up to Mrs. Badalamenti and says how sorry he is that this has happened.

Larry Ruggiero says the "back-row lawyers" are calling Kennedy's defense a "charade."

"Actually," says Kennedy, "it's more of a dance than a charade. The point was: I had to get Badalamenti on without the government anticipating that he would refuse to answer."

The truth is, says Manny Moore, not just an experienced drug lawyer but a former prosecutor, the government *wants* Badalamenti to continue refusing to answer. That way, the jury gets the impression, "This guy's so arrogant, he puts himself above the laws of the United States."

1:20 P.M. The jury returns, and instantly notes the absence of a half-dozen defendants and family members. Defendants Vitale, Trupiano, Evola, Palazzolo, and Alfano are all at the hospital, standing by to give blood, and their wives are with them.

Leval thanks the jurors for their patience. The delay was irrelevant, he tells them. Certain defendants have asked to be absent. "You are to draw no inference."

Badalamenti is back in the box. Freeh asks: What is "the thing from four to five years ago?"

"If you'd like to know if it was drugs, it was not. If you'd like a full answer, I'll give you a complete answer. . . .

"As you well know, the U.S. government has put together from the Badalamenti group 400 tapes. . . . If all of them had been offered to the jury, there would be no need for an explanation because they altogether would be self-explanatory. . . . Out of those, the U.S. government took fifty, approximately, and sent them to Italy. Italy used them, and you know about it.

"If you'd like, I can explain. To begin with, it has reinforced an arrest warrant on Mafia and Mafia war charges for importation of weapons, recycling of currency, and drugs. When you spoke of 'the thing of four-five years ago': In his opening, Mr. Stewart slightly hinted at it. Later on, some testimony occurred which I hope to fight. Still, in order to support this thing of five years ago, out of these 400, you are using twenty, approximately, and explaining things along as you're doing in such a capable fashion, I have to give explanations of drugs. With the same, I have to give explanations of Mafia, Mafia war, importation of weapons and so on, all those things."

As Kennedy said in his opening, Sicilians *always* talk in code. To indicate his scorn, Freeh sits down. Badalamenti continues "explaining."

"Now, as of this thing of five years ago, as you say, it has a name, a name which has been given not by you, but by your office, and it is the same name given by Italy. I don't believe either is true.

"In any event, at this point I am incapable of explaining. You know that the way it has been put, this chapter is perhaps the most important chapter of my whole life. This is the reason why I cannot reply to the thing of five years ago."

"Are you finished, sir?"

"Yes."

Freeh asks that this so-called answer be stricken, and the witness directed to reply to his question.

Leval reads the jury an important instruction: Because this defendant has chosen to take the stand, he has given up his right to refuse to answer, and the jury may consider his refusal as part of the evidence against him.

"The government contends you should consider Gaetano Badalamenti's refusals to answer questions as deliberate evasion, based on his belief that true answers would show his guilt. . . . Gaetano Badalamenti contends his reasons for refusal to answer are different, and that they do not involve any consciousness of guilt on his part."

277

The refusal to answer, and its meaning, is a matter of *fact,* for the jury to decide. . . . But "you may not consider such answers or refusals to answer as evidence affecting any *other* defendant."

Freeh asks, "Isn't it a fact that the thing from four years . . . ago is a heroin source that you had?" No.

Isn't it a fact that "the modern one" is cocaine? Not true.

"Tell them you desire fish." Is *fish* a code word? Yes.

"For what . . . Is it a code word for money?" No.

For drugs? No.

What was it?

This question is simply not answered.

"Are you familiar with the phrase, *la stessa cosa?*"

"Of course."

"Do you understand that to be a common reference to a member of Cosa Nostra?"

"To speed things up, I refuse to answer."

Eleanore Kennedy leans over to a visiting lawyer and asks, "Would it ever occur to you that these were guns? Weapons he needed for the Mafia war? He won't tell the truth. The truth could set him free here. But it would screw him up there, and he won't do it."

. . . THURSDAY, OCTOBER 23, 1986.

THE COURTROOM.   By this next morning, positions have hardened. Badalamenti's face looks brutal, dark, choleric. It will be a difficult day.

Vito has been found to have three bleeding stomach ulcers, doubtless stress-related. But he is bleeding less now, and his age, twenty-eight, is much in his favor.

The government wants to strike from the record all of Badalamenti's refusals to answer, hold him in contempt of court, and not allow Kennedy to reexamine on his reasons for his refusals. As Freeh has said, "It is not a simple matter where this defendant is just refusing to answer. He says it could be, it could not be. He is *playing games.* He could sit up there and say: 'Look, Mr. Freeh, I am not going to answer you *one* question about this call.' " The prosecutor would then move on to the next call. But "he is not doing that. He is using the opportunity to testify in a very, very clever manner."

The Kennedys say Leval "is catching on" to Kennedy's defense, and has said, "You are trying to trick the U.S. government." He is angry.

He has said he will rule on the government's contempt request at the end of the cross, and will also rule on whether to permit Kennedy any redirect.

Badalamenti's refusals today are more adamant. He answers in brutish grunts. He has had a night to think about what has happened to Vito. By now, though, the Old Man's games seem like empty displays of Sicilian bravado, more childish than dangerous.

Teresa Badalamenti and Mrs. Evola put on their coats and leave the courtroom for the hospital. Badalamenti stares after them, and in his dreadful eyes is a look of profound longing.

Freeh puts more questions about codes, gets more refusals to explain. The prosecutor is doing everything he can to enhance the feeling among the jurors that Gaetano Badalamenti is personally insulting and deliberately mocking *them* by his refusals.

Do you know whether, on February 4, 1984, Mr. Alfano brought some drugs to Mr. Mazzurco in New York? No.

Will you tell us? No.

"Your Honor, that concludes my questioning for the morning."

Today's lunch hour is longer than usual. Lewis, Lombardino, Benfante, Novack, and Burke head downtown for seafood. The lawyers think Badalamenti's performance is worse today than yesterday. By the end of lunch, they have decided, as Lombardino puts it, "Badalamenti is going down the tubes, and dragging his family with him." Additionally, the lawyers complain, Leval's rulings are making a lot of bad law: bad law on multiple conspiracies; bad law on severance; bad law on what may be testified to by an expert witness, such as the "drug-language expert," Agent Tarallo; and bad law that says the Mafia is, in and of itself, a conspiracy.

The jury is back. The Old Man is still on the stand. His eyes glitter like the Ancient Mariner's. The unanswered questions stretch on and on. "I'm not going to explain . . . not going to explain." Leval is stifling yawns.

"Your Honor," says Freeh, gathering up his folders, "I don't have any more cross-examination."

Leval declares a ten-minute recess, and at 3:31 P.M. says, "Call the jury, please." It is time for redirect.

Michael Kennedy stands. Either he is a truly wonderful actor or a supermasochist—or he's got a defense to put on. He asks about Badalamenti's reply to the question "Are you now, or have you ever been, a member of La Cosa Nostra?"

The jury looks sodden with boredom. They avoid looking at the witness, always a bad sign.

Now Kennedy reads his client's answer: "Mr. Freeh, you know well, I would have big troubles in Italy . . ."

Freeh objects, but is overruled.

What did Badalamenti mean by this?

"I have already stated it," he begins, arrogant as before. "There is a proceeding against me in Italy. I believe that the investigation . . . started in 1982."

Freeh objects, is sustained, and Kennedy asks to approach.

Leval says Kennedy's client is giving off-the-wall, hearsay answers. Why should he be permitted hearsay testimony "about all kinds of facts that he thinks would favor his cause, [such as] suggesting that he wasn't at a meeting because he wasn't arrested"? Kennedy permits himself to hint to the court at his own exasperation with his client. "What he was saying—to be sure, it's convoluted, and that may be part of the Sicilian character, I don't know; it's also an affliction of the Irish—was that he faced a Mafia war charge. I think where he was going—to the extent that I can get him to go anywhere—is directly to that point."

Things get worse when Kennedy turns to Badalamenti's war record. He elicits that Badalamenti did personally fire on the Germans, but when Kennedy asks him to point to the place on the map where this happened, he cannot find it. At length he says, "The fact of the matter is that I cannot even locate Cinisi."

And on this weak note, the day closes. Kennedy's struggle to rehabilitate the Old Man has been valiant, but he is getting zero help from his client.

That evening Badalamenti tells his lawyer a long story, really a parable, which leaves both men spluttering with laughter. Kennedy is never certain what the story means, but for weeks he cannot get it out of his mind.

Once upon a time the other animals decided to elect the wolf King of the Forest. It was an extremely long, cold winter, and after a while virtually nothing could be found for the animals to eat. The whole community was slowly starving to death. The animals voted and decided that henceforth any food that was found should be brought to a central place where all the animals would eat it together, share and share alike. The wolf's job was to enforce the decision.

One day a young deer was walking alone through the forest and saw a single leaf, high in a tree. The deer was very hungry, and so he ate the leaf. Some of the other animals saw the deer, and captured him, and the deer was brought before the wolf. The little deer was eloquent. "Oh, please, sir! I didn't mean to disobey. But I was *so* hungry, I had to eat."

But the wolf was merciless: "You have disobeyed our law and you must pay for it with your life." So saying, the wolf executed the deer, and then—since the deer was dead anyway, and since the other animals had reached the starvation point—he ordered the flesh butchered and the meat shared among all the animals.

A short time later in this most desperate of cruel winters, word reached the wolf that a hungry lion roaming the frozen forest had found and eaten a stray lamb. Soon the lion was brought before the wolf. "I was so hungry," roared the lion, "that I *had* to eat."

Said the wolf, "Well, when you gotta eat, you gotta eat."

Kennedy had asked Joe Calluori what he thought the story meant. "I think it means that Mr. B. did not want to deal heroin, but he was forced into it; circumstances offered him no other choice."

"Yes," said Kennedy. "But what if Mr. Badalamenti was the deer?"

Eleanore Kennedy was consulted. "The Boss of Bosses would never liken himself to a deer," she said. "I don't think it's a story about heroin at all; it's about power. I think it means you must deal from strength. It expresses Mr. B.'s view of the world: If you are strong, you can do whatever you feel like."

. . . FRIDAY, OCTOBER 24, 1986.

THE COURTROOM.   When the jury is seated, Judge Leval makes a little speech. "Joe advises me that it was a year ago yesterday that I congratulated you on having been selected . . . and I never had any anticipation at that time that we would be celebrating the anniversary together a year later." This is greeted with affectionate laughter.

"I want to add also . . . my very genuine, sincere appreciation to you for the cooperation and patience that you have shown. I know that in many respects it is a great hardship and imposition on your lives, and I give you the most sincere and deep thanks of the court. . . ."

Now comes the new jury instruction the government has asked for. Yesterday Mr. Badalamenti said he believed his testimony was true, correct, and complete. "A witness has no legal right to decide when he will answer, and when he will not. The court has ordered him to answer. He has refused. He has no legal right to refuse to answer, and his refusals have been in violation of law."

"Good morning, Mr. Badalamenti."

"Good morning, Mr. Kennedy." The Old Man's voice is noticeably stronger. He knows that Vito got two more pints of family blood last night, and is feeling better. Kennedy leads his client through a brisk review of his prior testimony about his World War II experiences as a soldier/deserter/partisan/civilian. His answers are good, and convincing. He is precise and modest, not grandiose.

"In 1950, did you tell your attorney you had rendered service to the U.S. Army in Sicily in World War II?"

"No, sir."

The answer seems devastating. But it will turn out that, once more, Badalamenti is being preternaturally precise. It was not he but his brother who made this statement. Why doesn't he say so? For the moment, Kennedy has no choice but to move along.

He shows Badalamenti the thirty-six-year-old document. In it, he is *asked* if he understands that he is under oath.

I don't remember that, Mr. Kennedy. The two of us were sitting there. I and the guy from INS, who spoke a little Italian, and less Sicilian. We had such trouble communicating, we wrote down our questions and answers.

Did you understand, then, that you were under oath? No, sir.

Kennedy reads from the document: "Gaetano Badalamenti stood, raised his hand, and was sworn to tell the truth."

"Did you stand?"

"Not that I remember . . . But I did *not* tell the truth!"

Why?

I would have got the person who brought me here, and also my brother, into trouble—which, after all, is the only thing they wanted to learn.

Why did you lie, in 1950, but under oath today you tell us he did help you?

"Well . . . my brother is dead."

This redirect of his client is a labor of Sisyphus for Kennedy. Watching his back as he stands at the podium struggling to dredge what he hopes will be helpful answers from his strange, fierce, oblique-speaking, Mandarin-minded client, one can almost see the back muscles straining under the Brooks Brothers suit.

Mr. Badalamenti, you admit to tobacco smuggling. Yet you deny drug smuggling. What in your mind is the difference?

"For me there is an abyss."

Describe it.

With cigarettes, only the state is being defrauded. It is quite different with drugs.

What is the difference?

"It hurts people."

Kennedy moves on. "Mr. Badalamenti, you were asked by the prosecutor if you were the Chairman of the Board of the Mafia, in Sicily. What did you mean when you said: 'If you need this for the Italian trial, you won't get it'?"

Because I believe that's relevant to Italy.

But the court has told you it is relevant here. You *must* answer. . . . If I were to ask you, as the prosecutor has asked you, would you answer *my* questions, Mr. Badalamenti?

No.

[Boldly] "Why, Mr. Badalamenti?" The lawyer's posture is very erect, his body half turned to the witness. His stance and bearing suggest a matador regarding the bull.

I have already said no. For two reasons. The first is a trial I am facing in Italy. The second is that, if I had received some information in confidence, I would not betray.

What do the Italian charges of Mafia association and Mafia war have to do with your refusal in *this* case, Mr. Badalamenti?

Because they would use them. In Italy. They've already used them up to now.

"Object!" Freeh demands the last sentence be stricken, and Leval sustains.

During the course of your testimony, did you see individuals in this courtroom whom you believed to be Italian magistrates?

"Object! Irrelevant." Leval sustains.

It may not be legally relevant, but it is difficult to see how the question could be more relevant from Badalamenti's point of view.

"You did say in one of the calls that you would like to come to the U.S. for an appointment, in 1983. What appointment?"

I wanted to have an appointment with Lamberti [he does not say which] and Pietro Alfano.

Why?

Mr. Kennedy, I do not think that these are things which concern this trial.

Do you refuse to answer *my* questions, Mr. Badalamenti?

Yes. Because they concern private family matters.

Freeh again objects, and asks that all the recent answers be stricken.

"I object to that! It's contrary to the agreement I thought we had," says Kennedy. They go to argue at the side bar.

Ivan Fisher has slipped into the aisle seat behind Eleanore. "An international jurisprudential first!" he exults. "He's defied the prosecution, defied the court, now he's even defied his own lawyer!"

Fisher wants to help. He has an idea. Kennedy should put an Italian lawyer on the stand to explain Badalamenti's predicament. "The government," he says, "has made it look like they've been screwed by Badalamenti—when in fact they are doing the screwing! If he says 'I belong to the Mafia' *here*, it's an automatic twenty-one years *there.*" If Fisher's former client Sindona, the billionaire banker, could not avoid being served cyanide while in Italian protective custody, what chance does Badalamenti have?

Kennedy asks a series of questions to bring out his client's prison history. Then: "You were asked if you knew Saca Catalano." (Saca is a cousin of Salvatore, found shot to death in 1983 in a parked car in Queens.)

"Yes."

"You said you were part of an association together . . ."—one of 114 defendants.

Yes. They called it "the Association of the 114." It was a trial in Palermo.

"In which you were convicted of being a member of the Mafia?"

"Yes, sir." Kennedy has found a clever way to show the jury that his client is a Mafioso without having it come from his own grim lips.

Yesterday you said that some words were code. For example—*tomato.* Have you ever used the word *tomato* to refer to the vegetable tomato?

Yes.

Have you ever used the word *can* to mean can?

Yes.

Kennedy, in a big voice: "In your conversations played in court, were you ever speaking of arms, or weapons, in coded fashion?"

Freeh's instant objection is sustained, and the lawyers are called to the side bar.

Inevitably Leval strikes the suggestion that the coded contraband commodity was guns, not drugs. But as Eleanore observes with a small smile, "You cannot unring a bell."

The Kennedy quandary had been: pound in the weapons defense now, or hold it back until final arguments? Kennedy is inclined to wait, so as not to reveal his strategy to the government until the last possible moment. Leval solves the lawyer's problem when he rules that Kennedy may not use his redirect as an opportunity to ask questions he did not ask the first time around. What has happened is that when Badalamenti was being questioned by his own lawyer, he did not admit that his conversations were code; he refused to discuss them. Then, on cross, he told Freeh, defiantly, yes, they were code. That admission took Kennedy completely by surprise. Now he wants to use the admission made on cross as a basis for further questions on direct. But Freeh objects, and Leval sustains. Otherwise Kennedy would get two turns at bat to the government's one turn; otherwise Badalamenti would in effect be rewarded, not punished, for stonewalling his own lawyer and opening up, in a limited way, to the opposition; otherwise the court would be giving Badalamenti an opportunity to mention arms or Mafia war or give any other self-serving evidence "that he refused to give to Mr. Freeh."

When the jury comes back, Kennedy says, "In the light of the court's ruling, I have no further questions."

Freeh has no further questions. The witness returns to his seat, smiling for the first time in a week.

Kennedy is right now silently playing a dangerous game: He has not said, "Defense rests." He is waiting to see whether or not the court will grant the government's motion to strike all the Badalamenti testimony.

The wait will be longer than anyone anticipated. Benfante has a witness waiting who must be taken out of turn, a convict brought here from prison to testify. The Bronx drug dealer Sadid Torres, whom the government has named as Mazzurco's cocaine connection, has already been convicted, and has spent more than a year in prison, on the basis of the coke found in his apartment in the April 9 raids. Torres is either very brave, very dumb, or very hungry. Despite the fact that he is almost up for parole, he is here to tell the jury he has never seen Sal Mazzurco before in his life.

Martin's cross is short and brutal. After exposing Torres as a crude and stupid liar, Martin asks: Isn't it true that between your conviction and your sentencing date, you tried to work out a deal, and that when you and your attorney met with Mr. Freeh, you told them you were *terrified* to testify against Mr. Mazzurco, and his people. . . ."

Screams of "Outrageous!" "Mistrial!" The lawyers assert that Martin deliberately threw in the phrase "and his people." He did it to tar all defendants with the same brush. The jury is sent out. A vicious debate ensues. The government asserts that when Freeh told the drug dealer, no deal unless he was willing to name his drug source, Torres had said he could not do that, "because he knew what Mr. Mazzurco and his people would do to him." Dave Lewis accuses Martin of "misconduct," which brings the riposte: "*This* from the man who brought us the questions on Agent Tarallo! *Thank you,* Mr. Lewis!"

Leval puts a stop to the squabble, but Torres has confirmed vividly the connection between at least some Pizza defendants and the lowlifes at the bottom of the dope ladder.

Benfante is in an Italian emotional fury, and can scarcely speak. "When the government takes it upon itself to do every illegal thing, including coercing this witness . . . because this man is terrified of the *government,* of Louis Freeh . . . If you want to gag me, or hold me in contempt, go ahead. . . ." Tears run down his cheeks.

In tones of a patient father, Leval says, "You elicited all this . . . it was perfectly proper impeachment. . . . I don't think I have ever seen a witness so properly impeached. . . ."

All defense lawyers in the room join in a motion for a mistrial. Martin defends himself. This man has come in here and given testimony that is just ridiculous. Motive—that's the key element. That power which "these people" have over men like Torres is exactly what the RICO count is all about. (RICO allows the government to charge that the Mafia, or organized crime, is itself the racketeering enterprise.)

Leval supports the government, though with the observation that the question should have been asked first at the side bar. Had it been, Leval would have recommended that the phrase "and his people" be left out. But "Mr. Torres on the stand is the worst thing that ever happened for any defendant in the case. It has just been a terrible bloodbath for the defendants."

The continual demands for, and denials of, a mistrial are no longer merely, or entirely, the ritualistic, *pro forma* posturings of a normal case. Pizza is no longer a normal case. Each day it continues, a mistrial becomes a less and less viable option for the court.

Over lunch, the attorneys say what they could not say in court: They *know* Martin's quote about Torres is incorrect. If it were true, it would certainly have been used at the bail hearing, and in the case in chief. Leval must know this. He may not be too familiar with RICO and 848s, but he has handled many bail hearings.

Ivan Fisher is next to the podium. Today he is in his thin phase, and the expensive new chocolate-brown suit he has chosen for his defense debut suggests a very tall Hershey bar. Fisher's strategy is to concentrate his attack on the three most damaging pieces of evidence against his client. The first is Sal Catalano's alleged meeting with Ganci and several other Mafiosi in Palermo's Piazza Politeana on Valentine's Day 1980, a few weeks before the alleged Bagheria farmhouse drug tests. Second is Ronsisvalle's testimony concerning the delivery to Catalano of heroin driven up from Florida. Third is Amendolito's claim that "Sal" gave him $1.5 million in cash on a Queens street.

Fisher insists his client has been railroaded, and he believes that if he can clearly disprove any one major facet of the government's story, he can then invite this jury to doubt the whole.

Several of Fisher's witnesses have been brought from Sicily to testify. While they are on the stand, Malerba occupies Kennedy's chair, the seat closest to the witness box, beaming silent, Sicilian encouragement in their direction. The first is Sal Catalano's mother-in-law, a smartly dressed woman with cropped grey hair. By the time she speaks two sentences, the minestrone of Sicilian names thickens to indigestible hodgepodge. Her name is Maria Catalano. Her husband's name is Sal Catalano. But neither she nor her husband was in any way related to defendant Catalano until he married her daughter. Both families come from Cimina, a village outside Palermo on the road to Bagheria, where it appears that practically everybody is named Catalano.

Mama Catalano gives her testimony in a gloomy monotone, to a diminished audience. Jurors #3, 7, and 12 are soon out cold, and five defense lawyers are absent—Benfante, Lombardino, Schechter, Bronson, and Burke. She describes her daughter's wedding reception, which, in keeping with Cimina tradition, took place at her home the Sunday after the Sunday wedding in church. Fisher produces a leather album of richly colored wedding photographs, and elicits from Mama Catalano a vivid description of a gay and elaborate Sicilian *sposalitsio*. Under Fisher's capable direction, she sketches something that sounds like the party scene from *Cavalleria Rusticana*.

Mama Catalano did all the cooking for all the parents, children, in-laws, brothers, and sisters in both Catalano families, including the brother of the bride, who is, of course, named Sal Catalano. Guests arrived all afternoon and evening to congratulate the newlyweds and present them with wedding gifts, many of which, according to Sicilian custom, were fat envelopes of cash. The bridegroom was present all the time, from noon until the last guest went home at about 10:30 P.M.

Fisher shows Mrs. Catalano the photograph of the unshaven man taken in the late afternoon of February 14, 1980, in the Piazza Politeana in Palermo. This is the picture the government says is defendant Catalano meeting with Ganci and two Mafia drug dealers a couple of weeks before the testing of the forty-one kilos of heroin in the Bagheria farmhouse. Fisher elicits from Mrs. Catalano that her son-in-law shaves every day. Defendant Catalano listens intently, a forefinger clamped to his buttoned upper lip.

Prosecutor Stewart is curt. He does not greet Mrs. Catalano by name. He uses her testimony to introduce a number of other photos of the wedding reception, which show that the party was attended by about 300 people, among them several top Mafiosi, including the Sicilian Mafia boss Leonardo Greco. She identifies other pictures. One is the late Joe Ganci, her grandchild's godfather, but she says she does not recall seeing him during any of the wedding festivities. She identifies a certain "Toto" Sal Catalano as a cousin of defendant Sal "Toto" Catalano, and a brother of Onofrio Catalano, who at the time of the wedding had a business renting out farm vehicles.

And what does Onofrio do now?

"Now he's a fugitive," she replies.

"The father of Salvatore 'Saca' Catalano and Onofrio Catalano is also named Salvatore, is he not?"

No. His name is Antonio. But everyone calls him Giuseppe.

Marshals whisper that Stewart's plodding style of questioning has earned him the jury nickname "Nitol." Former prosecutor Ruggiero says, "I would have asked her two questions: Mrs. Catalano, do you love your son-in-law? And two: You wouldn't want something bad to happen to him, would you?" Instead, Stewart is using the occasion to pump the witness for new Mafia names to start files on. "They really have the mentality of policemen, not lawyers," says Kennedy.

Fisher's second witness is another wedding guest, a small, fierce-looking, white-haired blacksmith. He is Vito Marcello, sixty-five, a close family friend of defendant Catalano. The lawyer gets straight to the point. "What time did you visit the Catalano household on that day?"

Between 3:30 and 4:30 P.M., and, yes, he saw Sal Catalano at the wedding reception.

Stewart again cross-examines. A government formula has already developed. First questions: name, address, previous address in the United States—all the data necessary to do a routine check on each witness's INS files. Mr. Marcello had spent almost one year in the United States in 1969, living with his mother-in-law in Chicago.

Stewart grills this witness much more closely than the last. He asks for his employment record, the date of his retirement, who invited him to testify in the United States, and where he has been staying in New York.

Then he switches to the man's awareness of a certain Mafia family in his little village of Cimina. Suddenly trapped into this taboo subject matter, the old blacksmith resorts to Sicilian rustic humor. "Mafia—what's that? I don't even know what it is! Is it something that one eats?" The answer is ruinous. Stewart sits down.

Fisher needs to check with the witness before redirect, and Leval orders a recess. When the players reassemble, before the jury is brought back, Fisher announces he will have no redirect. Stewart jumps to his feet, alarmed, to make an application to reopen the government's cross-examination. Vito Marcello's immigration file has just arrived from Chicago, he claims, and it contains damaging information. Fisher beams his most Babylonian smile. The government has attempted an ambush: Let Fisher wander in with a few innocuous questions on redirect, then sandbag him with the immigration file. Fisher has at least temporarily thwarted the ploy, and Stewart is livid. The blacksmith's file shows a forty-year-old armed-robbery conviction that resulted in a restricted U.S. visa. Leval rules against Fisher. He must keep his witness available for a further grilling by the government.

Fisher's next witness is his client's wife, Caterina Catalano, an attractive woman in her late thirties with neatly coiffed auburn hair and a conservative dress. She seems nervous and vulnerable. The lawyer phrases his questions in a friendly, down-home manner. "Know that guy over there?" He nods toward her husband. He takes great pains to establish that Caterina Catalano was with her husband all day February 14, 1980, except for forty minutes in the afternoon when he crossed the Cimina piazza to visit a butcher friend.

Fisher is at his humorous, disarming best, skillfully guiding the timid woman into giving a solid and warm performance. She talks concisely and pleasantly of meeting and marrying her husband, and moving to the United States. She explains various connections within the Catalano family and among her husband's friends. Joe Ganci was the godfather of their daughter. She is a close friend of Margarita Ganci, Joe's widow. Yes, she knows Baldo Amato; he became godfather to Sal's niece. Fisher turns to her various family albums recording the nuptial celebrations in Sicily and later at the Marina del Rey in the Bronx. He shapes her testimony into a sustained attack on the government's technique of guilt by association. In his hands, the lurid photos of mob figures resume their original shape as Mrs. Catalano's private photograph albums, and her description of family relationships and friendships completely explains the presence therein of such defendants as Amato and Ganci.

Stewart will cross-examine. He retraces the relationships that Mrs. Catalano has testified to, and challenges her to explain how she knows Frank Polizzi. The link is their late friend Ganci, who in this conspiracy has assumed a position and function akin to the universal joint. Stewart probes a little deeper. He wonders how close she is to her husband, and how forthcoming he is about his business activities.

Toto has never been away for any period of time when she did not know where he was. Really? Does she know what he was doing in the Dominican Republic? No, she was not aware he had been in the Dominican Republic. The prosecutor shows her Catalano's passport, stamped with entry and exit dates. So much for Mistress Goodwife. No further questions.

In the corridor she paces back and forth with her husband, speaking quietly in rapid Sicilian. Their intimacy seems to soften Catalano's masklike face and tough-guy waddle.

Leval permits Stewart to recall Marcello, the blacksmith, and question him about discrepancies in his immigration file. The Chicago address he gave Stewart does not correspond to the one he gave the INS seventeen years before. The old Sicilian says he was confused and forgot. This is exactly what Stewart wants, for it allows him to pitch hardball: "But you do remember exactly and precisely where you were between 3:30 and 4:30 PM on Valentine's Day of 1980. Is that your testimony, sir?"

Fisher's next witness is Dominic Tartamella, a small, stocky man with a cocky manner. Calling him is an audacious move, for he is the same Tartamella whom government witness Ronsisvalle claimed drove off with a kilo of heroin in a red Porsche back in 1978. His presence here lets Fisher send an unspoken message to the jury. "Look, this guy is on the street. If there had *been* any red Porsche, this man would be in jail."

The witness knows Ronsisvalle, but denies ever having driven a red Porsche, especially one containing heroin. Fisher uses Tartamella to introduce large color photographs of the Catalano Brothers Bakery, so the jury can see what a handsome, clean, prosperous establishment his client operates.

Louis Freeh, out for blood, puts on a ferocious cross. Tartamella becomes evasive. He cannot remember dates, times, periods of employment. Freeh produces a surveillance photo showing him in conversation with Amato on a park bench in Queens. Fisher's gamble is backfiring. Tartamella cannot give a satisfactory explanation of the meeting.

"It was because of a soccer game," he says, but there is not a ball, uniform, or player in sight.

The web of family, social, and criminal relationships in this multidefendant trial makes normal defense strategies risky. A perfectly innocent encounter or friendship may lead to an inexplicable criminal link somewhere down the line. The government has woven a very strong net; the more the defendants struggle to get out, the more tightly they become enmeshed.

Fisher pushes to his feet in a contained rage. He must get back to the one element of this testimony of value to him: "Did [Freeh] ask you a single question about the time that my client, Sal Catalano, was supposed to have gone in the Caffe del Viale and grabbed you, and told you to get in a red Porsche and drive it away?" Fisher turns on his heel, then spins back and adds, "Just one?"

"No."

The next witness is yet another Catalano. Benny Catalano is no relation to defendant Sal Catalano, but he is the brother-in-law of Joe Ganci, which means that defendant Ganci was married to a Margarita Catalano who is not related to defendant Catalano. Benny is a tailor, and his function is to tell how he helped defendant Catalano load suitcases into Ganci's car for a vacation, and noticed that Ganci's garage was filled with boxes of imported Fiuggi mineral water. Gourmet Ganci, a thirsty but finicky man, would drink no mineral water but Fiuggi. This accounts for the large number of boxes moving in and out of his garage.

Dick Martin goes straight for the jugular. "Ever see boxes of cash in Mr. Ganci's house." No.

"Ever see Mr. Ganci packaging kilograms of heroin?" No.

"Ever see any guns in his house?" No.

Martin is smiling at the jury as he heads back to his seat. Martin sits closest to the jury of all the lawyers, and he spares them few of his smirks of self-satisfaction.

... THURSDAY, NOVEMBER 6, 1986.

THE COURTROOM. Fisher's big finish challenges the most damning piece of evidence against his client, the handwritten note Amendolito said was handed to him on a deserted Queens street by "Sal," and led to the delivery of $1.5 million in cash. The scrap of paper bore the names "Sal" and "Vito," and a telephone number. The number still belongs to Alexander's Coiffure, a Queens beauty parlor owned by Sal Catalano's brother Vito. Fisher calls Vito Catalano, who admits that the note is written in his brother Sal's handwriting, and that the phone number is correct for his salon. He denies having received any phone call from Amendolito, and denies all knowledge of the man.

Freeh dismisses him with only one question: "Would you lie to help your brother not get convicted?"

Fisher rests. He may have introduced some doubt about the government's case against his client, but the prevailing mood in the courtroom is becoming one of disenchantment, and the sweet smell of self-delusion is wafting through the stale air.

Every night now the lawyers Gerry Di Chiara and Pat Burke meet with Joe Benfante and his diminutive client at Benfante's plush Broadway office. Badalamenti's refusal to answer questions about the phone calls has driven Mazzurco to insist upon also taking the stand. Kennedy believes that Mazzurco is being forced to testify by the sickly but powerful Sal Lamberti. Gossip has it that Lamberti has decided that, among all the defendants, only the little contractor is smart enough to get them off the hook.

The three lawyers work long into the night, running Mazzurco through mock cross-examinations and bombarding him with tough, rapid-fire questions. Later, to relax, the little Sicilian heads for the bar to down a couple of double brandies.

The next man named in the indictment after Catalano is Joe Lamberti, and Badalamenti's failure to explain the Al Dente phone conversations has left him in serious trouble, so serious that his lawyer has decided to side-step the phone calls altogether. Instead, Lombardino has lined up a small group of witnesses who will challenge other elements of the government case. If he makes his points well, he says, one or two doubting jurors are all he needs.

His first witness is a white-haired Sicilian, born in Borghetto, now living in Queens, who has known Joe Lamberti all his life. In June 1983, he relates, Joe Lamberti brought Giuseppe Soresi, another native of Borghetto, to see his old friend at his Queens apartment. Soresi is the man whom the government accuses of being the alternative supplier to Badalamenti and of making a drug-related visit to New York City. Lombardino seeks to show that his trip had a legitimate purpose; he was trying to buy the witness's Borghetto house. This testimony may also allow Lombardino to argue in summation that all Lamberti's dealings with Soresi, including their subsequent meeting in Sicily, had to do with real estate—not narcotics—transactions.

Lombardino next calls an architect who has had business dealings with Lamberti over the years. This seems like an attempt to provide an innocent explanation for the phone conversations with Mazzurco in which Lamberti speaks about meeting the "architect."

Lombardino's third witness is a muscular young construction worker who is swiftly eaten alive by Richard Martin. Carmello Marrabello testifies that he delivered a paint sample to Lorenzo DeVardo at a Bowery address. Again Lombardino is trying to amass sufficient evidence in his defense case to allow him to argue in summation that some of the tapped phone conversations are in fact innocent negotiations for building materials.

Without even a hello, Martin says, Who do you work for? His uncle Angelo, in the construction business.

"What would be the role in the construction business of a scale with traces of heroin?"

"Objection!" Lombardino roars. There is no good-faith basis for the question.

But he is overruled, and Martin snaps, "In the construction business, do you use .45 caliber ammunition? Guns with silencers? . . . What did your Uncle Angelo tell you you would have to do here when you came to testify?" Uncle Angelo, a large, somber, mustached man, is waiting in the back row for his hapless nephew to stagger off the stand. Martin's ire is such that the uncle will be lucky to get out of this courthouse without a subpoena.

Each time Lombardino has tried to plant the seeds of an alternative story, the prosecutors have effectively counterattacked. His last try is Giuseppe LoPiccolo, sixty-two, a big barrel of a man with a full head of white hair. When he is told to raise his right hand, it shoots straight out in the Fascist salute. Defendants guffaw. The jury chuckles.

LoPiccolo is a former longshoreman, now a dealer in precious stones, born in Partinico, Sicily, who has known Joe Lamberti for fifteen years. In September 1983 he was told of the arrival in New York of an old Sicilian friend, a jewel dealer called Vito Roberto Palazzolo, whom the government has already identified as a Swiss money launderer. LoPiccolo rushed to meet him, and a few days later called on Joe Lamberti to introduce his friend formally. Perhaps they could do some business together in precious stones. This story is Lamberti's explanation of his dockside rendezvous with Palazzolo that the FBI observed at the *Queen Elizabeth 2*'s berth in Manhattan.

Lombardino intends to argue that after witness LoPiccolo introduced Lamberti to the gem dealer, Lamberti and his brother-in-law Mazzurco began trading in precious stones with Palazzolo in Switzerland. This alibi would go some way toward explaining certain records found in Mazzurco's house, and the large sums of money found in the homes of both defendants.

Stewart crosses. The clash of styles is entire: the stiff, starched-collar government man taking on the Sicilian clown. LoPiccolo plays the country bumpkin, smiting his forehead when he can't remember a name, then snapping the answer back to Stewart as though the prosecutor were a fool to ask in the first place. It is crude peasant humor, similar to the Badalamenti performance, and no one enjoys the show more than the Old Man.

At one point LoPiccolo confuses the name of the Zurich gem dealer. The ensuing dialogue as Stewart struggles to ungarble the story sounds like Abbott and Costello doing their baseball routine, "Who's on first?" Badalamenti and Sal Catalano are doubled over laughing.

LoPiccolo says, "LoBaido told me, 'Do you know who's here? Vito Spitalieri.' " The witness strikes his brow and throws his hands up in the air, "No, Vito *Palazzolo,* damn it!"

"Which one is it?"

"Vito Palazzolo."

"You're sure now?"

"I swear to God."

"This guy is like Count Dracula! He changes back and forth."

"Object to Count Dracula," Lombardino barks. Jurors and defendants burst out laughing.

Only Pierre Leval is not amused. As soon as the clock hits 4:00 P.M. he dismisses jury and witness until tomorrow, with a firm instruction not to discuss his testimony with anyone. Tomorrow is Veterans' Day, a public holiday, but the judge is so eager to end this trial, he has decided to hold court anyhow.

. . . TUESDAY, NOVEMBER 11, 1986.

THE COURTROOM.   This morning, the courthouse is a tomb, no sound but the long lonely echoes of footsteps and the hum of the x-ray security machine at the courtroom door. The marshals ask each visitor to state his business. The courthouse is officially closed, and only persons involved in Pizza may pass the checkpoint.

In the courtroom Lombardino confesses to the judge that LoPiccolo has vanished, he knows not where, and so the lawyer is forced to put on his next witness. A marshal whispers in Lombardino's ear. Mr. LoPiccolo has finally appeared. He had arrived at the courthouse on time this morning, been told by the marshals at the door that the courthouse was closed for the holiday, and gone home.

Chuckling breaks out around the room when his lateness is explained. LoPiccolo gives an inane smile. Stewart is not smiling. His arms are filled with telephone transcript.

"Do you have a driver's license from New York? . . . Have it with you?" Yes. "Can I see it?"

The wily old man goes into an exaggerated search of wallet and pockets, punctuated by much head-slapping and arm-waving. "I do not-a have it here, it is impossible!"

Stewart is no match for this witness as an entertainer, but last night the New Jersey prosecutor did his homework. LoPiccolo has already admitted knowing defendant Mazzara. Stewart cuts through his buffoonery to bring out that LoPiccolo once visited Mazzara at his Roma Restaurant. Accompanied by more head-slapping and flurries of "can't remember," the witness says that he just dropped by Mazzara's restaurant by chance, no previous phone call, no invitation.

Stewart looks like a fisherman who has just hooked a big one. LoPiccolo had in fact phoned Mazzara four times on that day, and the FBI taped every call.

Stewart: "You went up there at a quarter to two, and you met him behind the pizzeria, didn't you?"

LoPiccolo: "Where behind? Inside the pizzeria? Why behind?" His answers are annoying and embarrassing. FBI men were staked out all around the restaurant that day. The old fool has not only wrecked whatever case Lamberti may have had; he has contaminated Mazzara as well.

"You addressed him [Mazzara] as Don Tanino because he is an important member of the Mafia, isn't that right, sir?"

"No, not even jokingly. I wouldn't even think of that!"

The Lamberti defense has been wretched. The overall defense case is little better. The impression is growing that it is impossible to get one truthful word from the mouths of some of these Sicilians. Worse, their testimony is insulting and demeaning to judge and jury.

While the Mazzurco defense is still in the wings, bright young Gerry

Di Chiara makes an astute comment: "What these guys were smuggling, and speaking in code about, may have been precious stones. Will the gem defense fly? It's just a story. But in a no-drug drug case, our story is as good as the government's. It's gotta be gems, or guns. So one of them is lying, Badalamenti or Mazzurco. Unless both of them are lying—and it's drugs."

The first witness for Mazzurco's lawyer, Benfante, is a bald gemologist in a black suit named Bluestone. Martin deftly puts the guy away in three. What is his fee for testifying here today?

"$3500." The jurors are horrified.

"Mr. Bluestone, can you make precious stones from heroin? . . . Do you ever use heroin in your business?"

Of course not!

"No further questions," says Martin smartly, and sits.

Benfante's next witness is Mazzurco's partner in certain construction work on "deteriorated apartments" in Harlem. In short, a slumlord. The lawyer elicits that Lamberti and Mazzurco had a $600,000 contract. The testimony sounds important, because of the references to "the architect" and "the engineer" in the phone calls.

The next witness is a white-haired lawyer who handled Mazzurco's real estate dealings, and who was retained to foreclose on Giuseppe Baldinucci's house. The implication is that Baldinucci's bagful of cash was some kind of delayed mortgage payment, not drug money. But Bucknam on recross brings out that the mortgage could not be foreclosed on because Baldinucci's property had by then been forfeited to the federal government. A few shouts and yelps from Lombardino succeed in barring an explanation of *why* Baldinucci's property was seized.

Sal Mazzurco, laughing heartily, is half turned in his chair, trying to flirt with Carol Novack. This supports the lawyers' contention that none of these Sicilians on trial understand their lawyers any better than the lawyers understand the clients. Without the soothing, Esperanto presence of Mario Malerba, these proceedings are at risk at any moment of grinding to a halt.

"May I proceed, your Honor?" says Bucknam. That depends on your question, the judge replies. Jurors #1 and 2 and several others smile with new-found comprehension of legal safeguards. One year and eighteen days into this trial, the sanitation man, the data processor, and the others have become fair amateur lawyers. When Bucknam asks if Mazzurco or Lamberti ever informed the witness what business Baldinucci was in, or ever asked *why* the property was forfeited, these jurors don't need to hear the answer; they have learned that answers are implicit in the questions.

It is two weeks before Thanksgiving. Leval announces that court will be held on Monday and Tuesday only of Thanksgiving week, and that there will be a Christmas recess from Friday, December 19, through Sunday, December 28.

For his debut on the witness stand, Mazzurco has chosen a funereal black suit, pink brocade necktie, and a haircut. The easels display yard-high blowups of pages from his famous red notebook. Benfante too wears a new suit. The tiny witness, now fifty-one, tells the jury he has been working to help support his mother and younger sister and brother since he was eight years old and his father died. They came to America from Borghetto when he was eleven, and he is now a citizen.

"How do you like this country?"

"I *love* it!"

Are you nervous as you sit there now?

Yes, I am.

The eleven-year-old Mazzurco immediately got a shoeshine job, and later worked in a grocery, a bakery, a fruit store, while attending a vocational high school and learning carpentry. He worked two years as a shipping clerk for a plastics company, and five years as an electroplater for a watch-case factory. Then he opened a fruit store with a brother-in-law. Martin is up to his old scare tactics, interrupting at every turn to be sure he gets all the family names and addresses.

In 1958 Mazzurco was drafted, trained as a tank gunner, and spent a couple of years in Germany. He was honorably discharged with the rank of sergeant, and remained two years in the reserves.

His brother-in-law Joe Lamberti is a boyhood friend from Borghetto. In the 1960s he and Joe started a construction company, then got into the bakery business, and operated a chain of subway food stands. By 1970 they had formed Lamberti Contracting Co.

Mazzurco is coming across as a forthright, intelligent, responsible, very hard-working man. Benfante brings out that he did contracting work renovating buildings for the same federal government that is now trying to put him in prison forever. By the late 1970s he was also a prosperous clothing manufacturer and made frequent buying trips abroad. He took a correspondence course in electronics, and learned to become a TV repairman. Ever since his job in the watch-case factory, he has been selling watches, jewelry, rings, and such on the side. Soon he was importing precious stones. He became involved in a casket company. He started Roma Imports, bringing in pasta products, tomatoes, mushrooms. . . . He is a classic all-American Horatio Alger hustler, a gifted, natural-born capitalist flourishing in the land of opportunity.

It was 1982 when Joe Lamberti and Ganci approached him to invest in Pronto Demolition, which was then in terrible shape. Bit by bit, he describes how hard work and sensible management policies nursed it back to health.

Recess. Pat Burke is talking about the Mazzurco defense. "He is a straight, hard-working guy who fell in with bad company, and they used him. This will fly with the jury, unless one of them figures out that, before the army, he had only menial jobs; after, he was always an investor. Where did he get the money?"

The defense moves to the date of the Zito visit to the Ganci house. The FBI tape is replayed. Jurors watch in silence as Zito again enters the house with his panda-paper-wrapped package. Mazzurco has brought along his own log of the day's events. He arrived at the Ganci home at 4:23 P.M. This fits nicely with the 2:55 P.M. phone call in which Ganci says to Joe Lamberti to meet at his house, not the pizzeria.

Mazzurco was talking to Ganci in his basement, he says, when someone, Joe's wife or daughter, called him upstairs. Mazzurco had no idea then that someone had come to see Ganci. Five minutes later, Ganci returned to the basement. According to his log, this caller must have been Zito, but Mazzurco never saw him.

. . . WEDNESDAY, NOVEMBER 12, 1986.

THE COURTROOM.   When Mazzurco takes the stand for the second day, he wears a different suit and different demeanor. He is no longer scared. But the jurors are still stone-faced.

Mazzurco acknowledges that he does know Giuseppe Baldinucci. The man once worked for him at Lamberti Construction, and since both men are from Borghetto, they also met at weddings and funerals.

The government has begun objecting to nearly every question, and Leval is sustaining. He finally tells Benfante if he doesn't have proper questions, this examination is over.

"I'm doing my best, Judge," the lawyer replies amiably.

In the recess, attorneys squabble. Burke has written out a careful cross-examination of Mazzurco designed to denature the harmful aspects of the phone calls. Benfante wants Burke to do the cross-examination himself; the jury will be more impressed with the silver-tongued Burke. Client Alfano objects to Burke's participation, doubtless because it would enrage Badalamenti. Burke and Benfante have become pals, and this is putting a strain on their friendship. Benfante says if Burke had "had the balls to say *no* from the outset [to Badalamenti's insistence on controlling all the family defense strategies] there'd be no trouble now."

Benfante blames Kennedy. Kennedy is saying he will not do the cross himself, and that his client wants no one in the Badalamenti family to have any connection with Sal Mazzurco.

In the courtroom, Benfante is still dealing with Baldinucci. Mazzurco denies knowing that Baldinucci had anything to do with narcotics, or that he was carrying heroin at the time of his visit.

Joe Benfante may seem like an Italian Joe Palooka, but he is enormously likable, and the lawyers say he has the largest practice of any solo criminal attorney in the city. It is a lawyers' axiom that no client understands how good or bad his attorney is. "Sal Mazzurco has no idea!" says Lewis. "Joe is charming to schmooze with. Mazzurco thinks the judge is continually ruling against him because that is what all judges do."

In the Mazzurco search, a Pino Europa Boutique shopping bag containing several packages of white powder wrapped in foil was found in the bedroom closet. The defendant says he knew the powder was plaster of Paris, because he had had it analyzed a year before. Why?

"Because of where I found it." A crew of workers assigned to clean up the Pronto Demolition premises had discovered a large cardboard box in the rear yard, and brought it to their boss. Inside was a smaller box containing a scale, as well as two wooden boxes holding four or five packages of white powder. Mazzurco had seen a similar scale when he worked in the watch-case factory.

"Sal, when you brought the white powder to the lab, did they tell you what it was?"

"Yes. Calcium sulphate," which is to say, plaster of Paris.

"Did you put the calcium sulphate in the closet personally yourself?"

Yes. He told his wife he thought it might be narcotics, and she advised: Don't leave it out in the open. Sal had his own suspicions as to the source of the powder, and mentioned them to his wife and to Joe Lamberti, but not to Ganci—who the jury is evidently now supposed to assume was Mazzurco's prime suspect.

Once Mazzurco got the results from the lab, he forgot about the packages in his closet. Now the story gets a bit strange. He did not know the other white powder—the stuff found by the agents in his garage—was lactose, which is to say, powdered milk sugar used in cutting drugs. He thought it was more plaster of Paris. "I did not even remember it. I had so many white powders in my garage: Plaster of Paris, cement in bags . . . my garage was a shambles."

In a recess, Eleanore says the Kennedys had been fearful that Mazzurco at some point "would shaft Mr. Badalamenti, his mortal enemy. He is still trying to kill Mr. Badalamenti. The Mafia wars are still *on*. That's why Sal Lamberti didn't want Michael to go last." Nor could Schechter budge his client, because Sal Lamberti feared a double cross by both Kennedy and Badalamenti.

This is not surprising. The World According to Badalamenti is a dangerous place. For months he has been telling the Kennedys that some of his codefendants are allied with the Corleonese in the Mafia wars. These men want to kill him, and have been trying for some time, perhaps ever since he was mysteriously kicked out of the Mafia and forced to flee Palermo the first time, in 1978. Sometimes, but not always, he has said, or hinted, that the leader of his Mafia enemies is Sal Lamberti, the oldest, most senior Mafioso in the courtroom.

Benfante next deals with Mazzurco's guns. He says he had them for both protection and target practice. The .38 was a gift from Ganci. He has never pulled a gun on anyone. He never sought a gun permit because he understood only one gun permit was issued per company, and his partner, Ganci, already had one.

And the scale found in his car? That related to his imported-Italian-foods business. He suspected his Italian suppliers had been short-weighting the pasta, and this scale is accurate to one-sixteenth of a pound. Benfante produces a subpoena from the city Department of Consumer Affairs relating to his charge of short-weighting macaroni products.

Discussing all these matters, Mazzurco has successfully played the part of a responsible, informed, competent businessman. Now his lawyer switches to the personal level. "Mr. Mazzurco, how do you feel right now?"

"Tired."

Mazzurco claims that his conversations on the tapes have been mistranslated, and that people he met with have been misidentified.

The day ends. Outside, the first snow of the season has begun. The Kennedys and Burke go for a beer. "I've heard a lot of bullshit," says

Kennedy, "but this was the worst testimony I've heard in twenty-five years! It's *inherently* incredible.

"Sal Lamberti is the one who really calls the shots. They all take orders from him, including Benfante." Whatever happens, Kennedy adds, "Mazzurco is doomed. If he falls, it may take some heat off Sal and Joe."

Kennedy reckons that "Joe Benfante probably is under orders to help out the Lambertis.

"But the bottom line is that Louis Freeh is going to tie twenty defendants to Sal Mazzurco. He'll drag everybody down, just because he took the stand."

... THURSDAY, NOVEMBER 20, 1986.

THE COURTROOM.   It is Mazzurco's third day of testimony, and lawyer and client look waxen with exhaustion. Benfante will flee to Florida the moment this ends. Yesterday Mazzurco was so tired he almost fell asleep on the stand. Today's testimony concentrates on his records and notebooks. At one point, Benfante holds up the red spiral notebook. The defendant says the notations represent "unit transactions."

"For what?"

"Precious stones."

"How much did *you* make on the transactions?"

"A little over $100,000."

Benfante distributes a packet of blowups of the notebook pages to each juror. He runs through the "unit transactions." "Page 50 summarizes the prices paid for stones . . . *4 at 130 = 520* means *four units at $130,000 per unit.* . . . Page 53: *540 = 4 at 135* means that 540 is the selling price, 520 is the buying price, so on four kilos of precious stones, Sal Mazzurco's profit is $20,000."

This is numerological gibberish, digital soup, and it goes on for many minutes, interrupted by long pauses, as Mazzurco struggles to explain his elaborate, eccentric record-keeping. Sal Catalano wears a constant sharklike smile; he enjoys this high-stakes numbers game. Louis Freeh licks his lips.

"Sal, tell the jury how you got involved in buying precious stones."

The story that follows ropes Mazzurco to the Badalamenti family for the first time. No wonder the Old Man preferred to keep his distance.

Mazzurco met Enzo Randazzo in Europe. They were introduced by Badalamenti. Mazzurco had met Badalamenti in Palermo, on the courthouse steps. He was with a friend who needed to see a certain lawyer, so they went to the courthouse, and the lawyer was there with Badalamenti. They talked about the clothing business. Badalamenti said he had a nephew in the business. Mazzurco met Randazzo the next day, in a shop run by the Badalamenti family on Via Leonardo Da Vinci. Later Randazzo had asked Mazzurco if he could find an American outlet for precious stones.

During this testimony, the faces of the Badalamenti family are absolutely expressionless. Vito is back beside his father, ivory-pale. A stranger could pick out which defendants are family members by their masklike impassivity.

Back in the United States, Mazzurco asked Joe Lamberti to help him find a buyer for the stones. He also got in touch with Santo Caruso, a friend of Randazzo from Houston, Texas, who said he would sell the stones there, on commission. Good, said Randazzo. He would find someone to bring the stones to America as soon as possible. In early May, 9.3 kilos of stones arrived. Throughout this testimony, Sal Lamberti is smiling.

During the break, the younger lawyers in particular are frantic. "This is terrible!" "Who does he think he's kidding!" "How tall are you? Five three. That's the first straight answer he gave." "Would you mind stepping back, Mr. Pinocchio." "He's gonna drag *everyone* down with him!"

Back on the stand, Mazzurco says he has flu and feels "unbelievably bad." He adds that, earlier, he was having difficulty understanding his own records. He makes clear that he himself never laid out money for the stones. He was only a middleman, a broker.

"How much profit would you make, for example, on a kilo of emeralds?"

Mazzurco says he "cannot answer individually." Stones are not "singled out." He "can only give figures for the entire shipment."

All the figures in the notebooks refer to gems. "If you *were* in the heroin business, would you make notes of it?" No, sir.

Your conversations with Gaetano Badalamenti, what were they about?

They were not about drugs.

Mazzurco did discuss the gem business with Badalamenti, Alfano, and Randazzo. In conversation with the last, he also discussed food and clothes, and gold ingots. Randazzo and Mazzurco later did business in garments and precious stones.

Lunchroom gleanings: At 1:00 A.M. this morning, Ivan Fisher called Mazzurco and told him, "Don't volunteer anything on Saca Catalano." Sal's late murdered cousin had been a gem dealer. Someone else called Mazzurco last night and threatened to burn a hole in him. Lawyers' consensus: Had Mazzurco done as Leval wished and taken a plea, he would have got seven years. This performance guarantees him twenty-two years at least.

Louis Freeh's cross-examination opens with one question, and a majestic roll call of statements. On April 9, 1984, do you agree you were in unfortunate circumstances? Yes.

Freeh lists some of the circumstances. Baldinucci was seen entering and leaving your house, and he had a sample of high-grade heroin in his pocket.

You were in Joe Ganci's basement while a heroin sale between Ganci and Zito was taking place right above your head.

Your palm print was on the tissue paper in the blue box in which the heroin was delivered.

A triple-beam scale, with traces of white powder, was found behind the spare tire in the trunk of your Mercedes.

You knew the Adamita brothers, and it was unfortunate that when they were arrested, one of them had your phone number in his address book.

You had a legal brief in your house relating to an international heroin conspiracy ring. . . .

Benfante: "Objection! . . . Move to strike . . . Demand a mistrial . . ."

This is overruled, and Freeh elicits that the brief was found in a bathroom closet and that Mazzurco was translating it from English into Italian, for no fee, as a favor to a friend.

You had a gun in your bedroom, next to your bed, which was loaded and had an obliterated serial number.

The deadly roll call is followed by a long sidebar argument concerning Mazzurco's postarrest statement.

In the lull, Kennedy whispers, "Bet you didn't realize Sal Mazzurco is Japanese. . . . Because what you've been witnessing is a form of hara-kiri." He adds that he believes Sal Lamberti deliberately ordered Mazzurco to give this testimony "in order to sink the Badalamenti group."

Freeh is back at the podium. Mazzurco denies he lied to the arresting officers on April 9. "Did you say anything to the FBI that was not true?" No.

Isn't it a fact that you were dealing in and speaking of drugs? No. Do you admit you have been involved with smuggling precious stones?

Benfante objects, and Leval once more summons him to the side bar. During the long bench conference, Mazzurco stares ahead or at the jury. Only the whites of his eyes are visible on his high brown forehead, little, piggy eyes.

Now for the phone calls. Mazzurco admits that Badalamenti and Alfano called him, and that he frequently called Alfano from his home.

Isn't it a fact you went to the jelly-bean store to call Alfano so there would be no toll record on your phone?

"When I started to speak to Mr. Badalamenti, there was an understanding that he did not want his whereabouts known."

Did you wait by the pay phone outside Ganci's Al Dente Pizzeria in freezing weather to get a phone call? Yes.

Did you smuggle something in? Yes.

Was it shirts? No.

Was it code? What you call code, I call speaking in a cryptic manner.

The conversations had nothing to do with clothing, did they? *Shirts* referred to something you were brokering into the U.S. You say it was precious gems.

"It was *precious stones!*"

. . . MONDAY, NOVEMBER 24, 1986.

THE COURTROOM.   In recent weeks, chief U.S. Attorney Rudolph Giuliani has scored major victories in two other courtrooms. Downstairs on the third floor, a jury has voted the heads of three of the five families of the American Mafia Commission—Carmine Persico, Tony "Ducks" Corrallo, and "Fat Tony" Salerno—guilty as charged. In New Haven, where Giuliani has for five weeks personally been prosecuting a number of New York City officials for municipal corruption involving a parking-meter scandal, the jury has voted for conviction on nearly all counts. The weekend papers and TV were filled with comment about Giuliani's two big wins. But this morning, all nineteen remaining Pizza jurors and alternates assure Judge Leval that they have read nothing, heard nothing, seen nothing.

Today Louis Freeh goes deeper into Mazzurco's records and notebooks. "Write anything about precious stones, gems, valuable rocks?"

No, he says, he was not buying or selling. He was acting as a broker, for a commission, dealing in aquamarines, emeralds, topaz, and beryl.

"This is not something you've read up on in the past few weeks, is it?"

"No, sir. I have been involved in jewelry since the 1950s."

"Of course you filled out a receipt when you got those stones?"

"No, sir."

Mazzurco is an obvious liar. It's embarrassing—to everyone but him. The little man does not even wriggle with discomfort. He looks at ease.

Freeh has provided the jury with government copies of the relevant notebook pages. Mazzurco says Joe Lamberti handled the actual cash.

"About one million in three months?" Yes.

Lamberti gave the money to the middleman, Caruso, who got it to Randazzo.

Freeh is incredulous. "You have no knowledge in what form Caruso got the million to Enzo?"

No. Joe Lamberti kept no records, and no other records exist. Mazzurco is glib, gives rapid answers, and does not seem to care that he is telling obvious bald lies. The jury is impatient and hostile: #3, the young, unmarried purchasing agent from Westchester, is having a yawning fit; #6, the blue-eyed Hungarian giggler, is holding her head in her hands, elbows propped on the rail; #7, the black South Bronx transportation supervisor, is beating out a rhythmic tattoo on his blue-jeaned knees.

. . . **WEDNESDAY, NOVEMBER 26, 1986. SAYREVILLE, NEW JERSEY.**   Court is in recess today. Tomorrow is Thanksgiving. This evening, the ruddy, hawk-faced defendant Gaetano Mazzara, Frank Castronovo's partner in the Roma Restaurant, does not come home. He has spent the day driving his lawyer Harriet Rosen around New Jersey preparing their defense. Late this afternoon he dropped her at a bus stop, went to visit his girlfriend at her bakery, and told her he was driving to New York.

On Thanksgiving evening, when he has still not returned, the girl-friend calls the police and reports him missing. Over the holiday week-end the government, saying it fears a mass bail jump, revokes bail on ten other defendants and incarcerates them in MCC.

. . . 9:00 A.M., MONDAY, DECEMBER 1, 1986.

THE COURTHOUSE CORRIDOR. People are here early. Court has not yet been called to order. Defense lawyers caucus in the corridor. Word has reached them that Mazzara's senior lawyer, Marvin Segal, is coming in. "It takes an act of God . . ."

Ivan Fisher has rushed back from a half-completed vacation, tan and thin.

Theories abound. Mazzara has fled to Italy. He has become a government informant. He has been kidnapped.

Kennedy says in a flat voice, "Someone blew him away."

Malerba agrees. "If they was gonna run, they would've all run."

Court is called to order. A number of extra U.S. marshals police the room. An unusual number of family members and friends of the defendants are in the room, but very few defendants. Segal stands up. "Your Honor, as of now, Gaetano Mazzara is unaccountably absent."

Now defendants Catalano, Greco, Polizzi, both Lambertis, and Mazzurco are marched in through the jurors' entrance. All are under arrest and each is guarded by his own marshal. After two nights in MCC, the men look rumpled and worn. The courtroom back benches are filled with their weeping wives and teen-aged children.

Castronovo is not here. He had undergone quadruple by-pass surgery in 1983, was diagnosed as suffering from acute angina last October, and has been absent from court since.

Cangialosi is in his regular seat. He has come in on his own recognizance. He is considered so marginal a defendant that no one had time over the weekend to accept his surrender.

Another well-guarded bunch of prisoners enters: the two Badalamentis, Sal Salamone, and their three marshals. The two sets of prisoners are like two troupes of circus ponies escorted by handlers to the center ring.

Segal tells the court Mazzara's wife is "incapacitated with worry," and he offers his own ominous opinion. "His absence is not a voluntary absence. I have concern for his well being." If Tommy Mazzara was going to flee, "it would have happened much earlier. . . . He had limited means [i.e., Segal has not been paid] and he has strong family ties." No money has been withdrawn from the bank, no clothes taken. Yet he has not been seen since late last Wednesday afternoon.

"May I hear from the government," says Leval.

Freeh stands. "His timing is not consistent with involuntary absence." The government believes Mazzara's function in the conspiracy was as a direct supplier of heroin to Ganci, or a receiver of drugs or money from Ganci, and he says the jury will draw this conclusion about Mazzara at the close of the Mazzurco testimony.

In the clear light of Monday morning, Leval asks Freeh to review the government's original Friday-night assumption—that Mazzara had fled, and that only swift mass arrests, based on the weekend bench warrants Martin persuaded Leval to issue, could assure the presence in this courtroom today of ten codefendants.

When the cops went to the Mazzara home, his partner, Castronovo, was already there, consoling the wife and children. Mrs. Mazzara refused to cooperate with the police. One son said, yes, their dad was missing, in a Subaru. Josephine DeMaria, the girlfriend, was also there. He had told her only that he was heading to 44th Street, in Manhattan.

"Absurd," whispers Eleanore. "If he *intended* to leave, the wife, not the girlfriend, would have seen him last."

"This is obviously a very serious matter. And most unfortunate," says Leval. "The most likely inference is that defendant Mazzara has fled, which would make him the second defendant in two months to attempt flight." The reference is to Enzo Randazzo's disappearance in October.

Martin says warrants had also been issued for Alfano and Evola, who had gone home to their families over the holiday weekend, but they were not served because court time would have been lost if the suspects were detained in the Midwest. He now wants Alfano held here, in MCC with the other incarcerated defendants, and Leval agrees, even though Alfano has not yet been formally arrested. He dispatches a marshal to the jury room to send them home for the day, and declares a recess. The marshals insist that the families remain seated until they have escorted their prisoners backstage.

Trooping out into the corridor, visitors notice Mrs. Catalano, in a red coat, weeping disconsolately in the back row. Martin makes a rare corridor appearance, and is immediately surrounded by the press. Major coverage tomorrow is assured.

In the courtroom, Ken Kaplan has agreed that his convalescent client will stay at home and in close touch with the U.S. Attorney's Office, and the government's application to revoke Castronovo's bail is accordingly withdrawn. The other remanded defendants are to be held in custody while each man's lawyer reargues his client's bail application. During the day, the already huge bail sums—$3 million each for Mazzurco and Catalano, $1 million for Cangialosi—are stiffened.

By day's end, everyone has had new bail fixed except Joe Lamberti. The government claims they caught him speeding away from his house carrying $20,000 in checks only moments after he got a call from the Mazzurcos that the FBI was there arresting Sal. Nonsense, says his lawyer, Lombardino. The checks were uncashable third-party checks, for deposit only, and his client was wearing only a sweater. Obviously he was rushing to help his brother-in-law's family. Leval is unpersuaded and orders Lamberti to remain overnight in MCC with the others, until their adjusted bail has been posted.

He dismisses the court and summons Mazzara's lawyers and the U.S. attorney to his robing room, where he renders an opinion he wants to be sure to keep from the press. "All of the information . . . justifies a finding that [Mazzara] has voluntarily absented himself. One recognizes that there could be surprises. . . . But at present the indication is that he did."

. . . TUESDAY, DECEMBER 2, 1986.

THE COURTROOM.   The circus troupes of prisoners and marshals reappear at 9:30 A.M. While awaiting a late juror, Leval says, "Let me express my special pleasure at seeing all the defendants here this morning." A nasty joke; nobody laughs.

The trial routine soon resumes, and Mazzurco climbs blithely back onto the witness stand as if nothing unusual were happening. He is about to be cross-examined by Michael Kennedy, acting to protect his client. Thus the "contradictory defenses," which the government anticipated and the lawyers feared, are about to clash head-on.

The jurors enter. Lawyers and defendants scan their faces. It seems impossible they have not read in the papers about Mazzara's disappearance.

Kennedy rises. "You understand that my job is to examine, and yours to testify?" Yes. "Why did you take the stand?"

"Objection!"

"Sustained."

"In your testimony, you tried to help yourself. Did you try to help anyone else?"

"Mainly tried to help myself."

"Try to hurt anyone?" No.

"Do you deny when you were talking to Mr. Badalamenti on the phone that you were following orders?

"Isn't it a fact *that you did not want to speak to Mr. Badalamenti at all?*"

"Yes."

"And this is also true of your conversations with Alfano?"

"Yes."

Kennedy hopes to use Mazzurco to establish that the conversations between Badalamenti and the New York group were in fact complicated moves and feints in the Sicilian Mafia war. This prospect plus anxiety about the Mazzara disappearance have got all defendants and lawyers sitting bolt upright. But the jury seems unaware of the added tensions. Most wear vacant stares; a few doze.

Did Mazzurco deal in firearms? He squirms, then denies, looking increasingly uncomfortable. Sal Lamberti whispers nonstop to Amato during this testimony. Badalamenti has by now told everyone but the jury that Lamberti is out to kill him.

Kennedy focuses on a piece of paper found in Mazzurco's Mercedes-Benz on April 9. The paper bears Alfano's address and phone number, and the number of a mail-order house that specializes in military and intelligence hardware, a sort of CIA outfitter.

Mazzurco was interested in a bulletproof vest referred to as a "body danger shield," soft body armor capable of resisting .22, .32, .38, .357 magnum, and 9 mm bullets.

Kennedy walks to the evidence cartons beside the prosecution table and holds up the two bulky bulletproof garments found in the Alfano house. Did he give these things to Alfano? Yes, when they met in Queens. Mazzurco is swallowing hard, dismayed by the direction the questions are taking.

"Did you like Alfano?"

Mazzurco squirms and mumbles an inaudible answer. Kennedy demands he repeat it.

"Yes, sir!" Mazzurco barks in a loud, unhappy voice.

You deny telling Salvatore Lamberti that you thought Pietro Alfano was a "jerk"? Kennedy towers over the little man. Mazzurco despised Alfano, and said as much in the phone calls. There was in fact a deep hostility between all the New York people and Badalamenti's Midwest group. This hidden mutual hatred and fear are the heart of the Kennedy defense. He tries to show the jury that Mazzurco truly dreaded having anything to do with Gaetano Badalamenti, and that what he feared was not the police or the FBI, but some other sinister force. Mazzurco is most reluctant to go along with this line, and his very reluctance underlines the point. He may be afraid now, just as he was back then when he had to get on the phone to the capo of the Losers.

Kennedy pushes him very hard. "Isn't it a fact that you dealt with Mr. Badalamenti because you had been *instructed* to deal with Mr. Badalamenti?"

"I was asked."

The lawyer reads from Mazzurco's previous testimony: "There was a worry that somebody would know that we had a contact with Mr. Badalamenti. And at the time, it was a taboo for anyone to be in touch with Mr. Badalamenti. Too many things had happened."

"Who imposed this taboo?" Translation: Who's the bad guy?

Sal Mazzurco's bad guy, it turns out, is the same as Ronald Reagan's. "Articles in the media," he says.

What did *you* mean by taboo?

This question produces the answer: "Something like witchcraft." Close, but not close enough.

Kennedy tries it another way. "Isn't it a fact there was a *Mafia taboo* against Mr. Badalamenti?" and draws the inevitable one-two punch: Object! Sustained.

Now Kennedy seeks to tailor his questions to make the jury feel the witness is refusing to answer, or being evasive, *because of* the very Mafia taboo he is not allowed to mention.

Isn't it a fact that you were afraid of Mr. Badalamenti's enemies? Isn't it a fact that you didn't want Mr. Badalamenti's enemies to know you were dealing with him? Isn't it a fact (and here the lawyer drops his voice almost to a whisper) that you were dealing . . . arms . . . with Gaetano Badalamenti?

Mazzurco denies having seen, let alone having delivered, the large cache of arms later found in Alfano's house.

Kennedy, quickly: "But you admit the two bullet-proof vests?" Yes. No further questions.

People filter out of the courtroom in clumps. The arrested defendants take their places beside the marshals and disappear into the back of the courthouse.

An hour later, the jury is not yet back, and Stewart is droning to the judge about some medical reports, when a distraught Harriet Rosen rushes into the half-empty courtroom.

"Your Honor!" Her face is ashen. Leval raises his hand to halt Stewart.

"Your Honor . . . my client, Gaetano Mazzara, has been reported to have been found dead."

A hush stills the room. Leval appears shocked. Some of the lawyers hurrying in late are halted in their tracks. But all the defendants sit absolutely poker-faced. Not one shows a trace of emotion.

Leval asks to hear from the government. Martin says he has been advised that the police have found a body, and documents in the pockets indicate it is Mazzara. The man may have been killed within the last twenty-four hours.

The mutilated body of Tommy Mazzara had been wrapped in two plastic garbage bags and left in a gutter on Gardner Street, in an industrial section of Greenpoint, Brooklyn. It was found at 10:20 A.M. this morning after two passers-by notified police that they had seen feet protruding from a bag. At first the police thought the man had been repeatedly struck in the head with a meat cleaver. Later they understood he had been shot twice in the head at close range. In his pockets they found his wallet and $700 in cash. He had been dumped just two miles from Knickerbocker Avenue.

Kennedy as lead counsel is the first to speak. "I extend my condolences to the Mazzara family. It is a deep tragedy to them."

The jurors are still in the jury room. The judge must first address the problem of what to do with them to isolate them from the effects of the murder. Already the courtroom is filling with news reporters, and television sketch artists have begun unpacking their pads and chalks.

Kennedy asks for a limited sequestration. Jurors should be kept isolated in a hotel until the inevitable furor quiets. All the lawyers want a mistrial. There is no way their clients can get a fair trial in the atmosphere that now exists. Kaplan is adamant that Frank Castronovo, the murdered man's invalid cousin and his alleged partner in money laundering and heroin dealing, cannot get a fair trial.

Leval will rule later on mistrial motions. Right now, he wants opinions on what to do about the jury. He listens with great forbearance to every lawyer on both sides who has anything to say. He is just deciding he will not sequester, but will tell the jury of Mazzara's death and instruct them collectively and individually to avoid newspapers, radio, and television for a number of days, when Marvin Segal bursts in, breathless and angry. He shunts Harriet Rosen aside to say, "May I make a statement?"

"Later," says Leval. "Bring in the jury."

They file in, and several look with surprise at the packed press and visitors' benches, which before lunch had been almost empty. Three courtroom artists begin to sketch the jury's collective portrait. All the lawyers and defendants have turned to stare at the box, trying to read their faces.

Leval addresses them formally. "Members of the jury, I have the sad duty to advise you that one of the defendants, Gaetano Mazzara, died today. We have just received the unhappy news."

Juror #13, the pleasant, round-faced black woman, gasps and places her hand over her mouth. #18, the red-haired Puerto Rican woman, also gasps. #2, a grey-haired retired telephone technician, glances at #1, the foreman, as if to say, "I told you so."

Leval tells the jurors they must be especially careful to avoid the media when they leave. Surely they know, or suspect, that Mazzara has been murdered. The word *died* has failed to convey the sense of urgency and danger that grips court and counsel. It feels very much, right now, as if the Mafia war the lawyers have been talking about has suddenly jumped its tracks and invaded this courtroom. Why the victim should be Mazzara is still unclear.

**. . . WEDNESDAY, DECEMBER 3, 1986.
THE COURTROOM.**   Before court convened this morning, Leval took pains to voir dire each juror individually, and he reports that not a single juror admits to having heard a word about the killing. Yet when they parade into the courtroom, nearly every one steals a covert glance at the empty third-row chair where Mazzara normally sits. When they are settled in their seats, Judge Leval cautions them still another time: Sometimes jurors learn things *inadvertently* . . . if any one of you *has* heard something involuntarily, do not tell any other juror.

The court attempts to proceed as usual. Several defense attorneys today wish to cross-examine Mazzurco, who at this point has become like a leper without a bell. Malerba, not Fisher, handles the cross for Catalano. Maximum distance is the name of his game, and he swiftly establishes that his client had no business relationship whatsoever of any kind with the now alas seriously tainted Mazzurco. They met briefly through Ganci, but Catalano never had anything to do with Pronto, and he has "never been to Sal's home, or vice-versa."

"Ever deal with Sal Catalano on anything? Precious stones? Pizza? Hot dogs? *Anything?*"

"No. Never."

Marvin Schechter elicits that Pronto had a business relationship with Sal Lamberti's company, BIG L Excavation and Demolition.

Paul Bergman reads back a lot of surveillance testimony, and asks interminable questions about Pronto's billing practices. Not until the very end of his examination does he come to the point: Before they met in MCC, Sal Mazzurco never once saw or spoke to Baldo Amato, or to Bonventre.

But Louis Freeh springs to his feet with a clear surveillance photo of Catalano entering the premises of Pronto Demolition. Mazzurco, Pronto's president, is swift to say that he has no idea what Catalano could be doing there. Nor does he recall meeting Catalano or Amato at the Bono wedding. Freeh drags out of him that he did see Catalano one time at the Glendale Social Club, a mob hangout similar to the Toyland Social Club.

Benfante continually objects "outside the scope," and is consistently overruled.

Rarely has the folly, and peril, of putting on a poor defense been more eloquently demonstrated. Far better to mount no defense, or just read back a bit of transcript to clarify the record, or demonstrate inconsistencies, and stake all on one's final argument. Before lunch, Marvin Schechter and Carol Novack, on behalf of defendants Sal Lamberti and Giovanni Ligammari, advise the court of their intention to do just that. In the following days, attorneys Lewis, Koppelman, Burke, Leitman, and Di Chiara will do the same for defendants Evola, Vito Badalamenti, Alfano, Palazzolo, and Cangialosi.

Ruggiero refrains from putting on a case for a different reason: He feels the evidence against his clients is legally insufficient. One phone conversation shows Trupiano *refusing* to make the drive to Florida; it would require him to close his pizzeria. In another, Alfano says to Palazzolo, "I just spoke to Rudolph Valentino Trupiano, and he won't participate." Ruggiero does not want to risk inadvertently increasing the scant evidence by putting Mrs. Trupiano, or any other witness, on the stand. The Vitale evidence, he feels, is insufficient for similar reasons.

"I think I have a good chance to get my guys off," he says. The irony is that acquittals for Trupiano and Vitale could seal the fates of others, because the jury after all this time will feel it must convict some defendants. Ruggiero has felt from the beginning that the government has included his clients in the conspiracy for just this reason: They are intended as human loss leaders.

When Mazzara first disappeared, Ruggiero thought he had fled, "and I was glad for him." Later he thought he might have decided to cooperate with the government. "He was such a sweet guy, he might have said to himself: Rather than put my family through this, make them live with me in jail, I'll cooperate."

Newsday has published a story speculating that Mazzara might have decided to work for the government, and Ruggiero is impressed, because when he worked in law enforcement he participated in similar schemes. "I thought Dick Martin had perhaps permitted Mazzara to become an informant. It's very, very risky, to plant a spy in the enemy camp," but Ruggiero knows Martin well, and thinks the tactic would appeal to him. He would instruct his spy to converse with the attorneys, learn as much as possible about their trial strategies, "and then another U.S. attorney debriefs him, and filters out the stuff that he thinks Martin may be able to use." That way, Martin himself remains clean. "Dick Martin is famous for constructing these 'Chinese walls.'"

Something else has been bothering Larry Ruggiero about this case, something that has only recently started to come clear in his mind. Mazzara's murder triggered these musings, though Ruggiero still cannot figure how his murder fits into the overall picture. About a month before the murder, Ruggiero had noted Mazzara and Catalano taking long corridor strolls together, talking urgently during every recess. "Tommy was looking very troubled, as if something very wrong was happening. Also, Sal Lamberti is a very heavy character, and now *he's* taking long strolls with Catalano."

Ruggiero has started to think that Badalamenti "may be throwing the case. The Mafia-war defense was a good one. It could have worked. It would have explained the guns, and the conversations. It would have got big headlines in the press, and been very effective with the jury. It would sound like real Mafia stuff: The Old Man whispering to his gang, 'Get next to those guys in New York! Pretend! Pretend!' Then you have Pete Alfano sitting with his arsenal, and Badalamenti saying, 'If they wanna come over the ocean, *let 'em* come over the ocean!'

"Sal Lamberti tells his people, 'Just keep him talking. Watch him! At all times we must know where he is.' And this evil old man is saying the same thing about *them*. 'Always know where your enemies are.' *Read* the Alfano conversations. They're fencing! It's obvious. So why wouldn't the Old Man permit it? Why did he stop Kennedy? *Why?*"

. . . FRIDAY, DECEMBER 5, 1986.

THE COURTROOM.   The place is once more in turmoil. Last night U.S. marshals and FBI agents raided an apartment in Greenwich Village south of Washington Square and arrested the fugitive Enzo Randazzo. The apartment had been rented by his new American girlfriend, and she is currently downstairs in the courthouse waiting to be brought before a grand jury, which will determine whether charges should be filed. The jurors, ever unaware, play bridge in the jury room and await their summons to duty.

Martin is on his feet, defendants and lawyers listening intently. Randazzo's discovery is an indirect result of the government roundup of defendants after Mazzara's disappearance. The agents traced all phone calls made by Alfano and Palazzolo from their seedy hotel room. A great many of the calls were to a dial-a-porn telephone service; one call went to an apartment two blocks from the hotel. The agents raided the shabby apartment and found Randazzo, as well as notes on Mazzurco's testimony, and court papers filed after Randazzo's disappearance. Martin's story does little to support the image of a billion-dollar ring of international drug dealers.

The government wants Randazzo's lawyer, Larry Schoenbach, disqualified from further representing his client. Martin will not say why in open court, but he implies that Schoenbach knew something of Randazzo's whereabouts. Freeh goes further and argues that Schoenbach, who during this hearing is seated in his former front-row seat, should be told to leave before the jury enters. The young lawyer may very well find himself on the witness stand, hence he should be barred from the proceedings like every other potential witness. The government also wants bail rescinded for Midwest defendants Alfano, Palazzolo, Trupiano, and Vitale, all of whom stayed in the dingy hotel whenever court was in session.

The courtroom atmosphere is tense, disturbing. Shock waves from the Mazzara murder have touched all trial participants, and now a defense lawyer seems threatened with possible criminal prosecution. Leval, again appearing stunned, asks Schoenbach if he intends to remain. His departure would make life easier all round. But the bearded choirboy defiantly insists on staying, at least for a while. Leval postpones his decision. For now, Schoenbach can sit in the visitors' benches. As for the out-of-town defendants, they must remain within the confines of the courtroom, or the corridor immediately outside, or risk forfeiting their bail.

Such is the grim setting in which Paul Bergman waits impatiently to launch what he considers a strong, well-made defense case on behalf of Baldassare Amato. At last the jury enters, and a pleasant, friendly looking woman in an expensive dress slides into one of the spectator benches. She is Baldo's wife, Madeline Amato, and beside her sits a thin, black-haired young man, almost certainly Baldo's brother. But his face is wolfish and his hair unkempt, his conservative clothes do not hang well, and he lacks his brother's easy nonchalance.

Earlier in the case, Bergman scored a major victory by proving that the FBI misidentified another man as Amato in a photograph purporting to show the clandestine exchange of $100,000. To reemphasize his win, he has brought along several yard-wide blowups of the photos to show the jury. Bergman has made clear repeatedly that he has no use for understatement, and he intends to exploit the Bureau's mistake to the maximum.

His main witness is Amato's younger brother, Vito, who now swaggers up to the stand. Vito arrived in the United States in 1969, along with the rest of the family, and took up residence in the Bensonhurst section of Brooklyn. In 1975 they bought a Manhattan deli at Second Avenue and 84th Street. Both Vito and Baldo have worked there as managers. In 1982 a fire badly damaged the interior. The insurance company paid the Amatos $200,000, and the family decided to open "the only authentic Italian café bar in New York," Café Biffi.

The construction work on Café Biffi did not go well, so they fired the original designer and turned to the contractor Sam Conovo, the same Sam Conovo whom Mazzurco had claimed was represented by the initials "SC" in his damning red notebook. At this point Bergman, who is performing this direct with much smiling and snappy marches between podium and witness stand, wants to introduce as evidence Sam Conovo's business card. Martin bounces to his feet and asks for voir dire. When Martin approaches the stand, Vito stiffens.

Bergman resumes his examination by announcing that the business card was merely to refresh the witness's memory—a classic example of Bergman overkill. Vito Amato has become dangerously keyed up by the confrontation with Martin.

Café Biffi had serious problems. Not only did the original construction firm have to be fired, but work permits were held up because of building-code violations. Did Baldo Amato confer with Joe Ganci about this work? Yes.

By lunchtime, Bergman has skillfully laid the groundwork to explain the gathering at the Café Biffi construction site in March 1984 of Ganci, Catalano, Polizzi, Mazzurco, Joe Lamberti, Bonventre, and Amato.

In the cafeteria, other lawyers worry about the particularly charged-up atmosphere of the coming cross-examination. Martin can be ferocious, and he has smelled blood.

The prosecutor waits for the witness to settle down in his seat and sip a glass of water, then moves to the podium to flourish his épée right under this young wiseguy's nose.

When did Vito Amato last see Cesare Bonventre?

In late 1983.

But Vito was at Café Biffi when Catalano, Bonventre, and friends arrived for their March 1984 meeting. "So you saw Mr. Bonventre in 1984?" Yes.

Martin has drawn first blood, but the cut is so fine, Amato appears not to have noticed.

How did Vito and Baldo and family manage to pay $500,000 in construction bills between 1982 and 1984?

"I lived for two years on credit cards," he brags. "I worship Mastercard and Visa card."

Did he not have a second job?

"To be exact, in May of 1984 . . . I started a job as a banquet manager."

Switching subjects, Martin asks if he knows Dominic Tartamella, the man with the red Porsche who was a witness for Ivan Fisher. Vito Amato denies it. But Tartamella has already testified that Baldo Amato once worked for him. Martin adds that Tartamella attended the baptism of one of Baldo's children. Vito admits he does now remember Tartamella.

The prosecutor leads the witness into a long list of denials that he knows key Bonanno Family mobsters photographed outside the Bono wedding at the Hotel Pierre, and the Toyland Social Club in Little Italy. Just as the witness is once more becoming comfortable, the prosecutor drops the by-now ritual, reliable immigration hand grenade.

"By the way, you told us before that you worked as a—"

"Banquet manager."

"Beginning in May, 1984?"

"Yes."

"Isn't it a fact that you actually began working there in June of 1983?"

"Me? No, sir."

"You're sure of that?"

"I'm sure, yes."

"Let me show you a document. . . ."

Defense lawyers around the courtroom covertly glance at one another. Bergman is on his feet asking to see the document, and trying to conceal his despair.

The papers that Martin holds include Amato's application for U.S. citizenship, filled out just five months ago, saying he worked as a banquet manager from June of 1983.

The fool doesn't even recognize when he has been mortally wounded. His admission that he lied on his application could lead to charges of having filed a false instrument.

"Any other prosecutor would let this just wash over his head, but Martin's a sick bastard," one lawyer says later. "If he doesn't charge him, he'll certainly inform the INS. This kid is not going to get his citizenship."

Martin has caused profound depression in the defense ranks. After court, Carol Novack says she can hardly stand it any more; she hates the trial and is sickened by her sense that a malevolent giant is mechanically squashing foolish little people. An older lawyer says Bergman may have the singular distinction of managing to get a witness indicted.

The morale of several lawyers has hit bottom. They have watched a succession of awful witnesses. Bergman, who up until today had been mounting a strong if somewhat laborious defense, has completely blown it. His star witness has made a couple of stellar points for the prosecution: The meeting at the construction site was a Zip summit, and defendant Amato had an extraordinary amount of money to waste on construction.

Larry Bronson's defense of Sal Greco is focused on his client's need to prove that he was not in a Bagheria farmhouse in early March 1980 watching a heroin quality-control test. Bronson will show he was quietly, busily at home in New Jersey. He calls Greco's good friend and tax accountant, Justin Pisano, a man who keeps detailed date books.

Under patient examination by Bronson, the witness goes through a precise account of driving to the Jersey Shore three Sundays in March to go over Greco's accounts, and to visit nearby pizzerias with his client in order to compare their business with that of the Greco pizzeria in Neptune City.

Stewart's cross-examination of Pisano becomes this prosecutor's finest hour. He concentrates on the March date-book entries.

On March 2, yes, I drove down to see Greco, Pisano says, and we had a leisurely dinner.

"You told us yesterday you were in no rush, right?"

"Yes."

"And that's the truth, the whole truth, and nothing but the truth?"

"Yes."

Then what is this appointment for 7:00 P.M., with Troviatta?

Just a tax appointment. Early March is income tax time, and I made many Sunday and night appointments to service all my tax clients.

What is Troviatta's first name? Where does he live?

I don't remember. "I don't even think I do their taxes anymore."

Stewart remembers. He says Pisano was thirty-five miles away from Greco's pizzeria that night, in the heart of Manhattan, at Lincoln Center, at the opera.

Pisano emphatically denies this. He has only been to Lincoln Center once in his life, to hear Pavarotti.

Are you an opera fan?

Nope. Only been to one opera in my life, when I was in high school.

Stewart shows the witness, and the jury, the Sunday-evening newspaper opera listing for March 2, 1980, at the New York State Theater at Lincoln Center: *La Traviata*.

Bronson objects. "Misleading the witness, your Honor." His witness's tax client is named Troviatta—with two t's.

"And the advertisement for the opera is spelled T R A V I A T A, right?" Stewart asks.

"No. It's *La* Traviata," says Pisano gamely.

"La Traviata?"

"Right. I don't see the comparison to Troviatta."

"Except for time. *That's* a coincidence, isn't it?"

Pisano agrees, and Stewart directs him to look at the entry for two Sundays ahead, March 16, at one in the afternoon.

"Are you referring to Carmen? Carmen Sangari, who I no longer do?"

"Carmen Sangari?" Stewart produces the *New York Times,* and asks him to read aloud the opera listing for that Sunday afternoon. Pisano looks, and agrees that this is truly an amazing coincidence.

Spectators have begun to giggle. But Stewart is not finished. He directs the witness's attention to his diary entry for the following Sunday at 7:00 P.M. "Is that a tax client of yours?"

The giggling turns to guffaws. The notebook says "Barber of Seville."

Over the laughter, Pisano suddenly remembers that he had a girl-friend back then who was crazy about opera, and whose birthday was some time in March, so she "picked three operas she wanted to see—but we never made any of them."

"You just made that up, didn't you?" says Stewart, barely audible over the waves of laughter. Leval has turned crimson. Stewart remains, as usual, absolutely poker-faced, and the good-natured Bronson, shaking with laughter, has lowered his head to his desk, and tears are rolling down his cheeks.

. . . **MONDAY, JANUARY 5, 1987.**
THE COURTROOM.   A new year has brought no new vigor to the Pizza invalid. The cold, bleak courtroom still has a sickroom feeling. Generally speaking, the defenses are not working. One lawyer, Mike Querques, intends to try something new; not a wonder drug, to be sure, more like legal chicken soup, but, as they say, it couldn't hurt. Querques has lined up a colorful cast of witnesses to speak for the big, kindly, sorrowful-faced Frank Polizzi, whom the government has painted as a key source of investment capital for drug deals. Querques intends to show that the restaurateur and builder, at least six times a millionaire, came by his money the hard way: He earned it.

Felix Busby is a mechanical engineer who worked with Polizzi on Sally Mathis Gardens, a community construction project of some 150 apartments in the Brownsville section of Brooklyn. Polizzi was the general contractor, and Busby is here to say that the job was racked with problems. Brownsville is a poverty-stricken, crime-ridden ghetto dotted with abandoned buildings and vacant lots. Unemployment is widespread, and competition for the precious jobs on the construction site became cutthroat. Three minority pressure groups tried to lean on the contractors to hire their people. The FightBack and the Free At

Last coalitions were black; the Fair Start Coalition lobbied for Hispanics. These groups would invade the building site and try by picketing and sometimes by threats and violence to get their members hired. Somehow Polizzi kept the project going through it all.

TV quiz-show producers would kill to snag a character as colorful as Querques's next witness. "Mrs. Susan Reddick," the lawyer announces, turning dramatically toward the back of the courtroom. A sixty-three-year-old black woman, round as she is tall and dressed in a white fake-fur Cossack hat, Irish knit cardigan, flowery blouse, and a pair of substantial leather boots, stomps up the center aisle. She carries a heavy coat over one arm, and a handbag capable of transporting a good portion of the trial transcript. She takes the oath, sits, and gives the jury a thorough inspection.

Querques looks as pleased as a puppy. Mrs. Reddick has lived in Brownsville for some forty years, and now occupies one of the Sally Mathis Gardens apartments.

"How many children in your family, Mrs. Reddick?" Twelve.

Yes, there "sure was violence" while the apartments were under construction. In fact, Susie Reddick took a job as security guard to prevent "theft and such."

"Who was the contractor?"

"Well, I calls him Mr. Frank. I'm not sure his real name." Querques has Polizzi stand up. "Yeah! That's the Boss!" she shouts enthusiastically.

"What violence took place while you were there, Mrs. Reddick?"

"Well one guy got shot, one got bust in the haid, one got cut. The coalitions they all foughts with each other—you know, the FightBack Coalition and the Free At Last Coalition. Mr. Frank, he work through it all."

"Did you live in fear, Mrs. Reddick?"

"Sure did. I was shot at."

"Did you do anything to protect yourself?"

"Sure did. Got me a shotgun." Defendants, jurors, and lawyers shake with laughter. The whole courtroom loves her.

Dick Martin stands to cross. Even he, most ruthless of interrogators, would not dare beat up on this woman. He makes a quick point about concealed weapons. "Mrs. Reddick, you didn't hide that shotgun under your dress did you?"

"No, sir. I carry it for all to see."

The prosecutor sits down.

Mrs. Reddick throws her coat over her arm, picks up her bag, and heads for the rear door. The room almost bursts into applause. Badalamenti gives her his most courtly bow.

Querques is scoring high on two fronts; he has sanitized his client's millions by rooting them in the American ethic of hard work, and he has established the violence in Brownsville to explain the two handguns discovered at Polizzi's house by the FBI.

The lawyer's next witness is equally forthright and personable. Jasper Canella is Frank Polizzi's cousin, and the cook and business partner at their restaurant. He is a jolly, round man endowed with both humor and street smarts. Were he on the payroll of a Madison Avenue advertising agency, he could sell pasta by the ton.

Joe Ganci was one of Canella's best customers. He remembers him as a lively, boisterous man who enjoyed the company of his friends. He talked about food, about life, about women, and when he was with his girlfriend Carol, he was a very happy man.

Bob Stewart opens his cross with a standard government knockout question. "Mr. Canella, do you believe in the Mafia?"

Canella laughs. "Sure I believe in the Mafia! I read it in the papers, on TV. The President's having a Commission on it, fer Chris' sake."

The prosecutor is taken aback by the candor, and spends far too long trying to crack Jasper Canella's belief in Frank Polizzi. It is a hopeless task, and the roly-poly witness exits, still smiling.

In light of the miserable performances by Badalamenti and Mazzurco as witnesses in their own behalf, Querques has decided to put on not Frank Polizzi but his good-looking wife, Cecilia. She will explain the family's wealth and social connections.

The blonde, forty-six-year-old American-born mother of three tells the court that her husband is an extremely hard-working man. He held down two jobs all through their courtship. As his construction firm and his motel complex grew, he worked long, late hours. Yes, she accompanies her husband to many Sicilian social functions—weddings, christenings, graduations, funerals. At these gatherings she came to know the Catalanos, the Amatos, the Lambertis, and the Ligammaris. They all attended the Bono wedding, the marriage of Joe Lamberti's daughter, and the baptism of Sal Catalano's child.

The woman is under a great strain, and her voice trembles. Querques moves to a key moment in the evidence against her husband. At eleven o'clock at night on June 8, 1983, Frank Polizzi was seen meeting with the suspected money launderer Filippo Salamone, brother of defendant

Salvatore Salamone, in the parking lot of Polizzi's Belleville Motor Lodge, in New Jersey. Salamone had driven from Bloomsburg, Pennsylvania, a three-hour journey. The two men talked, and the agents saw Salamone handing Polizzi a brown grocery bag.

Querques is leaning firmly on the podium, head turned toward the jury, trying to catch the eye of those jurors ready to nod off. "At any time in the year 1983 did your husband ever bring home a bag of fish?"

"Yes, he did." Cecilia Polizzi tells how she awakened one morning to find a two-pound bag of *sarde* sitting on the kitchen counter. *Sarde*—fresh-caught sardines—is the essential ingredient for *pasta al sarde,* a concoction of macaroni, fish, raisins, and spices, probably first introduced to the island in the tenth century by Arab invaders. It is considered the Sicilian national dish.

Querques seeks to prove that the bag Salamone gave Polizzi that night at the motor lodge contained sardines. He holds up a brown paper grocery bag, closed at the top, obviously full.

"Have I asked you to duplicate the package" your husband brought home?

"Yes, you have."

"Is this the duplicate you made this morning?" Yes.

Querques asks Mrs. Polizzi to display the contents of her paper bag to the court and the jury. She holds up two ice packs and two pounds of half-frozen smelts, explaining that fresh sardines are out of season. With a great flourish Querques produces another paper bag, folded and stapled—the same one jurors, months ago, watched the agent fold to resemble the bag he saw Salamone hand to Polizzi in the dark parking lot.

Querques asks Mrs. Polizzi to transfer the fish from her bag to this one, so the jury can see that this one is big enough to contain two pounds of fish, with ice packs. The whole thing is pure theatrics—and theater turns to accidental hilarious farce when Cecilia Polizzi picks up her bag. The melting ice packs have soaked the paper through, and the fishy cargo drops out the soggy bottom, splashing brine in all directions and destroying Polizzi's entire case. The prosecution need not even argue that a grocery bag that contained fish and ice could not have remained intact on a three-hour drive on a June night. The defense has just dramatically proven the point.

... **WEDNESDAY, JANUARY 14, 1987. THE COURTROOM.** All of the lawyers have had their shot. Kennedy must finally rest his case. Instead of calling an Italian magistrate to explain Badalamenti's legal problems, he calls a bearded, wild-haired cryptology expert wondrously named Dr. Cipher A. Deavours.

Kennedy flips a page on the easel, revealing his representation of the telephone code.

$$T = 1$$
$$E = 2$$
$$R = 3$$
$$M = 4$$
$$I = 5$$
$$N = 6$$
$$U = 7$$
$$S = 8$$
$$A = 9$$

The correct term for this is not a code, but a cipher, says the expert. Freeh appears furious at this late-hour witness, and Leval has indicated his displeasure. But the jury sits up, curious and expectant.

Kennedy turns next to the matter of the wiretaps. "If you were given thousands of cassettes of conversations in Sicilian, how would you go about analyzing them?"

"Translations are inherently distortions" of text, and "*cannot* be duplicates of the originals."

And if the speakers know each other well and have spoken many times?

Ah, that would make the process of decoding still more difficult. As he listened to the conversations, Deavours asked himself: Do words like "it . . . that . . . thing . . ." have a coded meaning? To find out, he analyzed seven key conversations in this case—Zito and Ganci; the Lambertis and Badalamenti; Badalamenti, Mazzurco, and Sal Lamberti, and so on. He also reviewed the testimony of Agent Tarallo.

Any problems? Kennedy asks.

Yes. The translations are "full of idiom," and idiom, when translated, "does not make sense." For example: To translate the English phrase "change one's mind" into idiomatic French, one would have to say, literally, "take out one brain and put in another," the expert claims. He finds "a lot of this sort of thing" in the wiretapped conversations.

The idioms "introduce an additional level of difficulty," making it especially hard to pick out code words.

The government offers repeated objections to this testimony. Leval thinks carefully before each ruling. This is critical evidence.

"*Are* there any code words?" Kennedy asks.

"Yes. I think 'shirts' is code for something." Also words like *acrylic* and *cotton,* and the small monetary amounts. But, no, he was unable to decipher the meaning of any of these code words.

Freeh is quivering like a terrier. If you were given a professional assignment to break the code in, say, the "twenty-two containers" conversation, would you tell us again, sir, how you might go about it?

Deavours is a rare example in this trial of a well-prepared witness. His answer describes exactly what the defense accuses the government of failing to do before making the arrests. "I would observe these individuals and try to catch them in the act of making a sale of drugs, to confirm that there were twenty-two of something in the sale."

Kennedy is about to rest the Badalamenti defense case when Benfante announces he wants to cross. Kennedy's face reddens, but he says nothing. Saying nothing is the single most important, most difficult thing a trial lawyer must learn—as these proceedings have amply shown. These men work essentially alone. They are virtuoso soloists; most have the egos of tenors and divas. To curb one's tongue is an unnatural act for them, requiring Japanese self-discipline.

Judge Leval calls Benfante to the side bar. "Are you sure you want to do this?"

The lawyer is enraged. "I resent that, your Honor."

Leval tries to calm him. "Don't get all huffy. Under pressures of battle, sometimes a hasty decision might be made. . . . I just want to give you a couple moments to think it over."

Benfante manages to rein himself in. "I'm sorry I reacted that way." A ten-minute recess is called.

Benfante announces he will *not* cross, and Kennedy rests.

The government does intend to put on a rebuttal case. Freeh is at the podium talking about "a seizure of six kilos of cocaine from an individual named Guido Cocilovo in Florida."

Defense lawyers are furious. Sixteen months into the trial, only days from summations, the government comes up with a massive amount of cocaine, which it promises to tie firmly to Salvatore Mazzurco. Eleanore Kennedy's direst fears have been realized. Bob Koppelman speaks for all when he says, "This is sandbagging, pure and simple."

Leval orders Freeh to proceed.

In 1983, the prosecutor says, Guido Cocilovo, a shipping broker, was stopped by railway police at the Miami Amtrak station as he was about to board a train for New York. A search of his suitcase turned up six one-kilo bags of cocaine. A search of his pockets produced an address book containing the phone numbers of defendants Mazzurco and Joe Lamberti.

Freeh asserts the right to introduce this evidence in rebuttal because Genay Leitman, in her defense case, had placed in evidence a number of translations of telephone taps she believed the government had been trying to suppress. One February 1984 conversation, between Alfano and Palazzolo, mentions someone called Cocilovo. When Freeh heard the name, it rang a bell. He remembered the Miami bust, and that it had some dim connection to Mazzurco. He asked the FBI to check further.

Agents reexamined the Florida evidence seized from Cocilovo and found a scrap of paper bearing his itinerary for the day of arrest. The same scrap also had the Pronto phone number and the notation "S. called twice."

It is too much. Rumors have circulated for months that the government had an ace up its sleeve. Now the defense must deal with a quantity of drugs larger than anything heretofore seen in the case. Koppelman requests that Freeh be placed under oath and questioned in a nonjury hearing to determine whether the prosecutor deliberately withheld the Cocilovo accusations from his main case, to wrong-foot the defense.

Freeh admits to Koppelman that the FBI and his office had considerable information on the drug courier. He had been dragged in front of a grand jury, immunized, then had refused to answer questions and been jailed for contempt. Right now he is locked up in MCC. He has been brought from Florida so that when the government asks him to testify, and he takes the Fifth, the prosecutors will have the right to read into the Pizza record statements he made to the Miami police.

Fine, says Koppelman, except that the Cocilovo mentioned by Palazzolo in the phone call was a different man! That Cocilovo was a casualty of the Mafia wars, a man murdered in Sicily in 1984, a year after the Miami cocaine bust. But Leval rules that Mazzurco's rambling, terrible testimony nonetheless provides ample grounds to introduce this evidence. The judge will consider the matter further over the weekend.

That weekend, Joe Benfante is pressed hard by certain of his brethren to visit Cocilovo in MCC and plead with him to testify, thus thwarting the government's move to read his arrest statement into evidence. But Benfante has had enough. "I'm finished with being the fall guy. Let somebody else go over and talk to the scumbag."

Ever since the collapse of the Mazzurco plea bargaining, stories have circulated that both he and Benfante were leaned on by other defendants to stay in and not deal. One lawyer claims Baldo Amato approached an associate of Benfante's and asked him to "encourage" Benfante not to take the plea. Several Badalamenti-group lawyers believe Mazzurco was forced onto the stand by the other defendants. The dead Ganci was insufficient to dump on; they needed a human sacrifice.

On Monday morning Leval announces his decision: ". . . no basis whatsoever for any finding that the government has behaved in any manner improperly . . . no reason why it shouldn't be offered on rebuttal."

The government wheels a small troupe of agents onto the stand to tell the story of the cocaine connection, and of mysterious boxes of books shipped by Cocilovo to Miami in 1979. That was five years before the Badalamenti phone call that mentions the "things of five years ago." The inference the prosecution will draw in the coming summations is obvious to the Badalamenti lawyers. The Old Man was the supplier "of five years ago," and the supplier at the time of the arrests—1984. In short, he was one of the New York group's primary drug sources.

With this damning testimony, the government rings down the curtain on its Pizza evidence.

7. *The Summing Up*

... 9:40 A.M., **TUESDAY, JANUARY 27, 1987.**
THE COURTROOM. Both sides have rested. The time for summing
up is at hand: government summation first, then defense summation,
then government rebuttal. The government gets two turns at bat, and
the last word, because it always bears the burden of proof, just as the
defense never loses its presumption of innocence.

The big prosecution table, for so long heaped with bags of heroin,
piles of weapons and ammunition, body armor, drug paraphernalia,
and mountains of documents, is swept bare. The government attorneys
seem no longer to want to sit there. All of them are on their feet while
defense lawyers make last-minute arguments. After a while, Freeh is
relaxed enough to sit; Martin never is.

Leval inquires how much time each attorney will need for summation, tots it up, and says that fourteen and a half days, or three full
five-day weeks, "will be pretty rough on the jury. . . . My guess is that
the jury will be very fed up. . . . I caution you not to abuse, or alienate
[them] by just going on. . . ."

He asks the marshals to escort the jurors in. By now, only six alternates remain.

"Ladies and gentlemen of the jury, you have now heard the evidence in this case. We move now to a new phase—summations. It is now more important than ever that you don't discuss the case, and don't read newspapers."

The jurors appear newly grave and sober. Even when Leval tells them summations may take three weeks, perhaps a bit longer, no juror flinches, or, indeed, appears to react at all.

Children's puzzle books invite the reader to connect the numbered dots. If the child does it in the right order, the random dots organize themselves into a pattern; a picture appears. Lawyers making their summations invite the jurors to do the same. To make the jurors' task easier, to *insure* that they make no wrong connections, the prosecutors have supplied them with red 410-page loose-leaf chartbooks studded with maps, visual aids, all the appropriate symbols for phone conversations, plane trips, money transfers, car surveillances, and such. One chartbook, as thick as the Manhattan telephone directory and "personalized" with the juror's own number on its cover, lies this morning on every jury chair. Despite all the earlier cautions from the bench that charts are not evidence, but summaries of evidence, these jurors have now been outfitted with books that are summaries of summaries to help guide them through the extensive evidentiary thickets and swamps ahead.

In addition to their printed guides and maps, the jurors can count on a live prosecutor to lead them by the hand. Martin announces that Louis Freeh will do the first part of the summation for the government. The little podium has been wheeled directly in front of the jury box, with a cup of water on top, and a carton of evidence sitting alongside.

This is the grand finale. All the attorneys are here, stunt lawyers included. The key FBI men are on hand. All five of Leval's attractive young clerks have joined him on the bench. The judge has had his robe dry-cleaned. The jurors look attentive and alert. It is 9:59 A.M.

"Mr. Freeh, you may proceed."

"You have had an opportunity to observe this international drug conspiracy over ten years and four continents. . . ."

Defense attorneys intently scan the jury faces.

Freeh opens with a locker-room pep talk: Don't let yourselves be intimidated by the length of this case. You can handle it! We are confident you will reach a verdict.

"Extensive investigation was necessary to penetrate this complex network." Freeh takes the jury on a whirlwind tour of the money-for-drugs, drugs-for-money story, and for a finale cites $50 million in cash that the government can actually trace; 4,000 pounds of morphine base; and 2.5 kilos of high-quality heroin the government bought from Zito. He adds that the defendants were about to receive cocaine from the Badalamenti group when they were arrested. Leval listens thoughtfully, nibbling his thumb.

At 10:32, Freeh sits, and Martin stands to explain the charges. He has a new chopped haircut, blunt delivery. "All defendants are charged with conspiracy." All were made members, or associates, in a secret criminal organization known as La Cosa Nostra, and all are bound together by a secret code. The object of the criminal enterprise is to enrich members of the conspiracy. All but three—the two Badalamentis and Alfano—are charged under RICO. "That's the charges. For the next couple of hours, I'll explain them.

"The existence of the Mafia is virtually unchallenged in this case"—a good point, which Martin cannot resist embellishing with a sneer—"except for Vito Marcello, who asked if Mafia is something you eat."

Now, his main point. No better example exists of how the Mafia works than the manner in which Gaetano Badalamenti testified. True, he sat on the stand and gave an oath. But *he* chose the questions he would answer. Gaetano Badalamenti *defied* this court. He defied the law of the United States, and that defiance brought this kind of witness: Sadid Torres, Dominic Tartamella, Vito Amato.

Martin recaps Buscetta and his Mafia history. Turn to page three in your hymn books, ladies and gentlemen of the jury, to see the chart COMMISSION OF LA COSA NOSTRA, and follow along as Richard Martin sings the beautiful old refrain: How the Mafia is organized like a family, and how Palermo is divided into Mafia family territories. He goes through it all again, jurors #1, 2, 4, and 8 in particular paying rapt attention.

We submit: What Gaetano Badalamenti opposed was not drugs, but the Corleonese. And *to this day* Badalamenti wants that power back. Why? Because power equals control.

Now, regarding Gaetano Mazzara's trip to Bagheria . . .

At this point, the summation phase becomes indistinguishable from the evidence phase, and jurors' eyes begin to glaze over.

In the recess, lawyers compare notes. Fogelnest thinks Martin is very good. Segal thinks Freeh was good, Martin not, because he got too detailed. Fisher calls Martin "terrible," filled with mistakes.

It is 10° outside, and not much warmer in the courtroom. Leval has ordered the marshals to maintain punitive climate control in order to force the jurors to remain awake.

Martin ridicules the Troviattas and Carmen. He produces the opera-minded accountant's 1980 date book. "This book is a faked, fabricated alibi for Sal Greco, and this says more about the truthfulness of Contorno's testimony than anything else." The most obvious lie was when he told you he was meeting with Greco at Sal's Pizza in Neptune City. Sal Greco didn't buy the Neptune City pizzeria until 1982, two years after this book was compiled. "This book was a calculated lie to keep Sal Greco away from Bagheria."

In the next recess, the defense attorneys agree Martin is doing much better, focusing in, being specific. The faked opera diary is devastating. "That's stuff they can take to the bank!"

It is past 4:00 P.M. when Martin gets down to the Ronsisvalle testimony. "Most important, Ronsisvalle was sent to Florida . . . the same place Badalamenti and his family were sending dozens of pounds of cocaine from." Martin for once sounds overly expansive. There has been no testimony whatever to this effect. But a lawyer arguing in summation, on either side, has latitude to say almost anything, and courtroom etiquette expects the other side to keep silent. So in Martin's world Florida belongs to Badalamenti now, no room for Colombian coke by the ton or Jamaican hash by the boatload. It's all so simple. Miami, the nose-candy capital of the world, has been downgraded to the status of a Sicilian staging post in order to be hammered into the government jigsaw.

Next, more of the government's off-the-wall money figures. In all, Luigi Ronsisvalle delivered more than 300 kilos of heroin. He carried 600 pounds to Chicago in 1977 and 1978. "Just his deliveries alone brought in $14 million to $45 million—and it only cost $12,000! . . .

"By 1980, this enterprise was in full operation. It continued to April 9, when these men were arrested and brought here for you to judge.

"It's been an honor to address you. Thank you very much."

. . . WEDNESDAY, JANUARY 28, 1987.
THE COURTROOM. This morning the jurors appear swathed in sweaters and lumberjack shirts. The 6'-by-20' money-laundering chart, which Freeh will call "the monster chart," is back in place.

Where did this cash money come from? he asks. From the sale of shirts, or pizza, or precious rocks? And where did it go? *We* say, from the sale of narcotics. Look in your books, pages 27–30; they give you bench-mark prices for heroin and morphine base in Italy, year by year.

Two groups handled the money: the Catalano group and the Badalamenti group. Evola and Alfano flew it to Brazil on their bodies. A startling new charge; jurors are very attentive.

More news. Mr. Phelan at E. F. Hutton tipped off Vito Roberto Palazzolo in Switzerland. He got a $15,000 Cartier watch for his trouble. As Freeh talks, jurors eyeball the monster chart. Now he refers them to their red hymnals, to follow the money washing, channel by channel, down the ever-flowing river. Freeh is in good form, gesturing with his left hand, a fine schoolmaster-lecturer. Martin, hyperalert, makes tiny notations, following every word. "None of this money is reported. . . . Now Amendolito returns to the U.S." and meets a courier at JFK who has the money from Castronovo. The jurors' eyes begin to glaze over again. This is too hard to follow, except for #8, the accountant, who studies his charts, shakes his head, bobs his chin. The thicket of numbers is his normal habitat. In him the government has a sure-fire guilty verdict.

Freeh presses on, free-handedly reciting his financial begats and interpreting code: Sprouted onions are green, i.e., cash. Some jurors are now deep in their red books, following carefully, unquestionably impressed by this oceanic evidence.

"Your chart of weapons to protect the conspiracy, page 68, shows the relationship between the money launderers and the drug distributors in this case." Page 68 looks like something ripped from an illustrated firearms catalogue. Closer inspection shows that only six of the seventeen high-powered weapons pictured, all bought in Bloomsburg by Sal Salamone, and reported to the government on the ATF forms, are part of the evidence in this case. Two were found in Carol Giuliano's New Jersey apartment; two in the ceiling of Sal Greco's Neptune City pizzeria; and two more in another pizzeria, belonging to one of 283 unindicted coconspirators in the case.

. . . THURSDAY, JANUARY 29, 1987.

THE COURTROOM. By the third day, the red hymnals are crumpled and soiled, and the bags of heroin are back on the table. Bucknam is now at center stage, performing with old-fashioned, debate-team technique. His boss, Giuliani, has slipped in to watch his maiden performance. He's good. His assignment is to delineate the role of each defendant, and in his presentation the distinctions between these men with such similar names and faces clarify as never before. Each time he indicates the blue shirt box that contained Mazzurco's heroin, his forefinger points straight down, self-assured as a Roman emperor's thumb. He has a genuine flair for reading dry surveillance reports, pointing out patterns, and translating them into dramatic actions. He is roly-poly in body, but sharp-nosed and smart, a legal armadillo.

In the corridor, loud noises of attorneys whistling in the dark. Calluori: "So he's pointing out patterns; correlation is not causation." Ryan: " 'I submit' means *we don't know.* " Kaplan: "Mazzara's a dead man and can't defend himself. And that buries me." Bergman: "In a case of this complexity, each juror will rely only on *his own* view of the evidence."

Bucknam lays out a spate of creative government deductions, presented as facts: Another distribution network was run out of Temperance, Michigan, by that man over there, Sam Evola. Pete Alfano supplied cocaine from the Evola house. Sam Evola admitted his guilt at his arrest. His statement, "You can't prove nothin' on me," acknowledges there was something to be proven. He said the cocaine found in his house was a sample of the kilo of 95% pure cocaine he had sold. It was so good because it came straight from the top, says Bucknam: from Badalamenti, through Alfano.

Another creative deduction: The cluster pattern of phone calls following Mazzurco's call to Cocilovo means, "we submit," that Cocilovo was dispatched to Florida *by* Sal Mazzurco and Joe Lamberti. When Mazzurco flew back from Italy and declared a 200-pound box as "used books, no value," the destination was Miami, and the broker's name on the Customs slip was Cocilovo. These books *"are* the stuff from five years ago."

Stewart's summation divides defendants into the "core group," the "distribution group," and the "smugglers." He has not talked five minutes before Lamberti and Greco and jurors #5 and 10 have nodded off. Soon even Badalamenti is drowsing.

On April 28, 1983, says Stewart, Joe Ganci does something unusual. He goes to a different pay phone, not his regular one, to get a special call from Italy, "and Frank Polizzi is standing right outside the booth. Why? He's there to *vouch for* Ganci, to get the overseas supply and quality control problems solved, and get the heroin pipeline flowing again."

Stewart's assertion is a good example of the sort of thing permitted attorneys on both sides in their summings-up. That a man observed standing outside a phone booth is in fact there to "vouch for" the man inside the booth, who is talking to someone in Sicily—even though the "outside man" never speaks on the phone—is creative deduction, not fact. The further assertion, that his purpose in standing there is "to get the overseas supply and quality control problems solved, and get the heroin pipeline flowing again," is baroque ornamentation of the original creative construct.

Then comes a "major meeting" at Casa Polizzi Restaurant, attended by Ganci and Joe Lamberti, Amato and Bonventre, Castronovo, Mazzurco, Ligammari, and others, with Frank Polizzi doing all the talking. This Frank Polizzi—again, seen but not heard—this "rich man" who solves the big "pipeline problem" in Europe by "vouching," at last gives the Pizza cast a character like the fictionalized Mafioso whom movie fans recognize: the sinister, shadowy Godfather who blinks an eye, and all changes, and someone offscreen is doomed to die.

. . . FRIDAY, JANUARY 30, 1987.

THE COURTROOM. On this snowy, soggy morning, his Honor finally gets fed up. Court has been called for 9:00 A.M. At 9:40 Judge Leval says, "The record will reflect that, after numerous absences on the part of juror #308, over the objections of counsel, I am proceeding without him." (During jury selection, each juror was assigned a random number to protect his anonymity.)

So the jurors are down to seventeen. A juror the defense favored is gone, and alternate #1 moves onto the jury proper. She is a thirty-four-year-old social worker/welfare assessor from the Bronx, a woman who smiled at left-wing lawyer William Kunstler when he visited the courtroom, and whose eyes filled with tears at the news that Mazzara had died. She is considered the most defense-minded person in the box.

In the break, Eleanore says, "All the lawyers are brain-dead. How could they not object to the loss of number 308? He was our second-best juror! Pierre Leval is hand-picking this jury!"

Freeh is back. He'll try to finish today, he says, "but please note there are 200 pages still left in your books." By now, Leval is following along in his own copy of the red book, nodding and bobbing his head as he traces the government's argument.

Mazzurco is in nearly every conversation Freeh now cites. Listening, the real-life Sal Mazzurco sits half-sprawled in his folding chair, hands thrust into his pockets, face turned away from the jury, wearing a dreamy expression, as if he is reliving these high moments of his life.

The red book at last over, Freeh reattacks Badalamenti's war record. Zito's three heroin bags get held up once again, like tired chorus girls. Toward the end, Freeh's three fellow prosecutors have turned to stare, along with him, at the jury, presenting to the spectators four left profiles of ill-masked anxiety.

... MONDAY, FEBRUARY 2, 1987.
Defense summations will begin shortly. Each lawyer considers his summation the pinnacle of his case, the ultimate dangerous game, the moment he has been building toward for sixteen months. To even matters out, the nineteen defense lawyers remaining in the case will speak in reverse order to the indictment, feisty little Joe Ryan leading off for the Eagle Cheese Company owner, Filippo Casamento.

A sense of renewed vigor pervades the courtroom. Leval has decreed that the first three spectator rows, nearest the jury box, be kept empty for the duration; this effectively isolates the jurors from the "congregation." Row four is a frieze of grieving Sicilian matrons, sons, and daughters, here to support their men. Badalamenti smiles at the women almost sunnily, if this term may be applied to so craggy and darkly smoldering a visage.

Ryan wears his combat gear—formal dark-blue suit, expensive pale silk tie, very close shave, ferocious expression. The lawyer is Irish-furious. He has asked since last week for certain government exhibits, charts, documents, and just moments ago has heard Freeh say, "Your Honor, they don't exist any longer. They were disassembled."

"What's the difference between this and destroying evidence? Oh, yeah, I remember," he snorts derisively. " 'The charts are *not* evidence.' "

At 10:07 A.M., preceded by hearty offstage laughter, the newly sweatered jury marches into the box.

Freeh has a few more pages to finish off in the song books, and then he bids these seventeen jurors and alternates farewell. "It's been a long case, lots of evidence. You, the jury, are now in charge of that evidence. Using the government information book, we know you can handle that evidence to reach a verdict. You have a unique expertise to handle this evidence, after sixteen months—more time than it takes to train a new FBI agent." He conveniently forgets that in the matter of evaluating evidence, these jurors have no training whatsoever, only conditioning. "You *can* do it. . . . If you tore out a couple of pages of your books and handed it to somebody, he might have some trouble. *You* won't!" All jurors look solemn as high-school seniors on graduation day. "We know you will find each and every defendant guilty as charged."

Ryan distributes to each juror a slim black notebook to replace his dog-eared red one—the defense view of the Casamento evidence. He eschews the podium and wears a lapel mike, which gives him freedom to pace. He asks his little rooster-faced client with crinkly white hair to please stand. "Four days," says Ryan, speaking very slowly. "Four days' evidence in one and a half years." The jurors look at Ryan, always a good sign. "Bet you thought the only way you hadda serve your country was in the army. You never dreamed, when you got your jury notice . . ." He grins. Then, serious: "*You* are now the judges in this case. You have more power than Judge Leval.

"They told you on nine occasions that my client dealt drugs." The jurors watch Ryan carefully as he runs down the evidence point by point. His manner is good, yet the dots seldom connect. He presents a series of random-seeming scenes, ideas, themes, which lack a thread to follow. Also, when he imitates Bucknam or Freeh, he becomes a shrieking, finger-pointing cartoon of the prosecutor he used to be. This late in the day, caricature and overstatement are counterproductive.

"In years of investigation, why was there never a wiretap on Eagle Cheese, or the Casamento home? Why no searches even?" This point is good. Yet Ryan has begun to seem like a man sealed in a plastic bubble, talking and listening only to himself. Despite his somewhat *outré* mannerisms, however, the lawyer may be planting a few seeds of reasonable doubt. His argument would be stronger without the eccentricities.

Ryan circulates his own set of photos of Ganci leaving Casamento's grocery store carrying boxes. The top of his cardboard box is clearly open, folded down. In tones of highest outrage, he declaims, "They have the *temerity* to tell you that's a box of money for drugs, when they

... don't ... even ... know what's in that box coming out of a food store on Avenue U in Brooklyn."

He approaches the easel. "Filippo Casamento was *held hostage* in this room for sixteen months! Mr. Casamento is Sicilian, from a large family. He worked construction with Tomasso Buscetta. But not even Mr. Badalamenti could say Mr. Casamento was Mafia!

"They got drugs from Zito! What have they got from Casamento?" He rips the top sheet of paper off the easel. Underneath, he has inked in large letters:

NO GUNS

NO DRUGS

NO MONEY

NO CODE

NO MAFIA

It's a neat Perry Mason finish. The lawyer hurries to put his arm around the shoulder of the genial little man in maroon sweater and glasses. "This is the last moment you'll have to see Mr. Casamento. May you reach the right, true verdict in this case."

In the corridor, Benfante is kidding around. "I'm gonna try that. Gonna rip off the paper and have a sign, '*All* the drugs, *all* the guns, *all* the money.' ... Gee, what if Joe had grabbed two sheets of paper by mistake?"

When court reconvenes, it looks like an art school. Four modest, cheap wooden easels are set in front of the jury box. The jury appears very interested. Mike Querques begins with a thank-you "for being super-people, super-jurors," and a plea: "For Mr. Polizzi, I need your intelligence, your integrity, your conscience and your fairness. ... I'm not talking about reasonable doubt. I'm talking about absolute, total innocence! Frank Polizzi is an—an American tragedy! Because of this prosecution and its lack of—of calibre." He uses no notes. He needs no mike. He works from a bent-knee crouch, like Groucho Marx.

"I was born plain. I was raised plain . . . but very well. And I *am* plain. Nothin' fancy about me. I'm going to try to talk to you very plainly, in a dignified way.

"What scares me to death is the *complexity* of this case. Why [stage whisper]—why is it scary? . . . 150 individuals are involved! Lawyers have two [words] for this—*spill-over*, and *rub-off*. It's as if I stood back 50 feet and threw half a bucket of water at juror #5."

The charges? "Fol-de-rol!" Pacing, gesturing, Querques is full of fire and brimstone, as much fun to watch and hear as Elmer Gantry—and not much more likely to save anyone, including Polizzi. It's a *performance,* but it does not persuade.

. . . TUESDAY, FEBRUARY 3, 1987.
THE COURTROOM.   Today Querques's easels display eight home-made charts, each abloom with varicolored Post-it notes, typed index cards, and handwritten memos in a profusion of hues and styles. In fact, these hodgepodge exhibits depict—and clarify—the overlapping, messy, asymmetric sequence of events better than the government's fancy graphics. Though not as easy to read as the government's neat rebus squares, they are actually more coherent.

"We are going to school," says Querques. First he brings out calls, ignored by the government, which unmistakably concern Ganci's marital problems. Then he shows that the coded conversations the government has put in evidence *also* refer to domestic problems. "So Frank Polizzi, Ganci's longtime friend, is a man in a vise." He was trying to soften the effect of Ganci's love affair on the wife, on the family. "Does he run away? Or does he take it like a champion? . . . *You* should have such a guy as a friend!"

As for Pizza's lovebirds, the plain man puts it very plainly indeed. "I suppose, if you are fiftyish, and you fall in love with a twenty-year-old girl, you can feel sorry for him." At this, the drowsing elderly juror, #4, opens his eyes. "But what brought Joe Ganci to Belleville? I call her *The Magnet.* Youth! Beauty! Passion at 50! *The Magnet* brought him—not Frank Polizzi!"

Next Ken Kaplan is up, to save Frank Castronovo, a herculean task. The Roma Restaurant owner has two major problems: the Bagheria farmhouse and Amendolito's boxes of cash.

Kaplan's first target is "the professional criminal and liar" Sal Contorno, the government witness who placed his client at Bagheria. "Is this the kind of person we want to bring to these shores? What business will he go into in his new homeland? The murder business, bank fraud, or perjury?"

The point is good, but the jury seems not in the mood to listen—a frightening notion for any lawyer. The government "needed Contorno desperately," Kaplan says, "to put Castronovo in the narcotics business." In short, Castronovo was not in Bagheria any more than Catalano was, or Sal Greco.

Kaplan has an even greater problem with the government's main witness against his client, "that snake oil salesman" Amendolito. There is no way Kaplan can deny the many cash shipments from the Roma Restaurant, so he says: "I'll answer the question, was there money in the boxes? Absolutely! My client gave Amendolito large sums of money in boxes. But my client was in no conspiracy, and broke no laws." This is lawyering by the *sauve qui peut* principle: Admit only what you have to, and try to put a spin on that, so it doesn't quite say what it appears to. Seventeen dubious faces look back from the jury box.

Castronovo is no dope dealer! "If he's such a big, rich guy, how come he works all day long in his pizza apron, a slave to the Roma Restaurant, even after his bypass operation and despite his kidney stones?"

The government says his client *knew* this was drug money. But the government cannot tie this money to any drugs. They cannot even prove Castronovo knew what was in the boxes. From the look on the jury's faces, there is no need to prove it; it's self-evident.

Kaplan turns to his bigger problem. "Amendolito has testified that *he* didn't know it was drug money." And the government has chosen to credit that testimony. "Pretend to credit" might be more accurate. "Watch out for the big government juggernaut, Ladies and Gentlemen." This line can never hurt. But it's doubtful it helps much with a jury that, after sixteen months in the care of marshals and of shepherd Pierre Leval, seems to have a galloping case of Stockholm Syndrome and may well view itself as part of the government.

Kaplan's whole presentation is professional and workmanlike. He calls Amendolito "an ex-defendant who's shaking Mr. Freeh down, for money," a line that recaptures the jurors' attention. They already know he's a lying, greedy braggart. When Kaplan suggests that he is collecting undercover cash from many sources, not just Castronovo, most seem to accept the idea. One cannot tell about #6. She has developed a habit of leaning forward and resting her chin on the jury rail, giving the eerie effect of a Medusa in the jury box.

Kaplan ends by ridiculing the most dangerous charge, the 848, which asserts that his client is the boss of a continuing criminal enterprise. On the list of at least five people whom Castronovo is alleged to have managed, organized, or supervised are "some individuals he doesn't know, and some who are *his* boss." Kaplan rests, knowing he has done the best he could for his deeply imperiled client.

By the next day, the jury appears lackluster, burned out by pleas and shouts. It has spent the late morning listening to Larry Bronson try to destroy Contorno and rehabilitate the opera patron, Pisano, a feat on a par with raising the dead.

Bob Fogelnest, the sometime eccentric of the defense team, now takes his shot. His client, Sal Salamone, is clearly on the fringe of the conspiracy, and the lawyer has spent the trial distancing himself from any faction, sometimes siding with Kennedy, sometimes exploding into wild shouting matches with prosecutors—another sturdy, single ego in this pack of legal loners. Now he wants the jury to acknowledge Salamone's similar isolation, and consider him separately from his codefendants.

"It's obvious that you can't join a Mafia drug conspiracy if you don't know of it." Sal may have bought guns in Bloomsburg, and he may have had people changing currency. But it was his brother, Filippo, who was the Mafia man. And his brother kept Sal in the dark.

Fogelnest reminds the jury of the expert on Mafia membership, the undercover agent Joe Pistone. It was Pistone who informed the jury that a made guy had to be neat and tidy, no beard, no mustache. Fogelnest whips out a scraggly photograph of his client. "Look at this! We're talking hippie here. Does this look like a made man to you?"

The lawyer has captured the jury's attention. He talks to them in everyday phrases and short, sharp sentences. "Could you be used by the Mafia and not know it? Sure you could. Mr. Bucknam told you that. They use people who have no knowledge that they are being used."

To prove it, Fogelnest has made a tape he calls "Sal's Greatest Hits," an edited version of Salamone's telephone conversations with a man he enlisted to exchange money. On it, Salamone threatens to sue the man to recover $3,500 that was not returned.

You heard the tape, the lawyer says. "Are those the words of a man who is up to his ears in a Mafia international drug conspiracy, that he would jeopardize . . . by going to court over $3,500?"

As a finale, Fogelnest invites his young client to stand, then turns to the visitors' benches. "Back there is his family." A dark-haired, simply dressed young woman with tired rings around her eyes stands up and pulls a young boy and an angelic little girl to her side. "They pray that you will be able to do this job."

Gerry Di Chiara, favorite lawyer of the female jurors, is wearing his best double-breasted suit and his biggest smile. He intends to finish as he started, with charm. His client, the little dark-skinned truck driver buried at the far end of the second row, is the unluckiest man in the case. In March 1984 trucker Giovanni Cangialosi lost his driving license in Sicily and came to New York looking for work. By April he found himself in jail.

Di Chiara suggests a criterion for jurors to use in considering their verdicts. "If at the end of this trial the defendants were hooded, and after your verdict the hood with the name Cangialosi on it was pulled off to reveal a member of your family, would you be happy with your verdict? Thank you."

Pat Burke has been designated by the Badalamenti-group lawyers as the man who will lay out for the jury and connect and interpret for it the crucial phone calls proving that what is really being spoken about is not narcotics but the Mafia war, the same bloody conflict that since the late 1970s has decimated the Sicilian Mafia, and is now reaching across the Atlantic to embroil and imperil Sicilians in North and South America. It is a heavy assignment.

Burke's summation is done without notes, and in simple language. He has invented a bland, overarching metaphor to bind together his unwieldy, somewhat wobbly, sometimes abstract, often reticulated heap of evidence. "We're going to all be detectives here, ladies and gentlemen," he begins. "Why would it be, fellow detectives, that a deposed Mafia leader living in hiding down in Brazil, why would he contact people who have Mafia connections in New York, knowing that there is communication between New York and Sicily?" Knowing, therefore, that any conversation with New York is a potential risk to his cover.

Wasn't the government "telling us that up here in Michigan somewhere is a narcotics supply network that he could tap into . . . *without* any risk of communication [of his whereabouts] to Sicily?

"One other important question. We understand from the other detectives in this case that twenty-two kilograms of a valuable commodity . . . had actually been delivered to Florida. . . . But for some reason a deal broke down over $10,000." The government's own expert told us that just one of those units, not twenty-two, would be worth $70,000. So twenty-two are worth $1,540,000. So why would a deal like that break down over $10,000, "especially when you know that the people who are supposed to be coming up with the money are millionaires." These are our problems.

The jury is very intent—a good sign.

"All we know about Pete Alfano is his unknown residence, Oregon, Illinois, west of Rockford, and that he has been there since 1967."

Well, what do we know about Gaetano Badalamenti? What did our four live witnesses say? Tomasso Buscetta knew scores of people in the Mafia. Second, a fellow named Contorno was a Mafia soldier. Third, "that vermin, Ronsisvalle," knew Mafia people on both sides of the Atlantic. Fourth, Agent Pistone knew members of the American Mafia. *Not one* of these people told us anything connecting Mr. Badalamenti to narcotics.

Burke strolls to the props. "These two blackboards will be our detectives' notebooks," which we carry with us. This easel will be our chart that we keep back in the office. Periodically we will note our conclusions on the chart. From 1967, when Alfano came to the United States from Cinisi, to 1982, we know nothing about Pete Alfano. But in July 1982 his passport shows us that he was in Brazil. Where is Badalamenti then? In Brazil. And Sam Evola is also in Brazil at the exact same time. We know that the three men met. We heard it from live witnesses.

"Who is this man Sam Evola, who has been seated over there for all these many months? He, too, is obscure. The big question: What is his and Alfano's business with the man in Brazil? Well, we know that Alfano is from the same town as Badalamenti, Cinisi, and that he is related through marriage." Burke reminds the jury that Mrs. Alfano's maiden name is Trupiano, that her brother is the defendant Trupiano, and that the other two Trupiano sisters are married to defendants Vitale and Palazzolo. The jury has seen Evola's "very attractive wife, who has been here most of the trial, seated with her aunt, Mrs. Badalamenti." Her name is Christine Badalamenti Evola, and she is the daughter of Mr. Badalamenti's older brother, the grocer he told us he lived with and worked for in the 1950s.

So what was discussed at that meeting in Brazil? Burke answers his own question: Badalamenti wanted to set up communications with the United States, because he had left money there many years ago. He had invested in land, and made some personal loans, "and now he was in some need, and he wanted to receive that money back." That was one part of his plan.

So, think for a moment. As a good detective, which fellow do you choose to be your representative in the United States? Obviously, you'd chose Alfano. He is less visible. He lives in a town nobody has ever heard of. The other one, Evola, is too traceable. He is married to your favorite niece, and lives in Michigan, where you once lived, and invested in land.

The TERMINUSA code was designed to communicate between the United States and Brazil. Only two people had it besides Badalamenti: Alfano and Evola. And it was a one-way code, a way to locate Badalamenti in Brazil and allow him to remain hidden. The purpose was to set up a system of communication within a very safe network.

"Who else was in Brazil? Do you remember, fellow detectives?" A long pause here; jurors look blank. "It was Tomasso Buscetta." He told us he met with Badalamenti there in June, July, August, and September of 1982. The last time they met was March 1983, and Buscetta told us Badalamenti asked him to return to Sicily with him. "Why? So that he could take over control again."

Burke walks to the easel. "Now we're back in the office." He picks up the marker and writes: "BADALAMENTI PLANS: 1) hide 2) communicate in a secure fashion with the U.S. Why? Money. 3) Sicily," and comments, "He had some plans in relation to Sicily."

Next, we learn from passport entries that Alfano makes two more brief trips to Brazil, in August and in October. This tells us that Badalamenti has chosen Alfano, not Evola, as his most secure U.S. contact and messenger.

"Next what do we learn? Very intriguing fact, detectives." The entry into the case of the New York element. Let's write down the first clue, Burke continues. In December 1982 and again in February 1983 someone traveled from New York to Brazil. Bet you don't remember who it was. It was Joe Lamberti! But Badalamenti told us he and Joe Lamberti did not meet.

"March 8, 1983, we get a big break. Know what that is?" FBI wiretaps go onto the home and business phones of a Mafia narcotics dealer, Joe Ganci. And in the same month comes the very first phone contact from Brazil to Oregon, Illinois. We have a toll record only, no conversation.

It is very quiet in the courtroom, everyone listening intently to the courtly Irish lawyer. "Within a month" of the toll-record call to Oregon, Illinois, comes the first phone call from Oregon to New York.

Here another fellow enters our evidence bank—Enzo Randazzo, nephew of Badalamenti. Randazzo is a "will-o'-the-wisp. . . . He can appear and disappear without a trace!" You have seen him in this courtroom, but "he is no longer here."

Although Burke does not mention it, four nights earlier, on February 5, Randazzo was taken from MCC under heavy guard, escorted to JFK, and put aboard a plane to Italy. He is now in a Rome jail awaiting trial on the same charges he faced in this courtroom.

"You can't follow his movements." His passport does not give good clues. We know he was in New York in the summer and fall of 1982, but there's no record on his passport. We see a picture of him in the United States in 1983, but again no record on his passport. He was also in Brazil, March 7 to March 9 of that year, and the passport indicates he left Brazil again May 20. It does not say where he went.

Thank heavens for the wiretaps. "The real evidence is in the calls, not in the government's book." But their book does not list the exhibit numbers of the calls, so it is hard to look them up. Also, the book does not list all the calls. Nor does it always reproduce calls it does list in their entirety, which "may have been an attempt to make things more difficult for you."

So look at our first good clue, Exhibit #7337, the June 27, 1983, call on the Ganci tap. Joe Lamberti is talking to Ganci, and he says, "We have to meet." He is very anxious. He has already broken two appointments with "the doctor"—who could be Badalamenti. He says, "We should see to free . . ."

And Ganci interrupts. "Lookit, lookit! It will be freed tonight or tomorrow. That guy should come." Ganci is trying to calm him down.

But Lamberti's next words are important. "Look. We are stringing it out. It's already been three months! Later, he'll come by." Well, three months ago was March, just the time Randazzo left Brazil.

"Later, maybe, he could come by. And if we lose . . . you understand what will happen?" These are very strange words for a narcotics conversation. Now think, detectives. *Could* this "he" be Gaetano Badalamenti?

Ganci says, "He told you that they will be going over there." Where does he mean by "there"? To Sicily? Who is "he"? Randazzo?

For the first time in this trial, the two Lambertis and Mazzurco, who is holding his head in his hands, are fully alert. Pierre Leval is very intent. Burke is reading bits of conversations the jury has not heard before.

"Joe Lamberti says, 'If he [Badalamenti] says, Let's meet there, rather than here, what should we do?'

"Ganci replies, 'I don't know.' "

Burke pleads. "Take the *transcript!* Look at it!

"Joe Lamberti says, 'We always drag things out. And we are embarrassed. Because if we lose it—what will we do then?' "

Burke reads more of this "very important call" and interprets Lamberti's words to Ganci as meaning: This guy said he's coming sooner or later. And he wants to meet. But what do we do if he says, "Let's meet here, rather than there?"

"Ganci replies, 'I don't know.' "

Then, says Burke, there is a long pause, a real pause. Lamberti is truly anxious. This was left out of the book the government gave you. He says, "We always drag things out. And we are embarrassed. Because if we lose it—forget about it!" Is this drugs? No. At that time, the summer of 1983, New York was awash in drugs. That was the time the Zito deal was on.

Then Joe asks, " 'Then who will hear them? The others . . .' and he doesn't finish the thought, but Ganci knows what he is talking about."

Ganci may know, and so may Burke, but despite his very careful analysis, little if anything is coming clear. Sicilian obfuscation still prevails.

What do we know about the plans of the New York group? Burke asks. One, they "will meet *here,* not there. And if we lose it . . . the others."

We have clear evidence—airline reservations and conversations—that on June 30 Pete Alfano came to New York, received some money from Mazzurco, and returned home. The agents saw Mazzurco go to Ganci's house and get the money. Since they saw Ganci peel it off a roll of bills, it could not have been an immense amount. True, the agents lost Mazzurco on his way to La Guardia to hand over the cash. But that night "he tells Ganci that he met with the doctor's nephew," and "he left happy, and we should be seeing each other at the earliest."

Who is *we?* "I suggest it is Badalamenti."

Remember what Badalamenti said he was doing in Brazil in the summer of 1983? Remember that he and his family used phony passports and traveled to Europe to see his brother, who was very ill? Now, on July 19, Ganci calls Joe Lamberti again. *Again* this call is not numbered in your government guidebooks. What does he say? "You know the doctor from far away? He has to go over to *that* side." We know that "that side" means Europe. And Lamberti's reply? "We have to see what has to be done. We must let *him* know right away." The big mystery: Who is *him?*

Burke is still speaking very slowly and quietly. "It's July, 1983, and we have yet to hear one word about narcotics. Look at the *real* clues, not at the government's preposterous scenario."

In August Randazzo is in New York. August 7 Mazzurco tells this to Ganci. August 9 Mazzurco calls again, and says, "I talked to that guy. I put him off." In other words, says Burke, the New York group cannot figure out what Enzo and his uncle have on their minds. Mid-August, Alfano comes to New York, under a phony name, to meet with Enzo Randazzo, who never stays *anywhere* under his own name.

Next, in September, a very intriguing meeting, in Queens. Four people who are connected to Badalamenti—Alfano, Trupiano, Palazzolo, and Randazzo—the will-o'-the-wisp that no one knew was there. They meet with *Mazzurco.* We have pictures.

The prosecution theory is that the Badalamenti group is supplying bad things *to* the New York people, says Burke. He suggests that in reality the New York people are arming the Midwesterners in anticipation of an outbreak of Mafia war in the United States.

Well, you know now what happened. "They bring body suits— armored vests!—back to Illinois." The jury sits absolutely rigid.

At the next meeting, someone gives money to Randazzo. October 2 he drops out of sight here. October 3 he enters Brazil. It says so in his passport.

October 10 provides "a crucial clue . . . that is excluded from your charts," says Burke. Joe tells Mazzurco: "Yesterday they called me from the other side."

Sal asks, "Good or bad?"

Joe says, "Only to give their regards. They wanted to know if there's any news regarding him."

Sal says that everything possible is being done to stay close . . . and to always stay close. . . . But you know what shape he's in. Worse than a snake!

Burke spreads his hands. "Now, ladies and gentlemen, does that sound like a narcotics deal? No, it sounds like they are trying to stay close."

October 13, Mazzurco tells Alfano, the messenger, "Make a call to that guy, and tell him to talk to me."

Something is going on in Brazil in October 1983. Buscetta is arrested, along with Leonardo Badalamenti, Vito's younger brother, and both men have false IDs.

Next Mazzurco calls Sal Lamberti, who says, "I'm concerned that we're going to be suckered in by those who are more stupid than we are." What does this tell us? That there is *an essential lack of trust* between New York and the others.

November 29, Alfano calls Mazzurco. He hasn't heard anything. "I lost the line," that is, the code doesn't work any more. "It's midnight here," meaning, I'm in the dark. The TERMINUSA code has broken down.

December dawns. Still no evidence of drugs. Several futile efforts are made to get in touch with Badalamenti.

December 4, Alfano at home calls Mazzurco at home, and Mazzurco asks for Badalamenti's phone number. Alfano can't, or won't, give it. They talk about suits.

Alfano becomes exasperated, and says: "I'll put him in touch with you directly. I'm a pizza maker, not a tailor."

This has no meaning in a narcotics context. What it means is that Alfano's getting fed up with being the messenger, and will try to put Mazzurco, who owns a clothing boutique, in touch with the clothing importer, Enzo Randazzo, directly.

December 17, Mazzurco tells Sal Lamberti: "I spoke with Pete Alfano. I asked about the Uncle."

Lamberti says, "Hey! Let it be, young man."

Mazzurco gets defensive, and says, "Oh no, it was only natural. It came up in the conversation. It's nothing you should be concerned about. I wasn't making it look like we were prying. . . ."

Burke turns to the jury. "These communications indicate something's afoot—but not drugs. Badalamenti's main interest is in his own security!"

It is striking how careful and skillful Burke is being about not dumping on anyone else, especially not on the government, the FBI, or the DEA. His detailed presentation of what he says is the correct interpretation of the calls has been offered utterly without rancor.

Now it's February 1984, Burke continues. The Midwest taps begin. "Thank God they put those taps on then!" They show that what is in the mind of the New York group and what they say to others is not necessarily the same.

The taps in the Midwest, when Alfano speaks to his relatives there, are much more forthcoming. Those people reveal what's in their minds. Whereas in the New York-to-Brazil and New York-to-the-Midwest calls "it's parry, thrust, parry, thrust." Their speech is always guarded, clouded.

In early 1984 Pete Alfano becomes a human yo-yo between the Midwest and New York as he and Evola struggle to raise money in Michigan for Badalamenti. *"Thank God* it is the government taps which will tell you what was really going on!"

Kennedy has been listening carefully and taking notes. Lunch with the Badalamenti-group lawyers in the cafeteria is a wild scene. Benfante has been acting insane, pounding the walls and shouting, and is now in the men's room. His client, Mazzurco, the gem importer, is now enlarged to a warmonger in the Mafia wars.

Ruggiero is at pains to explain his *paisan* to the others: "Everybody's dumping on him—the judge, his client, other attorneys. He can't take it. He's cracking. They're all leaning on him."

Kennedy says, "He's got a short fuse."

Eleanore adds, "But why is he dumping on us? Trying to hurt us? He's gonna get up and destroy us!"

Kennedy says, "That's okay. The more *he* dumps on us, the better we look." He adds that Martin and the government are fond of Joe. "He's the court jester here."

Kennedy has a graver problem. Badalamenti has just told his lawyer he wants no summations given, none by Kennedy, none by Koppelman. "He's taking a dive. He won't last two months in an Italian jail, but he doesn't want to tell the world that he hid, that he fled from his enemies."

Taking the long view, Kennedy thinks his client sees it wrong. "If he doesn't plead, and if he's convicted of drugs here, his life is over."

The lawyers stroll out into the corridor. From the men's room, located in the stairwell at the end of the corridor, the ranting, raving voice of Benfante can still be heard. Moments later, when the upset lawyer reappears, Kennedy slings an arm around his beefy shoulders, and soon they are laughing together.

Burke's careful presentation continues all afternoon.

Middle of January, Mazzurco calls Joe Lamberti. "You remember that man we used to call 'the grandfather'? The guy down there? I read it in the Italian newspapers. They say perhaps some nephew of his killed him."

"Oh, good!" exclaims Lamberti, in English.

"I suggest, ladies and gentlemen, that there is far more afoot here than the prosecutor would have you believe." These calls are not on your charts because they suggest a completely contradictory view of the evidence.

By February there are urgent conversations about money. But it's clearly not drug money. The people in the Midwest are truly poor people, and they're trying to scrape together some money for the Old Man. They ask, How do we get the money to Badalamenti without exposing him?

February 8, Badalamenti calls the Lambertis direct, at the Al Dente pay phone. Alfano is unaware of this call. The Old Man first asks to speak to Joe Lamberti. He's told, "He's not here." That's a lie. Because the FBI sees him there at Al Dente. So you know that the two groups do not always tell the truth to each other.

Next Badalamenti tells Alfano, "Take some money to Fort Lauderdale." But canny Badalamenti has divided his confidential information among various people, so that no one person has the whole message. "One person knows the town, Fort Lauderdale. The other person knows the place, the Howard Johnson motel."

The government claims there is a fight over $10,000. They "claim that nobody wanted to travel to Florida because of this Cocilovo business—

which came into the trial as an afterthought." Cocilovo, incidentally, says Burke, was arrested way back in June 1983. "So why is it the meeting can't take place? It's not the $10,000, and it's not Cocilovo . . . [that's] not what this is about." It's about picking a place where they can have this meeting. "Not there but here," says Badalamenti. "No," says the other side, "I want it here, not there."

Enzo keeps calling, from Europe, asking for money. "He can't afford to pay his hotel bill." Burke shrugs, and spreads his hands. "Some drug dealers! These are little people, doing little jobs in the Midwest—and the proof is in the phone calls.

"The commodity was not drugs, but money, and the money was supposed to go to Badalamenti."

Burke is coming down to his grand finale. You hear Alfano's brother-in-law say, "Hey, Pete, did you hear about Augustinello? They got him in *Germany*. Not even in Sicily! Not even in Italy! Wow! Do you think they could cross the ocean?"

"In the beginning, the prosecutor told us that we would hear of millions of dollars coming out of pizzerias all over America. Well, look at it and ask yourself what *evidence* there is of millions of dollars coming out of that little man's store in Oregon, Illinois? There is none!

"It is wrong to put this case all in one big basket, with 5,000 ethnic Italian names thrown to the jury. It's wrong!"

In April Alfano went to Madrid. And someone followed Alfano, as Badalamenti had feared all along would happen.

But before Alfano flew to Madrid, he made a trip to New York. It was March 30. Mazzurco picked him up at the airport, and Cangialosi was there. They went to Pronto and met the two Lambertis. Cangialosi carried away a very important clue. . . .

When Alfano gets home, he tells Evola what happened. "I was there with all three—not Cangialosi, because Cangialosi is really nothing. I told them: Friends of mine, if you all say you love him, we have to show him." He is angry that things are not working. You jurors know from the evidence that Alfano has no idea what these New York people think of him, "that they call him an idiot . . . call him a jerk. He doesn't know that they say . . . after they have spent a day with him, 'I'm sick to my stomach with that guy.' "

At the meeting at Pronto, "Alfano says, 'If you love him, this is no way to treat him.' The question in his mind is: 'Will you find him, or not?' What he says is, 'What can I tell him? They love you, but they want to stay home?'

"What *they* is he talking about?" Burke's voice is cracking, his face reddens. "There are no narcotics records in the midwest—none! Pete Alfano is not a narcotics boss. Madrid is not a drug haven, but is a haven." His summation ends with his voice breaking with compassion for his poor-soul client.

In the corridor, the other Badalamenti attorneys urge Kennedy to pay no attention to Badalamenti's latest mad request—that he wants no summation. "Do it anyway!" they urge.

To do so, and defy his client, would be not guerrilla lawyering but Kamikaze lawyering.

"He didn't really mean it," says the wise Koppelman. "It was just a Sicilian gesture."

Dave Lewis now begins to sum up for Evola. It does not go well. "Ladies and gentlemen, you're tired," he begins. "And I'm scared." By the end of the afternoon, he has put four actual jurors, not alternates, fast asleep. It is only his tenth summation, and he really is scared.

The jury is sent home, and Leval announces his plans for deliberations. The jurors will be sequestered, and he wants to tell them the bad news soon. He is genuinely taken aback that the defense is still so strongly opposed to sequestration. "It's done in *every* case of this sort. In the state courts, it's required."

Paul Bergman is on his feet, containing his rage. "In a ten-day trial, you can expect two days' deliberation. In *this* trial, you're asking that the jury be sequestered two months! . . . There is *no way* this jury can begin to assemble and understand this evidence . . . in less than a month of deliberation." This surprise impassioned speech is Bergman's finest hour in sixteen months of trial.

Leval gives an inch, but no more. "I'm willing to say it's not a *fait accompli,* but a likely possibility."

"I'd say that's a distinction without a difference," says Fogelnest politely. In fact, it is just one more tiny increment of perhaps necessary hypocrisy from the bench. Leval facing this roomful of lawyers often finds himself in the posture of a lion tamer armed with only a chair and a whip.

Burke asks Judge Leval to remove the ever-sleeping female juror, #9, and put in an attentive alternate.

Martin says he does not think "apparent inattentiveness is real inattentiveness." He maintains that he and Freeh have never, ever discerned any juror "actually, totally asleep." When the twelve jurors and five remaining alternates reappear, Leval again courteously reminds them to stay alert.

It is now Larry Ruggiero's turn at bat. He asks his two clients to stand up, and tells the jury, "Trupiano is the one on the left." He says this knowing that no juror can identify either of these small, dark men. Some lawyers might have a difficult time of it.

In measured, scornful tones, Ruggiero tells the jurors they are "part of a historic case," not because it has gone on so long, but "because it is a deliberate attempt by the government to manipulate and destroy the famous presumption of innocence" that in our system cloaks every defendant. My clients have sat here sixteen months, they have lived for two and a half years, since their arrests, for fifty-three minutes of evidence against them. Why? Solely because they have a distant relative alleged to be a high-ranking Mafioso.

"*You* have sat here for 10 months before you heard the name Vitale . . . 12 months before you heard Trupiano!"

He begs the jury not to rely on the government's unfairly edited chartbook, but to look at the complete translations of the conversations. He has had blowups of these made and sets them before the jury on the easels. "Ask yourselves, why would the government *omit* crucial evidence which could show my clients' innocence?

"Because the government wants to *win.* They want it so much that they take a group of people, and a group of crimes, and put them together without ever specifying which person did what crime! Freeh in his summation said, 'The evidence . . . shows that the two defendants Vitale and Trupiano also became available and wait at the ready to make the trip to Florida in this case, which never comes.'

"Ladies and gentlemen, apparently my clients are being accused of 'ready and waiting.' "

It's "prosecutorial zeal" that makes the government edit phone conversations so as to *leave out* anything favorable to the defendant. The lawyer turns to his large pasteboards and reads aloud several conversations in full. They are difficult to follow, but Ruggiero explains that Trupiano is telling Pete Alfano about a man called Galbo, and about Alcamo, a town in Sicily. In the next conversation, Galbo, talking to Alfano, refers to someone called Agostino. "They went and cleaned him up there . . . after the day they took out that guy at Cinisi."

Ruggiero interprets. This Agostino Badalamenti, a nephew of Gaetano, has been murdered in Germany, "the day after somebody was murdered in Cinisi. I submit to you . . . that what has broken out . . . in Cinisi . . . and Alcamo . . . is a Mafia war. *That* is what's going on!" Mafia wars, he assures them, "are incredibly brutal, unlike anything you've ever imagined in your lives. . . . And when you come back from lunch we are going to see a little bit more of it."

After lunch, Ruggiero reads more conversations, which make clear there has been still another murder in Cinisi. As for the late Agostino Badalamenti, his murder could have been "revenge on his brothers, maybe," says Alfano.

"Unbelievable!" replies Trupiano. "Let's hope they don't come across the ocean!"

Alfano replies, "Just like they go over the ocean, so can others do." Ruggiero, who speaks Sicilian, interprets this clumsily translated bit as, "Just like they can *go* over the ocean, the people in Italy who are doing these things, the people in Europe—Germany—who are killing these people can *come* over the ocean.

"And the government has the nerve to claim this is a narcotics conversation!"

When the Palermo newspaper arrived, sent by Palazzolo's frightened Aunt Lia, the Midwesterners learned more. Agostino was "cut up piece by piece, and tortured."

Most of the absent first-string lawyers have returned for summation, intent on grabbing the spotlight for a few solo twirls meant to dazzle the jury, and the client, while the stunt lawyer sits in the shadows. But Genay Leitman is permitted to do her own summation, and it becomes her best moment. Slim, fresh, and outfitted in a becoming new purple frock, she keeps it simple and sweet.

Her client is not even related to the Swiss money launderer Vito Roberto Palazzolo; nor to Giralamo Vito Palazzolo, or Filippo Palazzolo, who have also been mentioned here. Emmanuele Palazzolo, "that sweet soul in the corner of this room," is the shy, slim man in the khaki jacket. She asks him to stand up. She tells the jury that his mother, aunt, brother, sister, and many nieces and nephews still live in Cinisi. They telephoned him about the Mafia murders there; they sent him the Sicilian newspapers. Emmanuele is terrified for the safety of his family. His aunt Lia warns him that the family phones are tapped in Cinisi, "and we learn finally that the American Badalamenti family is fearful that they might be the next victims, that the killers might cross the ocean.

"A check was found on Mr. Emmanuele Palazzolo. Well, let me tell you: Drug dealers don't write checks. Drug dealers don't rent cars with credit cards, as Emmanuele did. Drug dealers don't act like Hansel and Gretel and leave a trail of breadcrumbs."

Leitman seems near tears. She paraphrases Blackstone's *Commentaries on the Laws of England:* "It is better that ten guilty persons escape than that one innocent suffer."

She says, "When I first addressed you one and one half years ago
. . . I told you that Emmanuele, like many immigrants . . . came to
America because he believed in its values and he wanted to build a
better life. I ask you to show Emmanuele that this great country truly
is a country where freedom reigns, and justice prevails."

Robert Koppelman, Vito Badalamenti's lawyer, looks like a schol-
arly, handsomer Woody Allen. He has said almost nothing for sixteen
months, and there is no reason to anticipate that he will give the most
eloquent summation in this case. Vito, his pallor accentuated by his
dark red sweater, sits quietly at his father's side. The jury, too, is
attentive. Koppelman's long silence is paying off before he even opens
his mouth.

Vito Badalamenti is charged only in Count One of the indictment,
the lawyer explains. But the conspiracy he is charged with being a
member of is massive. "You have seen the charts; they were up here
for most of the trial." The massive conspiracy encompasses Swiss bank
accounts, Turkish and Bulgarian narcotics, drugs from Benny Zito,
drugs from Bagheria, $60 million, and big, known, Mafia-connected
drug names like Rotolo, LaMattina, Crespo, Aiello, Musullulu. "Now
Vito is not charged with just a part of that conspiracy, not charged with
just trying to help his father. He is charged with the whole thing!
. . . To find Vito Badalamenti guilty on Count One is to find him
criminally responsible for *everything.*"

Robert Stewart promised in his opening statement, Koppelman continues, that he would prove Vito operated out of Brazil negotiating drug
deals and delivering drugs. "What happened is exactly the opposite."
We all sat here for a year and a half, and we heard not one word against
him. "There is no testimony that he sold drugs, that he bought drugs,
there is no evidence that he agreed to buy or sell drugs, there is no
evidence that Vito was present when any such discussions occurred,
there is no evidence that has been presented in this case that Vito
Badalamenti possessed drugs, there is no evidence that he was present
when someone else possessed drugs, there is no evidence that he spoke
about drugs, there is no evidence that he passed a package to anyone
or received a package from anyone, there is no evidence that Vito had
drug records. He had no drug paraphernalia. There is no testimony that
he had a gun, or that he had huge amounts of money."

His voice appears in *none* of the thousands of hours of phone calls.
The evidence of this massive conspiracy is based mainly on the phone
conversations. How can you be a member of the conspiracy without
one word on the tapes?

353

There are many Vitos mentioned in this case: Vito Grimaldi, Vito Aiello, Vito Roberto Palazzolo, Giralamo Vito Palazzolo, Vito Randazzo. "Any number of Vitos. None of these are my Vito." He points to the pale young man. *"That* is my Vito."

By personalizing the name just the least bit, by his repeated references to "my Vito," Koppelman has begun subtly to mock and scorn these prosecutors. It gets worse when he mentions a piece of blue paper found in the Joe Lamberti search. On one side it bears Alfano's name and address and telephone number, and on the other side is written "Vito," and the telephone number of a lawyer in Brazil.

The government has insisted that the Vito on the blue paper is "my Vito." If they are right, they have tied the Badalamenti family much tighter to the guilty-seeming Lambertis and Mazzurco. But they are wrong, and Koppelman is able to prove to the jury that they *know* they are wrong. He shows them heaps of documents seized both in Madrid and in the United States, documents that show the full name of Badalamenti's nephew Enzo is Vincenzo Vito Randazzo, and that he frequently calls himself Vito, and lists himself in the Milan telephone directory as Randazzo, Vito. *This* Vito is the Vito on the blue paper, Koppelman demonstrates, and the government must have known as much all along.

"Didn't they *notice* any of these documents? [Pause] This is really very nasty stuff, because that young man's life depends on this." Then an acerbic aside. "You know, nobody likes to get up here, as Ms. Leitman said, and accuse government lawyers. For a couple of reasons. One, you don't like to think it's true. Two, most jurors don't want to believe it.

"But when it's there, you've got to do it.

"And . . . it . . . gets . . . worse." By now, all jurors and lawyers and defendants are wide awake, listening carefully.

Koppelman slowly lets it get worse, revealing as he does so a sure command of drama and pace. He has earlier handed out copies of the few conversations in which "my Vito" is referred to. "I'm not going to tell you Vito was not involved in some sort of Machiavellian intrigue," he acknowledges, and concedes, "It's obvious *something* is going on. But it has nothing to do with drugs." The government's pursuit of Vito Badalamenti "is an effort to save a sinking case. This case is sunk."

He asks the jurors to look at the conversation in which Alfano asks Gaetano Badalamenti, "But didn't I ask you . . . wasn't I supposed to go there, where your oldest son told me?"

Koppelmen first suggests to the jury that they take the statement at face value. If you accept it, if it's not code, or a slip of the tongue, what does it prove? Yes, it says "oldest son," and Vito is the older son. Leonardo Badalamenti is the younger son, though he is bigger than Vito. "This one sentence, these two words . . . out of hundreds of thousands . . . are supposed to convince you of something beyond a reasonable doubt?" This one sentence is supposed to make you forget that there's *no other* evidence against my Vito?

Of course it doesn't prove that. The courtroom has fallen utterly silent. One would like to see the prosecutors' faces just now, but all four are bent over their table, backs to the room. The jury is staring at Koppelman. Pierre Leval, also staring, makes a note, stops, then begins to write vigorously.

"But what makes it really bad is that this transcript does prove something"—not against him, not against my Vito—but "against them. If not *them,* against Agent Russo."

Koppelman now slowly, carefully demonstrates that Russo, the government's chief translator on this case, has translated the Italian words for biggest son as oldest son, in order to implicate Vito. The lawyer produces another translation of the same conversation, made by a different government translator, in which Alfano asks, "Wasn't I supposed to go there, where your biggest son told me?"

"How did they work this magic?" Koppelman's voice deepens. "How did biggest become oldest? How does a transcript that doesn't help their case become a transcript that does help their case? How do we, all of a sudden, out of the air, get a transcript that's a reference to Vito? It's easy—Agent Russo changes it." And not content with changing the question, he also changes the answer! He has Badalamenti reply, in English, "Yeah."

"Like he agrees it's the oldest son." But look at the non-Russo translation, by the other government translator. In that one the Old Man replies, not "Yeah," but "Eh?"

Koppelman glares. "Eh? becomes Yeah. Biggest becomes oldest, and now we *have* some evidence against Vito Badalamenti. It is a disgrace! You wouldn't send a dog to the pound on this kind of evidence." Juror #5, the young black data processor, shakes his head in open-mouthed disbelief.

"Whether you like Vito or don't like him, one thing you know. He is not a dog. He is a flesh-and-blood human being, just like the rest of us. If you cut him, he bleeds, just like the rest of us. And he's entitled to a fair trial, if nothing else."

Koppelman has brilliantly orchestrated his summation so as to show the jury the government making dumb mistakes, and then show them making deliberate mistakes, and finally show them falsifying evidence—all this to nail a young man who has already spent three years of his life in jail with no evidence against him.

Koppelman's summation is dramatic proof of something Ivan Fisher had said many, many months ago: Give them the truth and a jury will always recognize it.

It has lasted forty-five minutes. When recess is called, Vito's mother, in an aisle seat, is in tears. Each member of the family bends to whisper a word or pat her shoulder as they leave the courtroom. Eleanore Kennedy too is weeping. "If they don't vote not guilty for him, we're all sunk," she says. Ivan Fisher, from his great height, blows his nose.

"He walked him out!" Kaplan gasps with admiration. Leval, meanwhile, has walked off the bench looking like a man who has his tail between his legs, under his robes. He is an honorable man, and he seems ashamed.

In the corridor, other lawyers crowd around Koppelman to offer congratulations. His angular face is Old Testament stern as he tells them, "Pierre Leval *knows* Vito Badalamenti is only in this case for one reason: so the jury will compromise—let him go, and keep the father. Leval has known for three years that they had no evidence," he adds bitterly. "Read my Rule 29 motion. It's all there."

One pattern emerging in the defense summations is that almost everyone has props. The government of course has its AR 15 rifles, bundles of cash, and bags of heroin. Against these, the defense sets its homemade charts, special photographs, and substitute chartbooks, which give a different picture of the evidence from the massive government summaries. Bergman has a little cutout cardboard storm cloud, a whimsical reminder of a reference Stewart made to "defense storm clouds gathering."

Bergman's summation is soon wandering lonely and cloudlike from Long Island parking lots to Russo's translations to Amato's relationship with the Catalano family to Bonventre's Ferrari. It is authentic Bergman: Why use ten words when you can say it in ten pages? At one point he mentions "the Badalamenti importation." Although Kennedy's face cannot be seen, his back seems to tighten.

Day's end comes with Bergman's promise that tomorrow he will try to be brief. The jury would be more likely to believe him if he promised to saw off his own leg in front of them.

After court, the Midwest defendants gather at the foot of the courthouse steps to catch a couple of cabs uptown. Alfano and his wife, Palazzolo and his wife, Vitale and Trupiano and Badalamenti's niece Christine Evola are all heading back to the spartan Washington Square Hotel in Greenwich Village, where they have been staying for most of the trial. Since they cannot afford to dine in restaurants, they will stop at a deli on the way. Sam Evola is not with them. As the family translator, he has been summoned to MCC to work with Badalamenti and Kennedy on the summations.

Sixth Avenue in the heart of Greenwich Village is bustling with commuters rushing home, heads covered by wooly hats, faces scarved against the cutting February cold. The aroma of freshly ground coffee and cured meats wafts out to the street from Balducci's delicatessen. Pete Alfano emerges from the expensive gourmet shop carrying a big grocery bag of bread and cheeses and salami. The other defendants and wives straggle out behind him.

No one notices the red four-door Chevy pull up to the curb at the corner of Ninth Street. Alfano and his party are wandering south on Sixth Avenue. Two men step from the car. A burly man in a leather jacket comes up behind Alfano as he is walking past the Black Rock Cafe. Leather Jacket sticks a .38 revolver into the small of Alfano's back and fires three times. The gunman and his accomplice sprint around the corner onto Tenth Street as pandemonium breaks out behind them. People scatter in fear, traffic on Sixth Avenue screeches to a halt. Passers-by see the gunmen jump into the back of a blue van waiting on Tenth Street and speed off toward Broadway.

Two men lie on the ground. One bullet has lodged in Alfano's spine. Another has traveled through his body and struck Ronald Price, a passing transit worker, in the thigh. Within minutes, the first ambulance from nearby St. Vincent's Hospital arrives.

At MCC, Kennedy is deep in discussion with Badalamenti and Evola when Dave Lewis hurries in with the bad news. The Old Man takes it with absolute, stoic calm. The two lawyers head for St. Vincent's.

A small group of press photographers and reporters has set up camp outside the Emergency Room entrance of the modern hospital. A uniformed cop guards the doorway, and two detectives have taken up positions inside the waiting area. The other defendants and wives are being guarded in a protected waiting room on an upper floor.

Kennedy and Lewis feel certain the shooting is a direct result of the "war" defense. Badalamenti's enemies—either the Corleonese or their surrogates among the other Pizza defendants—have retaliated against the Badalamenti group. Kennedy phones the FBI and asks that the other Badalamenti-family defendants be placed in protective custody. Federal agents collect Evola, Trupiano, Vitale, and Palazzolo at the hospital and drive them to join the Old Man and his son in MCC.

At the Kennedy office, Eleanore Kennedy is worried. She has been unable to find Pat Burke, Alfano's lawyer. He has not arrived home. A call to his athletic club has proved fruitless. No one remembers seeing him at his parking garage. His wife learned of the Alfano shooting at 6:00 P.M. Over the past months, Jane Burke has heard Pat talk continually of Mafia wars and the murder of Tommy Mazzara, and by the time her husband pulls into his driveway, soon after 8:00 P.M., she is nearly distraught. Burke had spent the evening in an upper room of the New York Athletic Club, catching up on mail and writing to his eldest son. He knew nothing of the shooting.

It is after 10:00 P.M. by the time the Kennedys, Joe Calluori, and Bob Fogelnest sit down to a late-night meal in a Third Avenue café. Fogelnest is convinced that the shooting of Alfano is a message, a warning to Kennedy to halt the war defense. He thinks Michael's life may be in danger and urges him to refuse to continue with the case. Eleanore also sees it as a warning, but she supports her husband's decision to continue. Later, at home, she and her husband will debate for hours the wisdom of having asked for protective custody for the Badalamenti group.

. . . THURSDAY, FEBRUARY 12, 1987.

THE COURTROOM. The air crackles with apprehension and nervous excitement, just as on the day of the Mazzara killing. Reporters, TV sketch artists, and relatives fill the spectator benches. All defendants wear scarily perfect poker faces. It is not wrong to imagine that the previous night's shooting was ordered by someone in this room.

Leval looks shaken. The newspapers and TV are full of the story. His main concern is the jury. He did all he could to diminish the impact on them. The moment Martin called last evening and told him of the shooting, he ordered the marshals and his clerks to make contact with every juror and alternate and warn him or her not to watch TV, read a newspaper, or talk to another juror. One juror was at the movies, in a theater only a few hundred yards from the shooting, and had to be paged—by name.

"Hey, Judge!" It's Kennedy, shouting through the doorway. He is trying to push past the marshals attempting to stop him from bringing newspapers into the courtroom. "Can I bring in these newspapers?" He is defiant, purple with fury. Leval signals for him to come ahead.

The judge proposes this morning to question each juror individually about what he or she has heard. Not good enough! Kennedy demands a mistrial. "It is impossible to proceed in an atmosphere of fear, intimidation and chill. I feel it personally . . . so do some colleagues. And some defendants.

"The war that we have been talking about as a somewhat abstract proposition . . . has in fact entered this courtroom and filled this courtroom with death, blood and gunshots. . . . I ask your Honor to, regrettably, declare these proceedings at an end."

Burke adds, "It's a real fear, your Honor, and it's one engendered . . . by the fact that so many disparate people from so many disparate groups have been brought together in one forum to test their criminality for so long."

Leval polls the lawyers. All but one want a mistrial. The holdout, Bergman, proposes that every other defendant be severed, leaving him alone to go one-on-one with Martin.

Koppelman adds that courthouse security has been beefed up to the point where the place looks like an armed camp. Dozens of new agents and marshals have appeared. A fair trial in this martial atmosphere is impossible.

The greatest concern is the jury. Leval agrees to admit a committee of lawyers to his chambers while he voir dires each juror individually. When he reports back to the courtroom, his hands are shaking. After the judge's report, Kennedy, as a member of the defense lawyers' committee, officially requests additional voir dire of four jurors. #3 is the one who was at the movies. His mother has been fearful of his safety ever since hearing that his name was broadcast on the theater's public-address system. #4 saw a headline, MOB HIT. "Both words as significant as anything I could imagine," says Kennedy. #7 feels "personal concern." The obese #10 has heard "They killed another one."

Leval agrees to ask the additional questions, "assuming, as I think is extremely likely . . . that trial will proceed," but he would first like to hear from the government.

Martin wants the jury sequestered. Otherwise daily voir dire might become necessary. The press uproar can be expected to continue. The jury must be protected from "non-evidence and speculation," particularly so close to the end of the trial. To sweeten the pill, they can be told that the trial will be accelerated during the time they are locked up, and the end will come sooner. The government asks the court to "tell the jury that Pete Alfano is hospitalized as the result of an injury or incident that has nothing whatsoever to do with this case." Hollow gallows laughter from spectators and defense lawyers; not a sound from their clients.

Ivan Fisher opposes sequestration. It would reinforce the untoward idea that the jury is in physical danger. Nor is Catalano's primary interest, at this point, a speedy trial. Fisher cannot recall a single paragraph in all four government summations that did *not* mention his client's name. Catalano is entitled to, and expecting, a lengthy summation.

Burke objects that Alfano has a right to be here. He asks Leval to sever his client, and tell the jury his severance has "nothing to do with their determination of the guilt or innocence of the others."

Fogelnest points out that now the government wants to sequester, but when the defense sought limited sequestration, after the Mazzara hit, the government was opposed. These jurors were told originally that they were anonymous to protect them from the media. If the court immediately sequesters them after the Alfano hit, they will interpret it as protection from another source, and that would undoubtedly "prejudice the defendants."

Bergman advises: Do precisely what you did when Mazzara was killed. Tell them "exactly what happened," coupled with a very strong instruction to avoid any media exposure. Judge Duffy did this at the time of the murder of Big Paul Castellano, and the Court of Appeals approved.

Benfante says sequestration "communicates danger." We need a cooling-off period, especially in view of the defense arguments under way right now, summations "which are actually pointing to a New York group as having an ulterior motive other than drugs to talk over the telephone between two continents . . . a motive . . . to set up the other defendants in the case for a hit." Benfante has just laid out the Kennedy/Burke charges against his own client, Mazzurco, more clearly than they have ever before been articulated. His point is that the Alfano ambush validates those very arguments.

Kennedy has heard enough. He sees a plum opportunity to fault Leval, and will take full advantage. "At the time of the Mazzara hit, we asked for limited sequestration" because of media contamination. The court denied it. "Now we see the government talking out of the other side of its enormous mouth," and the obvious reason, as Kennedy formally stated in his letter to the court written late last night, is the known fact that sequestered jurors are always more likely to convict.

Martin responds that the Mafia war is not *evidence,* only argument. The defense has sought a mistrial to strengthen its argument; but if it doesn't get it, it wants the court to tell the jury something that is not evidence. In effect, the defense is asking the court to bolster its own argument. Worse—and here is the real zinger, the real proof that Martin knows his man—if the jury is not sequestered today, the defense will argue on appeal that the media-generated prejudice was so strong that a mistrial should have been granted. And who knows what wild things tomorrow's press, or the next day's, may say?

Lewis stands. "Your Honor, it really boggles my mind that the government, which has been pumping out the canard that heroin has been distributed through pizza parlors . . . *as late as yesterday* . . . is now so worried about what the press is going to say." Sequestration would help the government win convictions, not through evidence, but through increasing the climate of fear. Furthermore, "I can tell you from my contacts with . . . the DA's office last night that they think this shooting may indeed be related to this case, and were pursuing that theory as of 1:00 A.M. this morning."

Leval replies that sequestration is far more appropriate now than at the time of the Mazzara murder, when it was "universally" requested by the defense. Now, the trial's end is in sight, and he would hold court weekends, and there's a good chance the trial would end in a week or two.

Kaplan interrupts, seeming near tears. "The facts have been misstated." He led the prosequestration fight after Mazzara, whose partner is his client. Then, the jury was ignorant, and "your Honor summarily rejected the idea of sequestration." This time the cat is out of the bag! How can you compare them?

Koppelman adds, "You have told us over and over how wonderful this jury is. They never read the papers, they never listen to the radio, they are going to forget everything they have been instructed not to hear, because you tell them to do so." What's changed?

After a brief recess, Leval says he has considered all the suggestions, and "I am convinced the correct action for me to take is to sequester the jury."

Kennedy at once asks, "Will you say it is at the request of the government?"

"I will tell them it is my decision." Whether to hold court on weekends will be their decision.

Martin gets the last word. "Some defendants are in protective custody already. The government is moving to remand the remaining defendants for the protection of the defendants. Also to prevent flight—which we think an even greater risk now than before. One, we're very near the end of the trial. Two, some defendants may be especially concerned by the shooting of Alfano."

Outside, tiny snowflakes continue drifting down. Leval's deliberations on whether to sequester or not must be considered in light of the fact that he almost certainly has been informed by Martin that three suspects in the shooting are about to be arrested, and that Giuliani will be holding a press conference. So he knows that even more sensational news is about to hit the screens and papers.

There is no court on Friday, February 13. To minimize the pressure on all hands, Leval has wisely given the jurors a day off to pack bags and make the necessary arrangements to be absent from their homes for some days. Court will reconvene Saturday morning, and Saturday evening the jurors and alternates will be taken to the undisclosed hotel where they will be housed, under the close supervision of the federal marshals, until after they have reached their verdict. Court will be held again on Sunday, with an hour or two off for those jurors who wish to attend religious services.

Friday morning, Giuliani's office announces a press conference at 4:00 P.M. Reporters learn then that the FBI has earlier arrested three suspects in the Alfano shooting. Frank Bavosa, of Newark, New Jersey, has admitted taking part in the ambush. The fat man who fired the shots was Philip Ragosta, thirty-three, of Brooklyn. The third man on the street that night was Giuseppe Amico. All were picked up in early-morning raids.

Rudolph Giuliani stands at the podium, Tom Sheer at his side, and says with unabashed delight, "Another myth has been shattered about the mob, that they can do these hits and get away with it. . . . The rules are changing."

But changing rules had nothing to do with it. That the FBI was able to solve the case so quickly was a kind of gift from Tommy Mazzara. The weekend Mazzara disappeared, Leval, at Martin's request, had issued bench warrants for ten defendants. Pete Alfano and Sam Evola had escaped arrest only because they had gone home for the weekend, and such a move would have kept them locked up in Michigan during possible trial time. But the FBI was taking no chances. Sunday afternoon, they shadowed the two men to Chicago's O'Hare Airport, and another FBI surveillance team was waiting at Newark Airport when they landed. This team followed the defendants' car on the twenty-six-mile haul to Manhattan, and at one point noticed that a blue Cadillac was also following. When everybody reached the Washington Square Hotel, the mysterious blue Cadillac, with three men inside, lingered at the door to watch Alfano and the other Midwest defendants check in. As the FBI closed in, the Cadillac sped off and disappeared in traffic. But the FBI had noted the license number. The Cadillac had been rented at Newark Airport by a Frank Bavosa, of Roselle Park, New Jersey. The FBI checked out the house and spotted Bavosa's blue van parked nearby.

When the news broke that Alfano's shooters had fled in a blue van, the FBI arrested Bavosa, raided his home, and discovered a 9 mm pistol and ammunition. Bavosa confessed to his part in the shooting, and gave the names of Philip Ragosta and Giuseppe Amico, who lived in Bay Ridge, Brooklyn. In Ragosta's home, still another team of agents discovered two notes. One said, "The end is very near! Believe me!" On the other was scribbled the figure 40,000. Bavosa told the FBI that the three men had been hired by a third party to carry out the hit for the sum of $40,000. As for Bavosa's blue van, the agents found it parked a few blocks from Amico's house.

The FBI also had evidence that, back on November 28, Bavosa had traveled to Oregon, Illinois, and had checked out the Alfano family's pizzeria. From at least mid-November then, perhaps earlier, someone had gone to a lot of expense to stalk and try to kill Pete Alfano.

At the end of Giuliani's news conference, Sheer hints that the FBI has information on the organizer of the hit.

That evening, Benfante calls Di Chiara to say he has been approached by a lawyer who throws a lot of work his way. Would he care to represent Philip Ragosta? Benfante does not, but he wonders if Di Chiara wants the case?

"Are you crazy?" Di Chiara can scarcely believe his ears.

Next morning Benfante calls the Kennedy office to tell the lead counsel that his associate Joe Candia had represented one of the hitmen at arraignment, but that Candia has decided to withdraw from the case. Mario Malerba's office then takes on representation of Ragosta.

Late Friday evening Burke returns to the hospital and finds his client in bad shape. A bullet is lodged in his spine, and any attempt at removal could be life-threatening. Pietro Alfano is expected to live, but he is permanently paralyzed from the waist down.

... SATURDAY, FEBRUARY 14, 1987.
THE COURTROOM.   Paul Bergman proves the perfect shock absorber for the Alfano trauma. His droning, meandering arguments soon throttle everyone back to Pizza pace. Eyes droop, heads drop. Midmorning he announces, "Getting back to Sigmund Freud," and a few attentive heads shake; has he mentioned Sigmund Freud before? And in reference to whom? Wasn't he speaking about "What is the evidence?" Bergman mercifully winds up his remarks on that subject, begging the question: If there is no evidence, why this gargantuan defense?

In the afternoon, the jury gets a rare opportunity to meet Steven Kimelman, absentee lawyer for Giovanni Ligammari. Throughout the sixteen months of trial, the poet/stunt lawyer Carol Novack has sat faithfully taking notes, occasionally objecting, dutifully trotting up to the side bar. Today her boss takes over the center ring. Kimelman has a snappy, precise delivery. He is clearly a seasoned legal veteran, but he has no sense of Pizza metaphysics, and his timing is an affront to Pizza sensibilities. This Ship of Fools has been at sea for many moons; the journey is almost at an end. Kimelman is like the celebrity with the house seats who pushes past the queued-up public outside a hit Broadway show.

Once inside, he shows no more delicacy. Ligammari's lawyer dumps on everyone. "Ligammari didn't stand by the phone. *He* didn't attend meetings. *He* didn't travel to Italy. Ask the government to show you *his* bulletproof vest. He had nothing."

The performance style of each lawyer is different, and often surprising. Marvin Schechter speaks for Salvatore Lamberti in a lyrical, birdlike tweet. He punctuates his predictable narrative of misunderstood phone calls and sloppy surveillance with swooping sounds, silly faces, stiff, corny gestures, and eyebrows awaggle, like a ham actor. His client, the man Badalamenti calls the second-highest-ranking Mafioso in the world, listens to his lawyer with one stubby-fingered hand splayed over his pale face like a starfish gripping a chunk of coral. Schechter has an evangelical manner, and little gift for summarizing. He burrows through it all again—the Brazilian phone calls, the instructions to Mazzurco, the Pronto meeting—and comes out the other side, almost three days later, with voice roughened, nerves shot, and the jury catatonic.

Another lawyer says sadly, "He is married to a public-relations executive who has convinced him that he knows absolutely every detail of this case, and that he has the unique ability to explain it to the jury. He started off well, good jokes, patient, slow delivery, but has become hysterical and is now in some sort of fugue state."

. . . TUESDAY, FEBRUARY 17, 1987.

THE COURTROOM. Now the jury must hear from the embattled, scorned, spat-upon Joseph Benfante. Speaking slowly and pacing thoughtfully, he begins by thanking Judge Leval "for being gracious enough not to leap on me from the bench." Then he thanks each of his brother attorneys by name. "Great move!" whispers Fisher.

He turns to the jury. "I'm told you have nicknames for every one of us. I don't want to know mine—or I'd probably never practice law again." This brings forth much tittering from a jury that for months has referred to him as "Goodbody Nobrain." Thanks to the marshals, the whole courthouse knows about it, including, almost certainly, Benfante, who has just brilliantly made the nickname work *for* him. His entire summation will follow the same pattern: Find a way to make the bad stuff you're stuck with operate in your favor.

After a long, soft, flattering opening, his voice hardens. "This is a trial of our 200-year-old legal system. Shouldn't we be able to remember individual witnesses? Be able to remember individual testimony? This is a trial that tests due process!"

Then he mocks it. "If I were Rudy Giuliani, I'd hire three experts in paleontology and archaeology, tell 'em to go to darkest Africa, show me where the first *Mafioso* was born. I'd tell the jury—you're gonna be here five years! The Darwinian theory of the Mafia. The first code words . . ."

The jury is already smiling fondly when he says, "If this is the longest criminal trial in federal history, I gotta get credit for being the most destroyed lawyer that ever was!" Bigger smiles from the jury. Modest dimpling from Benfante.

"I've been on the Pizza case three years! My daughter's only five! . . . I've probably been overruled more times than Ronsisvalle." Leval does not laugh, nor Mazzurco; but the rest of the room is loving this.

His summation is near-inept, wanting in coherence, lacking in style—exactly what the jury expects from Benfante/Mazzurco. "What did I do wrong? I could be a mummy from all the Band-Aids I took in this case! . . . But they let Benny Zito get *away*. With $625,000! He's probably on some beach, with chorus girls. Ganci's dead. And I'm here, stuck with this case!" Uproarious laughter.

"Mr. Tomasso Buscetta tells you Gaetano Badalamenti had nothing to do with drugs. *So what are we all doing here?*" Stronger laughter. Benfante has said all the things the other lawyers wanted to say, but didn't dare. A brave lawyer with nothing to lose, like Benfante, gains a paradoxical advantage: total credibility.

Tony Lombardino wears a florid red silk kerchief in his breast pocket, and his horn-rimmed half-glasses bobble almost at the tip of his bulbous nose. His summation on behalf of Joe Lamberti seems designed to give the client his money's worth; it is orotundity and bombast writ large. He tells "this incredible" jury that they are now twelve judges, and swiftly invokes images and events from God to Shakespeare ("The first thing we do, let's kill all the lawyers." —*King Henry VI, Part II*, Act IV, scene 2) to George Washington to World War II to the Inchon landing. In the course of this, he lays a very heavy burden on this jury. More than any previous attorney, Lombardino batters away at each juror's individual responsibility for his client's future liberty. But one sees very little reasonable doubt in these seventeen faces, the only seventeen people in this room who do not know that the shadow of Mafia war is present in the courtroom today, as surely as the ghosts of George Washington and General MacArthur.

The lawyer describes his client as a successful businessman who lives quietly with his wife and three daughters in a modest home in Baldwin, Long Island. He owns part of Pronto Demolition, Roma Imports, and Upskate. "Joe Lamberti's problems started when he met Joe Ganci. . . . Ganci is a drug peddler, no doubt about it." In short, the "not me, it's the other fellow" defense, with the other fellow safely dead. At regular intervals, between spurts of rhetoric—"a mad, rabid dog running down Pearl Street doesn't deserve to be convicted on this kind of evidence!"—the jury guilt-trip theme reappears.

"Mr. Stewart, who is writing as I speak to you, may say to you, 'I made a mistake.' But four or five days later, you can't call Judge Leval and say: 'Judge, I made a mistake, because the *prosecutor* made a mistake.' It will be [the big voice drops to a hoarse whisper] . . . just . . . too . . . late. . . ."

He picks up a copy of the government's thick chartbook. "Don't *go by* this bag of tricks!" He smashes it onto the podium. "Close that book and throw it away!"

Why did these defendants use public phones? The real reason? "Mr. Badalamenti had fled Sicily. There was upheaval over there. Is it so hard to believe that bloodshed was occurring? Is it so hard to believe that these guys shoot people? . . . So hard to believe that just maybe Joe and Sal Lamberti were just scared stiff, and they didn't want no phone calls coming to their house?"

Recess. Lombardino, a chain smoker, has his cigarette lit before the last juror is out of the room. As Catalano passes the seated Badalamenti, he nods a formal Sicilian good morning, as if they were meeting in church. Rumor has it that Catalano may be remanded by the end of the day, because of further developments in the case against Alfano's would-be assassins. Martin is pushing for it.

Lombardino goes back to work. At 10:45 A.M. Freeh checks his wristwatch and exits briskly. He is due in a downstairs courtroom to appear for the government in the arraignment of Patsy Conte, Sr., on charges of contract murder in the Alfano shooting. Representing Conte will be Malerba's associate, Manny Moore. This same Patsy Conte has been a shadowy background figure throughout the Pizza trial. He is the uncle of the man who hit Ronsisvalle in a traffic accident on Knickerbocker Avenue. He is also the man Catalano and Ganci stopped to visit in October 1981 on their way to have lunch with the head of the New York Mafia Commission, Big Paul Castellano. FBI agents have testified that Amato and Bonventre frequently were seen hanging around outside Conte's big Knickerbocker Avenue supermarket.

Now Conte is charged with the Alfano hit. To appreciate the ruthlessness and scope of the Mafia war, if indeed Mafia war is behind the Alfano shooting, the jury needs to know this. But they sit in the box like a dozen eggs, cocooned in innocence, swaddled in ignorance.

At 11:00 A.M. Manny Moore slips into the courtroom and speaks softly to Malerba, both men holding their hands over their mouths. Tony Lombardino is still busy trying to defuse the evidence of Joe Lamberti's phone calls and his stealthy dockside meetings. Meanwhile, Catalano leans forward to confer first with Malerba, then with Moore. Patsy Conte, Sr., is a close, long-time associate of Sal Catalano.

In the recess Eleanore says, "If Catalano gets remanded today, we're going to reopen the case." Malerba is in a huddle with Bucknam. Lewis is saying, "Sal Catalano doesn't *have* to be involved. He gets his piece either way. That's what being a boss means—you have to do very little." Other lawyers say that Lewis believes it is the Lambertis, not Catalano, who are behind the Alfano shooting.

Fisher asks Kennedy to ask his client whether it would be okay for him to argue to the jury "Badalamenti has an aide, Alfano. Catalano has no aide." It is not okay.

Two floors beneath Pierre Leval's chambers is the small courtroom of Judge Nina Gershon. Today it is packed with press. Manny Moore has left Malerba and Fisher on duty in Pizza, and come downstairs to this court to represent the firm's newest client. Now fifty-four, Patsy Conte, Sr., is the son of a Sicilian grocer who developed his father's business into the family empire—twelve supermarkets in the New York area. He is also a director of the huge Key Food Supermarket chain, which controls seventy-eight supermarkets in the five New York boroughs.

The squat, bespectacled man with dark hair and a toad face was arrested as he was about to board a plane for his holiday home in Puerto Rico. Now he is being arraigned on federal murder-for-hire charges, namely, that he "ordered and directed" the shooting of Pete Alfano. The government claims Conte offered a $40,000 contract to wipe out Alfano: $10,000 to each of the hitmen, and $10,000 for expenses.

Kennedy, a master of the inventive defense, could not have come up with a better scenario to illustrate and illuminate the shadowy progress of the Mafia war. But the law requires that the Conte case be kept forever separate from the Pizza case, lest it prejudice the case against defendant Catalano by shredding his presumption of innocence. So the Pizza jury will never hear that the attempted murder of one defendant has now been linked, by the government, to another defendant on the opposite side in the Mafia war.

Moore pleads Conte "not guilty," and the judge rules that he be held at MCC to await a bail hearing. A few hours after Conte is arraigned, Giuliani once more joins Tom Sheer at the rostrum of the FBI's press-conference room. Sheer displays ten weapons seized from the Conte mansion on Long Island. Giuliani describes the close personal Conte-Catalano connection. The reporters write it all down. Next day the *Post* front page screams SUPERMOBSTER! The story says Conte packs his garbage in Gucci shopping bags.

So far, no government official is prepared to comment on what motivation may have lain behind the shooting.

2:32 P.M. It is time for Ivan Fisher's summation. Catalano, leaning forward for a last-minute chat with his attorney, looks more animated than ever before. "Here comes Henny Youngman," murmurs Kennedy when Fisher gets to his feet.

Government arrogance is Fisher's theme. "Has it occurred to you, ladies and gentlemen," that Contorno and Dick Martin had never met "when Mr. Salvatore Catalano was yanked out of his home and made a defendant in this case? . . . And has it occurred to you . . . that Mr. Ronsisvalle had not yet come up with the notion that it was Mr. Catalano who produced Mr. Tartamella who with a red Porsche filled with heroin [sic] when Mr. Catalano was yanked from his home and arrested . . ." Fisher is saying that Contorno and Ronsisvalle did not become government witnesses until months after the April 9 arrests. But the lawyer's delivery is so breakneck that his point may well be lost on the jury. He asks the same question about Amendolito. He is pacing wildly, taking the full width of the courtroom, from the jury rail to the translators' booth, making himself a human pendulum. Jurors #3, 5, 7, and 8 appear mesmerized.

"Mr. Catalano was not in the farmhouse in Bagheria. It was *said*. It wasn't a mis-*take*. It was a *lie*. Mr. Catalano never . . . delivered to Tartamella a red Porsche with heroin. That was *said*. It was not accurate. It is a *lie*." A rhythmic beat is established.

"Mr. Salvatore Catalano did not meet, greet and hand over $1.5 million to Salvatore Amendolito. . . . It was *said*. It is not accurate. It is a *lie*."

Fisher is now pacing backward, as well as forward, never turning his face and body away from the jury. "I'm not here to wage the great wars others seem to want to wage. I want to focus on discrete, limited issues . . . the ones in the indictment. . . . I'm leaving out Mafia-ness. . . ."

This sounds like a swipe at the Badalamenti group, Kennedy in particular. Fisher's tone of voice is rising, becoming shrill, and his pacing has increased. He is talking about Ganci's garage, and how he keeps it stocked with cartons. The government suggests these are cartons of drugs, or money. In fact, they are Ganci's favorite, indeed, only, beverage—imported Fiuggi mineral water. Except that Fisher calls it Fiuggi criminal water. Twice.

Fisher's summation has become overkill, a Niagara of words, cascading and splashing from a great height, free-flowing, difficult to follow, benumbing in length. It lasts, not ten minutes, but all the next day. Three moments stand out. One concerns Contorno. "He repeatedly lied to you. . . . It would behoove a man like that to be absolutely *straight!* But he was absolutely a pretzel, a real warp-job. This is a desperate man . . . in a terrible, terrible fix. He got on the wrong side of some terrible

battle over there. He was connected with the Stefano Bontate family
. . . on the losing side," in the Mafia war, and the Corleonese were
shooting at him, trying to kill him. There was a price on his head. Even
in prison he would not be safe.

Several jurors are asleep before 11:00 A.M. They return from recess
carrying coffee containers. Fisher, who knows he's losing it, but is too
keyed up to stop, says, "It appears I've driven you all to drink. Please
don't let the lacklustre quality of my performance let you not pay
attention. . . . Please, please, please get what I'm saying." But it grows
harder and harder to do so.

The second moment is when Fisher tells the jury that each time
Ronsisvalle has testifed for the federal government, the prosecutor has
written to the New York State Parole Commission urging early release
in return for Ronsisvalle's "cooperation." When he testified in Miami
before the President's Commission on Organized Crime, the chief government lawyer wrote to the Parole Commission. When he gave information to the FBI in 1979, Special Agent Trahan wrote the letter.

"He comes up to the Southern District of New York and agrees to
give testimony. And what happens? A letter from the United States
Attorney himself, Rudolph Giuliani, to the New York State Parole
Commission . . . for the purpose of persuading them to let this guy out
early! Do you think Mr. Giuliani asked him first, 'Listen, Luigi, have
you recovered from your penchant for killing people? I mean, is it okay
now for us to let you out? Would it be responsible on my part to put
you in the [Witness Protection] program, where no one even knows
what your name or your background is?' . . . Do you get what's involved
when the United States Attorney . . . writes a letter to the . . . Parole
Commission on Luigi Ronsisvalle's behalf [despite] the man's agreement to kill one of his own assistants!" *This* is the arrogance of power
that Fisher had begun his summation by talking about.

In the corridor, Catalano is huddled with a brassy blonde in short
skirt and red stiletto-heel pumps. On closer inspection, she turns out
to be Mrs. Catalano, the same woman who appeared before this jury
looking like a nun in mufti, a Sicilian mouse.

Burke is telling other lawyers that yesterday he formally asked Judge
Leval to reopen the defense case, on the basis of new evidence that
defendant Alfano had been targeted for death, and the FBI knew it but
had failed to warn him.

This afternoon Burke intends to pay a quiet call on Tom Sheer and
try to find out why he and his client were not tipped off to the fact that
for the past several months Alfano was being stalked by a would-be

assassin. The FBI has interior guidelines that require them to do this, says Burke. If the story about the Bovasa surveillance proves true, "Pete Alfano has a helluva civil damage suit!"

Fisher spends hours attacking the Amendolito testimony. For a finale he places two tiny stereo speakers on the jury rail and replays the FBI tape on which Amendolito describes the man named Sal who gave him the $1.5 million on a Queens street corner.

He was, "tall and skinny, not muscular, wearing a T-shirt." Fisher shows the jury a Catalano wedding picture. "This is how the tall, skinny guy looked . . . in Palermo when he got married. Please note his skinny double chin."

He turns to his client. "Would you step forward, please?" Catalano slouches toward the jury box. Fisher tells him to remove his jacket, tie, and shirt. Abashed, Catalano strips down. "This is what *this* guy looks like!" The jury sees a beefy, slope-shouldered man wearing an undershirt and a sheepish grin. In the spectator section, Mrs. Catalano bursts into tears. The humiliation is too much to bear.

As for Fisher, he seems on the brink of coming unglued. His hands tremble as he reaches to gather his exhibits. His tirade is dissolving into garble. By now it is all showmanship, and very little coherent theory. In the spectator section, Fisher's assistant is drowsing. Let us mercifully draw the veil.

. . . FRIDAY, FEBRUARY 20, 1987.

THE COURTROOM. The Kennedy-prepared chartbooks for the Badalamenti summation do not please the prosecutor. Martin raises a terrible fuss about having received the 150-page books less than an hour ago. Kennedy explains that his tiny staff has just finished making them. The job had kept them up all night for three nights, after working twelve straight days. In any event, the books contain nothing but excerpted transcript, in proper sequence. "Had we had a weekend . . ." The source of the time pressure, everyone realizes, is the sequestered jury.

Martin cries, "Unfair! . . . Your Honor, every page has something on it we would object to." Leval suggests Kennedy Magic Marker out the government's objections. These turn out to be such pernicious phrases as "Mr. Kennedy: Thank you." and "The Court: Overruled."

It is sandbox-level harassment, a calculated attempt to get the Badalamenti summation off to a poor start. Kennedy endures the nit-pickery without complaint, and for a time the courtroom falls silent except for the *skr-e-e-e-e-k* of Magic Marker inking out the offending phrases.

10:12 A.M. The jurors enter, bright-eyed, carrying coffee mugs. "We have come a long way together," Kennedy tells them, since first he spoke of the tangled web. At one point he sat nine months without uttering a single word, silently awaiting one piece of evidence about the charges against his client. Badalamenti is charged with conspiring to deal drugs, and with maintaining a continuing criminal enterprise to deal drugs—the dread 848 count. But the total evidence against him comes down to five phone conversations "of a highly mysterious nature. That's it."

Kennedy is searching for ways to describe this trial. It's like what happens when you explode a neutron bomb. It destroys all living things, and leaves only buildings and inanimate objects. "That is what was happening here. Humanity was being blown out of this courtroom." The trial was also glacierlike, moving "imperceptibly . . . forward, crushing everything in its sight. Chilling everything in its sight. Numbing everything in its sight." Only you, the jury, can bring some humanity and warmth back into this room.

He will talk to them for about three hours, "an hour of your time for every year that Gaetano Badalamenti has been in jail."

Among the hundreds of law-enforcement people from three continents who testified here, the only ones who accuse Gaetano Badalamenti of dealing drugs are these four gentlemen. He nods toward the prosecutors, then walks backward, maintaining eye contact with the jury until he reaches the blackboard. On it, he writes DANGEROUS DANCE. "When Gaetano Badalamenti is speaking on the telephone," he says, "it is clear . . . that no matter what he is *saying*, something else is going on." That something else is the dangerous dance.

Let me begin at the beginning, Kennedy says. Badalamenti said at the outset he was not guilty. "I am not a drug dealer. I didn't intend to deal drugs. I didn't agree to deal drugs. I didn't conspire to deal drugs. I didn't encourage others to deal drugs. . . . I did none of those things."

Certain other things he did not contest. He said that is my voice on the phone conversations of January 20 and of February 8, 9, 14, and 19. These people are my family. As to the Mafia, I do not admit it, I do not deny it, I do not contest it. Mafia is not the charge here.

"Come back with me now, to the mid-1970s," Kennedy says, like an impresario flourishing before his hand-picked audience of twelve the printed program of the evening's events. His client listens intently, brows knit.

"Gaetano Badalamenti is head of the Commission of the Mafia, '75, '76, '77. He is expelled in '77, '78. He is forced into exile." The Mafia war is on—not war "over the control of drugs, as the prosecutors will probably try to convince you. It is a war between those who are opposed to drugs within the Mafia, and those who want to deal drugs and get the money." Mr. Badalamenti unfortunately is on the side of the losers. He goes into exile with his immediate family, and they take on a new name and identity. Others of his family are being killed in Europe. Uppermost in his mind is to protect his wife and sons, and also the American wing of his family.

"It is from this beginning that the dangerous dance starts. . . . He decides upon a plan." What are his resources? He knows that a boyhood friend and neighbor, Salvatore Lamberti, has quite recently, in 1982, emigrated from Sicily to New York. Also in New York are Lamberti's cousin Joe, and Joe's brother-in-law, Sal Mazzurco. He knows that his trusted nephew Enzo has had an on-and-off business relationship with Mazzurco since Sal Lamberti introduced them in the late 1970s. If Badalamenti approaches Sal Lamberti, "he may be able to negotiate the defense and protection of the American wing of his family." He knows he must be very careful in his approach to Lamberti. The Sicilian heroin dealers are out to kill him. They are looking all over the world for him. Remember that Buscetta called it "ferocious persecution!"

"If your enemies are looking all over the world for you, why not cause them to believe that you . . . are going to come . . . to a meeting at some particular place? Namely, [to] Salvatore Lamberti in New York City . . . This may cause them to focus their energies. . . ." Kennedy twists an imaginary spyglass. "The dance begins." Martin turns to scowl at Kennedy, his face expressing outraged disbelief.

Badalamenti mainly wants to keep open the lines of communication, Kennedy says. He does not know much about New York. He "doesn't know Ganci. [He] does not know that Sal Lamberti, Sal Mazzurco and Joe Lamberti are in partnership in Pronto Demolition with Joe Ganci. Obviously, Gaetano Badalamenti doesn't know that Ganci is a heroin dealer. Obviously [he] doesn't know that Joe Ganci is in league with the Sicilian heroin dealers, Gaetano Badalamenti's arch enemies, who have been trying to kill him for years. He only knows Sal Lamberti."

He tells Alfano and Enzo: You keep that line open. But don't let him know where I am.

For some reason, Ganci also wants very much to keep the line open. But he assigns that task to Mazzurco and the Lambertis. He himself wishes to remain completely in the background. Ganci's three partners don't want to meet Badalamenti, don't want to talk to him, don't want anything to do with him, but they pretend to go along. Kennedy promises later to review the conversations with the jury and make all this clear.

But what is Ganci's agenda? "We don't know that until Mr. Cangialosi, the messenger, appears on the scene . . . and is given a message, I suggest, by Ganci." Kennedy is careful to say that he does not mean to suggest that Cangialosi understands the sinister message he is to carry back to Sicily. "If he did, he would not have needed to write it down." Also, the sender would not want his messenger to know its meaning.

And what is Ganci's message to the Sicilian heroin dealers? He is positioning the targets. "The doctor is in Nice," it reads. "The nephew is in Zurich. The nieces and nephews are in America."

Recess. As soon as the jury leaves, Cangialosi's lawyer, Gerry Di Chiara, again requests a mistrial. He first asked this when Alfano was shot, begging the court to prohibit Kennedy from making this argument, "because now my client has been changed into the Messenger Of Death." The prejudice this causes is "insurmountable . . . considering the fact that two of the defendants in this case are no longer present, and we know the reason. I believe the jury knows the reason," he pleads.

"Your motion is denied."

The Badalamenti women all carry rosary beads. In the corridor, Benfante embraces Kennedy. "I *love* it!" he exclaims.

The jurors have left their red notebooks on the jury rail. When court resumes, Kennedy asks them to put their "prosecutorial prayer books . . . homogenized hymnals" under their seats, because the evidence against his client is not in them. "His life hangs by his voice."

Back to the dangerous dance. The note found in Cangialosi's pocket and given to him by Ganci was Badalamenti's death warrant, intended for his enemies, telling the Sicilian drug dealers that the *dottore*—Badalamenti—was in Nice ("Thank God at that time he wasn't! Their information was several months out of date"); that Enzo Randazzo was in Zurich, and the nieces and nephews were in America.

Juror #4 looks alert for the first time in months.

Moving into September, more steps in the dangerous dance: Mazzurco meets with four members of the Badalamenti family at the Charcoal Grill in Queens. Why did the Midwesterners fly to New York, but go home in a rental car? Kennedy suggests that it was because Mazzurco had just given them the two suits of body armor, which they could not carry or wear through the airport's metal detector. "Bear in mind what I told you the dance was about." Badalamenti wants the lines of communication kept open. He "wants ultimately to defend, and protect, the American branch of his family."

A few days later comes another meeting at the Charcoal Grill. This time Mazzurco gives some money to Enzo Randazzo. What's all this about? "We find out on the 10th day of October," when Mazzurco and Randazzo have a long conversation about sweat suits and shirts that "even this paranoid prosecutorial team says was a legitimate clothing conversation." Martin's sharply tailored shoulders shake with derisive silent laughter.

Conversations at the end of October show us that the wily Badalamenti now has the New Yorkers convinced he is "over there," and not "down there." That is: He is hiding somewhere in Europe, not South America.

In November, when Buscetta and Leonardo Badalamenti, the younger son, are arrested in Brazil, the father becomes preoccupied with family problems, and the people in the United States don't hear from him again until mid-December, when he attempts to speak directly to Sal Lamberti. This doesn't work; there is a mix-up in telephone numbers. It is January 20 when the two old friends, if they are friends, finally speak directly.

And what do they talk about, after going through the ritual Sicilian formalities? Here Badalamenti makes his first major step in the dance. "You must come over here in March," he says. "And we'll pick asparagus together."

"Well," said Kennedy, "the only place you can find asparagus in March in Europe is Sicily."

Martin swiftly objects; Leval sustains.

You know any other place? Kennedy asks.

No asparagus-harvesting timetable is in evidence, replies the court.

By early February it is clear that Mazzurco and the Lambertis want nothing to do with Badalamenti. We see them ducking him. When Sal says, on February 8, you gotta speak to my cousin Joe, the Old Man says, okay, let me speak to Joe. Sal says Joe is not available. But the FBI has told us Joe is fifteen or twenty feet away, in the pizzeria. "So they are lying to one another . . . ducking one another." You see this again in the calls on the 9th, the 14th, even the 19th.

"Whom do they finally slough off most of the calls on? The low man on the totem pole, I suggest, Mazzurco. These are not people who are dying to talk, to make a deal for drugs. These are people who are extraordinarily wary of one another: mistrustful, distrustful, deceitful."

February 19 is the conversation about the twenty-two containers and Fort Lauderdale. The FBI rushes to set up a massive Florida surveillance at the Howard Johnson motel. They cordon the place off, bug the rooms, install hidden TV cameras, says Kennedy. But nobody shows up! Why? Because the phone conversation was just fantasy, lies, more Sicilian double-talk for the sake of keeping the lines open. Ganci must keep "pressing, pressing Sal Lamberti" and the others to keep in touch, because they are resisting.

"When Joe Lamberti hears that Gaetano Badalamenti has been killed—which was misinformation—he says *Good!* Because he doesn't have to deal with him any more."

The jury is very alert, the foreman in particular; comprehension is visibly dawning on several faces. Some are on the edge of their seats. Several attorneys also are listening intently. Kennedy seems to be offering a coherent explanation of the sparse and bizarre facts these people have been listening to for months. He is connecting the dots.

The February 19 conversation is also the one in which the Old Man is pressing for money. On the stand, he refused to say why, so his lawyer will explain. "I suggest that because they were stalling, because they were dancing . . . he *knew* that if he pressed them for money . . . they weren't going to come up with any."

The government has a different explanation. They say that the New Yorkers' failure to come up with $10,000 is what blew the Florida dope deal. "Ridiculous! There wasn't any 'deal,' " the lawyer says sadly. "They wanted a *meeting.* Ganci wanted to find out where Gaetano Badalamenti *was,* so he could execute this death warrant. I wish it were not so."

Kennedy reviews the flight to Madrid, and Stewart's promise in his opening that the government would prove Badalamenti and Alfano went there to pick up narcotics. "He made that up!" If the prosecutors "genuinely believed" Madrid was a rendezvous for drugs, they would have waited a day or two longer, until the conspirators led them to the drugs. It is far easier to imply drugs, in the charges, than to prove drugs, under the rules of evidence. The truth, Kennedy suggests, is that the government pounced when it did because by that time the FBI had listened to enough conversations to realize there *was no* drug deal. Hence they had to strike immediately, while it was still possible to pretend a deal was in progress.

Kennedy embarks on a nuts-and-bolts review of the Buscetta and Contorno testimony, confirming his client's expulsion from the Mafia, and the fact that—according to the government's own witnesses—this happened *at the same time* as the Mafia was getting into drugs. The lawyer also manages to get in a kind word, or even an exculpatory phrase, about nearly every one of the non-Badalamenti defendants—an extraordinarily graceful performance.

At the break, Ivan Fisher tells Kennedy, "The jury didn't even *remember* Buscetta's testimony!'

When he resumes, Kennedy pounds in the point: "Buscetta testified for days and days and days . . . mentioned name after name after name after name after name in connection with drugs." But never Badalamenti. Instead, he says the Old Man refused to deal drugs! "Extraordinary!" Kennedy repeats. "He takes what is a terrible case—because they have *no* evidence against Badalamenti, and he makes it worse!"

Now Kennedy says a few words in careful Sicilian, which cause the defendants, the interpreters, and some spectators to break up. With a smile, he repeats the old Sicilian saying in English: "It wasn't very good parsley to begin with, and then the cat went and peed on it."

Taking no chances of being misunderstood, Kennedy makes clear he means that Buscetta was the cat. But—like Badalamenti's fable of the wolf in the forest—the parsley proverb is susceptible to many differing interpretations.

The rest of Kennedy's summation emphasizes the total lack of drug evidence against his client; the government's herculean efforts to smear his client; the failure of Agent Tarallo's drug figures to match the numbers mentioned in the conversations; the fact that not one dollar in the enormous money-laundering chart was traced to Badalamenti; and Martin's calculated attempt to falsify the dates when the Mafia got out of cigarette smuggling and into heroin in order to impeach Badalamenti. Kennedy reads eight instances of this from the record, all in testimony by government witnesses.

Buscetta and Contorno do more than raise reasonable doubt that the Old Man dealt drugs, says Kennedy. If they are truthful, they prove he was innocent! But remember, it is the government, not the defense, who invited you to accept the truthfulness of these Mafia turncoats. If the jury rejects their testimony as inherently incredible, he reminds them, they have also heard from "the cream of narcotics police from three continents"—seven men with more than 150 years of law-enforcement experience—and not one said one word about Gaetano Badalamenti dealing drugs.

However, since "this case is predominately a smear as a substitute for evidence," I anticipate that the government on rebuttal will now say it's not heroin, it's cocaine.

Kennedy deals delicately with Badalamenti's disastrous performance on the witness stand. His client is a man who makes his own decisions. He wanted to defend himself on the stand. The lawyer does not really know why, having taken the stand, he refused to answer questions. "I wish I did know. I know he is not suicidal. I know he faces twenty-one years in Sicily. So he had to make a choice, an awful choice." Judge Leval was right to order him to answer. "But as human beings, we can understand." For an instant, Badalamenti looks at the jury with a trace of longing, as if he hopes that they will view him as a human being.

The lawyer moves on to discuss the character of Badalamenti: He would never lie, he would never betray his oath, no one could ever get a secret out of the Old Man, not even by torture. The subject obviously means a great deal to Kennedy, but it may be a hard sell with this jury.

Kennedy returns to the theme that upsets the prosecutors most. "You don't call a man a liar—unless you know." Badalamenti did not lie to you, though he sometimes refused to answer. These people [the prosecution] were just slinging mud. Freeh spent *days* asking Badalamenti questions he *knew* Badalamenti could not answer. "They take every shot in the world! Why? Mud . . . mud . . . mud." He pantomimes throwing mud into the witness box, and the jury box. "Why? Because they don't have anything else to throw. . . . Mud is no substitute for evidence, and we have to clean this courtroom up." *You,* he says, can walk away, leave this mud at their feet. You don't have to clean it up.

Kennedy returns to the basic honesty of his man. "He admitted cigarette smuggling . . . denied drug smuggling." When I asked him the difference, he said there was an abyss, a chasm, a monstrous gap. Cigarette smuggling is tax fraud. Drugs hurt people, he told us.

It is 3:27 P.M. Kennedy asks for a brief final recess. In the corridor Fisher marvels, "Kennedy is *becoming* Gaetano Badalamenti, for the jury. They like Mike Kennedy."

In his peroration, Kennedy repeats, "Gaetano Badalamenti is a . . . remarkable man. To become the *capo di tutti capi* of all the bosses in Sicily requires an extraordinary man . . . extraordinary character."

He asks the bottom-line question: Why Gaetano Badalamenti? Why did they go after *this* man? "Why concoct such a gigantic case with no evidence? . . . The government went after him because of who he *was,* not what he did. Because, without him, this is just another drug case. It's not page i. It's page 52.

"Without the Boss of Bosses, there is no prosecutorial romance . . . careers are not going to be made, promotions gotten, ambitions filled." At this, Martin repeats his silent, shaking laughter.

"God save us from ambition. . . . Ambition is a disease of the mind. But when we have power, as you soon will, we must be careful with power. We can't be arrogant with it. We can't crush people with it and smear people with it.

"Now, why would these four fine gentlemen abuse their power? Ambition. Ambition causes illness. Ambition causes tunnel vision. It causes deafness . . . retrograde amnesia . . . it causes you to disremember, it causes foot-in-mouth disease.

"These prosecutors aren't witnesses. They didn't take any oaths. They are accusers . . . and they are arrogant, ambitious accusers." Kennedy is speaking slowly, pacing, standing way back from the bench, a long-shot point of view.

"He is here because of who he is. He is also here because of who [sneer of contempt] *they* are. . . . So don't be afraid. But please God, be careful. It's a life. It's . . . a human being."

3:51 P.M. and it's all over. Mrs. Badalamenti is shaking, in tears. In the corridor, Kennedy embraces her. Koppelman, standing off to one side, says quietly, and in some surprise, "Michael Kennedy is not an anarchist. He is an advocate of the system!"

. . . SUNDAY, FEBRUARY 22, 1987. FOLEY SQUARE, NEW YORK. It is the jury's second working Sunday. The empty streets around the courthouse are like a city evacuated by a bomb threat.

Today begins the government rebuttal to three weeks of defense argument. Richard Martin is laughing as he steps before the jury and tells them, "I'm sure after the past three weeks, when you heard us accused of those terrible crimes, you thought that [we] would be in some federal prison on conspiracy and obstruction charges." He stops laughing. "You've been in the Twilight Zone for the past three weeks. Now we're back."

The defense dumped on the dead and the missing, he says. They handed up to you people they said were guilty: "Ganci, Bono, LaMattina, Zito, Baldinucci, Filippo Salamone, Soresi, Vito Roberto Palazzolo and somebody in Sam Evola's family. If the prosecution is so right in identifying these men, then how is it that we're so wrong about all of the defendants?" Martin laughs again. "If Joe Ganci had been a defendant in this courtroom, not one of these men would stand up and say he's a Mafia dope dealer."

Martin glows with confidence. He alternates his professions of faith in the prosecution's work—"If you feel that after 16 months of trial that all of the evidence in this trial was faked, rigged . . . then acquit them. Send them back to those wonderful tomato and shirt businesses"—with stinging denunciations of individual defendants—"You better go home and look around your house and see if somebody snuck in and put guns in the ceiling . . . like they apparently did to poor Mr. Sal Greco."

Then back to his confident mode. "They [the defense attorneys] didn't actually stand up and say: Mr. Martin, I accuse you of lying, of cheating, of rigging." Defense lawyers' heads are thrown back in disgust. In private and in open court, they have accused the government in general and Martin in particular of dishonesty from Day One.

Martin turns first to the Badalamenti group. The very fact that the Midwest defendants put together a united defense is in itself an indication of guilt, he says. He dwells on two major holes in the Badalamenti-group defense. First, the Old Man was up there on the stand. He could have verified all the claims of the group's lawyers. Instead he said nothing. Yet "his word must not be questioned, you are told."

Second, there is a clear pattern of cocaine dealing by this group. Jurors sit up straighter. Look at the phone calls between Badalamenti-group members in May/June 1983. This was the time of the Cocilovo deal, and those calls tie them right into it. Mr. Burke sought to ignore these conversations.

Sam Evola had cocaine in his house, and he admitted to federal agents that it was a sample, part of a one-kilo quantity.

Mazzurco and Alfano were dealing coke in September at the Charcoal Grill in Queens.

Alfano's travels back and forth from the Midwest to New York in late 1983 and early 1984 were cocaine deals.

A big Florida cocaine deal was being set up that required the participation of Trupiano and Vitale. They were willing to "take a walk." Martin rereads critical calls between Alfano and other Badalamenti-group members to emphasize his point. In Martin's scenario, the Badalamenti group's cocaine dealing has the unity of purpose and troop coordination of a military advance.

Central to Martin's attack on the Mafia-war defense is Joe Lamberti's

1983 trip to Brazil. If the jury concludes that Lamberti did in fact meet Badalamenti in Brazil, then the whole argument that Badalamenti was hiding from the New York group goes down the drain. Further, Lamberti had "Vito's" Brazilian telephone number in his car.

Martin turns and faces Vito while he ridicules Koppelman's argument. "Nobody *ever* called Vincenzo Randazzo 'Vito,' " he asserts. The Vito in Lamberti's note was Vito Badalamenti. Koppelman heckles Martin with constant interruptions, worrying him like a terrier. At one point he forces a sidebar, in which Leval orders Martin to rectify his false interpretation of a Brazilian document.

When the jury leaves for lunch, Badalamenti-group lawyers remain. They angrily denounce Martin's repeated use of the Old Man's failure to answer questions as proof of the government's version of events. Leval dismisses all objections. "His [Gaetano Badalamenti's] non-testimony is part of his testimony. The jury is also allowed to consider his non-testimony as evidence that he was lying in other testimony."

MARIO MALERBA,

fifty, the one defense lawyer who did not give a summation, is the man who probably knows more about this case, at least on the defense side, than anyone in the courtroom. On this Sunday, which marks the beginning of the government's rebuttal summation, the mannerly, inscrutable Sicilian, smooth-skinned and ruddy as a nut, is at last ready to talk a little about the case and the people he understands so well.

The setting he chooses is one of the dozens of excellent Italian restaurants at which he is a known and valued customer. Like his late client Ganci, Malerba has a taste for life's finer things.

Malerba was Joe Ganci's lawyer for many years. After Ganci's arrest on April 9, his attorney sought a medical severance. By then, Ganci had terminal lung cancer. At that time Emanuel Moore, Malerba's tough, snappy associate, was representing Catalano. Manny Moore is an uncommonly busy man. In addition to his legal work, he owns a large farm in New Jersey, and is a major supplier of Chinese vegetables to Chinatown markets and Chinese restaurants in the New York area. Moore and Malerba also operate a one-plane airline, which weekly flies planeloads of mostly Chinese gamblers back and forth to Las Vegas. As a trial lawyer, Moore could be termed a specialist in organized-crime cases. When Moore said he did not care to be tied up in a trial that might last eight months, Malerba brought in Fisher.

After Malerba won the medical severance for Ganci, he sought to stay on the Pizza case, as co-counsel with Fisher for Catalano. Louis Freeh at first objected, later withdrew his objection, "and Judge Leval did a very nice thing for me: He said okay."

As soon as the Pizza case ends, Malerba and his wife, Jo, who recently retired as chief surgical nurse at Flushing Hospital, in Queens, are taking a special vacation. Their tickets already are bought for a flight to Helsinki, Finland, followed by a night sail to Leningrad, so that Malerba can realize his long-held ambition to tour the Winter Palace, the Hermitage, and other pleasure domes and playgrounds of the tsars. Malerba is diabetic, and feels slightly run down from his Pizza labors, but generally in good health. He drinks brandy-and-soda.

Malerba knows the Pizza prosecutors better than any of the defense lawyers with the possible exception of Marvin Segal, whom he much admires. He knows that Martin has one adopted child; and that he and Freeh both became new fathers during the Pizza trial. Stewart has children in college. Bucknam is unmarried. He knows that Martin, win or lose (which he also knows is inconceivable), leaves the U.S. Attorney's Office after this case to take a plum job in Rome, where he will be dealing not in criminal matters so much as in matters of international law.

Malerba was born and raised in Ridgewood, Queens, the nephew and grandson and great-grandson of physicians. His own father was a liquor dealer. Malerba sometimes wishes he too had been a doctor, "because it would have been less hectic." But he always knew he wanted to be a criminal lawyer. He was a wild youth or, as he describes himself, "I was not a very nice boy. . . . I saw a lot of injustice." He did well academically at Brooklyn College and at Baltimore Law School. He was a good athlete and boxed in a Golden Gloves tournament in which he was finally defeated by middleweight Coley Wallace, who later became a professional. During his "bad boy" phase, he lived for a time in Dublin, Ireland. The lawyer and his family still live in Queens, and they have a big summer home in Southold, Long Island. Except perhaps for Segal, Malerba believes he has the largest practice of any attorney in the Pizza case. On occasion disarmingly candid, he says he follows his profession "for two reasons—cash, and vanity."

Of Judge Leval and Paul Bergman, Malerba observes that they have the same problem: Both are highly intelligent men, but entirely lacking in street smarts—a quality Malerba prizes very highly, and with which he himself is well endowed.

"Any street kid could take Leval over," he says. "Michael Kennedy probably believes the judge is intellectually dishonest. I think he is honest, but he firmly believes that these men are guilty, and he must deliver the Holy Grail. He sees himself as the man on the white horse who must bring these dangerous criminals to justice.

"Dick Martin is a good street man. Freeh is the best street man in the case." Bergman, lacking street smarts, plays into Freeh's hands over and over. "I don't know Larry Bronson very well, but he and Lombardino don't get caught in that. Bucknam is not street smart. Fogelnest has very good street smarts; he's a brawler, a skinny little fighter. He has emerged as a favorite of mine, a friend. If I get any other cases, I'm gonna give 'em to Fogelnest. He is *not afraid.*"

Malerba invariably polls jurors, and plans are set for Manny Moore to be standing at the jury exit to nab the Pizza jurors as they leave the building after their verdict. Fisher and Malerba will post themselves in the courtroom "to take the verdict," which will go on for some time. The Pizza verdict sheet is fifty-nine pages long. Malerba thinks Leval will permit the jurors to talk, once the verdict is in. Lombardino has predicted that the judge will clamp an airtight lid on the Pizza jury, "but he doesn't know Leval at all."

Like the other defense lawyers, Malerba finds the Pizza courtroom atmosphere uniquely oppressive, depressing. "The bottom line is that this case shows the extent to which the government will go to win. There's no brakes on the thing; they will go to any extreme to get a conviction."

Malerba says that prosecutors are a different breed of lawyer. "A young man goes into the U.S. Attorney's Office, or the DA's office . . . he is not taught *justice;* he's taught to *win,* the Vince Lombardi ethic. He's taught: Learn this trick, learn that trick, to maximize chances of winning. It's basic. He's a good kid, but he's taught that means don't matter, only ends. The inevitable result is that these are bad guys.

"Once he has enrobed himself in that theory, he's on his way. From now on, he's *always* a prosecutor. He may go home and have dinner with his wife, make love to his wife . . . and the next morning he's still a prosecutor. Nothing else interferes. It's too strong. He looks up at the picture of the Big Man hanging on the wall—Giuliani. He does not have one scruple in his entire body! The only ones who can withstand it are the ones who get out."

Although the defense attorneys were sometimes at one another's throats during the evidentiary phase of the trial, and on occasion close to fist fights, by summation they appeared to be a more or less unified group or, as Malerba puts it, "despite some falsehoods, we presented a stew that somehow tasted good at the end."

Careful chef and tireless stirrer of the stew was Mario Malerba, who was three times more active backstage and offstage than he ever appeared to be in the courtroom. Without his tactful, vigilant presence, the defense team could have self-destructed on countless occasions. Although Michael Kennedy was lead counsel, and a man of formidable reputation, his late arrival on the scene, his unfamiliarity with most of the other Pizza lawyers and with organized-crime cases in general, and, most of all, the ingrained hatred and suspicion most of the other defendants had for his client would have made his position as defense capo untenable without the quiet presence of Malerba as his *consigliere*.

Asked who he thinks made the disastrous decision to put Badalamenti on the stand, Kennedy or his client, Malerba says firmly, "I know Tanino very well. It was his idea to testify. He thought he could *show them*. Even the smartest wiseguys err, you know, and he did. He misjudged. Also, he did not understand the American psyche."

Midway through Badalamenti's testimony, "I saw Tanino at MCC," says Malerba, implying, as always, a happenstance encounter. "I told him, 'Get off. Tell Mike: No more.' But it was too late. He is not the type of man who should go on the stand. The jury really hates Tanino!"

After lunch, Dick Martin attacks each member of the Badalamenti group, one by one, chopping with the fervor of Sweeney Todd. Sam Evola? He admitted his ounce of coke was but a sample. Palazzolo stashed an unloaded .38 under his mattress. Martin's Catch-22 argument is that the fact the weapon was unloaded proves its purpose was not for defense of life and property, but for future use in connection with drug deals.

Finally Martin turns to face Badalamenti and Kennedy. " 'Oh, what a tangled web we weave . . .' " he mocks. "How can Badalamenti even walk back to his chair with all that web of his own creation tangled around him?"

Martin's eyes have turned the color of ball bearings. This man, he says, got on the stand and refused to answer. "Who was it who directed that witness not to answer? It was Mr. Kennedy himself."

Kennedy: "Objection! That is a false statement."

"Overruled."

Martin ridicules the Mafia-war defense. It's an elaborate story strung out by the lawyer to divert attention from his client's drug dealing.

Kennedy likes to ignore Buscetta's testimony that "Mr. Badalamenti's expulsion from the Mafia had nothing to do with dealing or not dealing drugs."

The Messenger of Death argument is another defense smoke screen. Badalamenti was involved in dealing drugs with the very same Sicilians whom Cangialosi knew. "It's just an elaborate story designed to distract you from the evidence."

Martin does not discuss the meaning of the note. He moves back to his old argument, put forth fifteen months ago, that Badalamenti's expulsion from the Mafia came well after the Sicilians took over the U.S. heroin trade. "Deliberate distortion!" Kennedy had bellowed then.

"When Contorno had those discussions with those five separate narcotics suppliers in 1977," Martin repeats, "he told you that they were *already* in the heroin business."

"That is a false statement!" Kennedy shouts. Leval wants no rerun of that bitter battle and calls an immediate sidebar, then compels Martin to correct the date he had fudged to improve his argument. "I have been asked to remind you that Contorno . . . puts the date as '77/'78."

Next he intensifies his assault on Badalamenti, declaring that the monies in Mazzurco's red notebook were not revenues from precious stones, but drug profits funneled directly to the Old Man.

He got "$7 million in a year and a half. . . . Vito Randazzo" was the courier.

This last takes a moment to register. Vito? Then lawyers' heads shoot up; they glance at one another for confirmation. Lewis is nodding, smiling like a Babylonian idol. One or two jurors are suddenly alert; most snooze on. It is now 6:00 P.M. and even the ever-attentive Leval is not sure that he heard it. He sends the jury out before checking with the court reporter to make certain Martin did indeed say "Vito Randazzo," the very name he has ridiculed as "never, ever used."

Martin the hatchet man having just chopped off his own toes, the defense lawyers head home reasonably happy.

. . . MONDAY, FEBRUARY 23, 1987.

THE COURTROOM. This morning Louis Freeh makes his last pitch. He attacks the defense use of "lawyers' argument," his term for crafty oratory, and sets about rehabilitating Sal Amendolito. Okay, so he couldn't identify Catalano as the man with the $1.54 million, but then he saw the man for only twenty minutes in his entire life. Freeh seems to imply that an exchange of $1.54 million is an event easily forgotten.

Dick Martin returns to deliver the final prosecutorial *coup de grace* to the defendants he savaged in cross-examination. First on his list is Vito Amato and the March 6 meeting at "the only authentic Italian coffee shop in New York, Café Biffi.

"Was Salvatore Catalano supplying cannoli? Was Ganci talking about bringing pizza? Was Frank Polizzi going to bring over bags of sardines? Was Joe Lamberti there to discuss samples of paint from DeVardo in Italy?"

Martin turns next to Fogelnest's defense of Sal Salamone. Before he utters two sentences, Fogelnest objects and is overruled. Martin is trying to say that it is not necessary to show Salamone sitting and talking drug possession, prices, and shipments in order to prove him part of the conspiracy. In the next three minutes, Fogelnest objects six times. At the sixth, Leval cautions, "Don't argue in front of the jury, please."

Martin moves to Salamone's weapons purchases, and in the next five minutes come four more Fogelnest objections. Leval instructs the jury to disregard them. Fogelnest wants to approach. Leval tells Martin to proceed. One minute later Fogelnest again objects, and Leval snaps, *"Mr. Fogelnest,* if you don't sit down and stop making improper arguments . . . I am going to have to take action. Now, don't provoke me. Sit down."

Fogelnest has supplied his punctuation for the jury.

After lunch Martin moves like a seasoned actor toward his own dramatic conclusion. He dismisses Bronson and Sal Greco as the team that presented the "Night at the Opera" star, Pisano. As for Castronovo, clearly he has been part of the conspiracy since its start, back in 1980, with Amendolito.

Martin has saved his best wine for the end. "Mr. Querques had one last joke for you. You recall that when Mr. Querques stood before you [with] the bag [of] sardines . . . the bottom of that bag had melted through—and ripped!"

Everyone in the room knows the next line. Martin hits it at full volume. "That bag of sardines was just a fish story! Frank Polizzi, like the other men in this case, is guilty."

The prosecutor pauses a moment, looks around, "So that's it. The years of investigation, the years of preparation, the year-and-a-half of trial will be over, except the most important part. That is *your* evaluation of proof. Thank you."

8. *The Decision*

THE COURTROOM. It is 9:45 A.M. when Judge Leval says, "Members of the jury, you will see that I have distributed to you in your seats two thick documents . . . the indictment, and my charge."

It is unusual for a judge to provide jurors with written copies of his charge, but probably essential when seeking a verdict of this length and complexity. The charge alone runs to 114 pages. Count 1 is the conspiracy charge. Every defendant is charged with conspiring to violate the narcotics laws of the United States.

Counts 2–11 are charges of operating a continuing criminal enterprise in violation of U.S. narcotics laws (the 848s).

Counts 12–15 concern violations of the laws of the United States in connection with transfers of money.

"Count 16, on page 108 . . . called the RICO law, alleges that they conspired to conduct the affairs of an enterprise through a pattern of racketeering activity."

The jurors do not look thrilled to have this added "aid" to their deliberations. But they dutifully follow along as Judge Leval begins to read Count 1 aloud. "From on or about January 1, 1975 up to . . . about the 30th day of April, 1984 . . . the defendants, and other conspirators both known and unknown . . ."

The defendants listen to the reading more intently than the jurors, as if they are still straining to understand these charges against them.

By 10:20 jurors have begun to drowse. Leval halts for a "stretch-break" and commands, "Stand up!"

By 11:00 the full horror of what they are going to have to do appears to have begun to dawn on these unfortunate seventeen jurors and alternates.

After lunch, Leval takes up the fifty-nine-page verdict sheet, first reminding the jurors that *"your recollection* of the event controls."

They may send him a note at any time, "but do not reveal in the note what your standing is on the issue. . . . Juror #1 is your foreman. He sends the note through the marshal. . . . I remind you again: Your job is to consider each count, and each defendant, *separately."*

Individual verdict forms are distributed. "Do not be intimidated by the size of the form. . . . Pages 2–32 cover Counts 2–11; pages 33–36 cover Counts 12–15; pages 37–59 give you a separate sheet for each defendant on the RICO. . . . OA stands for Overt Act; RA stands for Racketeering Act. . . ."

Juror #2 is rubbing his eyes with his fist. #4 is asleep. #5 keeps turning to look at the clock over the rear doors. #6 is whispering to #7. #8 is tapping his fingers and feet in some private rhythm.

At 3:17 P.M. the jurors and alternates are sent out, but not yet to deliberate. Once they are gone, Judge Leval says that five alternates are too many. He recommends excusing two.

It is 3:28 P.M. when the twelve actual jurors again leave the room to begin deliberations. Now Leval must speak to the five alternates. "You may feel your time has been wasted. . . ." Five stoic faces look back at him, waiting for the ax to fall. "Alternates will wait apart, but will come into the courtroom whenever the jury comes in. . . . I hope you are not disappointed. . . ." A marshal leads them out so that the *coup de grace,* cutting their number from five to three, may be delivered offstage.

The lawyering is over. The long wait begins—a traditional time for strong drink. Burke, Ryan, Lombardino, and Benfante elect to celebrate in Irish style, with pint tumblers of Guinness stout at Eamonn Doran's Midtown pub. The word spreads, and most other lawyers quickly agree to attend. En route, Burke stops by the hospital, where he learns that Alfano's condition has further deteriorated. When Alfano was told of his paralysis, he became despondent. He says now he would rather be dead. Today blood clots were discovered in his lung, and he has been returned to Intensive Care, no visitors allowed.

In the drably furnished waiting room, Evola, Trupiano, and Vitale speak with animated hands, surrounded by the now-silent women. Christine Evola and Alfano's wife, Christina, sit with five or six plastic "I Love New York" bags bundled at their feet. Mrs. Alfano's belongings are stuffed inside. Pietro's transfer to Intensive Care means that she can no longer stay in the room with him, and must join the other members of the family at their current residence, a run-down Midtown hostelry sometimes patronized by the many hookers who work the neighborhood. The family had fled their Greenwich Village hotel after the shooting.

Christina Alfano whispers to her sister Fanita Palazzolo between deep pulls on her cigarette. Emmanuele Palazzolo sits like a gerbil in one corner, lost and afraid.

Joe Trupiano tells Burke that Mrs. Alfano is stone broke. Alfano had no medical insurance, and his wife does not know what to do next. If she files for welfare, it may alert the hospital that her husband has no means of paying his bill, in which case they might move him to another hospital, where he would not get the same first-rate treatment.

Burke says he will try an approach to the Crime Victims Compensation Board. He does not tell them he has no idea whether this will work. He would very much like to file a civil suit against Patsy Conte and try to tap into some of the supermarket millions. But each time he raises the subject, the Alfanos seem uneasy. They have some fear they will not speak about. Burke feels a growing conviction they will never move against Conte.

With a promise to return tomorrow, Burke leaves the forlorn group huddled in the deserted waiting room and heads uptown to the Irish bar. He is bitter about the condition in which the Badalamenti defendants have been left by their leader. "He's supposed to have money all over the world, and he leaves these people in stinking flea-hole hotels. Some Man of Honor! Some Godfather!"

The front bar of the Second Avenue pub is jammed with lawyers. Fisher, Malerba, Moore, and Schechter stand in their overcoats, taking small sips of the bitter black stout, their presence a courtesy to the more seasoned drinkers. The Kennedys have already left. Farther down the bar, Lombardino has lined up several creamy pints of Guinness for late arrivals.

The lawyers, after sixteen months, are Pizza junkies. They find it hard to talk of anything else. Di Chiara is deeply upset by Kennedy's summation. "Jesus, he really dumped on me. Nobody noticed me during the trial until—wham!—Kennedy hits me with the Messenger of Death. I thought I had given Cangialosi a shot, and the next thing, the lead defense counsel kills me." He shakes his head.

Lombardino worries about the jury. He distrusts them. They've settled down together as a government team, he says. The party gathers around a big table, anxious to drown their misgivings in thick, dark beer. They have little optimism, only a faint hope that perhaps they fed doubt to one juror, or two.

. . . THURSDAY, FEBRUARY 26, 1987.
THE COURTROOM. The first full day of deliberations begins with a jury note that suggests they are finding even the rebus-like government chartbooks too much to handle. They have asked for Paul Bergman's index to the government's charts, the one he presented to the jury during his summation. This document could properly be termed a summary of a summary of a summary, and most defense lawyers object strenuously. The index concentrates, hence intensifies, the government's unfair portrayals of their clients. They win, and Leval sends a return note: "This index was prepared for summation and is not available to you during deliberations."

Later the jury requests surveillance reports for the days surrounding the big Café Biffi meeting of March 6, 1984.

No one expects serious movement for many days. Defendants, relatives, lawyers, and marshals rest, like sailors becalmed.

. . . 10:00 A.M., FRIDAY, FEBRUARY 27, 1987.
THE COURTROOM. Leval, looking extremely grave, calls the court to order. Standing behind him, off to the side, is a tall individual in a slate-blue suit whose hair is almost the color of blue steel. He is the special marshal who, since the Alfano shooting, has been assigned as Leval's personal bodyguard.

The judge bangs for silence and says, "A family member of one of

the jurors received a phone call in which an unidentified male caller said
... 'I been watching you. I know where you're at. I want you. I will
get you.' "

The juror in question is #12, the plump black woman who formerly
was alternate #1. She learned of the threat when she called home last
night from the hotel where the jury is sequestered. Her daughter, who
received the call, said the caller sounded like a black man, and told her
mother she was not frightened. The marshal assigned to monitor all
jury calls in and out of the hotel overheard this conversation, and did
not consider the so-called threat worth reporting. But this morning the
conscientious juror herself told Judge Leval about it.

#12 is considered by all to be the best defense juror in the box. If
she is removed from the jury, many feel, the loss to the defense will be
irrecoverable. Others feel that new alternate #1, a twenty-six-year-old
security guard of Puerto Rican ancestry, is also a defense-minded juror
and would be an acceptable substitute.

Leval has already interviewed both juror #12 and her daughter. The
mother said she too is unperturbed by the threat, feels "I can be fair
and honest," and wants to continue. Leval has four choices: He can
replace the woman with an alternate and have the jury begin their
deliberations over again. He can accept her word that she is unafraid,
and keep her on. He can remove her and continue with eleven jurors.
He can grant a mistrial. The mistrial idea will receive no consideration.

Freeh requests "that the juror be excused and we proceed with eleven
jurors."

The defense vote is unanimous: Juror #12 must remain.

Judge Leval seeks time to talk with her once more before making a
final decision. He calls a recess.

The defense lawyers, furious, accuse the judge of jury-shopping. Says
one, "The first time we really knew he was jury-shopping was when he
fired the other #12 for lateness. He didn't cost us nearly as much time
as the days off for the foreman juror who had the operation." The
original #12 was a young Hispanic railroad-track worker. Several lawyers say that an eleven-person jury would be especially unfair in this
case, because it is so big and so long. "He's taking a helluva risk,"
someone says. "If another juror falls, it's an automatic mistrial. A
ten-person jury is illegal."

Schechter corrects him. "No. *U.S.* versus *Stratton* leaves open the
question of a ten-person jury. Read Rule 2-B. It says it is preferable to
go to eleven, rather than bring in an alternate and start from the
beginning. But this has happened after less than two days' deliberation.

And the excuse to dump her is so slight, especially since the possibility of additional voir dire exists."

Kennedy: "Who wants to bet he throws her off?"

Leval sweeps back in. "My decision is that this juror must be excused for cause. There are several reasons. . . . Whatever she may state to be her present attitude . . . there is absolutely no way of controlling the possibility of change in that attitude, and the circumstances are such as to be very frightening to a juror in her position. . . .

"Jury deliberations can be very emotional, very outspoken, and it's simply a very high likelihood . . . that she will communicate that.

"Therefore I have made the decision to excuse the juror." For Kennedy, this is the last straw. He looks straight at Leval. "In my considerable experience, it is the most intellectually dishonest judicial ruling I have ever encountered."

Leval shoots back, in a deadpan voice, "I am flattered. You have selected me out for special praise in the past . . ."

Kennedy breaks in. "You deserve it."

". . . and I am always glad to hear an admiring word from you, Mr. Kennedy."

The rest of the jury will be told, "Members of the jury: For personal reasons, Juror No. 313 must leave the jury. Please continue your deliberations."

Kennedy throws up his hands in disgust and walks out of the courtroom. In the corridor several other defense counsel now think all is lost.

Why did Leval accept #3's assertion that he could be fair, despite being paged by name in the theater, and refuse to believe the same from #12? several lawyers ask.

"The whole system sucks," says Ruggiero. "I got an offer to become a half-partner in a Chinese restaurant. I'm gonna take it. At least I won't have to deal with liars."

Fisher says, "I'm disgusted. I'd rather be in some more honest business—like renting limousines! That juror is being punished for her honesty. But we made a bad mistake here. We weren't playing with a full deck. We should have asked Pierre Leval to read us his conversation with the juror. Because we kept learning new things as he kept talking."

Schechter makes the best point. "Why didn't anyone say: Judge, this is an anonymous jury! Therefore, either it must have been a crank call or it came from the government?"

Leval has ordered that his additional voir dire of #12 be sealed, and despite several requests, filed at intervals by Ivan Fisher, this portion of the record remains sealed.

The waiting, the card games, and the siestas begin again. In the afternoon the court clerk rounds up the lawyers: A note has been sent out asking to see Mazzurco's red notebook. The jurors appear to be advancing through the charges at a rapid rate, bad news on top of bad news for the defendants and their lawyers.

The defense consensus about the remaining eleven jurors is that this jury is very tough, very determined. Every one left *wants* to be here, because by now they all *knew* how to get off, if they'd wanted to. They are not at all intimidated by this process. They entirely believe they can understand this case. They have no notion that few if any of the defense lawyers comprehend its full and massive entirety.

. . . SATURDAY, FEBRUARY 28, 1987.
Once more Foley Square is virtually deserted. Joe Benfante drives up in his flashy red Mercedes sports car, the 560 SE he bought through Bronson's German-car import business. He extracts two folding beach chairs to use for naps during the lawyers' poker game. As he steps off the elevator, the court clerk announces another jury note. Considerable time is required to round up the congregation. Lawyers are at their poker game; defendants huddle in smoke-blue corners on the oaken benches; Badalamenti and the other incarcerated defendants must be brought from their backstage holding pen.

When all are gathered, Leval reads the note. "Can Item 4 under the conspiracy count also be considered as one of the two racketeering acts required under the RICO statute?" The lawyers and Judge Leval debated and resolved this issue many months ago. Leval says he will write "Yes, you may," signed "Judge Leval" on a Xerox of their note and send it back in.

What might sound to the nonlawyer like nothing at all is in fact a very bad sign, says Kennedy. The note must mean the jury has already decided that Catalano is guilty of item 4, the continuing-criminal-enterprise charge—the Bagheria farmhouse meeting. Now they have received the okay to go on to find him guilty under RICO.

... SUNDAY, MARCH 1, 1987.
LUNCHTIME IN THE COURTHOUSE. The day is chill and
rainy. Benfante has decided it is time to catch up on lost sleep, and has
brought a more comfortable beach chair. Under a cloud of smoke in
an empty courtroom, Malerba, Bergman, Lombardino, and Koppelman are deeply involved in a poker game. Koppelman is on top, and
Malerba doing well. His client, wearing an expensive faded-leather
bomber jacket, looks over Malerba's shoulder at his hand. Catalano
looks much more comfortable now than in his too-tight court suit, and
very much the tough street wiseguy.

Out in the corridor, Casamento and Amato are spreading a large
white tablecloth over the big oak table that normally holds forbidden
newspapers. The defendants have decided that, if they must spend
Sunday in the courthouse, they may as well eat well, and have brought
in a complete Sicilian picnic. The table is covered with aluminum trays
of potato croquettes, fried chickpeas, calamari salad, and other delicacies. Sal Catalano has brought boxes of sweet cannoli from his bakery,
reputedly the best cannoli in Queens. Everyone is invited to partake,
including the marshals guarding the courtroom. They decline.

Mario Malerba feels like a hot lunch, and perhaps some wine. The
many restaurants in the courthouse vicinity are all dark and locked. But
Malerba raps hard on the door of the Pasta Pot, until at last the owner
himself peers out, recognizes the hungry lawyer, embraces him, and
hurries personally to cook and serve his old friend a delicious meal: ziti
with *pomidoro* sauce, wine on the house.

Malerba is a shrewd analyst of juries, and claims to have hand-picked
this one. By now, he says, they have already made their decisions as
regards the main defendants. He anticipates "bad things," especially
after the loss of #12. Other potentially prodefense jurors are "hurting
without her." He thinks she especially liked both Manny Moore and
Joe Benfante, and agrees the prosecution was anxious to get rid of her.
His sight line in the courtroom offers him a head-on view of Juror #2,
the retired telephone company technician, a man who he believes has
a strong moral sense and is "repelled by sleaze." He infers this from
#2's long-ago answer, during voir dire, that Jimmy Breslin does all his
reporting from a barstool. Now #2 has "seen Dick Martin's sleaze,"

seen him attempt to imply that a vote against the government would be a vote against their beloved Pierre Leval: "If you call *us* frauds, then you must include the judge." (The line had brought five or six Objections! and two shouts for a mistrial from the defense.)

Malerba handicaps each of the other ten jurors, reeling off backgrounds, courtroom mannerisms, and other observations with photographic accuracy. An example of his encyclopedic knowledge of courthouse scuttlebutt: One former juror, since dismissed, was the wife of the detective who administered the polygraph test to Malerba's late client Cesare Bonventre after the Galante murder.

Malerba can expertly delineate the personality differences among Bonventre, Amato, Ganci, and Catalano, all of whom he has represented at various times. Bonventre was a flamboyant womanizer. Amato is more sensible. Ganci was always extravagant and always needed money. Catalano is a quiet man, of moderate, modest appetites, happy with his lot, and "not given to throwing money around." He has no taste for high living, or "finer things, fun, or good conversation." He drinks only Coca-Cola, and drives a nonshowy car. "Yet it was he who pulled them all out."

If the Pizza defendants "go down," as Malerba suspects they will—though he would never say so, in or out of the courthouse—he does not care to speculate what may happen to the Knickerbocker Avenue community. He worries that, should Catalano get life on the 848 charge, he might well commit suicide to spare his wife a life tied to an entombed man. Catalano adores his four-year-old daughter, and "would be driven to the point of crack-up" if he were forever separated from her.

. . . MONDAY, MARCH 2, 1987.

THE COURTROOM.   The jury retired to consider its verdict at 3:28 P.M. on Wednesday last, so this morning the jurors are in their fifth day of deliberations. Some lawyers hang out in the cafeteria, others work at their tables in the courtroom, catching up on seventeen-month backlogs. Defendants and families are gathered in huddles.

11:15 A.M. The jury sends out its twenty-sixth note. They ask for a clean verdict sheet, and surveillance reports for July 22, 1983. "We've checked four or five times. There is no such evidence," says Freeh. Ken Kaplan, who has just arrived, says helpfully that the jury probably means the 24th, when agents surveilled a Ganci-Mazzara meeting. Shouts of "Kenny!" from shocked lawyers lounging on the back benches. This is scarcely a time to assist the enemy. The charge the jury seeks information on is on page 57 of the verdict form, just two pages from the end.

At 3:20 P.M. Fisher is pacing the corridor, drinking his fifth or sixth large Coke of the day, when a bevy of excited young women pushes past him into the courtroom. They are secretaries and clerks from the U.S. Attorney's Office, and they smell blood. Behind them come extra marshals. Sal Catalano stops pacing and looks at them. Something is going on.

3:35 P.M. In the silent courtroom, Kennedy is seated in his front-row seat, head bent low, Manny Moore behind him massaging his shoulders. Most of the other defense lawyers straggle in. Burke, Querques, Fogelnest, and Malerba are not here. The one window is wide open. John, keeper of the earphones, is hurriedly setting them out on defendants' chairs. No one is sure what is happening. The jury has been out less than five full days.

Lombardino says loudly, "This is it." As though to confirm his statement, all five prosecutors and Agent Rooney arrive, their arms heaped with books and verdict sheets, led by a smiling Dick Martin. More marshals appear; eventually there will be more than two dozen, standing like sentries on all four sides of the room.

Leval sweeps in, his face closed, followed by his entire staff. Kennedy takes time to grasp Badalamenti's hand formally and then that of every other defendant.

The judge announces in his most solemn voice, "There is a note from the jury. . . . It reads as follows: 'We the jury have reached a verdict.' " The room is utterly silent. A little tinkle of an offstage bell is heard, and the eleven jurors and three alternates are escorted in. They do not look at the defendants.

Leval and the beer-bellied foreman begin working their way through the fifty-nine-page verdict sheet, beginning with the all-embracing narcotics conspiracy charge. "How do you find the defendant Gaetano Badalamenti?"

"Guilty," the foreman replies.

"Sal Catalano?"

"Guilty."

Eight more times the juror repeats the word. Mazzurco, both Lambertis, Ligammari, Amato, Alfano, Palazzolo, and Evola all go down.

Occasional moans or gasps escape from the wives and children jammed onto spectator benches. But the men are utterly expressionless.

Then Leval asks "Vito Badalamenti?"

"Not guilty."

Bob Koppelman drops his head back onto the high back of his chair, as if dead. Vito does not move.

Trupiano? Vitale? Cangialosi? All guilty. Then, "Salvatore Salamone?"

"Not guilty." A gasp from the spectator benches. Sal's wife starts to cry.

Greco? Castronovo? Polizzi? Casamento? All guilty. The foreman's throat is drying up. The clerk gives him a glass of water. He turns to Counts 2-11 on the verdict form, the dread 848 charges, with their mandatory sentence of ten years to life. Seven men are charged. Five are guilty: Badalamenti, Catalano, Joe Lamberti, Castronovo, and Alfano. Sal Lamberti is not guilty, and neither is Sal Mazzurco. Benfante's face splits into a jack-o'-lantern smile. Schechter beams. Their clients, like all the other defendants, remain poker-faced.

The foreman next reads the decisions on each of the five criminal acts in each 848 charge. His enumeration of crimes proved and not proved is bewildering in pattern. Badalamenti has been found guilty on all counts across the board; he is convicted of committing twenty-five separate offenses, including importation of twenty-two kilos of cocaine (the twenty-two containers) and distribution of cocaine from Evola's house.

Catalano is found to have supervised fifteen named persons, including Ronsisvalle, Benny Zito, and Joe Ganci, and to have committed twenty-nine offenses, including possession of heroin in the Bagheria farmhouse, shipping the Milan forty-one kilos, possessing with intent to distribute five different multikilo quantities of heroin listed in Mazzurco's red notebook, and the attempted importation of twenty-two kilos of cocaine (the same twenty-two containers) into Florida.

Joe Lamberti is found to have supervised six people, including DeVardo and Cangialosi, and committed twenty-six offenses, including the Zito drugs and the twenty-two containers, but *not* the Cocilovo drugs.

Pietro Alfano is found guilty of organizing eight people, including his wife, and committing forty-five offenses, including attempted importation of the twenty-two containers, and forty-two instances of telephone facilitation of drug dealing.

Frank Castronovo is guilty of organizing six people and committing twenty-three offenses, including possession with intent to distribute the multi-kilo amounts of heroin listed in Mazzurco's red notebook, and distribution of the Benny Zito drugs. But he was not at the Bagheria farmhouse, nor is he connected to the Milan forty kilos.

The foreman moves on to Counts 12-15, the banking violations. Catalano, Castronovo, Greco are guilty on all money counts. Salamone is guilty of two fiscal misdemeanors.

Count 16 is the RICO charges, lodged against all defendants except the two Badalamentis and Alfano. The foreman's voice gets stronger as he reels off the word *guilty* fifteen times. The only hiccup occurs when he pronounces Salvatore Salamone "not guilty."

Some of the jury's conclusions seem eccentric. The government's allegation that Joe Lamberti met Gaetano Badalamenti on his trip to Brazil is ruled not proved. Nor are Baldo Amato's telephone conversations with Joe Ganci, although detailed over six numbing days of testimony.

Joe the clerk now polls the jury and asks each in turn to confirm his verdict. For the first and last time their eleven voices are heard as each speaks the simple three-letter word.

4:45 P.M. Leval asks the marshals to escort the jury back to its room for a few moments. Kennedy is talking quietly to a standing Badalamenti. The clerk returns the glass of water to its regular place on the witness stand.

Leval now has seventeen convicted men on his hands. Time to reorganize the seating. Marshals begin herding the men into the two front rows. Sal Salamone holds up two fingers to his wife and calls out, *"Due! Due* misdemeanors!"* Five marshals station themselves at one end, and ten marshals at the other, of two rows of seated, defeated Sicilians. A dozen more marshals lean against the back wall. Two or three stand at each courtroom exit. Sitting quietly in the next-to-last row, Rudolph Giuliani, surrounded by aides, is writing out a statement for the press.

Martin moves to remand everybody immediately, "to protect the community, which deserves a break from these defendants." Leval agrees. Martin would also like to argue the forfeitures now—the property seizures permitted by statute for defendants convicted on the RICOs and 848s.

"No! I'm emotionally and physically drained!" shouts Lombardino.

"I simply cannot keep the jury," says Leval.

This time Freeh challenges. "We're dealing with millions of dollars' worth of property. . . . The court is denying the government a right we have under the statute." He has a suggestion: Why not ask the jury? A note is sent to them and swiftly answered. "We the jury do not wish to participate in the above-mentioned proceedings."

Leval orders the jurors brought back in, then swings round in his leather chair to speak to them. He overflows with admiration for their intelligence, for their perseverance, for the fortitude of the alternates. Then he turns to the matter of jury secrecy. "I suggest to you that each of you has a kind of a bond, a kind of an understanding with the other jurors, that what each of you had to say to the other jurors in that jury room should remain your secret, the jury's secret. The jury speaks to the world once, when it says 'This is our verdict,' and I would suggest to you that you think of the value of letting that be the only time when the jurors speak to the world."

Leval pauses to let his words sink deep, then adds, "I cannot tell you how deeply I have been impressed with you. The jury is excused. You may return to your lives."

Not one juror looks again at the room, or any of the people in it. One alternate kisses one of the marshals on the cheek. Then they are gone.

. . . TUESDAY, MARCH 3, 1987.
THE CORRIDOR OUTSIDE JUDGE LEVAL'S COURTROOM.

Inside the courtroom, savage bail arguments are in progress. With the jury discharged, protocol is far less formal, and those lawyers whose presence is not required inside hang around outside smoking and discussing the verdicts.

Last night Bronson, Fisher, and Bergman had gone to dinner together and concluded: "No matter what we said, it wouldn't have made any difference. It was, finally, a *fait accompli*. When you have a sequestered jury, and you give them a 120-page indictment, plus 350 pages of other materials and charges, and 410-page chartbooks, they simply could not have even read all this, plus the fifty-nine-page verdict sheets, in less than two full days. So when did they deliberate?

"It defies imagination that a jury could come back in less than two weeks in a case like this."

Paul Bergman: "I'm devastated. I never expected this. The government never expected it. I've been doing this fifteen years—and I've never complained about a jury. But this is a fucking outrage! A travesty, that that jury wouldn't see through this."

Harriet Rosen: "The chartbooks came into this trial allegedly as aids to the jury, and then became gospel. They are going to change the rules of evidence. In future, prosecutors will make up all sorts of incriminating charts, and when they are challenged they will say to the judge, 'But your Honor, we used the same thing in the Pizza trial and it will save time.' It is a very bad precedent. The government will benefit from the bad legal practices they have managed to use in this case. I don't believe anybody could get a fair trial under these circumstances."

Bob Fogelnest: "I had an innocent client. Factually innocent. [But] I think the criminal justice system has broken down. The jury system simply cannot accommodate this sort of thing. These jurors were cheated. The public's been cheated.

"And while the prosecutors sit in there congratulating themselves, I can walk out onto the street, I can walk *around the corner from this courthouse,* and buy all the heroin or coke I want! There is not one less grain of dope available on the street today because of this case."

Mario Malerba: "I knew Sunday that it was coming. That's why I wasn't here Monday when they came in. I couldn't bear it. Those jurors—they'd had it. If Pierre Leval had not sequestered them until Day One of deliberations, they would have deliberated for two weeks. That's the maximum sequestration a jury can bear.

"If you start a big trial with an anonymous jury, search everyone going into the courtroom, flood the place with marshals, then sequester the jury, you've done everything to secure the inevitable conviction.

"Giuliani is now the man on the white horse. Those thrilled with his exploits are tomorrow's jurors."

Eleanore Kennedy: "This result was inevitable. Four things buried us. I call them the four coffin nails. Any one of them could have done it. With four, defeat was assured. Nail One was Leval's original refusal to sever. Nail Two was the anonymous jury. Nail Three was the extreme length of the trial, which made jury recall of evidence impossible. Nail Four, Leval's jury-shopping."

"Judge is on the bench! Oyez! Oyez!" comes the ritual cry once more down the granite hall. What a pleasure it is for these exhausted, defeated lawyers to know that, after today, they will not have to answer it.

In the courtroom, the brutal bail arguments continue. The government's position is that all these men are dangerous criminals, and now that they have been convicted, they will surely flee unless locked up to await sentencing. Martin is on his legs and baying like a bloodhound, demanding no bail for Sam Evola. Evola has been dealing dope *during* this trial, Martin claims, using his sons as drug couriers.

This is too much for Christine Evola, who rushes up to the chief prosecutor: "You bastard! You couldn't wipe my husband's shoes!"

Schechter fights furiously to keep Sal Lamberti out of jail. There is no violence in his record, no guns, no murders. Of all the defendants in this case, *none* had a greater opportunity to flee during the trial than the semi-invalid Lamberti, who recently had a kidney removed, and during the trial was allowed to stay at home for months at a time. Since his arrest, Lamberti has been rushed to five different hospital emergency rooms. He cannot get proper food and medication in jail. "To flee would be life-ending for him!"

Unmoved, Freeh says the jury's verdict compels preventive detention, "both on flight and violence grounds." The government had information that Lamberti planned to leave the United States to meet with Gaetano Badalamenti.

"Not true!" bawls Schechter.

Fogelnest is mad enough to invite Freeh to "step outside and I'll sue you."

Depressed by the spectacle, some observers wander downstairs to the empty courtroom where Gaetano Badalamenti waits with his lawyer to be indicted on criminal contempt charges for refusing to answer the government's questions. The judge and government prosecutor have not yet arrived.

A different atmosphere down here: The Pizza spotlight has been switched off, and the chief defendant now looks rather like the Wizard of Oz—a grizzled, wizened little man, no longer a figure of menace, standing alone in the empty courtroom, ignored by the solitary marshal dozing on a bench. No one else is present but the Kennedys, both of whom tower over their client.

Eleanore bends her head down to him and asks, with a melting smile, "When are we going to go pick asparagus together?"

"In thirty years," he replies in English, his tone fond and tender. Then he glances over his shoulder at the judge's high-backed chair and gives a rueful shrug. "With *this,* thirty-five."

"But do not worry." He smiles at her. "The asparagus will still be there."

9. *April 1988: Epilogue*

ON JUNE 22, 1987, Pierre Leval sentenced Gaetano Badalamenti to a term of forty-five years in prison, with a stipulation that he serve no more than thirty years. This stipulation was added to meet the requirements of Badalamenti's Spanish extradition agreement. Neither Kennedy nor Badalamenti had anything to say, nor did they stand for the sentencing.

Badalamenti is presently confined in the federal penitentiary in Marion, Illinois, a tomblike, underground dungeon considered to be the worst prison in the federal gulag.

Salvatore Catalano was sentenced to forty-five years, and shipped to Leavenworth, Kansas, "the second-worst place." Also in Leavenworth is Filippo Casamento, serving thirty years for his second heroin conviction.

Judge Leval sentenced Salvatore Mazzurco to twenty years for narcotics conspiracy and fifteen years on the RICO conviction, to run consecutively. He is now in the Tennessee federal penitentiary in Memphis.

Joseph Lamberti was sentenced to thirty years on the 848 charge. He resides in the penitentiary in Terre Haute, Indiana.

Salvatore Lamberti is serving twenty years for narcotics conspiracy in the penitentiary in Lompoc, California, one of the relative garden spots of the federal system.

Frank Castronovo is in Bastrop, Texas, doing twenty-five years on the 848. Giuseppe Vitale is in the same jail, serving his five-year sentence.

Salvatore Greco is serving twenty years for narcotics conspiracy in Alrino, Oklahoma, and grieves on top of his other troubles to find himself the only Sicilian for miles around.

Giovanni Ligammari was sentenced to fifteen years for narcotics conspiracy and sent to the prison at Talladega, Alabama, where he enjoys the company of Giovanni Cangialosi, who was sentenced to twelve years.

Salvatore Salamone was sentenced to five years for failure to file currency-transaction reports, for making false statements, and for conspiring to do both. Most of this time had been served by the end of trial. During the trial, Fogelnest had managed to get the Pennsylvania gun-running charges overturned on grounds of jury bias.

After the trial, Salamone fired his lawyer, "to beat me out of my fee," says the newly clean-shaven, clean-cut Fogelnest. The government retried the gunrunning charges. The new lawyer lost, and Salamone is doing eighteen years in the Texarkana, Texas, federal penitentiary.

On the last day before he was to be sentenced, Sam Evola decided to plead guilty to RICO and narcotics conspiracy. His reason, said his lawyer, was a promise from the government that the Evolas would not have to forfeit the family home. Dave Lewis also emphasized that Evola's admission of personal drug dealing could not be considered as an admission that the Old Man dealt drugs.

Judge Leval sentenced Evola to fifteen years, and he is now in Black Canyon, Arizona. Lewis believes the guilty plea cut five to ten years off his sentence.

Judge Leval sentenced Emmanuele Palazzolo to twelve years for narcotics conspiracy. He is serving his sentence in Petersburg, Virginia. Giuseppe Trupiano was sentenced to one year on the same charge, has served his time, and is now a free man.

On the day of his sentencing, Frank Polizzi stood up and made an impassioned, rambling, sometimes pathetic plea for leniency. Judge Leval sentenced him to twenty years. He resides in the Oxford, Wisconsin, federal pen.

At the conclusion of the Pizza trial, Paul Bergman filed a mistrial motion on grounds that Amato's defense had been severely prejudiced by the inclusion of the Galante murder in the government's opening statement. It was May 3, 1988, before Baldo Amato was sentenced. The cause of the extraordinary, fourteen-month delay was Bergman's extremely prickly demand that his client was entitled to a mistrial. In return for dropping the mistrial motion, the government finally agreed to drop its big narcotics-conspiracy charge and permit Amato to plead guilty to the lesser RICO charge. Pierre Leval sentenced Amato to a five-year term. Bergman's agreement with the government also ruled out any further charges against Amato for anything relating to the Pizza case.

Ten days after imposing sentence, Judge Leval granted Amato three months' bail so he could put his affairs in order before surrendering to a federal prison. According to Bergman, Leval also agreed to write a letter to the INS recommending that they not move to deport Amato as a resident alien.

On Friday, May 13, lawyer and client embraced and kissed on the streets of Chinatown in front of MCC. When Pat Burke was told of Amato's fate, he was stunned. "Wow, that's great lawyering, unbelievable lawyering. Who would have thought it?"

Vito Badalamenti, the only Pizza defendant found not guilty, has yet to see one day of freedom. The INS had obtained a deportation order against him, and he and the U.S. government are still trying to agree on a suitable country of destination. Soon after the verdict, he was shipped to the MCC in Chicago, where he is still being held. His present lawyer is a former head of the New York office of the INS.

In Italy, Enzo Randazzo was acquitted in March 1987 of charges identical to the U.S. Pizza charges. He lives in his old apartment in Milan, is still listed in the Milan phone book as Vito Randazzo, and still deals in clothes—shirts and sweat suits.

On June 6, 1987, Judge Leval issued a court order:

> It is hereby ordered that no attorney or defendant or party (or person acting for or on behalf of any attorney, defendant or party) shall, without prior permission of the court, communicate or seek to communicate with any juror or take steps seeking to learn the identity or location of any juror.
> New York, NY
> June 6, 1987
> so ordered: Pierre N. Leval, U.S.D.J.

Defendant Lorenzo DeVardo had pleaded guilty in mid-trial. His sentencing was postponed until after the verdict. In July 1987 Judge Leval sentenced him to four years for possession of a revolver. His lawyer, Jim Moriarty, kept his client on the street for a further eight months through a series of plea negotiations and leniency motions. Finally, on February 29, 1988, DeVardo was ordered to report to the federal prison at Milan, Michigan, to serve his time.

On July 17, 1987, Pat Burke won a mistrial for the crippled Pietro Alfano on the grounds that he was absent without his consent during a portion of his trial. Burke managed to have him released to his local hospital in Rockford, Illinois, while awaiting a retrial on all charges. The government appealed the mistrial decision, and pledged to retry the entire case against Alfano if necessary. By August Burke had worked out a deal with Louis Freeh for Alfano to plead guilty to narcotics conspiracy and RICO, in return for which the government would drop the 848 charge. On August 14 Alfano made his plea in a phone call from his hospital room to Judge Leval's chambers.

On October 21, 1987, Mrs. Alfano wheeled her husband into a small courtroom in Manhattan's federal court building, and Judge Leval sentenced him to fifteen years for narcotics conspiracy, with no forfeiture of property against his family. He remains paralyzed, and currently is incarcerated in the federal prison medical facility at Springfield, Missouri.

Three days after Alfano's sentencing, a special front-page story in the *New York Times* reported that the Reagan administration's war on drugs was a joke.

"There is no major drug crusade," said Senator Alfonse M. D'Amato, Republican of New York, a leading critic of the administration's handling of the drug problem. "It is a sham."

Three months later the *Times* ran another front-page drug story: CHINESE CRIME GROUPS RISING TO PROMINENCE IN NEW YORK. "As the Mafia declines and Chinese criminal activity spreads . . . some law-enforcement officials say they fear that Chinese organized crime could eventually achieve as much wealth, power and influence as Italian organized crime has had over the last half century. . . .

"Chinese criminals are a particularly difficult target for law-enforcement agencies because they often speak dialects the police do not understand and use aliases that they constantly change. In addition, they work in temporary alliances that have neither the structure nor the predictability of traditional Italian organized crime groups.

" 'They are following a trend almost identical to La Cosa Nostra,' " said Thomas Sheer, on the eve of leaving his post as head of the New York office of the FBI to become a risk management consultant with a company that advises major American corporations on the potential terrorist threat to future overseas investments.

A year later, in March 1988, New York citizens and officials were shocked, outraged, and up in arms when a young police officer was shot and killed as he sat alone in his parked patrol car. Patrolman Edward Byrne, twenty-five, was a clear victim of disorganized crime, just another tragic victim of the Queens crack wars. The senseless murder again drew forth thinly veiled laments for the good old days. "With $20,000 and a gun, anybody can play," groaned the president of the Citizens' Crime Commission, Thomas A. Reppetto. "If there had been some Grand Council [like the five-family Mafia Commission] and a hit like that [were] submitted, it would have been turned down!"

Ronald Goldstock, a combination policeman/scholar of organized crime who heads the New York State Organized Crime Strike Force, reminded people that in the United States, unlike Sicily, organized crime traditionally has discouraged hits on law-enforcement figures. In the 1930s, for example, fellow mobsters ordered the execution of Dutch Schultz to prevent him from carrying out his threat to assassinate a special prosecutor, Thomas E. Dewey.

On December 17, 1987, in Palermo, the maxi-trial ended in resounding defeat for the Mafia: 338 defendants were convicted on a cornucopia of criminal charges and sentenced to a total of 2,000 years behind bars. All of the Pizza defendants, of necessity tried *in absentia,* went down along with everybody else. Most prominent among the witnesses had been the turncoats Tomasso Buscetta and Salvatore Contorno. One of the 114 defendants acquitted in the maxi-trial was murdered just one hour after his release from Palermo's Ucciardone Prison. "The Mafia organization continues to function punctually," said one of the Italian government prosecutors.

In February 1988 the Italian Court of Appeals threw out the maxi-trial convictions of all the Pizza defendants on grounds that their trial in Italy had constituted double jeopardy under the terms of the Italian–United States Treaty for Mutual Assistance on Criminal Matters, signed in 1982.

In February 1988 General Manuel Noriega, the Panamanian strong man, was indicted by two U.S. grand juries as the world's biggest cocaine dealer. One of the first attorneys Noriega approached about his defense was Michael Kennedy.

In April 1988 a real pizza connection finally occurred: Kennedy,

Fisher, Schoenbach, and Moriarty joined forces and moved together into spacious new offices on Park Avenue. Lewis made a similar space-sharing arrangement with Fogelnest, and the newest arrival in their suite of offices was Joseph Calluori.

Kennedy's next trial after Pizza was the *pro bono* defense of Martin Sostre, a seasoned black prison-rights advocate accused of attempted murder. Despite the testimony of three eyewitnesses, Kennedy won an acquittal on all counts.

Ivan Fisher's next two clients were a doctor peripherally connected to the Joel Steinberg child-abuse and murder case, and an alleged Chinese dope dealer known as King Kon. Neither case went to trial.

Joe Calluori helped make new law in his first case when a New Jersey judge ruled that evidence obtained by electrophoresis—a technique for identifying bloodstains through genetic markers—is insufficiently scientific to be admissible in court.

Lewis and Fogelnest soon became involved, along with Anthony Lombardino, in another mob drug case. After eight months of testimony, a mistrial was declared because of alleged jury tampering.

Joseph Benfante also moved his office and now shares space with Bruce Cutler, the aggressive organized-crime lawyer who in June 1987 had won a spectacular "not guilty" verdict for Gambino boss John Gotti, on trial for RICO conspiracy. Benfante's star has been on the rise since the Pizza case. In the fall of 1987 he won an acquittal in a murder case in which the killing was witnessed by a passing taxi driver, and the accused killer was caught with the murder weapon a half block from the body.

Robert Koppelman won three more acquittals, two on murder charges, directly after his victory for Vito Badalamenti.

Schoenbach found himself back in Judge Leval's courtroom in another large RICO trial. This one involved the Westies, a group of Irish-American mobsters. "I like these long trials," he says. "You know where you're going when you get up each morning."

Gerald Di Chiara, lawyer for Pronto Demolition, began selling off the firm's trucks, buildings, and land in Brooklyn to pay back wages, liens, tax arrears, and the huge fines imposed by Leval on Mazzurco and Joe Lamberti.

Lawrence Ruggiero next tried a government corruption case in Miami. "I ended up being protected from the FBI agents and U.S. attorneys by a bunch of Colombians," he said. By trial's end the judge had referred the names of the federal agents and prosecutors involved to the Justice Department, with a recommendation to prosecute.

James Moriarty found himself representing a husband in a complex domestic dispute in Queens County Court. His client sought custody of his child on grounds that his ex-wife was an unfit mother: She had several times tried to have him killed. The mother, a Sicilian/American woman, claimed she was a battered wife. Her lawyer was Mario Malerba.

Harriet Rosen opened up her own practice and started the appeal process for Joe Trupiano. Lawrence Bronson, Di Chiara, Kenneth Kaplan, Joseph Ryan, and Marvin Schechter continued to represent their Pizza clients on appeal. The defense's joint appeal brief was submitted in June 1988, and the government was due to reply by September 1. The new lead counsel, on the appeal, Barry Fallick, does not expect a verdict until well into 1989.

Paul Bergman, Carol Novack, and Genay Leitman, as well as Calluori have entered solo practice. Ruggiero, Bronson, Kaplan, Malerba, Di Chiara, Moriarty, Querques, and Ryan continue in stable practices.

Larry Bronson took over Patsy Conte's case and was able to get the murder-for-hire charges thrown out. The government informant's memory as to who had put up the money for the Alfano hit proved unreliable.

On June 24, 1987, Marvin Segal filed a petition for Title II bankruptcy. In March 1988 he showed up in federal court in Puerto Rico representing an alleged member of the New York Gambino Family, Giuseppe Pellerito, on heroin-smuggling charges. Mario Malerba appeared on behalf of another alleged mobster on the same charges. Federal sources in New York stated that the two accused men worked for Patsy Conte, Sr. Malerba described the government's accusation as "ludicrous."

In November 1987 Bronson traveled to Sicily to arrange for the surrender to U.S. authorities of Rosario Dispenza, a minor Pizza figure. Dispenza was a major figure in a different drug case, and was important in Pizza only because a hundred-dollar bill seized in a raid on his Philadelphia home was the sole bill ever recovered of the government's marked $600,000 paid by Agent Hopson to Benny Zito. The remaining $599,900 has never been found.

One night in Palermo, Bronson called the U.S. Embassy in Rome and was startled to recognize the voice on an embassy answering machine. It was Richard Martin, now legal attaché to the U.S. ambassador in Italy.

While in Palermo, Bronson was secretly driven to a small mountain village and introduced to a tall, handsome young man—the fugitive

Benny Zito. Back in New York, Bronson called on Louis Freeh, now head of the Organized Crime Strike Force in the Southern District U.S. Attorney's Office, to discuss the surrender of his client Dispenza. It was agreed by all parties that Dispenza would surrender and plead guilty to money-laundering charges. Bronson expected his client to receive two five-year sentences, to run concurrently.

Robert Bucknam and Andrew McCarthy continue their government service in the U.S. Attorney's Office for the Southern District, as does Charles Rose in the Eastern District, and Robert Stewart with the Newark Strike Force in New Jersey.

Rudolph Giuliani looked for a while as if he was going to run for senator from New York on the Republican ticket, and would have had a chance somewhere between fair and good, until he ran afoul of Senator Alfonse D'Amato. He turned against the prosecutor for a display of overweening dynastic pride in attempting to name his own successor as U.S. attorney. For the moment, only, Giuliani is in his tent.

In September 1987 *New York Newsday* hinted at jury tampering in the Pizza case. A story recounting a new wave of gangland slayings said that a Brooklyn man had been murdered because of a botched attempt to bribe a Pizza juror. Pasquale "Paddy Bulldog" Varriale was a small-time hustler and gambler who hung out in the mob bars and social clubs of Bath Beach, Brooklyn, a tough Italian-American stomping ground for a horde of wiseguys, shylocks, and gamblers. The area adjoins the Bay Ridge home territory of Bonventre, Amato, Casamento, and numerous other recent immigrants.

In late 1986 Paddy Bulldog approached a high-ranking member of the Bonanno Family and said he knew a Pizza juror who might be bought. He was given $10,000 to make the payoff, but later claimed the juror got cold feet and refused to accept the money or go along with the scheme.

Paddy Bulldog did not tell his Bonanno Family contact about the juror's refusal. He rented a limo and drove with a friend to Atlantic City, where he blew the $10,000.

In early February 1987 he was lured to a pizzeria on Nostrand Avenue in Brooklyn, to discuss the possible robbery of a big-time shylock. A mobster friend who accompanied him that night had a handgun, and urged Paddy Bulldog to take it with him into the pizzeria. He refused, saying he knew these guys, and would be out in a few minutes.

He was never seen alive again. When the friend entered the pizzeria to inquire about Paddy, he was told no one fitting that description had come in. A few days later Paddy Bulldog's body was found, bound hand

and foot and wrapped in a garbage bag, in front of a church on Coleman Street in the Flatlands section of Brooklyn.

Four months later the bodies of two Bensonhurst brothers, Vinnie and Enrico Carini, were found in their cars, both shot in the head. The word around Bath Beach was that the brothers might have been responsible for luring Paddy Bulldog to the pizzeria. In September Paddy Bulldog's half-brother, Carmine, a made member of the Lucchese Family, was gunned down on the street as he walked away from the Big Apple Two-Way Radio Company on Bath Avenue. The Radio Company is a social club for a capo in the Bonanno Family.

Prosecutors and judges acknowledge that the Pizza Connection trial came about in part as a result of the government's increasing reliance on the RICO statute. Ever since such megatrials began in 1978, the criminal defense bar has denounced them as a dreaded, outrageous sacrifice of due process and Sixth Amendment rights to prosecutorial convenience and aggrandizement. But the Department of Justice has insisted that mass trials are essential for efficient, effective, economic prosecution, particularly of organized-crime cases, and recent Supreme Court decisions have upheld this view.

In late August 1987, about three months after the Pizza defendants were sentenced, a leading federal jurist, Chief U.S. District Court Judge Jack B. Weinstein, of the Eastern District of New York, decided the pendulum had swung far enough. The latest fashion in prosecutorial zeal—the so-called megatrial—had become dangerous and destructive to juries, attorneys, and judges alike, he said. It menaced the essential humanity that must be present in every area of our criminal justice system. It would be healthier, wiser, and cheaper to hold separate trials.

The case in front of him was *U.S.* versus *Gallo,* 86-CR-452(s), sixteen organized-crime figures charged with RICO conspiracy. Judge Weinstein severed the case into six separate trials. Over a period of a year, Douglas Grover, of the Eastern District U.S. Attorney's Office, won eleven convictions. Two defendants died or were presumed dead, two were acquitted, and one case was still to be decided.

In his celebrated sixty-eight-page opinion, Weinstein wrote the juridical equivalent of the little boy's statement "The Emperor has nothing on!"

"The courts must be scrupulous to avoid the spectre of guilt by association—or more likely, guilt by confusion," he warned.

"As chief judge of this court, I have observed judges . . . during . . . cases that last many months. The effect on the judge's health presents a serious matter of concern. The grinding tension of such a long, complex case, particularly where the judge is making rulings which are continuously on the borderline of probative force and prejudice, is debilitating.

"The worry about frequent adjournments, necessitated by the unavoidable problems of 18 jurors, 10 or more defendants, 10 or more counsel and any prosecutorial persons and witnesses and other personnel, all of whom must be present at all times, creates added tensions.

"The already overburdened docket reaches a breaking point, and the administration of justice in all the court's cases is unconscionably delayed. The judge effectively presides over a one-case court."

On the matter of mistrials, Judge Weinstein wrote that the need to avoid a retrial becomes so great that "the judge's ability to remain detached and objective is compromised," and mistrials become unthinkable, even when a defendant has disappeared or died.

The effect on juries is counterproductive. The jurors are removed from their normal lives for long periods and must sit silently in a courtroom for hours, day after day. "The process as a whole is undoubtedly draining, disorienting, exhausting and often demoralizing." They are required to perform the intellectual feat of applying evidence to some defendants but not to others, and to absorb huge amounts of information which must be assessed on the basis of its credibility.

The consequences to defense attorneys, particularly solo practitioners and members of small firms, are disastrous. Participation in such a case requires them to become virtually a one-client lawyer. As Weinstein put it, "Representation of one of these defendants virtually means sacrificing the entire remainder of one's clientele."

In a comprehensive piece on Judge Weinstein's decision published in the *National Law Journal,* the distinguished legal affairs writer Marcia Chambers said, "Experienced criminal lawyers who have busy practices view megatrials as a punishment from God." Some lawyers have begun to beg off. "Defendants unable to hire the counsel of their choice sometimes have turned to court-appointed and court-paid attorneys. The removal of highly qualified criminal defense lawyers, who often are experts in RICO, does not disappoint the prosecutor."

Chambers concluded that "these trials have become constitutionally messy and prohibitively expensive.

"If Judge Weinstein is right—and there is every reason to treat his extraordinary experience and sophistication with respect—the zeal to convict has led the Justice Department to damage the judicial system itself."

Cast of Characters

Cangialosi, Giovanni: 35; Sicily; arrived in U.S. 21 days before arrests

Casamento, Filippo: 59; Brooklyn, NY; owner of Casamento Salumeria and Eagle Cheese Co.; heroin conviction, 1972

Castellano, Paul "Big Paul": boss of New York Gambino Family; head of New York Mafia Commission; murdered 1985

Castronovo, Francesco "Frank," "Ciccio l'Americano": 51; Parlin, NJ; co-owner of Roma Restaurant, Menlo Park, NJ, with brother-in-law Gaetano Mazzara

Catalano, Onofrio: cousin of Salvatore Catalano; close associate of Ganci; linked to early money-laundering operations

Catalano, Saca: cousin of Salvatore Catalano; key figure among Zips; shot dead in Brooklyn, 1983

Catalano, Salvatore "Sal," "Toto": 44; Queens, NY, baker; alleged boss of Zips

Conte, Sr., Pasquale "Patsy": millionaire owner of Key Food Supermarket chain; closely linked to Salvatore Catalano and Gambino Family

Contorno, Salvatore "Sal": key government witness; Sicilian Mafia soldier turned informant

Corleonese: Sicilian Mafia family from mountain village of Corleone; dominant family among winning faction in 1980s Mafia wars

DeVardo, Lorenzo: 39; Queens, NY, painter and decorator

Di Chiara, Gerald: attorney for Giovanni Cangialosi; former Legal Aid attorney

Evola, Salvatore "Sam": 48; Temperance, MI, construction worker; husband of Gaetano Badalamenti's favorite niece, Christine

Falcone, Giovanni: leading Italian magistrate in drive against the Mafia

Fisher, Ivan: attorney for Salvatore Catalano; former Legal Aid attorney

Fogelnest, Robert: attorney for Salvatore Salamone

Freeh, Louis: assistant U.S. attorney, Southern District of New York; former FBI agent

Galante, Carmine "Lilo": boss of Bonanno Family; recruited native Sicilians for his Mafia family; murdered 1979

Galbo, Filippo: Midwest nephew of Gaetano Badalamenti; linked to Alfano network; referred to in Brazilian phone calls as "Salted Sardines"

Ganci, Giuseppe "Joe," "Il Bufalo": Queens, NY, pizzeria owner; partner in Pronto Demolition; key Zip drug dealer; deceased February 11, 1986

Giuliani, Rudolph: U.S. attorney, Southern District of New York

Giuliano, Carol: mistress of Joe Ganci

Goldstock, Ronald: Director, New York State Organized Crime Strike Force

Gotti, John: New York Gambino Family boss; came to power after murder of Castellano, 1985

Greco, Salvatore "Sal": 52; Oakhurst, NJ, pizzeria owner

Kaplan, Kenneth: attorney for Frank Castronovo; former assistant U.S. attorney, Eastern District of New York

Kennedy, Eleanore: paralegal; wife of lead counsel Kennedy

Kennedy, Michael: lead counsel; attorney for Gaetano Badalamenti

Kimelman, Steven: attorney for Giovanni Ligammari; former assistant U.S. attorney, Eastern District of New York

Koppelman, Robert: attorney for Vito Badalamenti; former district attorney, Bronx, NY

Lamberti, Giuseppe "Joe": 53; Baldwin, NY; partner in Pronto Demolition; cousin of Salvatore Lamberti; brother-in-law of Mazzurco

Lamberti, Salvatore "Sal": 53; Woodmere, NY; emigrated to U.S. from Sicily, 1982

LaMura, Joe: court clerk for Judge Leval

Leitman, Genay: attorney for Emmanuele Palazzolo

Leval, Pierre N.: U.S. District Judge, Southern District of New York, former assistant U.S. attorney, Southern District of New York

Lewis, David: attorney for Samuel Evola

Ligammari, Giovanni: 46; Saddle River, NJ, construction laborer; partner in Pronto Demolition

Lombardino, Anthony: attorney for Joseph Lamberti; former assistant district attorney, Queens, NY; former assistant U.S. attorney, Eastern District of New York

Losers, The: name given by Italian press to Sicilian Mafia faction defeated and persecuted by Corleonese in 1980s Sicilian Mafia war

Lupo, Faro: nephew of Randazzo living with Alfano before March 1984; joined Randazzo in Europe

Malerba, Mario: attorney for Giuseppe Ganci, Salvatore Catalano

Martin, Richard: lead prosecutor; assistant U.S. attorney, Southern District of New York

Mazzara, Gaetano "Tommy": 50; Sayreville, NJ; co-owner, with Castronovo, of Roma Restaurant, Menlo Park, NJ; body found December 1986

Mazzurco, Salvatore "Sal": 49; Baldwin, NY; partner in Pronto Demolition; owner of Pino Europa Boutique and Upskate roller-skating rink

McCarthy, Andrew: assistant U.S. attorney, Southern District of New York

Moore, Emanuel: attorney of counsel to Malerba; former assistant district attorney, Queens, N.Y.; former assistant U.S. attorney, Eastern District of New York

Moriarty, James: attorney for Lorenzo DeVardo; former Legal Aid attorney

Novack, Carol: associate attorney to Kimelman

Palazzolo, Emmanuele: 39; Milton, WI, pizzeria owner; nephew of Gaetano Badalamenti and brother-in-law of Alfano

Palazzolo, Vito Roberto: Sicilian money launderer; involved in Swiss banking operation; no relation of defendant Palazzolo

Pecosi, Lena: Italian-Sicilian translator for Gaetano Badalamenti

Persico, Carmine: boss of the U.S. Colombo Family; member of the New York Mafia Commission; buddy of Gaetano Badalamenti

Pisano, Joseph: attorney for Frank Polizzi

Pistone, Joseph: FBI undercover agent; infiltrated the Bonanno Family as burglar "Donny Brasco"

Polizzi, Francesco "Frank": 51; Belleville, NJ, millionaire owner of Belleville Motor Lodge, Casa Polizzi Restaurant, and Polizzi Builders

Querques, Michael: attorney of counsel to Pisano

Randazzo, Vincenzo "Enzo": 45; Italy; nephew of Gaetano Badalamenti; extradited from Zurich to New York

Ronsisvalle, Luigi: key government witness; hit man and drug mule turned informant

Rooney, Charles J.: FBI case agent for Pizza Connection investigation and trial

Rose, Charles: assistant U.S. attorney, Eastern District of New York; involved in initial U.S. approach to Buscetta

Rosen, Harriet: associate attorney to Segal

Ruggiero, Lawrence: attorney for Giuseppe Trupiano and Giuseppe Vitale; former assistant U.S. attorney, Southern District of New York

Ryan, Joseph W., Jr.: attorney for Filippo Casamento; former assistant U.S. attorney, Eastern District of New York

Salamone, Salvatore "Sal": 36; in custody, MCC; pizzeria owner; serving Pennsylvania sentence for illegal gun possession

Schechter, Marvin: attorney for Salvatore Lamberti; former Legal Aid attorney

Schoenbach, Lawrence: attorney for Vincenzo Randazzo

Segal, Marvin E.: attorney for Gaetano Mazzara; former assistant U.S. attorney, Southern District of New York

Sheer, Thomas L.: deputy director of FBI New York office; orchestrated April 9, 1984, arrests

Soresi, Giuseppe: Borghetto, Sicily, hospital porter; suspected heroin trafficker

Stewart, Robert: Department of Justice attorney, New Jersey Strike Force

Trupiano, Giuseppe "Joe": 35; Olney, IL, pizzeria owner; nephew of Gaetano Badalamenti

Vitale, Giuseppe "Joe": 44; Paris, IL, pizzeria owner; husband of Gaetano Badalamenti's niece

Chronology

1936:	Bonanno takes control of New York La Cosa Nostra
1943:	Gaetano Badalamenti deserts Italian Army
1943, Jul. 7:	Allied landing in Sicily
1946, Mar. 23:	arrest warrant issued in Sicily for Gaetano Badalamenti
1946, Oct.:	Gaetano Badalamenti stows away on S.S. *Saturnia* in Naples; arrives in U.S.
1957, Oct. 12:	Spano Restaurant meeting in Palermo devises Sicilian Mafia Commissione
1963:	Sicilian Commissione collapses because of interfamily war and Ciaculli Massacre
1964:	Tomasso Buscetta illegally enters U.S. at Canadian border
1969:	Sicilian Mafia Commissione reestablished under control of Gaetano Badalamenti, Stefano Bontate, and Salvatore Riina
1971:	Tomasso Buscetta expelled from U.S. by Immigration and Naturalization Service
1972, Nov.:	Tomasso Buscetta arrested in Brazil, extradited to Italy, sentenced to eight years in prison
1974:	Carmine Galante takes control of Bonanno Family
1976, Nov. 4:	Peter Licata, boss of Knickerbocker Avenue Bonanno Family, murdered; Sal Catalano takes control
1978, Nov.:	Gaetano Badalamenti expelled from Sicilian Mafia Commissione

1979, Jun. 19:   suitcase containing $497,000 wrapped in pizzeria aprons discovered at airport in Sicily

1979, Jul. 12:   Carmine Galante shot to death in garden of Joe & Mary's Restaurant, Brooklyn

1979, Jul. 31:   Baldo Amato and Cesare Bonventre appear for questioning in relation to Galante killing at Brooklyn district attorney's office

1980, Feb. 14:   Sal Catalano marries Caterina in Cimina, Sicily

1980, Feb.–Mar.:   Meeting in Bagheria farmhouse to test heroin

1980, Mar. 18:   41 kilos of heroin seized in Milan, Italy

1980, Jun.:   Salvatore Amendolito begins money laundering from New York to Switzerland

1980, Nov. 16:   Giuseppe Bono's wedding reception at Pierre Hotel, New York

1981, May 5:   murder of three Bonanno capos in Brooklyn results in Zips being given total control of heroin trafficking

1982:   U.S. and Italy sign Treaty for Mutual Assistance on Criminal Matters

1982, Sept. 8:   two of Tomasso Buscetta's sons disappear; feared murdered by Corleonese in Palermo

1982, Oct. 5:   FBI agents subpoena records of Franco Della Torre money transactions at E. F. Hutton brokerage

1983, Mar. 7:   FBI begins major wiretaps on Ganci, Castronovo, Mazzara, and other key suspects

1983, Jun.–Aug.:   DEA Agent Hopson purchases 2.5 kilos of heroin from Philadelphia drug dealer Benny Zito; Zito heroin supplied by Joe Ganci

1983, Sept. 26:   Sal Mazzurco meets Badalamenti Midwest associates Alfano, Randazzo, Palazzolo, and Lupo at Queens diner

1983, Nov. 17:   Sal Mazzurco exchanges package with cocaine dealer Sadid Torres in Bronx

1984, Jan. 20:   Gaetano Badalamenti calls Sal and Joe Lamberti at pay phone near Al Dente Pizzeria, in Queens

1984, Feb. 14:   Badalamenti calls Alfano and Mazzurco at same Queens pay phone

1984, Feb.:   Catalano, Ganci, Ligammari, Mazzurco, Sal and Joe Lamberti meet at social club in Queens

1984, Mar. 6:   Catalano, Ganci, Bonventre, Amato, Polizzi, and Joe Lamberti meet at site of Amato's Café Biffi in Manhattan

1984, Mar. 15:   Giovanni Cangialosi arrives in New York

1984, Apr. 7:   Pietro Alfano flies from Chicago to Madrid

1984, Apr. 8:   Alfano, Gaetano Badalamenti, and Vito Badalamenti arrested in Madrid; Enzo Randazzo arrested in Zurich

1984, Apr. 9:   massive FBI roundup; defendants arrested in New York, New Jersey, and Midwest

1984, Nov. 15:   Gaetano Badalamenti, Vito Badalamenti, and Pietro Alfano extradited to U.S. from Spain

1985, Sept. 30:   jury selection begins for "Pizza Connection" trial

1985, Oct. 24:   trial begins

1985, Oct. 29:   Sicilian Mafia boss Tomasso Buscetta testifies

1985, Dec. 2:   Sicilian Mafia soldier Salvatore Contorno testifies

1985, Dec. 16:   "Big Paul" Castellano murdered in Manhattan

1986, Jan. 4:   Mafia hit man Luigi Ronsisvalle testifies

1986, Jan. 30:   FBI Special Agent Joe Pistone testifies

1986, Feb. 11:   Giuseppe Ganci dies

1986, Feb. 13:   money launderer Salvatore Amendolito testifies

1986, Mar. 6:   "Great Gobi Desert" begins

1986, May 5:   DEA Agent Stephen Hopson testifies

1986, Jun. 19:   Enzo Randazzo pleads guilty to one immigration count

1986, Jul. 21:   Lorenzo DeVardo pleads guilty to weapons possession

1986, Oct. 8:   Great Gobi ends; government rests case

1986, Oct. 14:   defense case begins; Gaetano Badalamenti testifies

1986, Nov. 17:   Sal Mazzurco testifies

1986, Nov. 26:   Tommy Mazzara disappears

1986, Dec. 2:   Mazzara's body found in Brooklyn

1987, Jan. 15:   defense rests case

1987, Jan. 27:   government summations begin

1987, Feb. 2:   defense summations begin

1987, Feb. 11:   Pietro Alfano shot and wounded in Greenwich Village

1987, Feb. 12:   jury sequestered

1987, Feb. 13:   three men arrested for Alfano shooting

1987, Feb. 17:   Patsy Conte, Sr., arrested for organizing Alfano shooting

1987, Feb. 25:   jury deliberations begin

1987, Mar. 2:   jury returns its verdict

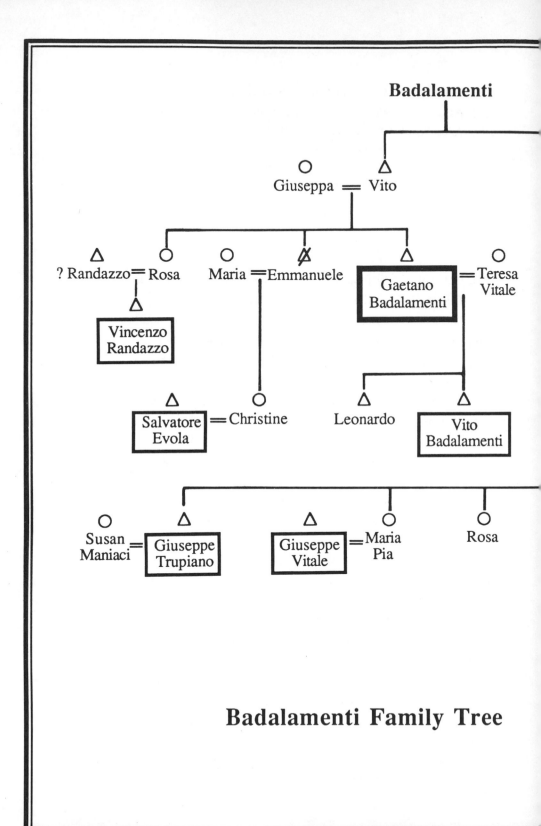

Badalamenti Family Tree

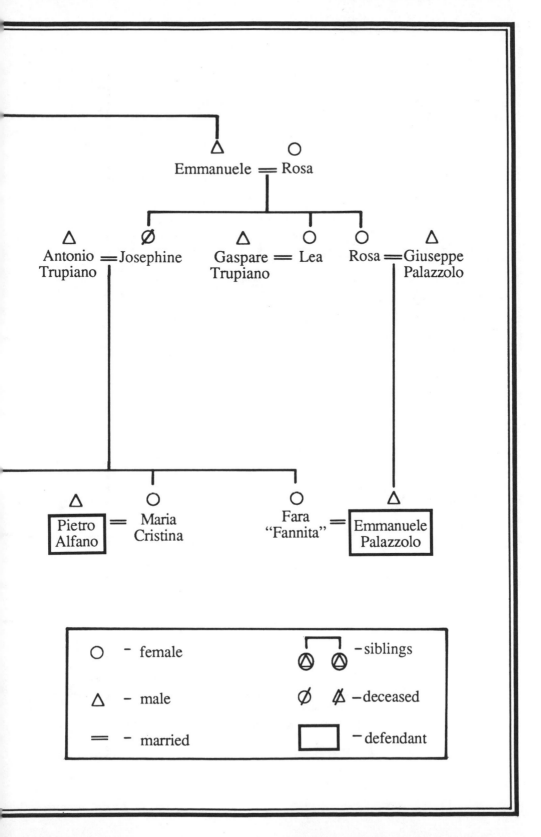

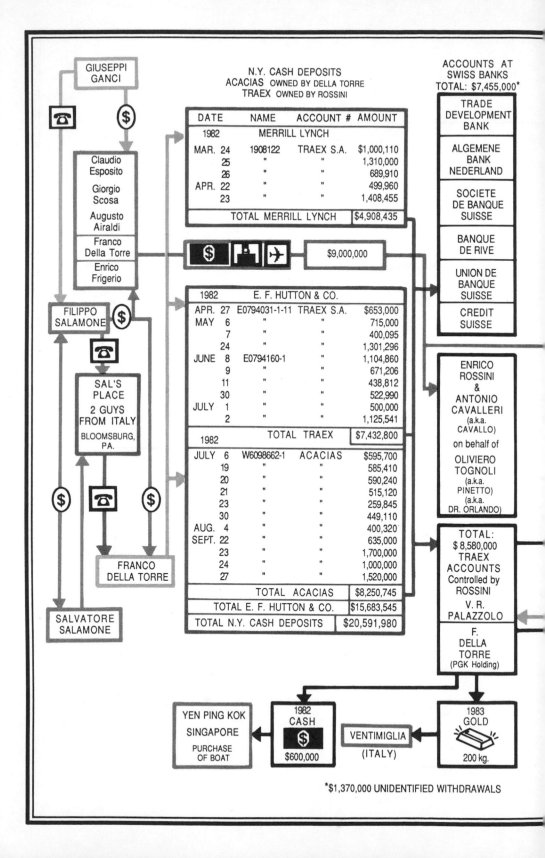

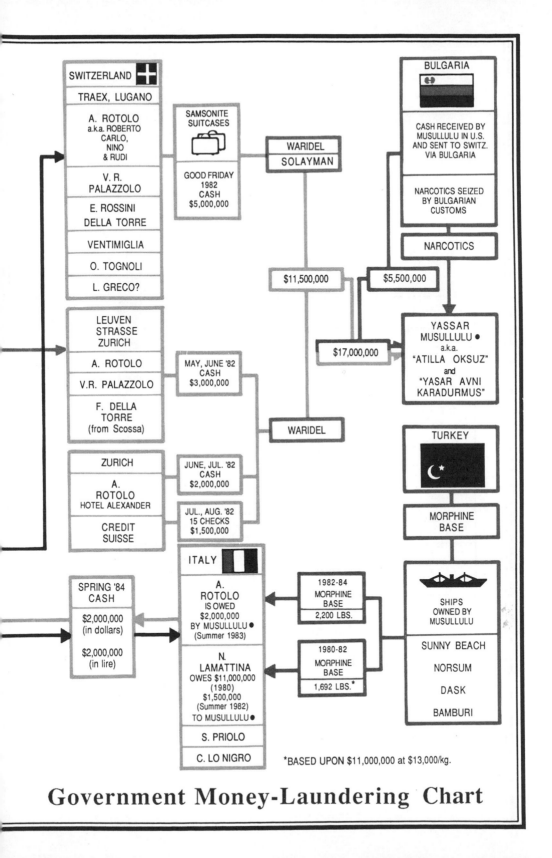

Government Money-Laundering Chart

Pizza Connection Trial Verdicts

			Michael Kennedy	Ivan Fisher/Mario Malerba/ Emanuel Moore	Anthony Lombardino	Joseph Benfante	Marvin Schechter
Count 16		RICO Conspiracy	■	✓	✓	✓	✓
Counts 12-15 Banking Violations	15	Failure to File Reports on International Currency Transactions	■	✓	■	■	■
	14	Failure to File Currency - Transaction Reports	■	✓	■	■	■
	13	False Statements	■	■	■	■	■
	12	Conspiracy	■	✓	■	■	■
Counts 2-11		Continuing Criminal Enterprise in Narcotics	✓	✓	✓	Not guilty	Not guilty
Count 1		Narcotics Conspiracy	✓	✓	✓	✓	✓
Defendants			Gaetano Badalamenti	Salvatore Catalano	Giuseppe Lamberti	Salvatore Mazzurco	Salvatore Lamberti

■ = Defendant not charged with this offense

✓ = Guilty

Defendant							Attorney
Giovanni Ligammari	✓					✓	Steven Kimelman/Carol Novack
Baldassare Amato	✓*					✓	Paul Bergman
Pietro Alfano	✓		✓				Patrick Burke
Emmanuele Palazzolo	✓					✓	Genay Leitman
Salvatore Evola	✓					✓	David Lewis
Vito Badalamenti	Not guilty						Robert Koppelman
Giuseppe Trupiano	✓					✓	Lawrence Ruggiero
Giuseppe Vitale	✓					✓	
Giovanni Cangialosi	✓					✓	Gerald Di Chiara
Salvatore Salamone	Not guilty		✓	✓	✓	Not guilty	Robert Fogelnest
Salvatore Greco	✓	✓	✓	✓		✓	Lawrence Bronson
Francesco Castronovo	✓	✓	✓			✓	Kenneth Kaplan
Francesco Polizzi	✓					✓	Michael Querques/Joseph Pisano
Filippo Casamento	✓					✓	Joseph W. Ryan
Vincenzo Randazzo	Pled guilty to lesser charge, deported 2/5/88						Lawrence Schoenbach
Lorenzo DeVardo	Pled guilty to lesser charge, 7/21/86						James Moriarty
Gaetano Mazzara	Murdered 12/86						Marvin Segal/Harriet Rosen

*Dropped May 3, 1988.

Index

INDEX

About the Author

SHANA ALEXANDER has pursued a varied and award-winning career as a journalist, lecturer, essayist, and author. She has been the editor of *McCall's,* a radio commentator for CBS News, a columnist for *Newsweek,* a writer and columnist for *Life,* and a commentator on "60 Minutes." She is the author of *Anyone's Daughter* (about Patty Hearst), *Talking Woman* (collected essays and autobiography), *Very Much a Lady* (about Jean Harris), and most recently the best-selling *Nutcracker.* She lives in New York City.

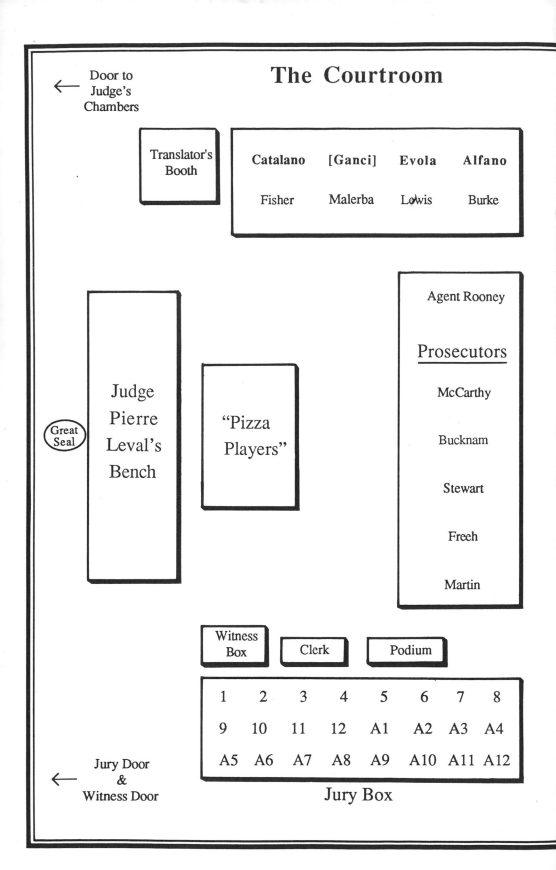

The Courtroom

Door to Judge's Chambers ←

Translator's Booth

Catalano   [Ganci]   Evola   Alfano

Fisher   Malerba   Lewis   Burke

Agent Rooney

Prosecutors

McCarthy

Bucknam

Stewart

Freeh

Martin

Great Seal

Judge Pierre Leval's Bench

"Pizza Players"

Witness Box

Clerk

Podium

1	2	3	4	5	6	7	8
9	10	11	12	A1	A2	A3	A4
A5	A6	A7	A8	A9	A10	A11	A12

Jury Box

Jury Door & Witness Door ←